Goodbye Cinema, Hello Cinephilia

Other Books by Jonathan Rosenbaum

Rivette: Texts and Interviews (editor, 1977)

Orson Welles: A Critical View, by André Bazin (editor and translator, 1978)

Moving Places: A Life in the Movies (1980)

Film: The Front Line 1983 (1983)

Midnight Movies (with J. Hoberman, 1983)

Greed (1991)

This Is Orson Welles, by Orson Welles and Peter Bogdanovich (editor, 1992)

Placing Movies: The Practice of Film Criticism (1995)

Movies as Politics (1997)

Another Kind of Independence: Joe Dante and the Roger Corman Class of 1970
(coedited with Bill Krohn, 1999)

Dead Man (2000)

Movie Wars: How Hollywood and the Media Limit What Films We Can See (2000)

Abbas Kiarostami (with Mehrmax Saeed-Vafa, 2003)

Movie Mutations: The Changing Face of World Cinephilia
(coedited with Adrian Martin, 2003)

Essential Cinema: On the Necessity of Film Canons (2004)

Discovering Orson Welles (2007)

The Unquiet American: Trangressive Comedies from the U.S. (2009)

Goodbye Cinema, Hello Cinephilia

Film Culture in Transition

Jonathan Rosenbaum

THE UNIVERSITY OF CHICAGO PRESS | CHICAGO AND LONDON

Jonathan Rosenbaum wrote for many periodicals (including the *Village Voice, Sight and Sound, Film Quarterly,* and *Film Comment*) before becoming principal film critic for the *Chicago Reader* in 1987. Since his retirement from that position in March 2008, he has maintained his own Web site and continued to write for both print and online publications. His many books include four major collections of essays: *Placing Movies* (California 1995), *Movies as Politics* (California 1997), *Movie Wars* (a cappella 2000), and *Essential Cinema* (Johns Hopkins 2004).

The University of Chicago Press, Chicago 60637
The University of Chicago Press, Ltd., London
© 2010 by The University of Chicago
All rights reserved. Published 2010
Printed in the United States of America

19 18 17 16 15 14 13 12 11 10   1 2 3 4 5

ISBN-13: 978-0-226-72664-9 (cloth)
ISBN-13: 978-0-226-72665-6 (paper)
ISBN-10: 0-226-72664-9 (cloth)
ISBN-10: 0-226-72665-7 (paper)

The following essays were originally published in the *Chicago Reader*:
"The World as a Circus" (December 1, 1989); "Movie Heaven" (April 5, 1991);"Wrinkles in Time" (February 18, 2000); "Unsatisfied Men" (May 26, 2000); "Art of Darkness" (December 5, 2003); "Prisoners of War" (June 18, 2004); "L.A. Existential" (October 1, 2004); "Marilyn Monroe's Brains" (December 2, 2005); "Introducing Pere Portabella" (November 10, 2006); "When Fable and Fact Interact" (August 31, 2007); and "Cinema of the Future" (November 15, 2007). Copyright © 1989, 1991, 2000, 2003, 2004, 2005, 2006, 2007 by Chicago Reader, Inc.

Library of Congress Cataloging-in-Publication Data

Rosenbaum, Jonathan.
    Goodbye cinema, hello cinephilia : film culture in transition / Jonathan Rosenbaum.
        p.   cm.
    Includes index.
    ISBN-13: 978-0-226-72664-9 (cloth : alk. paper)
    ISBN-13: 978-0-226-72665-6 (pbk. : alk. paper)
    ISBN-10: 0-226-72664-9 (cloth : alk. paper)
    ISBN-10: 0-226-72665-7 (pbk. : alk. paper) 1. Motion pictures. 2. Motion pictures — Reviews.
3. Motion picture producers and directors. 4. Motion picture actors and actresses. I. Title.
    PN1994 .R577 2010
    791.4309 — dc22

                                                            2010000440

⊗ The paper used in this publication meets the minimum requirements of the American National Standard for Information Sciences — Permanence of Paper for Printed Library Materials, ANSI Z39.48-1992.

To the memory of

NIKA BOHINC (1979–2009)

and

ALEXIS TIOSECO (1981–2009)

Contents

Introduction

I t's a strange paradox that about half of my friends and colleagues think that we're currently approaching the end of cinema as an art form and the end of film criticism as a serious activity, while the other half believe that we're enjoying some form of exciting resurgence and renaissance in both areas. How can one account for this discrepancy? One clue is that many of the naysayers tend to be people around my own age (sixty-six) or older, whereas many of the optimistic ones are a good deal younger, most of them under thirty.[1]

I tend to feel closer to the younger cinephiles on this issue, but I can sympathize with certain aspects of the other perspective as well. And both positions are entwined with attitudes about other technological and social changes that are far too complex and varied to be simply endorsed or condemned, especially insofar as we're still in the process of trying to figure out their full implications. Our terminology is developing at a far slower rate than our society, producing time lags that wind up confusing everyone.

Both of these positions as well as my proximity to each can be neatly illustrated with a brilliant, hilarious three-and-a-half-minute short, *At the Suicide of the Last Jew in the World in the Last Cinema of the World,* by David Cronenberg — who was born about two weeks after me and who stars in the title role, in a grizzled one-take close-up, preparing to shoot himself inside a men's room in the world's last cinema while two airheaded TV newscasters, male and female, offer a continuous and inanely cheerful offscreen commentary about him. This film was made for the sixtieth edition of the Cannes film festival, in 2007, along with thirty-two other shorts of the same length by other famous directors, issued on a French DVD with English subtitles, *Chacun son cinéma,* that I was able to order fairly cheaply (it currently sells on French Amazon for about ten euros, plus postage) on the final day of the festival so that I could watch it in Chicago on a multiregional player just a few days later. So in a way I qualify both as Cronenberg's Last Jew and as one of those dopey newscasters, equally untroubled by the loss of the last cinema because I can view this particular sketch feature at home.

Clearly the degree to which technology affects virtually every aspect of our culture — from the fax machine during the Tiananmen Square protests of 1989 to the mobile phone during the postelection protests in Iran twenty years later — has been equally applicable to film history, inside and outside the movie theaters. And my life and career have both been largely shaped by these changes, as a good many pieces in this collection show.

I t's hard for me to specify too precisely when my first encounter with cinema was, because from circa 1915 to 1960, film exhibition qualified as my family's business. My paternal grandfather, Louis Rosenbaum, opened his first movie theater, the Princess, in Douglas, Wyoming, around the same time that D. W. Griffith was shooting *The Birth of a Nation* in southern California. (The Princess's first program included A *Fool There Was*, with Theda Bara.) Later the same year, my grandfather built another movie theater called the Princess in North Little Rock, Arkansas, where he moved with his wife and four-year-old son, and four years after that he moved with them still again to Florence, Alabama, where he built his third, largest, and final movie theater to be called the Princess — this one also an opera house presenting an average of twenty-five stage shows a year, as well as films. A few of the famous people who appeared there during its first couple of decades (1919–39) were cowboy stars Gene Autry and Lash LaRue, violinist Mischa Elman, composer W. C. Handy (the composer of "St. Louis Blues," who'd been born in Florence), writer Carl Sandburg, former president William Howard Taft, and jazz musicians Gene Krupa and Fats Waller.

I was born a little after this period, in 1943. By this time, my grandfather had opened at least half a dozen other movie houses in northwestern Alabama and hired his only child, Stanley, to help him manage them. Almost a year before I entered grammar school, the Rosenbaums opened their biggest establishment, the Shoals — the fourth largest in the state, with 1,350 seats, named after nearby Muscle Shoals, with a sign whose flickering neon was designed to mimic the tumbling spillways at Muscle Shoals' Wilson Dam on the Tennessee River, one of the largest such dams in the world. So already, by the time the Shoals opened, I had been attending movies at the Princess and perhaps other Rosenbaum theaters for at least a year and a half. I can still remember being frightened a little by the supernatural trappings of *That Lady in Ermine*, the Shoals' opening attraction.

Once I could enter theaters on my own, my consumption of movies went up considerably. In Florence, the Princess, the Shoals, and the Majestic, all three of which could be found within the same three-block radius, generally showed about a dozen films a week, and I usually got to see at least half of these. Then, after the Majestic closed its doors for good in mid-1951, I generally made it to almost everything that played at the two other theaters, some of them occasionally more than once, for the next eight years — until I left for boarding school in Vermont in the fall of 1959.

A little more than a year after that, while I was still away at school, the theaters that were still open were sold — Rosenbaum Theaters having shrunk by then from nine operating theaters to five. My grandfather retired, and my father began teaching American and English literature at Florence State University, known today as the University of North Alabama. And less than a decade after that, in New York, I became a professional film critic — a practice that I then continued for almost eight years in Paris and London before resuming it back in the U.S. (on both coasts, and, since 1987, in Chicago).

In March 2009, I returned to Florence to give the keynote address for a conference on world cinema held at the University of North Alabama. This lecture was given for about two dozen people in the balcony of the Shoals Theater — which twenty-nine years earlier had stopped showing movies for good, closed its doors, and then reopened them only sporadically for a few local stage productions, concerts, and similar events, meanwhile repainting the auditorium's walls and ceiling and rebuilding and expanding the stage. The conference — a private event, closed to the general public, which continued on the university campus the following day — was timed to overlap with the start of an annual film festival, then in its twelfth year. The latter event was named after and founded by George Lindsay, a TV actor and University of North Alabama alumnus, and was open to the general public; it showed films exclusively on projected DVDs in various nearby shops and cafes. (All the local commercial movie houses in the area today are located in shopping malls several miles away and have no connection of any kind with the film festival.)

The night after I gave my keynote address, the Shoals launched the George Lindsay Film Festival with a tribute to two other journeyman actors who are mainly known for their TV work in the '6os and '70s, Rance Howard and Lee Majors, both of whom had recently been cast by a local woman filmmaker (who was interviewing them onstage at the Shoals) to play in a locally produced feature. This time, none of the balcony seats but most of the thousand or so seats downstairs were filled, and the evening began with projected DVD clips from various TV shows and features that the two actors had appeared in, including a few features — such as Howard in *Cool Hand Luke* (1967) and Majors in *Will Penny* (1968) — that four decades earlier had shown on the big screen at the Shoals, in 35 mm. Only now the screen, a mere fraction as big, was planted directly behind the two actors and hostess on the stage, who were seated in swivel chairs, and even though the brief excerpts from both of these

CinemaScope films were shown in the proper screen ratio, their impact was hardly the same. Perhaps no less depressing (and significant) was the fact that the festival event that was obviously the hottest ticket and that was handled the most professionally and conscientiously was the awards ceremony — clearly patterned after the Oscars, complete with full orchestra, standup routines, digital clips, and acceptance speeches — whereas a digital screening of the paltry prizewinners, held in a room with folding chairs at the festival hotel a couple of days later, was attended by practically no one.

I could mention many other changes that have taken place in Florence over the past half century. Politically speaking, the area was both Democrat and relatively liberal while I was growing up; today it's so staunchly Republican that I'm told that only about 10 percent of the local white population voted for Barack Obama. While I was growing up, movies played a central role in the life of the entire community, including every age group — a role eventually superseded first by television and then by the Internet, to the point where most movies now are designed to cater to teenagers and younger kids.

But even if the meaning and importance of filmgoing in Florence appear to have shrunk disastrously, I'm not persuaded that the overall changes in film culture everywhere are as bleak as I'm making them sound. Viewed from a different angle, film-viewing choices have expanded considerably, at least for those who care about having such choices, and it's been especially gratifying to me how many formerly unavailable films written about in this book have become accessible while I've been assembling it. ("For a movie lover," says my contemporary Tag Gallagher, in a recent interview on a German Web site about his excellent film analyses on video, "there's been no better time to be alive — with all due respect for those who claim that only nitrate is worth watching.")

But not everyone thinks that way, and part of the confusion arises from the fact that people nowadays don't always mean the same things when they use terms like "cinema," "film," "movie," "film criticism," and even "available" — terms whose timeframes, experiences, and practical applications are no longer necessarily compatible. Older viewers typically refer to what can be seen in 35 mm in movie theaters and read about in publications on paper. Younger ones are more likely speaking about the DVDs watched in homes and the blogs or sites accessed on the Internet. Furthermore, when the older group speaks specifically about what films are "available," they usually mean films showing in theaters — or videos found in rental stores — in their own towns or cities but nowhere else, generally excepting only rentals available by mail subscription though companies such as Netflix (although this has already expanded their potential choices quite a bit). Yet theoretically, this can also mean available for purchase through the mail, either nationally or (if one has a multiregional DVD player) internationally, and/or, among more hardcore and specialized cinephiles, via swapping or copying among friends and acquaintances, *or* obtainable by download through the Internet, legally or otherwise. In fact, after all the options get added up, even the potential meanings of nationality and territory get altered, along with those involving analog or digital means of communication and formats.

Quite often, of course, a greater number of possibilities means greater chaos — one reason, I suspect, why my most popular efforts as a critic over the past several years have been lists of my 100 favorite American films and my 1,000 favorite films — available, respectively, in my books *Movie Wars* and *Essential Cinema* (and on various online sites, easily found via search engines) — which propose personal canons as a practical alternative to a surfeit of possible choices. Much of this book, indeed, can be viewed as supplements to those proposed canons. And part of the potential chaos I'm speaking about, recalling in some ways the Patent Wars of a century ago, involves issues surrounding copyright and territorial rights versus various forms of piracy (or anarchistic appropriation) — some of which I address polemically in this book (e.g., "Film Writing on the Internet," "Trailer for *Histoire(s) du cinéma*"). For it surely matters that various films that were once literally or virtually impossible to see are now visible, sometimes by extralegal means (prompted in part by the ignorance or indifference of copyright holders, or in some cases by legal entanglements). One strong example is Rivette's twelve-hour serial *Out 1*, once regarded as the most unseeable of all major contemporary films. As of September 2009, it could still be downloaded for free with both English and Italian subtitles from a site called The Pirate Bay, even after this site was temporarily shut down on August 24, 2009, by order of a Swedish district court, and it may also be obtainable online from other sources as well. As the critic Brad Stevens recently wrote in his first "AVI" column for *Video Watchdog*, striking a cinephiliac chord that is characteristically both despairing and utopian (like *Out 1* itself),

> It is surely evidence of how widely cinema is still considered a second-rate art that one of its supreme masterpieces has been denied to British and American audiences; if a similar situation existed where literature was concerned, we would only be able to read English translations of Proust's *À la recherche du temps perdu* in the form of clandestinely circulated photocopies. Yet one

can hardly resist a wry smile upon discovering that *Out 1*, a work obsessively focused on conspiracies, has finally achieved widespread distribution thanks to what might described as an Internet "conspiracy."

And here is another cinephile/critic — Adrian Martin, writing in his column for *Filmkrant* ("World Wide Angle," July/August 2009, no. 312), reflecting more on the dystopian side of the new film culture and even resorting to some horror-movie imagery:

> Let us be honest. Despite the grumbles we all make or hear that IMDb [Internet Movie Database] is missing some important films, that it has a heavy bias towards the commercial mainstream, that it all looks so Hollywood and capitalistic — it is, by now, the Monster We All Have Sex With. And the scary children born of these couplings are beginning to appear, walking on the earth . . .
>
> Just as every living journalist now sneaks a peek at Wikipedia to verify (at their peril) facts and figures and names and places, everybody in the world of film, at whatever level, uses IMDb as the One Stop Shop for basic information. It has become as essential to us as email or Facebook or the mobile phone. I have even begun to spot serious university "media sociology" studies which forego old-fashioned "vox pop" sampling for a quick flick through the brain-dead "user comments" on Amazon.com or IMDb . . .

These are certainly perturbing and challenging signs of change, and having worked professionally as a journalist for well over three decades, I think that many of the best arguments to be made for saving some portions of this work are allied to whether or not they serve as chronicles of their own period(s). Naturally, I'd like to think that all fifty-four pieces included in this book do that in one way or another, even though they also reveal specific biases along the way. (Readers will note that I'm usually more of an old fogey when it comes to mobile phones than I am about DVDs.) But truthfully, the subtitle of this book, *Film Culture in Transition*, could have been used during any or all of those thirty-odd years, as well as during either of the two preceding decades of my formative moviegoing. I daresay that for better and for worse, film culture has pretty much remained in transition for all of its existence, and will continue to remain so. That is an integral part of its mystery and magic and its continuing emotional hold on us.

Although I've tried to make this collection as wide-ranging as its predecessors (*Placing Movies*, 1995; *Movies as Politics*, 1997; *Essential Cinema*,

2004) in terms of both its time range (regarding dates of original publication — in this case, covering a thirty-five-year span) and its subject matter, a recurring emphasis is on paradigmatic changes in the ways we view movies and think and write about them. This is reflected in my selections in several ways: I've included blog posts written for Web sites (both the *Chicago Reader*'s and my own, the latter launched on May 1, 2008) and articles or reviews written for film festival catalogues, Internet and/or paper publications, and books or booklets included with DVDs (in Australia, Spain, the UK, and the U.S.), as well as a couple of papers written for academic conferences. There are also many articles *about* DVDs, and one in particular about film writing on the Internet. The occasions for each piece differ, and this is part of my point: in the first section, my first essay was addressed initially on paper to a French cinephile audience, my second to a more mainstream American blog audience, the third to a French academic audience, the fourth to the readers of an American arts magazine that could access the article either on paper or online — and this shifting pattern continues throughout the book. (There's even a piece, on Raymond Durgnat, whose footnotes mainly exclude online sources — a situation I hope will change, if Kevin Gough-Yates will bring back the wonderful Durgnat Web site.) Although the precise placements of a few pieces border on the arbitrary — the separate essays on Luc Moullet in sections 1 and 4 both could have theoretically turned up in section 2, "Bit Actors" in 2 might have gone into 1 or 4, and the essay on Godard's *Histoire(s) du cinéma* in 4 could have turned up in either 1 or 2 — I've generally tried to respect the categories in each, so that these section headings provide far more shape to this book's contents than the overall chronology, which is deliberately jumbled.

The experience of retyping some of my earliest pieces in order to get them into digital form — thereby qualifying them for inclusion in this book, being posted on my Web site, or both — has been highly instructive, existentially speaking, as a way of testing their current relevance and/or resonance. In some cases, I've had to omit pieces due to space restrictions, but in most such cases I've posted these articles on my Web site and listed their URLs here, as supplementary reading — one clear illustration of the greater number of choices available to writers and readers nowadays.

Given how many editors and friends have helped me with these pieces over the years, I know I won't be able to remember them all now. But I should at least mention Eduardo Antin, Raymond Bellour, Janet Bergstrom, Nicole Brenez, Colin Burnett, Richard Combs, Richard Corliss, Gary Crowdus, Flavia de la Fuentes, Nataša Ďurovičová, Bernard Eisenschitz, J-C Gabel, Liz Helfgott, Penelope Houston, James Hughes, J. R. Jones, Craig Keller, Michael

Koresky, Kitry Krause, Michael Lenehan, Dennis Lim, Dana Linssen, Ron Mann, Lorenzo Mans, Adrian Martin, Ricardo Matos, Don McMahon, Jean-Luc Mengus, Mehelli Modi, James Naremore, Astrid Ofner, Mark Peranson, Richard Porton, John Pym, Mehrnaz Saeed-Vafa, Kate Schmidt, Milos Steh-lik, Alexander Strang, François Thomas, Andrew Tracy, Alison True, Rob White, and Nick Wrigley.

J. R.
Chicago, September 2009

Note

1. An earlier consideration of many of these issues and their generational aspects can be found in a collection I coedited with Adrian Martin, *Movie Mutations: The Changing Face of World Cinephilia* (London: BFI Publishing, 2003), which I hope can be regarded by the reader as a companion volume to this one.

Part 1

Position Papers

Goodbye Cinema, Hello Cinephilia

What is cinema?

Before one can even start to answer this question, it becomes necessary to acknowledge that one can't formulate precisely the same definition of cinema for France as for other countries. And the reason why one can't should be obvious: in France, an important part of this definition pertains to film as an art form — a distinction that is generally perceived elsewhere only as a minority position, and sometimes even as an elitist one. But if, on the other hand, one were to ask the question "What is cinephilia?," it starts to become easier to come up with a definition that applies everywhere. A seeming contradiction, it can perhaps be explained by saying that the "cinema" in "cinephilia" is not quite the same thing as "cinema" seen as a self-sufficient term, without reference to social forms.

Consequently, to answer the question "What is cinema?" from the vantage point of a cinephile living in Chicago, it is difficult to be very optimistic, but to answer "What is cinephilia?" from the same vantage point is a much more agreeable activity.

I

Regardless of where one is, whether one is speaking rhetorically or literally, there is usually the presumption that "cinema" is something that happens inside a theater, on a screen, which one watches with other people after purchasing a ticket. But more and more often these days, I'm beginning to think that this activity in much of the world currently represents an idealist model of what cinema consists of, and that it is no longer a practical description that applies to the experience of most people.

If more people today view films on television screens than inside theaters, one can see why this theatrical model is already something of a misrepresentation — perhaps even a nostalgic holdover from the past. Whether they're watching films on TV (with or without commercial breaks, cuts, alterations of the original speed or formats) or watching videos or DVDs that they've purchased or rented, the decision to see a film and how one goes about implementing that decision are already substantially different from what they meant traditionally.

Furthermore, insofar as films often figure as the central parts of advertising campaigns selling much more than films, it becomes important to ask precisely where the existential meaning of a film begins and ends — assuming that it can be said to begin or end anywhere in the affective life of the spectator. For it's surely obvious by now that we're all deeply affected by films that we never see.

This Christmas season, when I went to a branch of the Chicago post office to renew my passport, I saw that a placard on the service counter advertising various priority-mail bundles also had a tie-in ad for *The Cat in the Hat*, a studio live-action children's movie released last week. I haven't seen the film — which is based on a book by Dr. Seuss, the penname for Theodor Geisel, a writer whose works are less known outside the U.S. — and I have no interest in seeing it; everyone I know who's seen it despises it. But this doesn't mean it won't continue to have a strong presence in my everyday life. Indeed, seeing that ad in the post office made me reflect that the Stalinist dream of a planned culture may now have become realized more thoroughly in contemporary American culture than it ever was in Russia. (The only previous theatrical film I know connected to Geisel's work is *The 5,000 Fingers of Dr. T* [1953], a childhood favorite of mine, and when I once had a phone interview with him a quarter of a century ago, he told me that he was so unhappy with the experience of working on that film that he wrote only for television ever since, where he had more creative control. Now that he's dead, however, it's obvious that his estate doesn't share his compunctions.)

I *have* seen *21 Grams*, a hyperbolically depressing art film by Alejandro González Iñárritu that has been receiving a lot of mainstream exposure lately because of its cast (Sean Penn, Naomi Watts, Benicio Del Toro) and a sizable advertising budget. Thanks to this budget, an offscreen speech by Penn at the end of the film has been getting what seems to be more attention from the press than all the recent civilian deaths in Iraq and Afghanistan combined. The speech goes as follows: "They say we all lose 21 grams at the exact moment of our death . . . everyone. The weight of a stack of nickels. The weight of a chocolate bar. The weight of a hummingbird . . ."

Part of the attention paid by the press to this speech is to point out that this statement is completely untrue. But, with the recognition that "there's no such thing as bad press," this didn't prevent Focus Features from sending out, on consecutive days late last month, express packages with transparent bags of inflated plastic containing (a) a stack of five nickels, and (b) a chocolate bar inside a wrapper advertising 21 Grams, and (c) a made-in-China "hummingbird." I assume that if Focus Features were also capable of determining and then inserting the exact moments of our own deaths inside an inflated, transparent plastic bag, complete with a tie-in to the title of their film, they'd be sending that along to us members of the press as well, and probably gift-wrapping it in the bargain.

I try to guess how many packages containing twenty-five cents each were sent to members of the press, how many homeless people might have been fed with the same amount of money, and how much anyone was directly or indirectly persuaded to see this film because of this ridiculous and obscene advertising scheme. Are there any limits to what promotional departments will try, and do they even care whether they succeed or not? After all, a few years ago, in order to promote Peter Chan's The Love Letter (1999) — a Hollywood comedy that I liked far more than 21 Grams — DreamWorks actually sent out anonymous love letters to critics. Each one appeared to be written on an old-fashioned typewriter with a faded ribbon, much like an unsigned letter that circulates in the film, and this was done so persuasively that I'm embarrassed to confess that I was fooled into thinking it was a real letter addressed to me until I attended a press screening of the film, saw the same letter onscreen, and realized the emotional rape that DreamWorks' publicity department had cheerfully perpetrated on my feelings.

What I like to ask now is, was that imitation of a love letter "cinema"? If it wasn't, what was it? And if it was, was it more cinematic or less cinematic than Chan's film?

II

It's sad in some ways to see the old paradigms of cinema dying in the U.S. But the emerging paradigms of cinephilia in this part of the world — which could significantly be almost anywhere else in world — are exciting to me, and I don't believe that we're obliged only to lament the new state of things. If we start to think of cinephilia less as a specialized interest than as a certain kind of necessity — an activity making possible things that would otherwise be impossible — then it starts to become possible to conceive of a new kind of cinephilia in which cinema in the old sense doesn't exactly disappear but becomes reconfigured (something that, after all, has been happening with a certain constancy throughout the so-called history of "cinema").

The best DVDs being made today — DVDs of the best or most important films from the past as well as the near-present — are available to spectators across the globe, especially those who get into the habit of ordering them over the Internet, and sometimes from other countries. Today, for instance, it's possible to see the beautiful colors of the second part of *Ivan the Terrible* correctly, accompanied by superb historical documentation, anywhere one has a DVD player and the Criterion edition of the DVD, with commentaries by Yuri Tsivian and Joan Neuberger. Admittedly, this isn't the same thing as seeing a 35mm print of the film with incorrect colors and with less comprehensive documentation in Paris or New York thirty years ago, but can we really say with assurance that we're necessarily less fortunate today? Obviously the rules of the game are changing, both for the better and for the worse, and the fact that spectators in small towns will mainly choose to watch the masterpieces they couldn't see before in their own homes is only one reflection of current habits and practices. The disappearance of what Raymond Bellour has called "le texte introuvable" ("the unattainable text") and all the fugitive magic that this implies has to be weighed against the appearance of the film that one can now possess and casually browse through like a book, recovering favorite passages at will. Can films seen on television screens change one's life as films on giant theatrical screens could? I think so, but almost certainly not in the same ways, and possibly in certain new ways that are still evolving. Who's to say that future ciné-clubs can't be devoted to screening DVDs in casual surroundings — storefronts or schools, for example? Or maybe they can remain in homes while regaining some of their former status as public events.

In fact, only a few days after I saw ads for *The Cat in the Hat* in a Chicago post office, I attended a political meeting a few blocks from my apartment where I met for the first time about two dozen other people who despise George W. Bush as much as I do, and who want to find ways of getting him out of office. Their ages ranged approximately from early twenties to late seventies, and the occasion of our meeting was an opportunity to watch a film on DVD called *Uncovered: The Whole Truth about the Iraq War* — made explicitly by and for a rapidly growing and highly effective activist group called MoveOn, which currently has over two million online subscribers and which had organized the party, as well as over two thousand other parties like it that were being held in the U.S. at precisely the same time, most or all of them in private homes.

It's of course far too early to know if we have a chance of getting Bush voted out of office next November, but it was an evening that gave me some hope.

Strictly an agitational documentary detailing the lies and deceptions of the Bush administration, the film was neither presented nor received as art. Yet it afforded a communal experience that I think could be honestly and fairly described as a certain kind of cinema, and I have little difficulty in imagining such an experience transferred to some of the more conventional gratifications of cinephilia.

At one point, after we all watched the film in our hostess's living room and listened on a speaker phone to members of other groups at other parties around the country, we discussed how the film could be more widely seen in Chicago. Some members proposed — a little naïvely, I thought — that some local movie theaters be persuaded to show it as soon as possible; a prominent art theater as well as a commercial multiplex were suggested. I proposed, as an alternative, more partylike gatherings such as this one, where the film could be discussed and no one had to worry about convincing local exhibitors to change their booking schedules or worry about profits. I also suggested that one can envisage traveling programs of films on DVDs (and not only political or agitational films) that can be sold to individuals after the screenings, the same way that certain singers or musicians now sell CDs of their work after giving live performances. Ciné-clubs of this kind automatically have a potential that wouldn't be conceivable if one had to worry about acquiring 35mm prints and cinemas or auditoriums to show them in.

The issue, really, is how much arrangements of this kind can be made by audiences and programmers rather than by large companies. Will they entail new forms of the cinephiliac imaginary? Undoubtedly they will, although it is surely too early to predict all the new forms that this imaginary will take, except to stress that it will combine old and new materials, channels, ideas, experiences, technologies, and authors. In my first book, *Moving Places: A Life at the Movies* [published in France as *Mouvements*], almost a quarter of a century ago, I was already lamenting the end of a certain kind of cinema as well as a certain kind of theater, and a certain kind of social interaction that went with both. But it would be vain and foolish to claim that things of this kind ever end entirely, even if they change radically beyond our childhood recognition of them. The basic point is that there are still cinephiles much younger than myself who are full of excitement about films made even before the glory days of Louis Feuillade and Yevgeni Bauer (whose mise en scène in the 1913 *Twilight of a Woman's Soul* and the 1915 *After Death* are elegantly described by Tsivian on a new American DVD called *Mad Love*); and this situation isn't ever likely to change, even if the places and contexts where these films are seen and understood become radically transformed. And even if we can no longer claim with the same confidence that we can possibly know what the cinema is in all its manifestations and forms — any more than we could ever have made such a claim for literature or theater, at least if we acknowledge that comprehensive history isn't the same thing as contemporary access and fashion — we at least have the sophistication today of being able to recognize our ignorance to a greater extent than we possibly could have during the so-called Golden Ages of the past, such as the 1920s, 1960s, and 1970s. Even during the last of these decades, when Kiarostami was already making such masterpieces as *The Traveler* and *Two Solutions for One Problem*, most of us knew next to nothing about Iranian cinema, but today — because we know now that we knew nothing then — we're more apt to admit that there are possibly things going on today that we also don't know about.

At most, one can mention a few utopian principles as a starting point. Recently encountering the web site of an organization called ELF (an acronym for Extreme Low Frequency that can be found at www.extremelowfrequency .com), run by the independent filmmaker Travis Wilkerson — devoted to showing such films as Thom Andersen and Noël Burch's *Red Hollywood,* John Gianvito's *The Mad Songs of Fernanda Hussein,* Wilkerson's own *An Injury to One* (a remarkable experimental film exploring the 1917 lynching of union organizer Frank Little in Butte, Montana), and Billy Woodbury's *Bless Their Little Hearts,* to people "in theaters, homes, and schools" — I come upon a sort of manifesto that matches many of my own convictions. Let me cite the passages that strike me as being most relevant:

> The cinema is in crisis. It neither apprehends our reality honestly nor does it aid in imagining a different kind of future. It is suffocated by a set of anachronistic conventions dictated by the agents of commerce. Extreme Low Frequency (ELF) is a corrective action. It constitutes a conscious cine-rebellion. The chief activity of ELF is the propagation of new cinema waves. These waves will take an endless number of shapes, and confront an endless battery of problems. The new cinema mustn't be an "ism," nor an academic moment. To achieve its aims, the new cinema must become permanent.
>
> . . . The new cinema doesn't concern itself with technological debates, particularly the antagonisms of analogue against digital. It employs, without prejudice, any and all tools available to it.
>
> . . . The new cinema can exist only in a state as (un)finished and (in)complete as the world it intends to mirror and engage.
>
> . . . The new cinema refuses to recognize national borders. It identifies itself neither as fiction nor as documentary. Likewise, it is unconcerned with genre, which is useful only to the agents of commerce.

. . . The new cinema will strive to return popular culture to the people themselves.

Above all else: while studying the old, create the new.

These principles imply that, before one can even begin to answer the question "What is cinema?," one first has to determine "Whose cinema?" And maybe also "Where?"—at least if we dare to suggest that cinema is that indeterminate space and activity where we find our cinephilia stimulated, gratified, and even expanded. And if the audience can find ways again of claiming a certain cinema as its own, even if that means moving out of theaters, the possibilities start to become limitless. In spite of everything we might lose, and would hate to lose, we still have no way yet of determining all we might gain.

Trafic, no. 50 (été 2004): "Qu'est-ce que le cinéma?"; see also www.jonathanrosenbaum .com/?p=7024

In Defense of Spoilers

S ome people's obsessive preoccupation with spoilers has been driving me batty lately. It isn't only among moviegoers; many fiction readers are equally afflicted. Visiting a Thomas Pynchon chat room lately in conjunction with a recent prepublication reading of *Against the Day*, I find other Pynchon freaks breathlessly advising one another about whether they should read the short review of the novel that *Time* has already posted, which actually mentions — horrors! — one of the characters getting killed, something that happens, if I remember correctly, roughly a fifth of the way through this almost 1100-page novel. Percentage-wise, that's about as far as you have to watch *The Death of a President* before you witness the assassination that the title already announces. Honestly, does that spoil the movie for anybody?

Give me a break. Is this form of worry a fit activity for grown-ups?

My objections to spoiler-think are multiple, so I might as well set them down in a list:

1. Look at novels written from *Don Quixote* all the way through much of the nineteenth century, and you'll find spoilers even in the chapter titles — headings that habitually tell you what's going to happen before it happens. Hell, Pynchon pays tribute to that practice himself in his own first novel, *V.* How come nobody complained much about this practice for a good three centuries before it started getting readers and moviegoers so hot and bothered — mainly, it would appear, over the past decade? And what about the titles of certain plays? Should William Shakespeare have been horsewhipped by Elizabethan audiences for calling one of his comedies *The Taming of the Shrew*, thus giving away the outcome of the story? And what about *Death of a Salesman*?

2. The whole concept of spoilers invariably privileges plot over style and form, assumes that everybody in the public thinks that way, and implies

that people shouldn't think any differently. It also privileges fiction over nonfiction (although Terry Zwigoff actually once complained about some reviewers of his *Crumb* including the "spoiler" that Robert Crumb's older brother, Charles, committed suicide), and I'm not clear why it necessarily should. Why is it supposedly a spoiler to say that *Touch of Evil* begins with a time bomb exploding but supposedly not a spoiler to say that the movie begins with a lengthy crane shot? Is it a spoiler only to say that Dorothy travels from Kansas to Oz, or is it also a spoiler to say that *The Wizard of Oz* switches from black and white to color?

To be totally irresponsible and give a really big spoiler to Gilbert Adair's very enjoyable *The Act of Roger Murgatroid: An Entertainment*—his latest novel, an Agatha Christie pastiche that you'll have to order from England as I did if you're an American who wants to read it—the surprise ending isn't so much the identity of the murderer as it is the revelation that he's been narrating the entire novel in first person, just like Christie's Roger Ackroyd. This is something we haven't previously realized because Murgatroid, hiding under a different name, hasn't gotten around to using the first person until the final scene, so we've been assuming all along that what we've been reading has all been in third person.

The same novel, incidentally, has a wonderful epigraph, from Raúl Ruiz: "The real world is the sum total of paths leading nowhere." Metaphysically, I find this every bit as entrancing as the epigraph for *Against the Day*, credited to Thelonious Monk: "It's always night, or we wouldn't need light." . . . Am I guilty just now of subjecting the readers of both novels to spoilers regarding these epigraphs? How can I dare give away the delightful surprise of reading these sentences on the first pages of both books!

3. One thing that drives me around the bend about spoilers is that it's impossible to function as a critic if one can't describe anything in a movie or a book in advance. So if I'm expected to write a review of something, am I also expected not to analyze it?

4. The weird metaphysical implication of spoilers is that moviegoers and readers who fret about them want to regain their innocence, perhaps even their infancy, and experience everything as if it were absolutely fresh. From this standpoint, we shouldn't even know what films we're going to see in advance, or who stars in them, or who directed them, or what they're about, or perhaps even where they're playing. Just so we can experience the bliss of being taken there by benevolent parents.

Chicago Reader film blog post, November 14, 2006

Potential Perils
of the Director's Cut

Perhaps the biggest source of confusion regarding the term "director's cut" is the fact that it can serve both as a legal concept and as an advertising slogan, and both as an aesthetic theory and as an actual aesthetic praxis. In some instances, it can serve all of these functions, but I would argue that most of these instances occur in France — the only country, to my knowledge, where the legal concept is backed up by an actual law pertaining to les droits d'auteur. And even here, I've been told that this law is not always and invariably a guarantee of artistic freedom. A few years ago, while he was working on *Le temps retrouvé*, Raúl Ruiz told me in effect that in some cases it could function as a law that took on the characteristics of a deceitful advertising slogan — which is to say that it doesn't always function as an enforceable law, especially when larger sums of money are involved and various kinds of coercion are available to producers who want to impose their will on certain creative decisions made by filmmakers.

Even in the case of Ruiz's more recent *Klimt*, where the term "director's cut" still has a real meaning, it has apparently only been in France that the director's cut is being shown commercially. At the Rotterdam film festival last year, both the director's cut (which runs 127 minutes) and the producer's cut (which runs 97 minutes) were shown on separate days. I saw both versions and found that the producer's cut paradoxically and ironically seems to last much longer, to the point of tedium, because it comes across as a failed biopic whereas the director's cut, which clearly doesn't aspire to the status of a biopic, seems not only shorter but also more successful in terms of being more artistically coherent.

I should add that this state of affairs is quite common; I would also say that Jacques Rivette's original 169-minute version of *L'amour par terre* (1983) feels shorter than the 125-minute version that he was asked by his producer to edit—which is the only version that was commercially available until the 169-minute was belatedly released on DVD twenty years later. I would also argue that the longer version is more interesting, more coherent, and even more commercial—which is always or almost always the case with Rivette, especially if we recall that in 1968 the long version of *L'amour fou* performed better at the box office.

The case of *Out 1* is more debatable, of course—and less directly relevant to the concerns of this discussion, because both versions qualify as director's cuts: the 760-minute film of 1971 in eight episodes, made for (but rejected by) French state television, where Rivette hoped it would be run as a serial, and the radically different 255-minute version that he prepared in 1972, with a separate editor, for theatrical showings. But the issue of "longer" versus "shorter" remains pertinent to the more difficult task of discriminating between two or more director's cuts of the same material—which is surely an issue worth addressing, and one that challenges our usual terminology and categories. Are *Out 1* and *Out 1: Spectre* two different films, or two different versions of the same film? If we decide they're different films, our task becomes relatively easy. But if we decide that they're two different versions of the same film, don't we then have to construct, at least implicitly, a theoretical or Platonic model of this "same film" that necessarily qualifies as a third version? And don't we then have to judge the two versions according to how close each one comes to this model?

In order to make a distinction between aesthetic and business ways of dealing with this issue, it seems worth arguing that the long version of *Out 1* was never given an opportunity to function in commercial terms once it was rejected by French television—or at least it wasn't until it finally surfaced on cable television many years afterwards, in the early 1990s, long after its historical moment had passed. And because the serial is easier to follow as narrative and, as Rivette himself has noted, closer to being a comedy than the four-hour version, I believe it can also be deemed more commercial. Yet paradoxically, *Spectre* was created precisely in order to make *Out 1* more presentable—that is to say, more commercial.

As a final, preliminary comment on the sort of ongoing confusion that we typically encounter between aesthetics and business, let me cite a joke offered in 1971 by the screenwriter and director of Westerns Burt Kennedy, as cited by Richard Corliss in his 1974 book *Talking Pictures*: "I was driving by Otto Preminger's house last night—or is it [better to call this] 'a house by Otto Preminger'?"

Arguably, one reason why the film industry as a whole has encouraged and promoted the concept of a director's cut, even though it might appear to be counter to its own interests in certain cases, is that it enables a film's owner to sell the same product to the same customer twice. The mythology underlying this process appears superficially to be that every film has two versions, a correct one and an incorrect one. But in fact this isn't quite true. A better paraphrase of the mythology would be to say, more paradoxically, that every film has at least two versions — a correct one and a *more* correct one.

I should add that in François Thomas's French translation of the previous two sentences, in my abstract for this paper, which I approved last month, this particular distinction became somewhat simplified: "*Superficiellement, le mythe à l'œuvre est que chaque film a deux versions, une bonne et une mauvaise. En réalité, il sous-entend que chaque film a au moins deux versions, une bonne et une meilleure.*" On reflection, this is a journalistic simplification — and a necessary one, I should add, for the purposes of a brief abstract, but still inadequate in relation to the larger point I wish to make. The distinction seems worth making, because the term "more correct" in English is a barbarism — a little bit like the term "slightly pregnant" — and I used it to parody the sort of illogical leap sometimes made by large companies when they employ the term "director's cut."

As one example of what I mean, I'd like to quote my capsule review of something that's widely known as the "director's cut" of Joseph Losey's *Eva* (or *Eve*, as it's known in the U.K.), written a few years ago for the *Chicago Reader*:

A failure, but an endlessly fascinating one. Between making his only SF film (*The Damned*) and his first successful art movie (*The Servant*), black-listed expatriate Joseph Losey directed this 1962 film, adapted by Hugo Butler and Evan Jones from a James Hadley Chase novel, about a washed-up Welsh novelist of working-class origins (Stanley Baker) who unsuccessfully pursues a high-class hooker (Jeanne Moreau) while effectively driving his wife (Virna Lisi) to suicide. The film is pretentious and plainly derivative; I've always regarded as unwarranted and philistine Pauline Kael's ridicule of Antonioni, Resnais, and Fellini in an article of the period called "The Come-Dressed-as-the-Sick-Soul-of-Europe Parties," but she might well have included Losey's film, with its clear debt to all three. It's a painful testament of sorts (Losey himself can be glimpsed in a bar during a pan that also introduces the hero, showing his personal stake in the proceedings from the outset), though it makes wonderful use of locations in Venice and Rome and features an excellent jazz score by Michel Legrand (with a pivotal use of three Billie Holiday cuts). A decadent period piece and a sadomasochistic view of sexual relations, this singular, resonant, and at times even inspiring mannerist mess is far more interesting than a good many modest successes. Losey can't be blamed entirely for the film's disjointedness either; its producers mucked around with it, ultimately reducing it from 155 to 100 minutes. Labeling this rare 120-minute version with two kinds of Scandinavian subtitles — the longest surviving edition since the '60s — the "director's cut," as various publicists and reviewers have been irresponsibly doing, only adds insult to injury.

This review places the blame for misappropriating the term "director's cut" on "various publicists and reviewers," which is a way of personalizing the issue. But more objectively, I believe one could place at least part of the blame on advertising and journalism as institutions, both of which commonly feel obliged to represent both the meaning and the value of certain films in "twenty-five words or less," as the common expression goes. In other words, one can't simply blame publicists and reviewers for these abuses when the individuals in question are merely responding to the requests and perceived requirements of studio executives and newspaper and magazine editors. All these figures tend to regard both films and film reviews as commodities rather than as unique objects, with the consequence that many possible distinctions can get bypassed for the sake of what might be described as an "undisturbed" and continuous product flow. Nuances and ambiguities tend to get overlooked whenever considerations about the flow become more important than anything else.

One good example of what I mean is the 2004 version of Samuel Fuller's *The Big Red One* produced by Richard Schickel. To my mind, neither the 1980 release nor Schickel's alleged "reconstruction" of the original longer cut of the film qualifies as a director's cut. For one thing, Fuller was adamant about not wanting an offscreen narration, and an offscreen narration figures in both of the existing versions. If I had to choose between these two versions, I would choose the more recent one, although this isn't the same thing as calling it the director's cut. But in the kind of journalistic shorthand that we've become accustomed to, it automatically takes on the status of one.

On the other hand, we face a quite different dilemma when we encounter two or more versions of a film that *do* qualify as director's cuts. Consider the principal Italian version of Abbas Kiarostami's *Taste of Cherry* — which is missing the film's final sequence, a documentary sequence shot in video, that occurs in all the other versions of the film that I'm aware of. (Reportedly this sequence was shot by Kiarostami's son for a documentary about the making of *Taste of Cherry*, and Kiarostami's decision to include it was an afterthought.)

Soon after the film premiered at Cannes in 1997, many critics and various friends and acquaintances of Kiarostami urged him to cut the original ending, for commercial and/or artistic reasons. Half a year later, when I heard that Kiarostami himself decided to delete this ending from the version of the film opening in Italy, I was so upset and appalled by this decision that I wrote Kiarostami a letter and faxed it to him in Iran, urging him to reconsider this decision. At this point, I should add, the film had not yet opened commercially in the U.S., and I was especially worried about the film being deprived of its original ending elsewhere, especially because I regarded this ending then — and continue to regard it today — as a major asset of the film, not in any way a flaw. Although I didn't mention this in my letter, I believed that the changes in style and form represented by the final scene were comparable in some ways to the changes in the final sequence of Michelangelo Antonioni's *Eclipse*, which was reportedly cut from the film, and completely without the consent of Antonioni, when it showed at certain American cinemas in the early '60s, as reported at the time by the critic Dwight Macdonald in *Esquire* — a decision apparently made by certain exhibitors. In the case of *Eclipse*, it appears that the stated reason for removing this sequence was the fact that neither of the two stars, Monica Vitti and Alain Delon, appears in it, though of course this absence is part of the point of the sequence. In the case of the ending of *Taste of Cherry*, the actor playing the major character appears in it, but as himself, not as his character, and Kiarostami appears in the sequence as well; the point in this case is to reflect on the shooting of the film rather than on its fictional story. It's obvious in these two cases that without their final sequences, both films are quite different, and to my mind they're also quite inferior.

I was both surprised and gratified when Kiarostami wrote me back in English only two days later. He explained to me that for the Italian-dubbed version of the film, he decided, as an experiment, to show the film with the original ending in some theaters and without the original ending in some other theaters, and to see what the differences in audience reactions would be. In other words, one could conclude from his letter that there were in fact two director's cuts of *Taste of Cherry* in Italy, with and without the original ending, but that he intended to show the film with the original ending everywhere else, which suggested that the original version was the one that he still preferred. From this standpoint, the notion of "*une bonne version et une meilleure version*" continues to have some meaning, but not "*une version exact et une version plus exact.*"

Unfortunately, as far as I could tell, on the basis of the testimonies of various Italian friends, Kiarostami's experiment lasted only as long as his stay in Italy; after he left, the Italian distributor chose to show only the shorter version of the film, and the longer version basically disappeared. This raises the interesting and somewhat vexing question of whether or not the shorter director's cut of *Taste of Cherry* was still the director's cut after Kiarostami left Italy.

An important point arising from this example is that any director's cut has to be pinpointed in time for this label to have any meaning. To postulate that only one director's cut can exist for a given film implies the privileging of a particular point of closure in the filmmaker's creative decisions — a privileging that becomes quite arbitrary in some cases. Since there are many different subtitled versions of some of the later Straub-Huillet films employing different takes and therefore different editing, choosing one version over all the others may be capricious, and arguably the same thing might be true for the separate 1952 and 1953 versions of *Othello* edited by Orson Welles, as recently described by François Thomas in *Cinéma 012*, in an ongoing series of articles significantly titled "Un film d'Orson Welles en cache un autre." In this case, do we privilege the first thoughts or the second thoughts, and how do we defend our selection?

Once revision becomes an issue, any notion of a single director's cut has to be discarded. (The same considerations apply, of course, to revisions of literary works by their authors after their initial publication.) And how we evaluate the status of multiple director's cuts of the same film varies from case to case. To cite a rather extreme theoretical example, I'd like to quote something from Krzysztof Kieślowski regarding his original plans for *The Double Life of Véronique*:

> At one stage we had the idea of making as many versions of *Véronique* as there are cinemas in which the film was to be shown. In Paris, for example, the film was to be shown in seventeen cinemas. So we had the idea to make seventeen different versions. It would be quite expensive, of course — especially at the last stage of production — making internegatives, individual re-recordings and so on. But we had very precise ideas for all these versions. What's a film? we thought. Theoretically it's something which goes through a projector at the speed of twenty-four frames a second and, in fact, the success of cinematography depends on repetition. That is, whether you project in a huge cinema in Paris or in a tiny cinema in Mława or a medium-sized cinema in Nebraska, the same thing appears on screen because the film passes through the projector at the same speed. And so we thought, Why, in fact, does it have to be like that? Why can't we say that the film is handmade? And that every version's going to be different? And that if you see version number 00241b then it'll be a bit different from 00243c. Maybe it'll have a slightly different ending, or maybe one scene will be a tiny bit longer and another a bit shorter, or maybe there'll be a scene which isn't in the

other version, and so on. That's how we worked it out. And that's how the script was written. We shot enough material to make these versions possible. It would be possible to release this film with the concept that it was, so to speak, hand-made. That if you go to a different cinema, you'll see the same film but in a slightly different version, and if you go to yet another cinema, you'll see yet another version, seemingly the same film but a little different. Maybe it'll have a happier ending, or maybe slightly sadder — that's the chance you take. Anyway, the possibility was there. But as always, of course, it turned out that production absolutely didn't have the time, and that, in fact, there wasn't any money for it either. Perhaps the money was less important. The main problem was time. There wasn't any time left.[1]

Kieślowski went on to explain that there were in fact two versions of the film because he made a different version of the film's ending for America. In fact, although he didn't say this, the separate, "happier," and somewhat less ambiguous ending he edited for the U.S., which was four shots longer, was done at the request (or perhaps at the demand) of Miramax's codirector at the time, Harvey Weinstein, after the film showed with its original ending at the New York Film Festival in 1991 and Miramax had agreed to distribute the film. According to an article by Weinstein which I read years ago, and which I don't have access to now, Kieślowski congratulated Weinstein on the brilliance of his suggestion and said that it was better than his own original ending. According to Kieślowski himself, however, his thoughts about the matter were somewhat different and more cynical: "Of course I thought about the audience all the time while making *Véronique* so that I even made a different ending for the Americans, because I thought you have to meet them halfway, even if it means renouncing your own point of view."[2]

The difference between Weinstein and Kieślowski's accounts seems crucial. According to Weinstein — whose article was clearly an explanation of why he was so brilliant that he could only improve other people's films by reediting them, which he then proceeded to do with a large number of his subsequent releases, with or without the director's approval — the "true" director's cut of *Véronique* would be the U.S. version, precisely because he knew or understood Kieślowski's intentions better than the filmmaker did himself. (This is the same argument that was recently made to me by Michael Dawson — an American film technician who has already revised the soundtrack of Welles's *Othello* and plans to revise the soundtrack of *Chimes at Midnight* in the near future by adding the sound of neighing horses to one shot "because if Orson were alive today, I'm sure he would have done it himself.") According to Kieślowski — and, I'm happy to report, according also to Criterion, who just released the film on

DVD — the director's cut is the original one released everywhere except for the U.S., so that the American ending on the Criterion DVD is included simply as a bonus. But it's important to add that this distinction can be made only if we limit Kieślowski to one director's cut; if he'd produced seventeen director's cuts, as originally planned, the issue would be much harder to resolve.

Let me cite a more specific example of revision in the case of a film on which I worked myself — the only time in my life when I've ever been employed by a film studio. This was on the reediting of Welles's *Touch of Evil* by Walter Murch according to a studio memo written by Welles while the film was in its penultimate stages of postproduction — a project undertaken by producer Rick Schmidlin, on which I was hired to serve as a consultant. I was brought to this job because I'd originally published about two-thirds of this memo myself, in the fall of 1992, almost simultaneously in *Film Quarterly* in the U.S. and in *Trafic* in France. I was editing the book *This Is Orson Welles* at the time, published in France as *Moi, Orson Welles*, which chiefly consisted of a lengthy interview with Welles by Peter Bogdanovich, but also contained many documents, including an edited version of this memo by Welles, at least until my editor decided to delete this text for reasons of space. So I decided to publish the text elsewhere, as what might be described as an "outtake" from the book, and after having been turned down by both *Premiere* and *Film Comment*, this text was accepted by *Film Quarterly* and *Trafic*. [2009 postscript: Today, the full text of this memo is available only in Universal's three-disc DVD box set and on the web site Wellesnet.com.]

Some years later, the cinematographer Allen Daviau contacted me about possibly using this text in some fashion on the laserdisc of *Touch of Evil* that was then being planned, and still later this project was taken over by Rick Schmidlin, who then approached Universal with the proposal of following the instructions in the memo as closely as possible in a reedited and remixed version of the film.

It was clear to Schmidlin, Murch, and myself throughout this project that what we were undertaking was neither a "restoration" nor a "director's cut," and we went to great lengths to stress this fact in the pressbook that we prepared. One can't restore something that never existed previously, and nothing survives in Universal's *Touch of Evil* materials that qualifies as a "director's cut." Welles's own comments in the memo are unambiguous and unequivocal in this respect. To quote from two separate passages:

> My effort has been to keep scrupulous care that this memo should avoid
> those wide and sweeping denunciations of your new material to which my
> own position naturally and sorely tempts me. In this one instance I'm pass-

ing on to you a reaction based — not on my convictions as to what my picture ought to be — but only what here strikes me as significantly mistaken in your picture. It's sufficiently your own by now, for me to be able to judge it on what I take to be your terms alone, and to bring to that judgment — (after so much time away from the film in any form) — a certain freshness of eye.

And later on:

I ask you please to believe that what minimum criticism of that new material I am passing on to you, is made in recognition and full acceptance of the fact that the final shape and emphasis of the film is to be wholly yours. I want the picture to be as effective as possible — and now, of course, that means effective in your terms.

It was never the intention of Schmidlin, Murch, or myself to supplant the earlier versions of *Touch of Evil* that had already circulated. We hoped, in fact, that a box set devoted to at least three versions would be released by Universal [as finally did happen in 2008]. Speaking now only for myself, I would use the same term to describe what we did as the term used by Kiarostami: "experiment," which might have also been used by Kieślowski if he had edited seventeen separate versions of *Véronique*. But, as in the case of Kiarostami, our power to influence the reception of this experiment was limited to a period when we were still in some control over how it was being understood. Although we were happy to find that a large number of the original reviews of the reedited *Touch of Evil* took some trouble to differentiate what we had done from a restoration or a director's cut, thanks to our efforts, some of this emphasis vanished over time, so that some supposedly authoritative reference books have misrepresented our efforts by reverting to those terms — which, to all practical purposes have now become trade terms rather than aesthetic or material descriptions of our work.

The commodification of artworks ultimately affects not only their definitions and catalog descriptions but also to some extent their distribution. As astonishing as this may sound, all original invitations from foreign film festivals to show the reedited *Touch of Evil* were rejected by the woman in charge of foreign sales at Universal because, according to Rick Schmidlin, she was convinced that no one outside the United States had the least bit of interest in Orson Welles. Once she changed her mind, the film was of course shown all over the world, but arriving at this stage took some time.

More generally, the issue of commodification can sometimes affect the coordination between the technical realization of a DVD and its content. By chance, while writing this lecture I received in the mail a few DVDs from Australia containing commentaries by the Australian film critic Adrian Martin. One of these films was Luis Buñuel's *The Exterminating Angel*, and as many of you will recall, less than five minutes into the film, Buñuel deliberately repeats a brief scene of guests arriving at a dinner party at the same time that a couple of servants are leaving and the host is calling for his butler, showing this scene a second time from different camera angles. Martin's commentary deals at some length with this repetition and its significance — quoting Buñuel's own comments in *My Last Sigh* about several deliberate repetitions in the film, including this one, and how this one was even misunderstood by Buñuel's chief cameraman while the film was being edited, believing it to be a technical error even though this cameraman had shot both versions of the scene himself.

But through an absurd technical error on the part of the DVD company, which ignored Martin's commentary and arrived at the same erroneous conclusion as the cameraman, the scene's repetition was deleted — even though Martin, who was watching a more complete print while giving his commentary, discusses it at some length. So ironically, it might be concluded that one Surrealist non sequitur, quite deliberate, was replaced by another one, completely accidental, to anyone following Martin's commentary. In both cases, the viewer is apt to be puzzled by and perhaps a little incredulous about what she or he has just seen and heard.

I'd like to conclude by broaching a few of the ontological issues raised by the two best known versions of *Blade Runner*—namely, the original release version of 1982 and the so-called director's cut of 1992.[3] To complicate matters, the DVD of the latter version is explicitly labeled "The Director's Cut: The Original Cut of the Futuristic Adventure." But as we know from Paul M. Sammon's book *Future Noir: The Making of Blade Runner* (New York: Harper-Collins, 1996), none of the five separate versions of *Blade Runner* seen by the general public fits that description. On the other hand, one can certainly sympathize with the dilemma of a publicist who might have wished to represent accurately the nature and status of any of these five versions on a DVD box label — a list that doesn't even include what Sammon calls "Paul Gardiner's *Blade Runner: The Final Director's Cut*" — a sixth version that hasn't yet been shown to the public, and that is even less of a director's cut than at least two of the others.

What follows is a highly abbreviated account of a slapstick saga that Sammon devotes an entire book to recounting, and one that for me raises the same question raised by the woman in charge of foreign sales at Universal Pictures — namely, how the Hollywood studios manage to produce and distribute films at all, much less do so profitably. In 1989, a sound reconstruction consultant named Michael Arick discovered a 70mm print of *Blade Runner* in a vault. Eventually screened as part of a film series in Los Angeles the following year, this version turned out to be a work print that had been shown as a sneak preview in Denver, Colorado, on March 5, 1982 (which is incidentally the same day on which Philip K. Dick's body was cremated in Santa Ana, California), and then on the following evening in Dallas, Texas. At this point the film had neither a voiceover (apart from one brief segment) nor a happy ending, and the somewhat mixed audience responses persuaded Warners to add both these things. But it's important to add that the whole idea of using a voiceover had been hatched in mid-1980, after the project had been in development for about five years. According to Hampton Fancher, the main screenwriter, Ridley Scott, the director, "was the one who initially pushed the voiceover idea. That's why it's [in] so many of my drafts"—and Sammon adds that ample documentation exists to support this statement. But according to David Peoples, Fancher's cowriter, most of the voiceovers had been removed from successive drafts of the script in early 1981, with the original intention of restoring some of them in postproduction. And in fact, Harrison Ford recorded a voiceover three separate times—the first two times in late 1981, supervised by Scott, who subsequently decided, once again, to scrap almost all of it in either version, and the third time, after the Denver and Dallas previews, supervised by Bud Yorkin and mainly written by Roland Kibbee, after Scott had essentially given up on his own version.

If we flash-forward again to 1990, when the 70mm preview version was shown, Scott saw it and felt it was closer to his intentions than the 1982 release version. With this in mind, he proposed that Warners release a cleaned-up version of this work print as a director's cut. But he was too busy at the time working on *Thelma and Louise* to supervise this work himself—although a few months later, when he was less busy, he did try, without any success, to purchase the print from Warners. But by this time, Warners had begun to screen the 70mm print publicly more often in Los Angeles, with much success. Then Warners struck a 35mm reduction dupe print from it and opened it commercially in Los Angeles, billed as "The Original Director's Version."

Scott, who was back in London at the time, casting his film *1492*, wasn't even aware of this until someone belatedly informed him, in September 1991. He flew back to Warners in Los Angeles and proposed revising this version in order to make it a proper director's cut. They reached an agreement to proceed with this plan. But due to some misunderstanding and confusion, two different versions of this revision were then set in motion—one in London, carried out by Michael Arick, who followed Scott's detailed instructions, and the other one in Los Angeles, carried out by Peter Gardiner, who had a much more rudimentary revision in mind and was apparently unaware that Arick's version was also in the works. Scott, however, was so distracted by his work on *1492* that he wound up approving Gardiner's version instead of Arick's. Neither version, however, had the enigmatic shot of a unicorn that had been deleted during postproduction — an *idée fixe* of Scott's that was far more important to him than any other detail, and a shot that had subsequently been lost by the studio. So when Warners decided to release Gardiner's aforementioned *Blade Runner: The Final Director's Cut*, the sixth version cited by Sammon, without this shot, Scott threatened to place an ad in *Variety* and *Hollywood Reporter* publicly disowning this version.

Consequently, Arick was brought back and asked to prepare a third version of the director's cut in a month's time — ignoring most of Scott's former specifications, but omitting the happy ending and all of the voiceover and somehow contriving to include the shot of the unicorn. Arick finally found an outtake of the unicorn that Scott had rejected a decade earlier, completing his version in the nick of time.

As Arick put it to Sammon later, "I had to resign myself to coming up with a Director's Cut that was only a slightly modified version of the original theatrical release. But it was better than nothing." And Scott essentially agreed with this description: "The so-called Director's Cut isn't, really. But it's close. And at least I got my unicorn."

Scott's philosophical acceptance of this version as "close" significantly resembles the usual position of publicists regarding such matters — which is that in the final analysis, each film has two versions, a correct version and a more correct version. The notion that any version might be incorrect is one that belongs to history and aesthetics, but not to business.

To add a brief critical afterword to this account, I should confess that, as in the case of George Cukor's *A Star Is Born* — released in 1954, cut by Warners, and then partially restored in 1983, sometimes with stills to represent missing scenes — I mainly prefer the original release version to the later version that attempts to bring the work closer to its original conception. But I should add that the strength of *Blade Runner* in either version is more one of spectacle than one of narrative, and more a matter of visual design than one of narrative fluidity or cogency. I find the narrative periodically obscure in both versions, and the additional ambiguity of the second version is not one for me that necessarily enhances the story's ambiguities about which characters are human and what the characteristics of being human are. I would further argue that the commercial failure of the original release version can probably be blamed in part on the absurdities of the preview system itself — which I have written about elsewhere[4] as a kind of voodoo pseudo-science that relies on an audience forming its impressions and opinions immediately, as soon as a screening is over. Therefore, much of the debate about the relative merits of one version of the film over another is in part a displaced rationalization of a film that is relatively strong as spectacle and somewhat confused and unformed as narrative in all its versions.

Le mythe du director's cut (Paris: Presses Sorbonne Nouvelle, 2008), a collection co-edited by Michel Marie and François Thomas, adapted from a lecture given at a conference on "director's cuts" held at the Toulouse Cinémathèque in early 2007

Notes

1. *Kieślowski on Kieślowski*, edited by Danusia Stok, (London/Boston: Faber and Faber, 1993), 187–88.
2. Ibid., 189.
3. This paper was written prior to the release of *Blade Runner: The Final Cut*, which I subsequently reviewed in the *Chicago Reader* (November 1, 2007). See "The Actual Definitive Ultimate Director's Cut," www.jonathanrosenbaum.com/?p=15814.
4. *Movie Wars: How Hollywood and the Media Limit What Films We Can See* (Chicago: A Cappella, 2000); see especially 2–9.

Southern Movies, Actual and Fanciful: A Personal Survey

For a born Southerner such as myself, hailing from northwest Alabama, there are basically two kinds of movies set in the Deep South: authentic and inauthentic ones. The former are those done by filmmakers who consider it worth the trouble to film in the right locations, with the right actors, using the right accents while giving some attention to the local folkways. The latter are basically those who don't know and don't care about such distinctions.

The most obvious example of the first kind of filmmaker is Elia Kazan, who even went to the trouble of hiring a "speech consultant," Margaret Lamkin, for his celebrated stage production of *Cat on a Hot Tin Roof*, and then used her again on his film *Baby Doll*, to ensure that all the accents were letter-perfect. It's too bad that Richard Brooks didn't hire Lamkin when he made his 1958 film version of *Cat on a Hot Tin Roof*. And an even greater lack of Southern verisimilitude hampers the second Richard Brooks film of a Tennessee Williams play directed on the stage by Kazan, *Sweet Bird of Youth* (1962), even though no less than four of the same original actors were used — Paul Newman, Geraldine Page (admittedly, in the part of a non-Southerner), Madeleine Sherwood, and Rip Torn. Having seen this Kazan production, I can attest to the profound differences in overall feel and flavor between the play and the movie, especially when it came to handling locale.

Kazan, who'd spent some time in the Deep South as part of his leftist activities during the Depression, was partly reacting against the artificiality of *Pinky*, a 1949 studio-bound effort at Twentieth Century-Fox he'd been assigned to take over from John Ford. He vowed to do a better job on his subsequent films with Southern settings, and he was true to his word on *Panic in the Streets* (1950), *A Streetcar Named Desire* (1951), *Baby Doll* (1956), *A Face in the Crowd*

(1957), and *Wild River* (1960). The first two were set in New Orleans (though *Streetcar* was filmed exclusively in studio sets), *Baby Doll* in rural Mississippi, *A Face in the Crowd* in Arkansas and Tennessee, and *Wild River* in the same general area where I grew up, the Tennessee Valley (which extends from Tennessee to northern Alabama).

In all these movies, the local shadings are very conscientiously and meticulously rendered, even when the performances are highly stylized in other respects. In *Baby Doll*, for instance, the black characters, all minor figures in the story, comprise a kind of amused Greek chorus to the foolish goings-on of the white principals. One could theoretically object to the way such stylization conflicts with the naturalism of the on-location shooting, but the way the characters sound is as letter-perfect as Williams's dialogue. So when Baby Doll, played by Carroll Baker, delightfully defends her small-town sophistication by declaring herself with pride "a magazine reader," a whole tradition of strained Southern gentility gets pinned into place, and the way Baker pronounces it (roughly, "uh mygahzine reah-duh") makes it even more spot-on.

Among directors, Kazan probably had the most consistent track record of anyone. Three other good examples of ones who took the trouble to get things right would be Clarence Brown (a Southerner himself, who directed the memorable 1949 William Faulkner adaptation *Intruder in the Dust* on location in Oxford, Mississippi), Phil Karlson (a Chicagoan who directed what is in my opinion the best feature ever set in Alabama, *The Phenix City Story* — a seedy noirish docudrama about a crime-ridden town located next to a military base, filmed on location in 1955, with some of the town's residents used effectively in bit parts), and, rather surprisingly, Luis Buñuel — whose underrated and neglected 1960 Mexican feature *The Young One*, supposedly set on an island off the coast of Georgia, is uncommonly smart and accurate about depicting Southern Baptists.

The most obvious negative examples would be the absurd Hollywood skim job of William Faulkner's *The Sound and the Fury*, directed by Martin Ritt on the Twentieth Century-Fox backlot in 1959 (with none other than Yul Brynner pressed into service as Jason Compson); Otto Preminger's 1967 *Hurry Sundown* (set in Georgia and filmed in Louisiana, but truly taking place in some Never-Neverland derived more from other bad movies about the South than from the South itself); John Frankenheimer's 1970 *I Walk the Line* (in which Gregory Peck is supposed to incarnate a Southern sheriff). Last but not least, Alan Parker's 1988 *Mississippi Burning* is wrong about everything — Jim Crow segregation practices at lunch counters, the role played by the FBI during the Civil Rights movement, and the ways most of the people look and sound, just for starters. Yet this movie is so adept at dishing out pro-vigilante sensationalism — a trait it ironically shares with *The Birth of a Nation*, not to mention the 1996 *A Time to Kill* — that it made much more of a mark than a relatively accurate and sober as well as old-fashioned liberal account of the Civil Rights movement, Carl Reiner's *Ghosts of Mississippi*, also released in 1996.

Robert Altman's 1975 *Nashville* is a good example of a movie that's full of fine things despite the fact that it's pretty bogus as a depiction of where it's supposed to be set. (If you doubt my words, try talking to people who live there.) Admittedly, it was filmed on location, but Joan Tewksbury wrote the script after spending only a few days there, leading singer Brenda Lee to call the movie a "dialectical collage of unreality." Altman, I should add, had already done a somewhat better job in relating to rural Mississippi during the Depression when he'd made *Thieves Like Us* the year before *Nashville*; and a quarter of a century later, he would deal plausibly with that state again, this time in the present, in *Cookie's Fortune*.

■■■■■■■■■

I'm not trying to argue that fidelity to Southern reality should necessarily supersede other criteria when it comes to adapting material related to the South. Bertrand Tavernier, who once codirected a reputable documentary with Robert Parrish called *Mississippi Blues* (1983), also opted two years earlier to adapt Jim Thompson's pulp novel about a police chief, *Pop. 1280*, by transposing the action from the American South to French West Africa, and according to most accounts, the resulting *Coup de torchon* (*Clean Slate*, 1981) is a plausible fit.

Furthermore, it's worth stressing that a few irreproachable films dealing with relations between black and white characters in small-town settings that are putatively Southern manage to fulfill this agenda without emphasizing or even addressing any specifically Southern traits. I'm thinking above all of Jacques Tourneur's sublime *Stars in My Crown* (1950), in which an enlightened and imaginative preacher (Joel McCrea) manages to prevent a lynching by the local Ku Klux Klan of a black man (Juano Hernandez) who has refused to sell his property. And not far behind this masterpiece are two other underrated low-budget dramas that directly address interracial issues: Leo C. Popkin and Russell Rouse's *The Well* (1951), which charts the snowballing effects through which a simple accident involving a black girl slowly builds into a race riot, and Roger Corman's *The Intruder* (1962), adapted by Charles Beaumont from his own novel about a rabble-rousing Yankee racist stirring up Southern whites in a town whose high school is about to become desegregated. (Inspired by the real-life exploits of John Kasper in Clinton, Tennessee, Corman's film may have blunted the edge of its own story by planting its own events in a fictitious town in Missouri, but the loss was relatively minor.)

■■■■■■■■■

In the silent era, two of the most exceptional Southern movies are the afore-mentioned *The Birth of a Nation* (1915) — made by native Kentuckian D. W. Griffith, with all the racial biases that one might expect from a traditional white Southerner of his era — and the unjustly uncelebrated *Stark Love*, made a dozen years later in the Smoky Mountains of North Carolina by Karl Brown (1896–1990). An uncredited camera operator on *The Birth of a Nation* and many other Griffith classics, Brown broke into directing himself with this highly unorthodox and commercially unsuccessful Paramount release about Appalachian mountain folk — a love story shot on location with nonprofes-sionals for a total cost of about $5,000. Fondly remembered by James Agee, among others, the film was considered lost for many decades until film histo-rian Kevin Brownlow discovered a surviving print at a film archive in Prague in 1968. Although I haven't seen it in years, it persists in my memory as the most authentic film record that we probably have of the sort of Southern hillbillies caricatured in such Yankee-drawn comic strips as *Barney Google and Snuffy Smith* and *L'il Abner*.

The Birth of a Nation and the much later *Gone with the Wind* (1939) testify to the enduring popularity of Civil War stories recounted from Southern view-points. (Buster Keaton's *The General*, released the same year as *Stark Love*, of-fers a third example.) By contrast, Hollywood features that deal significantly or honestly with prewar slavery in the South tend to be few and far between. The best example that comes to mind, Richard Fleischer's well-researched and genuinely shocking *Mandingo* (1974), has been mainly dismissed in the U.S. as trashy camp — perhaps because it comes too close to the material facts of slavery as a tainted part of the American past to be faced squarely — but praised by some of the more discerning British film critics, most notably Andrew Brit-ton. (Significantly, I had to order my own DVD copy from Hong Kong.) Less shocking, but no less illuminating, are two clear-sighted movies made on the subject for American television by black filmmaker Charles Burnett, who was born in Mississippi, *Nightjohn* (1996) and *Nat Turner: A Troublesome Property* (2003).

The Civil War and, more generally, the South figure significantly in much of the work of John Ford as a kind of mythical watershed. To focus momen-tarily on just the four films Ford made with black actor Stepin Fetchit, only the first of these, *The World Moves On* (1934), which I haven't seen, partly takes place during the Civil War. But in the remaining three — *Judge Priest* (1934), *Steamboat 'Round the Bend* (1935), and *The Sun Shines Bright* (1953) — which are all set decades later, in the 1890s or shortly thereafter, the war remains as an almost constant reference point. *Judge Priest* and *The Sun Shines Bright* are both based on stories by Southern humorist Irvin S. Cobb set in Kentucky, while *Steamboat* moves up and down the Mississippi River; all three are nostalgic idylls that see that era in Southern history as somehow benighted in spite of the wounds and traumas left by the war.

■ ■ ■ ■ ■ ■ ■ ■ ■

Given all the pungent and reliable depictions of the South in American prose fiction, from William Faulkner to Flannery O'Connor to Harper Lee, it's a pity that so few of the movies adapting these authors have been up to the job. The most outstanding exception is John Huston and screenwriter Benedict Fitzgerald's impeccable rendition of O'Connor's hilarious first novel, *Wise Blood* (1979), which captures the novel's savage wit and its rural Deep South milieu with uncanny precision. In fact, if it betrays its source in any particular, this is in the highly subtle way in which an atheist director honors the brutal ironies of a devout Catholic writer. An absurdist, black-comedy parody of the French existentialism of Jean-Paul Sartre and Albert Camus, *Wise Blood* focuses on a disillusioned homeless cracker (Brad Dourif) named Hazel Motes who preaches a church without Christ, predicated on the nonexistence of God, and winds up becoming a self-tortured martyr to his own cause as if he were some version of Christ Himself. Textually, it's difficult to fault Huston for betraying O'Connor's story or tone in any detail, but one has to acknowledge that philosophically, at least, the film is coming from different place.[1]

It's also hard to fault any of the Southern styling in Terrence Davies' exquisite CinemaScope adaptation of the relatively minor, posthumously published novel *The Neon Bible*, reportedly written when its author, John Kennedy Toole, was a mere sixteen years old. This is all the more remarkable when one acknowledges that, like Huston, Davies, who hails from Liverpool, has no Southern roots of any kind, just a fanatical desire to do justice to a specific place and period (Georgia in the late '30s and early '40s).

By contrast, all the movie versions of William Faulkner I'm familiar with aside from *Intruder in the Dust* (which comes from a minor Faulkner novel) — and not counting the 1972 *Tomorrow*, a Robert Duvall vehicle directed by Joseph Anthony from a Horton Foote script which I haven't seen — are distinct disappointments. Douglas Sirk's *The Tarnished Angels* (1958), derived from the atypical novel *Pylon*, is most likely the best Faulkner movie, but this is in spite of rather than because of its Southern details (putting aside its flavorsome, expressionist, studio-shot rendering of some New Orleans revelry). Rock Hudson's version of a drunken reporter becomes acceptable only in the same way that Gregory Peck is as a kindly small-town lawyer in *To Kill a Mockingbird* (1962) — namely, after one agrees to ignore his phony and synthetic Southern accent. And as noted by one of its costars, Orson Welles, Martin Ritt's *The Long, Hot Summer*—vaguely derived from portions of *The Hamlet* by the screenwriting team of Harriet Frank Jr. and Irving Ravitch, who'd already mangled *The Sound and the Fury* for Ritt, and released the same year as the Sirk movie—comes closer to Tennessee Williams (arguably in its homogenized Richard Brooks form) than to any semblance of William Faulkner.

After their two stabs at Faulkner's work, Ritt, Frank, and Ravitch would come a bit closer to Southern authenticity with their much-acclaimed *Hud* in 1963 and *Norma Rae* in 1979. In between, the screenwriting couple had one last go at Faulkner—adapting his last novel, *The Reivers*, in 1969 for director Mark Rydell, which I've deliberately avoided. Along with Horton Foote (who also scripted both *To Kill a Mockingbird* and *Hurry Sundown*), it would appear that this couple cornered the Southern movie market for far too long.

To be fair, Hollywood movies have never had any sort of monopoly on ersatz depictions of the Deep South; in the realm of theater, Jean-Paul Sartre's *The Respectful Prostitute* and, to a lesser extent, James Baldwin's *Blues for Mister Charlie* are both sterling negative examples that arguably surpass those of Richard Brooks and Alan Parker in sheer obtuseness. Yet given the apparent remoteness of a former Harlem preacher like Baldwin from the feel and texture of Mississippi, it's all the more remarkable that Brooklynite Spike Lee, in his documentaries set respectively in Alabama and Louisiana, *4 Little Girls* (1997) and the recent miniseries *When the Levees Broke* (2006), should display such extraordinary sensitivity and insight into the lives and people of those regions. So there are no hard and fast rules about what produces a genuine grasp of and feeling for that part of the country. Even so, first-hand experience—whenever and however it comes—clearly makes a difference.

Stop Smiling, no. 31 (2007)

Note

1. From my DVD column in *Cinema Scope* (Summer 2009): "It seems that when this issue came up in a script conference about the film's final scenes during the latter stages of the on-location shooting, Huston wound up conceding to Dourif that "[at] the end of the film, Jesus wins." (See also my blog post "Flannery" at www.jonathan rosenbaum.com/?p=15255.) [2009]

À la recherche de Luc Moullet:
25 Propositions

1   "Every film by Gerd Oswald deserves a long review." —LM, 1958.

2   Many of you, perhaps most, have never heard of the man. So much the better. Not all news gets into newspapers, and not all movies get into theaters. The sculptor Paul Thek once proposed an interesting solution to the newspaper problem to me: Get rid of all of them, except for one edition of one daily paper (any would do), and pass this precious object from hand to hand for the next hundred years — *then* the news might mean something.

Living, as we do, in a time and culture where cinema is becoming an increasingly occupied and colonized country — a state of affairs in which a few privileged marshmallows get saturation bookings all over creation while a host of challenging alternative choices languish in obscurity — the need for legends has seldom been quite so pressing. Such are the established channels nowadays that even avant-garde films come to the viewer, if at all, in a form that is almost invariably preselected and predefined, with all the price tags and catalogue descriptions neatly in place. Given the need for legends that might gnaw at the superstructures of these official edifices, the adventurous filmgoer has few places to turn. Even in specialized magazines, one is most often prone to find duplications of the choices available elsewhere; and unless one lives in a megalopolis, the mere existence of most interesting films today is bound to seem almost fanciful and irrelevant.

Within this impossible setup, one is obliged to construct a pantheon largely out of rumor and hearsay: at one big state university, stories still circulate about the one time that a few students got to see half an hour of Rivette's 252-minute *Out 1: Spectre*.

Needing an emblem, agent provocateur, and exemplary scapegoat for a legendary cinema that by all rights should be infinite and expanding, I nominate the figure of Luc Moullet, patron saint of the avant-garde B film. Whether or not anyone chooses to second the motion is beside the point.

3   In the packet of press materials that LM sent me last May is one still of *Les contrebandières* showing Brigitte (Françoise Vatel) scaling a boulder over a waterfall that is possibly the grubbiest I've ever seen — even grubbier than what the film looks like. Most people would call it "substandard," and they'd be right. This is the unfettered register that LM's films occupy, breathe, and thrive in, a happy legion of the damned. Not even the $22 million spent on making Friedkin's *Sorcerer* look as impoverished and boring and artfully godforsaken and xenophobically unpleasant as possible could buy that sort of freedom and enlightenment.

4   LM on *The Tarnished Angels*: "One of the multiple styles of Douglas Sirk is marked by the filling out of nothingness, the higher bid, the incantation, yielding *Summer Storm* or *Written on the Wind*, which one could call filmed on the wind.

"When one has nothing to start with, all excess, all forms of expression are good. The effects of *The Tarnished Angels* are totally gratuitous. Faulkner's technique [in *Pylon*] presents and refines this same behavior, with inspiration alone dictating the tone. One couldn't care less about verisimilitude. Attempts, variations, disparate efforts: *The Tarnished Angels* is basically a faithful adaptation through the utilization of the camera and the direction of actors. The whole film is made up of short tracks, usually lateral, almost invisible, the camera perpetually strolling five or six meters above the ground. Why? No reason. Just Sirk's pleasure in making his camera move. . . . In art, there is only artifice. Let us therefore praise an artifice that is cultivated without remorse, which consequently acquires a greater sincerity rather than artifice masked by itself as by others under hypocritical pretexts. The true is as false as the false; only the archi-false becomes true." (*Cahiers du cinéma* no. 87, septembre 1958.)[1]

5   BIOFILMOGRAPHY: Born October 14, 1937, son of a mail sorter and a typist. Zellidja scholarship, 1954 ("Human Aspects of the Southern Préalpes"). An uncompleted degree in English. Often lists his profession as *habilleur de charbonnier* [dresser of coalminers] and helps his father run a tiny clothing factory. Film critic (1956–1966) for *Cahiers du cinéma, Arts, Télérama*, etc., championing the causes of Buñuel, Cottafavi, Godard, Hawks, Mizoguchi, Sirk, Solntseva, Ulmer, Vidor, and above all Fuller, timing the long takes of

Verboten! with his waterproof, anti-magnetic Reglia wristwatch; wrote *Fritz Lang* for the Seghers series, 1963, a book that Brigitte Bardot can be seen reading in the bathtub in Godard's *Contempt*. Apart from producing forty shorts and features (e.g., several by Eustache, Duras's *Nathalie Granger*, all his own films) and acting in his own films and others (e.g., Pollet's *L'amour c'est gai, l'amour c'est triste*), has scripted and directed the following films (the genre classifications are his own):

> 1960 — *Un steack trop cuit* (*Overdone Steak*), burlesque sketch (short). 1961 — *Terres noires* (*Black Lands*), social documentary (short). 1962 — *Capito?*, travelogue (short). 1966 — *Brigitte et Brigitte*, comic film (feature). 1967 — *Les contrebandières* (*The Smugglers*), adventure film (feature). 1970 — *Une aventure de Billy le Kid* (*A Girl Is a Gun*), western (feature). 1975 — *Anatomie d'un rapport* (*Farther Than Sex*), codirected and coscripted by Antoinetta Pizzorno, sex film (feature). Projects: *Genesis of a Meal* (1977), social documentary, and "*The Ninth Curve under Pordoi*, a film of no kind."

6   In all, I've seen one of the shorts and two and a quarter of the features, over a five-year period in three countries. In this lifetime, at least, I don't expect to have a chance to see many more. On May 18, 1972, I stumbled into the last twenty minutes or so of *A Girl Is a Gun*, dubbed into English, at a Marché du Film screening at Cannes; my records report that I saw at least portions of six other films that day, and about all I can recall, correctly or not, is Jean-Pierre Léaud's protracted skirmishes with Rachel Kesterber on some obscure mountain ridge, in color — somewhat reminiscent of the finale of *Duel in the Sun*,[2] but pushed to the level of excruciating lunatic farce, with a touch of Fuller's madness. Then, last year in London, I saw the only LM film distributed in England, *Un steack trop cuit*, and since then I've seen *The Smugglers* and *Farther Than Sex*, both in the U.S. All three of these are in black and white, and *The Smugglers* is the only LM film I've seen more than once. That's the extent of my exposure to his movies, and I am a lot luckier than most.

7   (LM, after complaining about the overbearing luxury hotel service accorded to critics at the San Sebastian Film Festival): "Writing, writing, always writing. I think, therefore I am . . . or rather, I think therefore I don't mop up, because there's nothing to mop up. I turn my sink faucet all the way, hoping in the depths of my being that it will explode and that I'll have to repair it, choke off a flood. There's running water in my sink, even hot water. But I'd rather be in the mountains where a liter of cold water costs a hundred francs, because then at least it's fun to calculate how much water I can consume. There's a bed in my room, even sheets, but I'd have preferred hay and a downy quilt, first of all because one's better off that way, and secondly because it permits amusing involuntary nocturnal slips and unexpected awakenings, where am I? What are my bearings? Dear God, how could I have lost my bearings? I want to take the stairs, but the zealous lift-attendant forces me into his elevator: he doesn't know that, as a *Touch of Evil* enthusiast, I don't ever draw upon my resources to struggle with him." ("Le Martyre de San Sebastian," *Cahiers du cinéma* no. 99, septembre 1959.)

8   Just for the record, it was LM and not Godard who first observed that morality is a matter of tracking shots (*"La morale est affaire de travellings"*), in the course of his remarkable "Sam Fuller sur les brisées de Marlowe" ["Sam Fuller in the Footsteps of Marlowe"] (Christopher, not Philip) in *Cahiers du cinéma* no. 93. When Godard picked up the idea and injected it into a *Cahiers* discussion of *Hiroshima, mon amour* four months later (no. 97), he gave the phrase more currency by standing it on its head: "Les travellings sont affaire de morale."

Much of LM's work can be seen in the shadow of pre-1968 Godard: use of Hollywood genres, along with a dismemberment of many of the *parti pris* of Hollywood narrative; an anarchist thrust often involving a flight from civilization; a deadpan, often boorish kind of humor in handling male actors that always makes one aware of the presence of *mug* in *smug* (Belmondo and Szabo in all their Godard appearances, Jean-Pierre Melville in *Breathless*, the louts in *Les carabiniers*, etc.); self-reflexive references to the film you're watching. Yet whether by design or default, most of LM's echoes of Godard tend to come off as rather devastating critiques of his mentor, perhaps because LM is a light-hearted humanist and Godard is not, so that, for example, *Les contrebandières* can be read as a "deconstruction" of *Les carabiniers*, just as *Les carabiniers* "deconstructs" the war film. LM has also alluded to an important class difference between them — Godard's bourgeois background versus his own peasant origins — which helps to distinguish their styles and attitudes.

It is characteristic of LM's quasi-invisible status that some of his wilder pronouncements — that *Rio Bravo* expresses "the finest of morals: that a man should earn his daily bread and not care about the rest"; that the moral of the story in *The Ten Commandments* "is extraordinarily Manicheistic. Just a straight line, no dialectics: Ramses stands for Mao Tse Tung, and Moses for De Mille himself" — have sometimes been ascribed to Godard, as in Gérard Gozlan's memorable attack on the *Cahiers* writers, "In Praise of André Bazin" (translated in Peter Graham's *The New Wave*). And when Godard's celebrated lengthy interview on *La chinoise* (*Cahiers* no. 194) was translated and abridged in the Winter 1968–69 *Film Quarterly*, it seems only natural that his praise for *Brigitte et Brigitte* was omitted: "Here is a revolutionary film, and if it isn't one, I don't see what could be. It's Moullet and others like him who should be entrusted with the movies that people like Quine or the Gaumont company are currently shooting. It's Moullet who should be making 'commercial' films."

9 LM: "I won't go on about the advantages that the richness of a budget can bring, these generally being rather well known. What are recognized less are the advantages of poverty. I think for instance that if *The Smugglers* had cost twenty percent less, the result would have been better because there would have been something in the film that emphasized this austerity. . . . One of the great advantages of poverty is to develop a sense of responsibility on the part of the director." (Interview in *Cahiers du cinéma* no. 216, octobre 1968.)

10 "Our Jarry," Rivette calls him. And when I asked Straub in Edinburgh two years ago which contemporary filmmakers he admired, he cited Mizoguchi, Ford, Renoir, Lang, Godard . . . and then LM: "I am willing to defend him until next year — things can change — even against all those who accuse him of being a fascist, which he is not. He's the most important filmmaker of the French post-Godard generation . . . especially for *Les contrebandières* more than for the other two."

11 Noël Burch: "Taking for his features grossly stereotyped subject material . . . Moullet then proceeds to subvert these platitudes through techniques which, though they have evolved perceptibly since his first feature, are still basically the same: a deliberately 'feeble,' almost vulgar humor; a disjointed, 'rickety' narrative, bristling with ellipses that generally don't quite 'come off'; a very personal contrast between a profilmic action which is almost trivial pastiche and landscape imagery which is often really grandiose (especially in *Billy*). His first two features, shot in black and white on something less than a shoestring, had a very special, pseudo-amateurish quality about them — the acting, in particular, was especially 'weak' — which endeared him to a few sophisticates — justifiably so to the extent that there had never been any films quite like them! — and quickly discouraged the bulk of art-film goers with their worshipful attitude towards glossiness. For *Billy*, Moullet had enough money to modify some of his basic options: production values are no longer 'symbolized,' they are actually there . . . yet of course in a derisive way." (From notes prepared for *Cinema Rising* on French independent cinema.)

12   INVOCATION: Dear readers, help us to deliver ourselves from our enslavement to production values, our ridiculous attachment to slickness which makes filmgoing in most sectors an exclusive subscription to the puerile pastimes and philosophies of stupid, vulgar millionaires. Help save us from the disease of wasted, useless wads of money heaped upon "projects" that never get scripted, or scripted but never cast, cast but never started, started but never finished, finished but never shown, shown but never seen, or seen but to no conceivable purpose, pleasure, edification, or profit to anyone. Help us to liberate ourselves from millions spent on awful movies designed to prevent us from seeing better movies, like *The Smugglers*, which cost next to nothing to make. Awaken with us to the profound truth of LM's statement to Roland Barthes in Pesaro in 1966 that *"Language is theft"* — language meaning the corporate studio styles and their decadent derivatives which have preempted the forms of reality and representation made available to us, which a consortium of investors, distributors, exhibitors, and "distinguished critics" have done their best to cram down our throats, making it our exclusive diets. Help us to understand, on one level, how the superiority of a cut-rate delight like *Dark Star* to *Star Wars* is a demonstrable fact that never had a chance to be demonstrated; or, on another, how an enforced gloss — not only on the screen, but on the mind — has kept the genius of a filmmaker like Michael Snow inaccessible to most spectators, perhaps even to you who are reading this. . . .

13   *Un steack trop cuit* is nineteen minutes long, and not very much happens in it. Although a second-unit director, cameraman, and editor are listed in the credits, virtually the entire action takes place in a small urban family flat when the parents are away, where Nicole (Françoise Vatel) fixes a steak for herself and her kid brother Georges (Albert Juross), which he loudly declares is inedible. He borrows sausages from a neighbor and gets Nicole to cook them, teases and flirts with her while she prepares to go out on a date, then goes into the kitchen after she leaves and methodically proceeds to smash the dishes. The curious thing about this plug-ugly effort with its diverse New Wave tropes and vulgar jokes (a copy of *Cahiers* used offscreen as toilet paper combines these categories) is its unexpectedly sweet and poignant aftertaste. After the adolescent hero's obnoxious treatment of his sister and his revolting table manners (loud sucking noises, spitting out pieces of food, picking strands of spaghetti off the floor and putting them on her plate, declaring that "At the sound of the third belch, it'll be precisely 7:49"), it eventually becomes apparent that the undercurrent of affection and complicity between these siblings is the film's true subject. The overall effect of this 1960 termite sitcom is to show up the *bêtise* of Godard's 1958 *Charlotte et son Jules* as pure coquettishness.

14   LM: "I contest a certain manner of reasoning which is founded on oppositions, like ugly and beautiful, human and inhuman, etc. I believe this manner of thinking is perhaps inherited from a certain materialism, but in spite of that it doesn't correspond to reality. It should first be subject to verification. For my part, I simply verify . . . that there are filmmakers who have a position on the human and those who don't. There are also those, like me, who have a position on intelligence and stupidity. . . . For me, there isn't intelligence *and* stupidity, but intelligence-stupidity. . . . My films are very much oriented around the problem of intelligence-stupidity (and there are a certain number of other problems around which they aren't oriented at all, such as sincerity and insincerity), so there is a sort of identification which is engendered, and in the final analysis, I don't know — can't know, don't want to know — if what I'm doing is a matter of intelligence, but when that's pushed pretty far, extreme intelligence rejoins stupidity. But stupidity derived from intelligence — that becomes a quality because it's something that one tries for. It's an effort. Thus, starting from the moment that one supposes one's self to be intelligent, the search for stupidity is an effort of intelligence, whereas if one is content to remain inside intelligence itself, that reverts to stupidity because there's an absence of progression.

". . . It is Chabrol who inaugurated at the start of the Sixties a sort of critique of stupidity which represented at the same time that effort I spoke of to move toward it. . . . What I like in *La ligne de demarcation*, for instance, is precisely the absence of a line of demarcation. One is in a perpetual uncertainty and that's what interests us: we don't know what the true direction of the film is, and we obviously can't know because there isn't one." (Interview in *Cahiers du cinéma* no. 216, op. cit.)

15   Distribution rights to *A Girl Is a Gun* were sold to forty small countries, although LM was unable to get the film distributed anywhere in France. There's a gag about this in *Farther Than Sex* when LM receives a phone call complaining that lions are keeping audiences away from his films. In America, the situation is even funnier: *The Smugglers* has been available for distribution from New Yorker Films for eight years, ever since it had a brief, disastrous New York premiere. But Dan Talbot is so gloomy about its prospects that it hasn't even been listed in any of his recent catalogs. To the best of my knowledge, Peter Wollen and I are the only ones who've ever booked the film for college courses.

16   LM: "There are films which reproduce life in a matter-of-fact way and try to hook the spectator through their plots. There have been so many films like this that one wound up believing that they all had to be like that, without any reason but force of habit. Like certain [other] recent films, *The Smugglers* marks a reaction against scrupulous reproduction and the plot full of interest, which has seemed to me to furnish an opening on life that's too limited and partial: it's a film that insists on the ridiculous value of all affirmation, and thus also this habitual aesthetic of cinema. The only criteria which presided over the film's conception and which should make it lovable or detestable are (a) the variety and breadth of the means of ridicule and of the objects submitted to ridicule; and (b) the sharpness and the suppleness of the ridicule.

"Such as it is, *The Smugglers* is presented as an attempt at a full, warm, and serene restoration of the playful potential inherent in the unanimity of deeds and thoughts.

"For me, *The Smugglers* is the best film of Robbe-Grillet." (*Cahiers du cinéma* no. 206, novembre 1968.)

17   "Man is a creature of habit, and the task of the artist is to try to break these habits."
—Jean Renoir.

"Who goes to the Music Hall? Communists!"
—movie producer in *Sullivan's Travels*.

The Smugglers is a movie about borders and barriers and how people live in relation to them — a movie about how to work within limits that sees filmmaking itself as a form of smuggling. It's no accident that Brigitte and Francesca (Monique Thiriet) smuggle Kodak Plus film in their packs along with food, LSD, and other staples; or that they go into a village at one point to shoot a documentary "about local problems, for distribution in China." Filmed in the High Alps with a Cameflex camera and Kodak Plus X film and inventively post-dubbed, *The Smugglers* takes place in two adjacent countries which remain nameless.

The adolescent hero (Johnny Montheillet) enlists Brigitte and Francesca in smuggling, although from where to where is never apparent, apart from elliptical bits of offscreen narration furnished by all three. Over a shot of a rushing stream, the boy says, "Look closely: this used to be a totalitarian state," while the camera pans to the right over the ground, then stops. "Now it was to know freedom and democracy. All at once, everything would change." The camera pans back to the left, stopping at the self-same stream as one hears church bells and the boy again: "Look at it now!"

Much of the time, the klutzy trio is in flight from both customs officials and the Smugglers' Union, except for odd moments of repose, such as when Brigitte does housework. (She washes and scrubs everything in the kitchen in a basin, soapbox included, then carries the basin to a craggy precipice and throws the objects down on the rocks. Shortly after a meal eaten awkwardly out of shells on the same spot, dubbed with Tatiesque noises of sucking and slurping and subsequent kissing, LM appears in a suit and with a briefcase, and calls a meeting to order with a cowbell. After sipping discreetly from a glass of water, he announces that "We've bought a helicopter to track down Union smugglers," and a cut to a helicopter in the vicinity confirms this.)

As narration and a panning camera both shift between the three heroes at a picnic table, the boy starts to pop grapes into his mouth as rapidly as possible — continuing incessantly at something like the speed that Sacha Piteoff deals out cards to Giorgio Albertazzi in *Last Year at Marienbad*. (Could this be why Moullet regards *The Smugglers* as "the best film of Robbe-Grillet"?) "I had to act naturally," he says offscreen. "My gluttony cowed and impressed them." In flight, one of the girls ignites a few weeds with a match and rum: "The Customs were met with a wall of fire." The boy, after trying repeatedly to mount a bike on another chase, eventually throws it down in disgust; he becomes bound, blindfolded, and gagged, and wanders around the rocks interminably: "They were hoping I'd fall into a ravine. They forgot how well I knew the area."

There's no question of how well LM knows the terrain of the Hollywood adventure film — every shot testifies to this knowledge — but he contrives to be diffident, leisurely, and honest about it, shrugging off the genre's heroic postures every time the physical effort becomes too tiresome. If Godard's characters in the sixties always come off a bit like retarded adolescents, they're never fully acknowledged as such; he treats them like heroes. LM treats his adolescents as something better, as people.

I could tell you more, but I won't. The last time I saw *The Smugglers* was seven weeks ago; I took copious notes, but memories are fast-fading, and anyway I lost over half these notes while house-cleaning last month. I don't have very much of this film now, and by the time this appears in print, I expect to have a great deal less. I want it back, but I don't know how to get it. In ten years' time, I doubt I'll have many fragments left, apart from the few peeks provided here, some of which may well be incorrect.

18   LM on *Jet Pilot*: "It is indeed remarkable that the ruses of Furthman and Sternberg would be in the same style, that they would apply to political or philosophical signification or eroticism. It seems that erotic verve would be indissociable from contempt for every collectivity, from the frenzied ex-altation of individuality within the framework of traditional social and moral principles. . . . The two highest summits of the genre are *Jet Pilot* and *The Fountainhead*." ("Sainte Janet," *Cahiers du cinéma* no. 86, août 1958.)

19   Suggested title for a hypothetical article in *Screen* about LM: "Suture/Self." (Ia, i) A special dividend: this pun would be comprehensible only to those who pronounce *suture* the English way, thus leaving the Francophiles out in the cold for a change.

   (II) It's highly unlikely that *Screen* would ever publish an article about LM because (IIa, i) none of his features is available in England and (IIa, ii) despite *Screen*'s professed aim of interrogating cinema as an institution, it has usually avoided the question of distribution; (IIb, i) *The Smugglers* is an anarchist film, and (IIb, ii) in Europe, unlike America, anarchy is nearly always assumed to have right-wing connotations, thus implying that (IIb, iii) as a right-wing direc-tor LM wouldn't qualify as representative or exemplary *or* relevant. Anyway, (IIc, i) comedy presupposes a loosening of mental corsets not very much in keeping with *Screen*'s practice, despite the welcome accorded in its pages to such jokesters as the Russian formalists and Roland Barthes.

20   THE CASE AGAINST LM: (1) Let's face it, he hasn't much of an eye, (2) he's lazy, (3) people never say intelligent things in his movies (although they sometimes try, e.g., LM himself in *Farther Than Sex*: "Film cans and sewer holes are always the same shape; this always frightens me"), (4) they make stupid faces, and (5) some of his actresses walk around in bikinis.

   And oh yes, one more thing: (6) He makes movies.

21   Near the end of *The Smugglers*, after Francesca has gone off on a train (the other two on a hillside wave at a receding train: how long did they have to wait around for that shot?), the boy goes to work at a quarry while Brigitte holds down an office job at a big company in Boulogne. Then the company computer goes haywire — paying the wrong people, if I remember correctly (I try to ignore plots, like all other vehicles, unless I'm driving: why miss all the scenery?) — and the couple returns happily to the mountains and smuggling and a variation on the film's opening shot, with the same odd electronic warble on the soundtrack.

   A curious prophecy: *Farther Than Sex* was financed by a real bank com-puter going haywire and accidentally sending LM a check for seven million francs — he tells you all about it in the movie. Or *would* tell you, if you could see it.

22   *Farther Than Sex* is a collaborative film, although I don't see it as contradicting LM's earlier work; as Jean-Pierre Oudart says of *The Smugglers*, "Moullet's film doesn't speak to us about the world, it is the world that speaks there; and the mechanism of subversion to which it submits itself functions without an author." Yet insofar as it can be considered half an LM movie, I would call it his *Scenes from a Marriage*, that is, a practical, modest work, not a breast-beating declaration of self-important anguish. Antoinetta Pizzorno and LM simply made an apparently straightforward movie about their relationship, with the glamour of neither Bergman's suffering nor their own — just the mundane sorrows and clumsy embarrassments of sexual problems as they're lived, reenacted, wrestled with. (LM: "I feel like I'm taking an exam." AP: "I'll whisper the answers.") Christine Herbert (our old friend Rachel Kesterber) plays AP and LM plays himself, but this doesn't become fully clear until AP herself appears in the final scene to demand another ending — like a character in one of Tex Avery's Screwy Squirrel cartoons — and LM mutters resentfully that "A guy's gotta make a movie in order to fuck the way he wants."

Here are excerpts from the only two American reviews I've read of the film, in *Soho News* and *Film Comment*, respectively, after it showed in the Museum of Modern Art's New Directors/New Films series last spring: (1) "Luc Moullet, who has been an interesting film critic in the past, shares that fallacy which seems to afflict the recent work of Jean-Luc Godard: he assumes that his rather simplistic notions of the dichotomy of life and art are new flashes from the outer limits." (2) "The script is puerile, the acting clumsy, the sound and lighting pre-Edisonian; and the sex, despite the blurb's contention [that the sexual revolution has not had an emotional equivalent], is non-existent — unless you're into blankets, which the actors go to great lengths to cover themselves with even during the throes of passion."

In response to (1), leaving aside what "recent Godard" could mean in this up-to-date New York context (*Pierrot le fou*, perhaps?), what LM assumes is not clear to me, but my own assumption is that his and AP's "rather simplistic notions" are more like old flickers from the inner limits, and ones that efface themselves out of existence through their relative nonchalance, leaving a very warm and human residue. (*New York, New York*, which must have cost a good thousand times as much to make, has even more simplistic notions, and leaves much less of a residue, whatever its other merits.)

As for (2), yes, the script is puerile and the acting clumsy — so are we all — and yes, I'm into blankets, I use them every night. "Pre-Edisonian" is hyperbole, of course, but if it were true, what could be more exciting? And so what if you don't see a lot of clinical, over-the-blanket sex — isn't that already available on every street corner?[3] What's so obligatory about it, much less interesting? If vulnerability has anything to do with sex or eroticism, a few shots of an embarrassed LM in his underpants adds up to a lot more exposure than anything waved about by anyone in, say, *Deep Throat*.

Not that I'd argue that *Farther Than Sex* is anything more than a minor appealing film — isn't that a rare enough commodity these days? So I'd quarrel, too, with the hyperbole of Rivette's remark in the English pressbook ("One can't go farther than *Farther Than Sex*": how do you say that in French?), and would tend to go along more with Eustache's blurb: "We can bet that this film will be a flop. That's the best for me: I'll plunder it more easily."

23   SELECTED SUPPLEMENTARY BIBLIOGRAPHY: Alfred Jarry, "The Crucifixion Considered as an Uphill Bicycle Race"; LM, "Le Cinéma n'est pas qu'un reflet de la lutte des classes" (*Cahiers du cinéma* no. 187, février 1967), "Jean-Luc Godard" (translated in Toby Mussman's 1968 Dutton anthology on Godard); Jean Narboni, "Luc Moullet, Notre alpin quotidien" *Cahiers du cinéma* no. 180, juillet 1966); Jean-Pierre Oudart, review of *Les contrebandières* (*Cahiers du cinéma* no. 208, janvier 1969); Richard Roud, "The French Line" (*Sight and Sound*, Autumn 1960).

24   Manny Farber — whose termite category could have been invented for LM — asked me a couple of months ago how formal analysis could account for the tenderness Straub displays towards the young waiter in *Not Reconciled*; I asked in turn how a proper formal analysis could avoid it. It would seem, from the available evidence, that LM has shown a comparable tenderness towards everyone he's ever filmed, and yes, Virginia, this is "work on the signifier." It's the signified of commercial cinema that gets short-changed in *The Smugglers* — not its production of meaning, which is indicated in virtually every shot. This makes some people angry because they want to forget they're at the movies. LM starts with the assumption that you want to be there.

25   Nevertheless, at one time or another, LM's films have defeated distributors, exhibitors, spectators, even projectors. At Filmex in Los Angeles last March, people who arrived to see *Anatomie d'un rapport* — not very many — were essentially informed that the 16 mm projector refused to contend with the film, and those who wanted to see it had to come back the following day. When I returned, along with an even smaller group of people, the projector grudgingly complied this time, but not without a couple of spiteful breakdowns. Every time I've seen *Les contrebandières*, the projector has obstinately refused to keep all of the image in focus at the same time; the gate usually seems to shudder and flinch at the very prospect.

Maybe cameras rebel against LM's cinema too; consider the awfulness of that still I cited from *Les contrebandières*. I wonder if the breakdown in representation implied by it may, after all, be a fair indication of what his films are all about: not a breakdown of the people and things represented, but of the sort of guff that money and idealism dress them up with. All I know is that the longer I look at that still, the more it inspires me. Like the best of LM's cinema, it is priceless — language that isn't theft, because it takes nothing from anyone, but offers, rather, a gift that anyone can have. If anyone will let us have it.

Film Comment, November–December 1977; corrected and slightly revised, July 2009

Notes

1. David Ehrenstein, T. Leo French [Bill Krohn], and John Hughes have all helped to nourish this article in various ways, for which I'm grateful. But for better or worse, all the translations are mine. Some of these are freer and hastier than others, and I apologize to LM and his compatriots if I've inadvertently stepped on any of their meanings.

2. Before making this film, LM described it as "a *mélange* of *Duel in the Sun* and *Les Dames du Bois de Boulogne*, or, more precisely, *The Shanghai Gesture* and [José Giovanni's] *La loi du survivant*."

3. In *The World of Nations*, Christopher Lasch aptly notes that a recent "development, widely mistaken for a 'revolution in morals,' is a growing literal-mindedness about sex, an inability to recognize as sexual anything other than the genitals."

Bushwhacked Cinema

When the history of American movies during the eight-year reign of George W. Bush (2001–9) eventually comes to be written, one might hypothesize that the commercial development of the mobile phone during the 1980s and 1990s and the introduction of the iPod during the first year Bush took office were crucial in setting the stage for some of the basic conditions of that era. Arguably for the first time, one could easily sustain one's ignorance about and indifference to one's fellow citizens even while sharing the same public space with them — on the street or in other public locations dedicated to some form of transport: terminals, buses, subways, trains, planes, fairgrounds, theme parks, and, above all, cinemas.

So the phenomenon of a U.S. president who, to all appearances, preferred to remain blissfully (and strategically) ignorant about the news and the overall state of the world, and ran his office accordingly, was part and parcel of this growing trend to eliminate the public sphere from American life and subdivide the entire culture and society into "special interest" groups and niche markets. Not that the news itself as it was reported in the U.S. was necessarily indicative of what was happening. In the freedom-of-the-press rankings done annually for 169 countries by Reporters Without Borders, the U.S. plunged from 17th place in 2002 to 53rd in 2006, with only a minor upswing to 48th place in 2007. (By contrast, the U.K. fluctuated between 21st and 28th place over the same period, with the Scandinavian countries, Ireland, and Canada leading all the others.)

During the same period, mainstream moviegoing continued its gradual shift from being a community activity, which it was during roughly the first half of the twentieth century, to being for the most part either a public activity for teenagers and preteens or a private activity conducted in homes. Yet at the same time, outspoken films critiquing the U.S. occupation of Iraq and Afghanistan — popularly known as "the war in Iraq and Afghanistan" — began to proliferate. Some of these were documentaries such as *Iraq in Fragments*, *The War Tapes*, *The Torture Question*, and *Gunner Palace*, which, like Michael Moore's *Fahrenheit 9/11*, performed the essential task of reporting basic information that the U.S. news had mainly failed to report. Some fiction films, such as Paul Haggis's *In the Valley of Elah* (which featured arguably better and more detailed work by both cinematographer Roger Deakins and actor Tommy Lee Jones than the more Oscar-friendly and apolitical *No Country for Old Men*), mainly decried the devastating effect that the horrors of the occupation was having on American servicemen; a few others, notably Brian De Palma's *Redacted* (which borrowed a page or two from his 1989 *Casualties of War*), protested the inhuman treatment of innocent local citizens. There were still other important features that dealt with the occupations indirectly — perhaps most notably Clint Eastwood's memorable diptych *Flags of Our Fathers* and *Letters from Iwo Jima*, which arguably wouldn't have materialized when they did if there hadn't been a pressing need to rethink some of the basic postulates regarding American idealism in relation to warfare.

With the striking exception of two 2004 documentaries — *Fahrenheit 9/11*, the most successful documentary in film history, and Robert Greenwald's *Outfoxed: Rupert Murdoch's War on Journalism*, which briefly (and miraculously) became the top-selling DVD on Amazon without a single theatrical showing — few of these films fared especially well at the box office. But this shouldn't minimize their impact: sometimes the quality of the viewers and the viewing counts more than the quantity, especially when changes of public awareness are at stake. And all this protest filmmaking was in dramatic contrast to the meager cinematic response to the comparably controversial war of the U.S. against North Vietnam between 1959 and 1975. The latter mostly yielded one mainstream flagwaver (John Wayne's 1968 *The Green Berets*), a few marginalized protest documentaries (such as *In the Year of the Pig* and *Winter Soldier*), followed by the Oscar-winning *Hearts and Minds* just before the war's end, and then several after-the-fact blockbusters, such as *The Deer Hunter*, *Apocalypse Now*, and *Platoon*.

Meanwhile, certain kinds of niche markets in videos and DVDs began to form new sorts of film communities. Most of these were structured not around common viewing situations but around the same films being viewed and then discussed on the Internet via web sites, blogs, and chatgroups. One important exception to this tendency, suggesting a new form of cine-club, was the sponsoring by Moveon.org of countless home screenings across the U.S. of a few documentaries by Robert Greenwald, one of them the already-mentioned

Outfoxed. (Others have included *Unprecedented: The 2000 Presidential Election, Uncovered: The Whole Truth About the Iraq War, Unconstitutional*, and *Wal-Mart: The High Cost of Low Price*).

The extraordinary success of Moveon — a family of leftist organizations boasting a 3.2 million membership and an uncanny ability to raise money and help galvanize public opinion in a hurry, started only a decade ago — largely stemmed from the way it worked almost exclusively through the Internet, even though it specialized in organizing local activities through email and online appeals and resources. This has provided a potential model for organizing certain niche markets in cinephilia, though so far the only widespread success of this trend has been in the political realm. To a few hardy and aggressive cinephiles, it has suggested other utopian possibilities involving art films, experimental films, and revivals that have only begun to be tested, in the U.S. and elsewhere.

What has made such radical regroupings seem especially enticing has been the growing alienation of much of the film audience from public cinemas, as well as the growing suspicion that the future of cinema may lie elsewhere — a development paralleled in some respects by the growing public disaffection with George W. Bush. Despite the attentiveness to polls shared by the White House and the Hollywood studios, it seems that the remoteness of both from the people they service can readily be perpetuated as long as the right kind of spin is there to inflect the discourse. Indeed, it appears that some time after the film industry discovered that audiences didn't necessarily have to like a movie for it to do well at the box office (so long as millions were spent on publicity and monopolizing the marketplace — which became easier once Ronald Reagan stopped enforcing the antitrust laws in the 1980s), Bush's own team was offhandedly letting the citizenry know that whether or not they supported the U.S. occupation of Iraq and/or Afghanistan had little to do with whether or not it would continue.

It's clearly much easier to launch military invasions than to curtail them. One way that both so-called "Gulf Wars" in 1990 and in 2003 were easily sold to the public was by marketing them as if they were movies and movie spinoffs — a trend especially evident in cable news logos and their accompanying musical themes during both periods. (It could even be argued that the voice of James Earl Jones on CNN served in part to evoke its earlier employments in *Star Wars* — perhaps the first major media demonstration that massive warfare could be celebrated more guiltlessly if it were shown from a cosmic distance, without blood, as if it were a video game.) As was pointed out in the preface of Larry Tye's *The Father of Spin: Edward L Bernays and the Birth of Public Relations* (New York: Crown Publishers, 1998), the "public relations triumph" that was the "selling of America on the Persian Gulf War . . . was crafted by one of America's biggest public relations firms, Hill and Knowlton, in a campaign bought and paid for by rich Kuwaitis who were Saddam's archenemies." And the syntactical confusion created after the September 11 attacks by such terms as "The Global War on Terrorism" or "War on Terror"—implying that a "war" can have a beginning but not a foreseeable end—clearly helped to keep the business of such an enterprise afloat in a state of semi-permanence. Thus the second "Gulf War" was packaged not simply as a sequel to the first but as an ongoing TV series designed to last indefinitely, or at least as long as it kept turning a handsome enough profit for the new wave of merchandisers.

The September 11 attacks, commemorated in such movies as Paul Greengrass's *United 93* and Oliver Stone's *World Trade Center*, offered the U.S. the unique possibility of joining the remainder of the planet in terms of shock and suffering, opening the way towards a greater global awareness. That Bush Jr. chose to steer the populace in the reverse direction has had many lamentable consequences, including a redefinition of "America" in terms of both exclusivity and empire. If the terrorist attacks were an "American" tragedy, this implied both that the terrorists were allowed to set the terms of the debate and that the citizens of eighty-six other countries who died in the destruction of the World Trade Center didn't count. A similar privileging of U.S. casualties over others in the occupations of Iraq and Afghanistan tended to make the claims of altruistic motives sound even hollower.

■ ■ ■ ■ ■ ■ ■ ■ ■

It's an interesting exercise to try to sum up the personalities and predilections of various U.S. presidents according to their tastes in movies. Dwight D. Eisenhower (1953–61) was a particular fan of *High Noon* (and westerns in general) while John F. Kennedy (1961–63) displayed special affection for *Spartacus* and *The Manchurian Candidate* (the latter climaxing in a political assassination that creepily anticipated his own, which later prompted its star and Kennedy's former chum Frank Sinatra to remove it from circulation for several years). In the *Guardian*, Julian Borger reported that Lyndon B. Johnson (1963–69) "had one favorite movie and he watched it more than a dozen times, sometimes on consecutive nights. It was a 10-minute homage to himself, sonorously narrated by Gregory Peck and made on the orders of the White House staff to introduce the new president to a skeptical public after Kennedy's assassination." The reported favorite of Richard M. Nixon (1969–74) was *Patton*, seen the same week in 1970 that he ordered the secret war in Cambodia.

I've been unable to discover the movie preferences of either Gerald Ford (1974–77) or the first George Bush (1989–93), but it's worth noting that Jimmy

Carter (1977–81) saw more movies during his four years in office than Ronald Reagan (1981–89) saw in eight — and more, indeed, than any other president before or since. (I suspect Reagan tended to shy away from films because they reminded him too much of what he associated with work — although apparently he and Nancy had a particular affection for James Stewart movies.) Bill Clinton (1993–2001) has expressed enthusiasm for *American Beauty*, *Fight Club*, *Schindler's List*, and *Three Kings*. And George W. Bush's movie interests, insofar as he has any, appear to be Austin Powers comedies, a few war films (*We Were Soldiers*, *Saving Private Ryan*, and *Black Hawk Down*, his favorite), and the Afghan film *Osama* — the latter of which was apparently viewed for information rather than entertainment. *Black Hawk Down*, incidentally, was also distributed by Saddam Hussein to his own troops for comparable reasons — supposedly for its insights into how to defeat American soldiers.

More generally, one could perhaps single out the younger Bush as the first and only U.S. president to date to have expressed no interest of any kind in any of the arts, cinema included. (Even Nixon, by way of contrast, saw fit to pay tribute to John Ford.) But if one could reduce the Bushwhacked years to a couple of movie paradigms, these might be Marlboro cigarette commercials and the Austin Powers comedy-thrillers — both nostalgic evocations of the American empire as perceived from the vantage point of the Cold War, roughly half a century earlier. The Marlboro commercial showed the Texan surveying his endless range as the purveyor of visionary machismo and manifest destiny, in strictly serious terms. Austin Powers, on the other hand, suggests good-natured self-mockery, coming much closer to the Bush many Americans presumably thought they voted for — the one they allegedly wanted to have a beer with.

■ ■ ■ ■ ■ ■ ■ ■ ■

Not having seen *Saw* (2004) or any of its three sequels, all of which featured torture as their main attraction, I can't pinpoint precisely what connects them to the torture of prisoners in Abu Ghraib and Guantanamo, which came to public light the same year that the series started. But the fact that the films' popularity peaked with its first sequel in 2005 (*Saw II* grossed $87 million domestically), the year after the infamous photographs of Abu Ghraib prisoner abuse first appeared online, does strongly suggest a connection. Those images quickly entered the public imagination, and Hollywood was waiting to exploit them.

Given that the overwhelming majority of Iraqi citizens sent to Abu Ghraib have never been convicted of any crime, and that expert advice tends to confirm that any information acquired from even guilty prisoners as a result of torturing them tends to be useless — precisely because people under this kind of pressure are apt to say anything, especially whatever they think the torturers want them to say — one might wonder why Bush has been willing to break treaties and other international agreements and tarnish American prestige simply for the sake of inflicting needless cruelty. The only plausible explanation I've come up with for this is that expert opinion on this subject, like the prediction or prospect of $4-a-gallon gasoline, hasn't yet reached the Oval Office, apparently because second opinions of any kind aren't being sought.

Given the cultural remoteness of most Americans from the everyday lives and fates of innocent Iraqi citizens, it's hard to shake off the suspicion that Bush's indefensible position on this subject may be typical rather than eccentric — that a good many Americans may not really mind if innocent Iraqis undergo torture, just as long as the facts of such injustices aren't shoved in their faces. Given the overall willingness of the American press to accommodate this desire for avoiding the facts, the process by which torture becomes a box office staple may indeed not be too difficult to understand. After all, it's been demonstrated repeatedly by the TV series 24 — launched around the same time that Bush became president and still popular today — that government-sanctioned torture continues to be dramaturgically sound and therefore saleable even if it remains questionable on practical as well as ethical grounds.

This may help to account for how Mel Gibson's *The Passion of the Christ*, in Aramaic, Latin, and Hebrew with English subtitles, managed to come in third among the top-grossing releases of 2004, just behind *Shrek 2* and *Spider-Man 2* and ahead of *Meet the Fockers* and *The Incredibles* — how, in short, the only feature among the top ten not made chiefly for kids and teenagers offered a veritable orgy of cruelty and suffering, complete with slow motion and masochistic point-of-view shots. Despite the title, I assumed this drama about the last twelve hours of Jesus's life would include something about his teachings, at least in flashback. But the Sermon on the Mount was reduced to two sound bites, and miracles and good works barely got a glance. The charges of anti-Semitism and homophobia hurled at the movie seemed too narrow; its general disgust for humanity was so unrelenting that the military-sounding drums at the end seemed to be welcoming the apocalypse (rather like the mass slaughter following the Mexican rebel's torture in *The Wild Bunch*).

According to the trade magazine *Boxoffice*, on March 30, 2008, *The Passion of the Christ* in fact placed eleventh in its list of "all-time domestic blockbusters," on the heels of (in descending order) *Titanic* (1997), *Star Wars* (1977), *Shrek 2* (2004), *E.T.: The Extra-Terrestial* (1982), *Star Wars, Episode I: The Phantom Menace* (1999), *Pirates of the Caribbean: Dead Man's Chest* (2006), *Spider-Man* (2002), *Star Wars, Episode III: Revenge of the Sith* (2005), *Lord of the Rings: The Return of the King* (2003), and *Spider-Man 2* (2004). It's a sobering thought that six of these came out during Bush's eight years and the only other films on the list that didn't qualify as fodder for kids were made during previous decades. But this infantilism can be ascribed to the preferences of the film industry as much as those of the audience, and this audience was plainly as Bushwhacked as the movies it attended. In more ways than one, its mind was elsewhere.

Time Out Film Guide 2009, 17th edition, edited by John Pym (London: Time Out, 2008)

What Dope Does to Movies

To the memory of Paul Schmidt

Consider how the camera cuts from Richie Havens's face, guitar, and upper torso during his second number in *Woodstock* (1970) to a widening vista of thousands of clapping spectators, then to a much less populated view of the back of the bandstand, where there's no clapping, watching, or listening — just a few figures milling about near the stage or on the hill behind it. What's going on? This radical shift in orientation and perspective — a sudden movement from total concentration to Zenlike disassociation — is immediately recognizable as part of being stoned, and Michael Wadleigh's epic concert film, which significantly has about the same duration as a marijuana high, is one of the first studio releases to incorporate this experience into its style and vision.

Or think of the way that *Blade Runner* (1982) starts: a long, lingering aerial view of Los Angeles in the year 2019, punctuated by dragon-like spurts of noxious yellow flames, with enormous close-ups of a blue eye whose iris reflects those sinister, muffled explosions. Or consider the zany, spastic contortions of Steve Martin en route to an elevator in *All of Me* (1984) — torn schizophrenically between his own identity and that of a recently reincarnated Lily Tomlin. Two hostile forces and divided wills twist his elastic, string-bean body into a wild succession of contradictory jazz riffs, a riddled battlefield careening this way and that under opposing orders.

Better yet, contemplate the hallucinatory special effects and the screwy changes of tone in Joe Dante movies like *Gremlins* (1984), *Matinee* (1993), or *Small Soldiers* (1998); the wide-angle distortions and fantasy premises of films like Bob Balaban's *Parents* and Raúl Ruiz's *Three Lives and Only One Death* (1996); or the ambiguous netherworld between thoughts and realities comprising Stanley Kubrick's *Eyes Wide Shut* (1999).

All of these experiences have something to do with dope. None of them would look or sound or play the same way today if marijuana hadn't seized and transformed the style of pop movies thirty years ago. This isn't to say that the filmmakers in question are necessarily teaheads, or that the people in the audience have to be wigged-out in order to appreciate these efforts. Stoned consciousness by now is a historical fact, which means that the experiences of people high on grass have profoundly affected the aesthetics of movies for everyone: filmmakers and spectators, smokers and nonsmokers alike.

It all started around the same time that movies as a whole got shaken up. Exploding sixties culture opened up the way to all sorts of outside influences. From England came the Beatles and the Rolling Stones; from France came the New Wave movies of Godard, Resnais, Rivette, and Truffaut; political models were exported from China and Cuba, religious models from India and Japan. Meanwhile, the herbal emblems of certain American minorities — the peyote of Indians, the reefers of blacks — got tossed into the same heady stew, adding a congenial flavor to all the rest.

What did dope do to the movies, exactly? First of all, it changed the ways that people looked and listened. Then it altered the ways that they accepted what they saw and heard:

> In Los Angeles, among the independent filmmakers at their midnight screen-
> ings I was told that I belonged to the older generation, that Agee-alcohol
> generation they called it, who could not respond to the new films because I
> didn't take pot or LSD and so couldn't learn yet to *accept* everything.

This is Pauline Kael, writing in 1964. The article in question is the introduction to her first collection of movie reviews, an essay that is significantly subtitled "Are the Movies Going to Pieces?" Clearly alarmed at the gradual erosion of audience interest in coherent, well-turned narratives and the growing enthusiasm for jazzy innovations from abroad, Kael could already see a relation between this shift in taste and the widening popularity of grass over alcohol, a change that was generational as well as cultural. Appropriately enough, this revelation took place at a midnight movie — one of those dark, damp retreats of the sixties where stoned consciousness first came into full bloom. As J. Hoberman and I explored at some length in the book *Midnight Movies*, marijuana and midnight screenings have nearly always been closely interconnected, if only because dope generally helps to foster a wider and more hedonistic spirit of aesthetic openness.

For many experimental filmmakers, the requirement placed on most films to tell a story often stands in the way of other possible pleasures that movies can impart. The tendency to savor individual moments which pot encourages, sometimes at the expense of the whole — a trend towards fragmented experience which TV has also promoted — made consistent and realistic storylines less obligatory than they had been in previous decades. The qualities of pure spectacle found in Stanley Kubrick's *2001: A Space Odyssey* (1968) and diverse psychedelic fruit salads such as Fellini's *Satyricon* and *Performance* (both 1970) were generally dismissed and disparaged by Kael and other members of her generation. But potheads passionately embraced these movies, caring more about what they had to show than what they had to say. Another older critic, Andrew Sarris, revised his negative opinion of *2001* somewhat after he returned to the film with the aid of a little herbal stimulation, and the fact that he could report on such an undertaking without embarrassment in the *Village Voice* is emblematic of the relative freedom and relaxation of that period.

With the advent of such purely visual masterpieces of the late sixties as *2001*, *Point Blank*, and *Playtime*, movies were beginning to resemble such purely aural experiences as record albums by the Beatles and Frank Zappa over the same period. They were becoming environments to wander about and wallow in, not merely compulsive plots that you had to follow, and sustaining certain contradictions — two-tiered forms of thinking where the mind could drift off in opposite directions at once — was part of the fun they were offering.

Other older critics retracted their original harsh judgments of *Bonnie and Clyde* (1967) after the film went on to become a box office smash with the youth market. Now here was a movie that had a detailed storyline — but one that was subject to frequent and abrupt changes of tone, as in Godard's *Breathless* and Truffaut's *Shoot the Piano Player*, where slapstick comedy and nostalgic romance alternated with tragic bloodbath violence. Just as a doper's stoned rap might veer in mid-sentence from a consideration of life to a consideration of toenails, movies were getting redefined as an art of the present tense where theoretically anything could happen, regardless of whether or not everyone in the audience came along for the ride.

The same year that Kael first acknowledged the influence of dope on film taste, Susan Sontag published her "Notes on Camp," which bore witness to a closely related phenomenon — the ironic appreciation of sincere art that was outrageously overblown. Sontag's examples ranged all the way from *Shanghai Express* to *King Kong*, expressing new routes to pleasure that could bypass the usual barriers between high and low forms of art. And if camp taste probably owed as much to gay sensibility as the learned pleasures of pot owed to black culture, there was a way in which these two minority interests often worked hand in glove. Consider the lasting success of *Reefer Madness* as a midnight camp classic long after it was released in earnest in 1940; and by the same token — or toke — one should add that stoned amusement helped to pave the success of such deliberate camp efforts as *Female Trouble* and *Beyond the Valley of the Dolls*, not to mention other midnight staples including *The Rocky Horror Picture Show*, *Eraserhead*, and George Romero's *Dead* trilogy.

If Robert Altman's movies in the early seventies — *M*A*S*H*, *Brewster Mc-Cloud*, *McCabe and Mrs. Miller*, *The Long Goodbye* — reveal the overall impact of dope on movie consciousness, representing a halfway house between the softer dope influence of the sixties and the harder edge it would take on in the early seventies — this is because they reflect so many of the stylistic changes reflected above, at the same time that they frequently allude to drugs in their plots. The use of overlapping dialogue and offbeat musical accompaniments (such as the Leonard Cohen songs in *McCabe*, the bird lectures in *McCloud*, and the multiple versions of the title tune in *The Long Goodbye*) created a dense weave that made each spectator hear and understand a slightly different movie — and, given that these were crowded, widescreen features, see a different movie as well. These movies were all spaced-out experiences which presented both bright communal activities (from army pranks to patriotic rallies to frontier-town gossip to hash brownies) to lonely, deranged individuals who stood outside these mystiques and pursued dreamy head-trips of their own. As a spectator, one was invited to identify with both positions — hearing the local prattle about whorehouse owner McCabe (Warren Beatty) and his legendary prowess with a gun, and sharing the same character's tongue-tied awkwardness and experience. Drifting between these contradictory options, one navigated one's way through Altman's languid zooms and uncentered camera movements like a doper gliding through different trains of thought, comically stumbling (like many of the characters) through hallucinatory environments where nothing was ever the way one assumed it to be.

■ ■ ■ ■ ■ ■ ■ ■ ■

I occasionally use marijuana in preference to alcohol, and for several decades. I say occasionally and mean it quite literally; I have spent about as many hours high as I have in movie theaters — sometimes 3 hours a week, sometimes 12 or 20 or more, as at a film festival — with about the same degree of alteration of my normal awareness.
—Allen Ginsberg, 1965

Let's say that early period [up through *Pierrot le fou*] was my hippie period. I was addicted to movies as the hippies are addicted to marijuana, but I don't need to because movies are the same to me. . . . [and] now I'm over this movie marijuana thing.
—Jean-Luc Godard, 1969

In more ways than one, The Movie as Trip profoundly altered the social trappings and atmosphere of filmgoing as well as the more purely formal and aesthetic aspects of the experience. In contrast to the quintessential communal experiences of movies like *Gone with the Wind*, *The Wizard of Oz*, and *Casablanca*—movies for and about communities—the no less emblematic *2001* of the sixties and *Apocalypse Now* of the seventies made each spectator the hero of a new kind of drama, which was staged inside someone's head. In some ways this environmental experience could be attributed to tapping the atmospheric possibilities of Dolby sound, but in other respects it might be regarded as a throwback to the German Expressionist movie tradition that characterized such silent classics as *The Cabinet of Dr. Caligari*, *Metropolis*, *Faust*, and *Sunrise*, and which subsequently became more Americanized and mainstreamed in certain Disney cartoon features like *Snow White and the Seven Dwarfs* and *Pinocchio*—not to mention Orson Welles's live-action *Citizen Kane*.

You might even say that traveling down the river in *Apocalypse Now*—a movie whose origins can be traced in part back to Welles's unfulfilled first Hollywood project preceding *Kane*, to adapt Joseph Conrad's *Heart of Darkness* in terms of the present, with the camera taking the role of Marlow—was a little bit like taking a ride in Disneyland, remaining passive and mesmerized while a parade of marvels and surprises glided past you or were heard from surrounding speakers. Whatever was happening was happening to you, the spectator, first of all, the character of special agent Benjamin L. Willard (Martin Sheen) only secondarily, and the drugged-out ambience of the trip as a whole—derived in part from Michael Herr's remarkable evocations of pot-drenched Vietnam combat experiences in his book *Dispatches*—made the surreal fantasy element that much stronger. Alas, this made the meaning of the war in Vietnam for the Vietnamese even more remote from American experience than it already was; the "real" drama of *Apocalypse Now* had little to do with the suffering and struggle of the native population and everything to do with Francis Ford Coppola, the viewer's true surrogate (who was actually shooting in the Philippines), penetrating the "heart of darkness" like Conrad's Kurtz and Marlow.

Screened at midnight, marijuana-drenched movies might have been experienced communally, but in more mainstream venues one could argue that they tended by design to atrophy into more private trips. To a certain extent, subsequent blockbusters like the *Star Wars* and *Indiana Jones* trilogies reflected some of the same amusement-park tendencies, because by this time video games and home viewing were beginning to replace theatrical screenings as the main form of movie experience.

This transition had something to do with dope, but was affected still more by the implicit social philosophies of the respective periods, which also helped to determine how dope was smoked. What began in the sixties as an almost tribally shared collective pastime—being stoned at the movies—passed through the Me generation of the late seventies to become a more private and individualized experience in the eighties and early nineties. Seeing a movie like the recently revived *Yellow Submarine*—a feature-length cartoon set to Beatles songs—back in 1968, in any large U.S. theaters that tolerated toking (and there were plenty of those back then), you virtually had a guarantee of getting at least a buzz whether you brought along joints or not. The air would be so thick with smoke that you could walk through sample whiffs of various grades on the way to your seat, getting slightly glazed in the process. Because it was more fashionable back then to share smoke with strangers, roaches were more prone to be passed down the aisles, creating a kind of spider's web of complicity between the different people in the audience, as well as between them and the events on screen.

As grass-smoking gradually returned to the living room, bedroom, and bathroom, where it first took hold in the sixties before the pastime became public, this return to relative privacy—a high to be shared with friends, but not with strangers—was reflected in the more insular and insulated pop movies that came out. Compare *2010* to *2001*, *The Cotton Club* to *Singin' in the Rain*, *Dune* to *Forbidden Planet*, *Gimme Shelter* to *Woodstock*: in each case the social context becomes narrower while the individual head-trip looms larger. Taking the movie home with you on video or DVD not only keeps you off the streets; it also leaves the movie untested as a site for social interaction, hence less amenable to certain collective experiences—unless one finds a way of making it more interactive again.

Perhaps only with the current global interconnections of the Internet and email are we beginning to return to comparable kinds of complicity in relation to movies—the renewed notion of a tribal community, reconfigured this time not in terms of viewing movies but in terms of discussing them and related subjects (and sometimes in terms of finding and swapping certain movies on DVD). Interestingly enough, this may also be affecting movie content; the fantasy-driven contradictions that dope-enhanced and dope-influenced movies used to embrace are making a welcome comeback, only this time they could just as well be labeled cybernetic as psychedelic in impulse—and the influence of musical sampling could be equally important. Who says that Forest Whitaker can't play a New Jersey samurai operating according to ancient warrior codes and working for the Mafia, in Jim Jarmusch's *Ghost Dog*?

Twenty years ago the conceit would have been labeled a doper's reverie; today it still can be read that way, but it also sounds like a fantasy hatched on the Internet.

Included in *Grass: The Paged Experience*, based on the film by Ron Mann (Toronto: Warwick Publishing, 2001), 118–22. An early version of this article appeared in *High Times*, March 1985; revised and updated, March 2000. See also www.jonathanrosen baum.com/?p=15471 and www.jonathanrosenbaum.com/?p=14850.

Fever Dreams in Bologna: Il Cinema Ritrovato, Cineteca Bologna, June 28–July 5, 2008

Ever since I retired a few months ago from my twenty-year stint as film reviewer for the *Chicago Reader*, perhaps the biggest perk of all has been freedom from the chore of having to keep up with new movies. In practice, this translates into more free time to keep up with old movies. So returning to one of my favorite annual pastimes, Il Cinema Ritrovato in Bologna — a festival that caters to people devoted to seeing old films in good prints — seemed only natural. Its twenty-second edition, the fourth one I've attended, was especially rich.

Held in the oldest university town in Europe — hot and muggy this time of year, and full of labyrinthine back streets — the eight-day event mainly takes place at three air-conditioned cinemas during the day and at the Piazza Maggiore every evening, where the grand public shows up for outdoor screenings. (There's also a jury that I've served on in previous years selecting the best restorations on DVD.)

Among this year's Piazza attractions were the restored French version of Max Ophüls's *Lola Montès*, the silent version of Alfred Hitchcock's *Blackmail* with a live performance of a new symphonic score by Neil Brand (a clever and effective pastiche of such Hitchcock composers as Bernard Herrmann and Miklós Rósza), and portions of the two major retrospectives held this year, devoted to Lev Kuleshov and Josef von Sternberg. And since all the restorations of Charlie Chaplin films are done in Bologna, some fruits of that labor are always included: Kuleshov's 1926 *By the Law* was accompanied by *The Vagabond* (1916) and Sternberg's 1928 *The Docks of New York* was preceded by *The Immigrant* (1917).

This laidback holiday for specialists, part conference and part festival, allows everyone to casually swap notes about films from 1908, early newsreels about suffragettes, a 1918 Italian serial, pre-Code Warners features, Marcel Pagnol comedies starring Fernandel, and '50s Hollywood CinemaScope classics — to cite just a few of the daytime programs. The colors in the *Lola Montès* restoration, based on the bit I sampled, looked garish compared to the richer hues in the restoration of the German version carried out a few years ago by the Munich Film Archives (which Ophüls's son Marcel, for obscure reasons, has chosen to suppress), and this impression was reinforced by the reactions of several colleagues. At one of the daytime sessions chaired by programmer Janet Bergstrom (who brought along Sternberg's son Nicholas, a former cinematographer himself), it was a revelation to finally catch up with an eye-popping five-minute fragment of *The Case of Lena Smith* (1929) — the most celebrated of Sternberg's lost films (and the focus of a fascinating 300-page anthology published last year by the Austrian Film Museum) — recently discovered by a film scholar in Japan.

Thanks to the rarity of some of the films, audience turnouts can sometimes be disproportionate to the films' merits. Sternberg earned much of his clout at Paramount by retooling *Children of Divorce* (1927), an unreleasable Frank Lloyd feature with Gary Cooper and Clara Bow, and this patched-up turkey is usually so hard to see that it drew a standing-room-only crowd, even though it was almost as uninspired and impersonal as Raoul Walsh's 1916 Ibsen adaptation, *Pillars of Society*, another scarce item shown. For me, the high point in *Children of Divorce* was seeing a trial run for a spectacular camera movement — a track into an extreme close-up — that Sternberg would employ to much better effect with Marlene Dietrich in his highly underrated *Dishonored* four years later.

Throughout the festival, Kuleshov and Sternberg proved to be rather strange bedfellows, offering an intriguing dialectic of what it meant to be pioneering mavericks in both Russian and Hollywood cinema of the silent and early sound periods and all the perils this might entail. On my first full day in Bologna, going directly from Sternberg's *Blonde Venus* (1932) to Kuleshov's *Horizon* (his first talkie, released the same year) produced all sorts of piquant contrasts. The former, about a German showgirl who winds up in America with a husband and a little boy, is the only one of Sternberg's seven films with Dietrich that's set even partially in the U.S. The latter, about a likably oafish Russian Jew immigrating to New York, is one of at least five Kuleshov films with North American themes and/or settings, even though Kuleshov never set foot on that continent.

Kuleshov — the teacher of Sergei Eisenstein, Vsevolod Pudovkin, and Boris Barnet, who virtually started his career by helping to complete the last film of the great prerevolutionary Russian auteur Yevgeni Bauer in 1917 — remains less known today for his films than for his famous montage experiment and "effect" (juxtaposing the same close-up of an actor with shots of a bowl of soup, a woman in a coffin, and a child to produce radically different meanings). In his *Biographical Dictionary of Film*, David Thomson characteristically introduces his own Kuleshov entry with the admission that he hasn't seen any of the films. And even those who've seen some of Kuleshov's better-known silents — *The Extraordinary Adventures of Mr. West in the Land of the Bolsheviks* (1924), *The Death Ray* (1925), or his stark Jack London adaptation, *By the Law* (1926) — may be initially put off by the eccentric, caricatural acting of his remarkable wife, Aleksandra Khokhlova (as much of a cult figure in a way as Dietrich, and one of the most striking presences in Russian cinema, at once mannered and terrifying). Due to her aristocratic family background, Khokhlova — whose granddaughter was one of the three curators of this retrospective — wound up being barred from acting after *The Great Consoler*, although she continued working in film by assisting Kuleshov with direction. Her own solo feature, the 1930 *Sasha*, confounds expectations by showing her as a skillful director of nonprofessional actors in low-key, neorealist performances.

If one starts out with the standard American bias of opposing propaganda with personal expression, one might miss part of what's distinctive about some of Kuleshov's freer assignments. Even *Forty Hearts* (1930), an educational documentary about industrialization, is full of wit and invention involving Constructivist animation and other kinds of lively filmmaking. Though the crippling restrictions of the Stalinist era ultimately drove him into formulaic children's films of varying quality, this retrospective proved that he maintained several strengths throughout his career.

The Great Consoler (1933), his greatest film, is not just an innovative masterpiece, but also one of the most profound reflections on the social utility of art to be found anywhere. As daring as any Alain Resnais film, it moves among three separate blocks of material. (1) In prison for embezzlement, William Sydney Porter, better known as O. Henry, is persuaded by the warden to convince a fellow prisoner, safecracker Jimmy Valentine, to open a locked bank safe without explosives in order not to destroy the papers inside, after the banker, who knows the combination, skips town with the funds. Valentine can do this only by painfully filing down his fingernails to sensitize his fingers, but the warden promises to grant him a pardon in return. Meanwhile, Porter is so impressed by Valentine's skill that he writes a famous short story, "A Retrieved Reformation," romanticizing Valentine's heroic exploits. But then the warden, reneging on his promise, refuses to release Valentine, forcing Porter to realize in despair that he and Valentine have both been used. (2) "A Retrieved Reformation," recounted parodically. (3) The effect of this story on one reader,

Dulcie (Khokhlova), a shopgirl who is being forced to prostitute herself by the same cop who convinced the prison warden to exploit Valentine's gifts. Even though Porter's escapist tale falsifies the truth, it also inspires and emboldens Dulcie to shoot the cop when he tries to exploit her in turn.

Emotionally and dramatically, this paradoxical conclusion anticipates the climax of Andrei Tarkovsky's *Stalker* (1979) by expressing both despair about the hollowness of idealistic fantasy and exaltation about the redemptive possibilities of art. What makes it all even more challenging is the nonstop playfulness, which at times creates narrative distractions. For instance, Dulcie's flatmate and fellow shop clerk is viewed only in silhouette and is a shrill, compulsive giggler, neither of which serves to clarify anything else in the plot. This may help to explain why *The Great Consoler* was denounced in Russia as formalist, effectively putting an end to Kuleshov's artistic freedom — and, in spite of being available with English subtitles (on film) in the U.K., has been ignored in the West ever since.

Indeed, the degree to which the early and radically experimental sound period of Russian cinema continues to be overlooked in spite of its riches never ceases to amaze me. Although Barnet's *Outskirts*, Pudovkin's *Deserter*, and Dziga Vertov's *Enthusiasm* are now all available on DVD, they've been almost as consistently ignored by critics as Aleksandr Dovzhenko's unavailable first talkie, *Ivan* — for me his greatest sound feature. Perhaps the most important achievement of the annual Bologna bash is to inspire these reevaluations.

Moving Image Source (posted online as "Hidden Treasures"), July 17, 2008. See also www.jonathanrosenbaum.com/?p=6079; www.movingimagesource.us/articles/obscure-objects-20080619; www.jonathanrosenbaum.com/?p=15969; and www.jonathanrosenbaum.com/?p=15830.

From *Playtime* to *The World*: The Expansion and Depletion of Space within Global Economies

My subject is the presence or absence of both shared public space and virtual private space in two visionary and globally minded urban epics made about thirty-seven years apart, on opposite sides of the planet — Jacques Tati's *Playtime* (1967) and Jia Zhangke's *The World* [*Shijie*] (2004), coincidentally the fourth commercial feature of each writer-director. Both films can be described as innovative and very modern attacks on modernity, and both have powerful metaphysical dimensions that limit their scope somewhat as narrative fictions. I should add that they both project powerful yet deceptive visions of internationalism that are predicated both literally and figuratively on *trompes d'oeil*, specifically on tricks with perspective and the uses of miniaturized simulacra. (I'm referring here to both emblematic sites, such as the Eiffel Tower in both films, and the scaled-down skyscrapers used in the set built for *Playtime*.) In this sense, among others, both films are social critiques about what it means to impose monumental façades on tourists and workers — visitors and employees — who continue to think small.

One significant difference between the roles played by these films in the respective careers of their makers is that *Playtime*, by far the more utopian and optimistic of the two films, was the first of Tati's features to fail at the box office, and it wound up bankrupting him, a disaster that I don't believe he ever fully recovered from. (Furthermore, Tati was pressured to cut the film during its initial Paris run, and although he later said to me and others that he preferred the original and longer version to all the others, this version apparently hasn't been seen since the 1970s and may no longer exist.)[1]

Although it's too early to judge the ultimate effect of *The World* on Jia Zhangke's career, it's worth pointing out that it's the first of his features to get official sanction from the Chinese government and the only one to date to show commercially in theaters (all the others have circulated illegally in pirated versions on video), despite the fact that it is probably more critical of contemporary life and conditions in mainland China than any of his previous features. Another paradox: the film has been shown in China only or at least mainly in a shortened version, although I've been told that the cuts haven't constituted any sort of political censorship and have been made only in order to show the film more times per day during its commercial playdates. So, ironically, the full 139-minute version can be seen in most countries where the film is being shown, but not in China.

I should add that in some ways I'm more interested in the differences between these two very great films than I am in their similarities. Quite apart from the fact that *Playtime*, set in Paris, was mainly shot on a massive set outside that city, built expressly for the film, and that *The World* was mainly shot in an already existing theme park in the vicinity of Beijing, the former film depends on a vision of public life that eliminates any sense of private space or private behavior, while the latter — which is often concerned with the vast discrepancies between (a) decrepit, claustrophobic private spaces and alienated private behavior and (b) the enormous and utopian public spaces in a theme park, specifically as seen from the vantage point of the workers in that theme park — never strays very far from that specialized turf. Both films might therefore be regarded as metaphorical as well as metaphysical statements about the modern world that employ public spaces in order to say something about it.

Another key difference between these films and their respective worlds and eras is the presence and uses in *The World* of mobile phones and text messaging. This seems especially relevant because the utopian vision of shared public space that informs the latter scenes in *Playtime* — beginning in a new restaurant called the Royal Garden at night, and continuing the next morning in a drugstore and on the streets of Paris — is made unthinkable by mobile phones, whose use can be said to constitute both a depletion and a form of denial of public space, especially because the people using them tend to ignore the other people in immediate physical proximity to them.

Moreover, the dystopian vision of alienated and alienating public space in *The World* also posits a single, utopian form of escape that is tied to these phones and expressed by the film's abrupt shifts into animation. One might say, however, that the same mobile phones providing a mental escape from the public spaces of *The World* have also obliterated the sense of shared public space that made Tati's vision of utopia possible. On the other hand, they also express and seemingly establish, if only temporarily, a kind of shared private space that otherwise seems very difficult for the characters in *The World* to achieve in other circumstances. Indeed, just about the only sustained intimacy that we find in the film, apart from the kind established through text messaging, is the friendship between Tao (Zhao Tao), the heroine, a professional dancer at the park, and an exploited fellow dancer from Russia named Anna (Alla Chtcherbakova). And significantly, these characters don't speak a word of one another's language.

I have little doubt that Tati, if he were alive today, could and probably would construct wonderful gags involving the uses of mobile phones. But I don't think he would be able to envision the public reclaiming community space in a modern city in quite the same way that he imagined this in the 1960s. More specifically, if he were making *Playtime* today, I suspect he'd most likely be inventing gags that involve mobile phones in the first part, and then would have to find a way of destroying or at least disempowering those phones in order to make way for the utopian creation of a community with a shared communal space in his second part.

Playtime, shot in 65-millimeter, often makes use of multiple and sometimes even conflicting focal points in order to grant the viewer an unusual amount of freedom and creative participation in scanning the screen for narrative details. Virtually the entire film is set over a twenty-four-hour period, following a group of American tourists in Paris from the time they arrive inside Orly airport at the beginning until the time they leave for the airport the next morning. And the overall visual structure, as was described by Tati himself, develops from an urban landscape of straight lines and right angles that gradually becomes curved and then round as the regimentation of both the architecture and various daytime rituals give way to a more relaxed, spontaneous, and festive atmosphere.

Within this world, there is no real hero or central character. Tati's Monsieur Hulot, who's just one figure in the crowd, appears at an office building early in the film in order to meet an executive for some unstated reason. They quickly lose sight of one another, and their day becomes a painful series of missed connections, where the architecture itself — in particular the spatial confusions created by reflections in glass panes — seems to conspire in their mutual disorientation. There are also many other male characters who resemble Hulot in terms of their height, weight, and dress, especially from a distance, adding to the executive's disorientation as well as our own, and thereby illustrating Tati's own democratic and nonhierarchical theory of comedy in which, as he put it, "the comic effect belongs to everyone." Most of the film's second half is set at a brand-new restaurant on its opening night, the aforementioned Royal Garden, where connections between people rather than disconnections predominate. Hulot, who finally runs into the executive on the street at night, purely by chance, also reencounters an old army buddy now working at the restaurant, who brings him along; the restaurant's décor gradually comes loose and falls apart, and the people there, including the employees as well as the clientele, take over the place, so that a kind of anarchistic and carnivalesque atmosphere prevails where public space essentially becomes reclaimed and reinvented.

All the main characters in *The World* are employees working at a theme park that features simulacra of famous sights around the world such as the Taj Mahal, the leaning tower of Pisa, the Parthenon, and even lower Manhattan with the World Trade Center towers still intact. The two main characters are a couple, the aforementioned Tao and Taisheng (Chen Taisheng), a security guard. Both of them, like Jia himself, come from Fenyang, a small rural town in northern China's Shanxi province where they were already a couple (and where Jia's three previous features were shot). Tao came to Beijing first, eventually followed by Taisheng, and their relationship now is much more tenuous than it was in Fenyang. Taisheng eventually betrays her with an older woman named Qun (Yi-qun Wang) who works outside the theme park in a sweat shop, making clothes that are precise imitations of brand-name items found in a fashion catalog. She works, in other words, in a business that is equally involved with simulacra.

Given all the grandiose dance numbers and other kinds of performances that we see at the theme park, all of which are based on representing ersatz versions of various foreign nationalities, *The World* can be regarded in some ways as a backstage musical. It's also a failed love story in which it's suggested that the synthetic environment where these characters work plays a role in making serious relationships difficult. Significantly, in *Playtime*, dance is seen playing a substantial role in bringing people together at the Royal Garden, and while nothing that qualifies as a love story develops, one nevertheless finds a kind of chaste romantic flirtation between a young woman named Barbara (Barbara Denneke) and Hulot—one that is partially thwarted when the mazelike obstructions in a shop prevent Hulot from delivering a going-away present to her before she departs on her bus. Hulot, however, succeeds in getting one of the "false Hulots," a younger version of himself, to deliver it to her just in time—a very touching illustration of the generosity of Tati's democratic vision whereby one Hulot can readily be replaced or supplanted by another.[2]

It's possible that the utopian vision expressed by Tati of a universal urban experience that can be transcended by an international community is no longer plausible in the same fashion—because even if the same technology is shared around the world, the social meaning of that technology can differ enormously from one culture to the next. There are times when I think that people around the globe have more in common today than they've ever had before at any other time in history—if only because the globe is being run by the same people and corporations who are doing the same things everywhere.

This idea is in fact already anticipated and satirized in *Playtime* by the posters we see in a travel agency extolling the virtues of various countries around the world. Each of these posters features an identical anonymous skyscraper resembling all of those that we see in *Playtime*'s version of Paris, where the more celebrated emblems of the past — the Eiffel Tower, Concorde, Sacre Coeur — seem to survive only as reflections on glass panes.

But there are other times when I think more pessimistically that we're kept further apart than we ever were before — subdivided into separate target audiences, markets, and DVD zones, territorialized into separate classes and cultures — in spite of our common experiences. This suggests that the technology that supposedly links us all together via phones and computers are actually keeping us all further apart, and not only from each other but also, in a sense, from ourselves. In other words, our sense of our own identities, including especially our social identities, becomes fragmented and compartmentalized, with the operations of Internet chatgroups providing a major illustration of this trend.

Perhaps this paradox about so-called "communications" impeding communication has always been the case. But I think the example of mobile phones illustrates such a cultural difference more vividly than any of Tati's examples, which are mainly related to architecture. Personally, I despise mobile phones when I encounter other people using them on the buses and streets of Chicago, because I experience them as a rejection of myself as a fellow passenger or pedestrian. One used to assume, whenever one saw a person walking down the street speaking loudly to no one in particular, that this person was insane. Today one commonly assumes that this same person is a sane individual speaking to someone else on a phone, but it might also be possible to assume that the implied rejection of one's immediate surroundings suggests another kind of insanity, based no less on an antisocial form of behavior.

Yet I have to acknowledge that for a young person who lives with her or his family and feels in desperate need of some kind of privacy, a mobile phone may also represent a kind of liberation. And for the characters we encounter in *The World* whose private spaces are invariably drab and unattractive, even if they spend most of their waking hours in the utopian spaces of a theme park, it seems that the only dreams that can truly belong to them as individuals are the ones that they can transmit on portable phones to one another via instant messaging. Indeed, according to a recent front-page story in the *New York Times* by Jim Yardley (April 25, 2005), "About 27% of China's 1.3 billion people own a cellphone, a rate that is far higher in big cities, particularly among the young. Indeed, for upwardly mobile young urbanites, cellphones and the Internet are the primary means of communication."

I guess I'm a universalist in Tati's sense insofar as I can view a film such as *The World* as being about what's happening in the world right now and not simply about what's happening in China — just as I can view *Playtime* as a film about the world in 1967 and not simply about France. In fact, I regard both films as being in advance of their own times, even literally so. *Playtime* was shot before France had parking meters, but Tati knew they were coming so he included them in his giant set. I don't know exactly what Jia is predicting about the future of either China or the world, but I think he feels the shock of capitalism more keenly in some ways than many of us currently do in the West, and out of that shock grows a need for a different kind of fantasy. His view is certainly much bleaker, because whereas for Tati utopia was a reinvention of what we already have, Jia sees it, in the shape of a theme park, as an emblem of something we've already lost.

World Cinemas, Transnational Perspectives (AFI Film Reader), edited by Nataša Ďurovičová and Kathleen Newman (New York/London: Routledge, 2009); derived from a lecture given on the final day of "Urban Trauma and the Metropolitan Imagination," a conference organized by Scott Bukatman and Pavle Levi held at Stanford University on May 5–7, 2005

Notes

1. I was privileged to work for Tati in Paris as a "script consultant" for a little over a week in early 1973. For more details, as well as some extended material about *Playtime*, see "Tati's Democracy" (*Film Comment*, May–June 1973) and "The Death of Hulot" (*Sight and Sound*, Spring 1983). An excerpt from the former, introducing an interview with Tati, is reprinted in revised form in my collection *Movies as Politics* (Berkeley: University of California Press, 1997); the latter is reprinted in my collection *Placing Movies: The Practice of Film Criticism* (Berkeley: University of California Press, 1995).

2. In his biography of *Tati*, David Bellos reveals that Tati was in fact romantically involved with Denneke — a German *au pair* who had worked for neighbors of his — during part of the shooting of *Playtime*. (See *Jacques Tati* [London: Harvill Press, 1999], 265.)

Part 2

Actors, Actors-Writers-Directors, Filmmakers

Kim Novak as Midwestern Independent

It's possible that the star we know as Kim Novak was partially the invention of Columbia Pictures — conceived, as the Canadian critic Richard Lippe puts it, both as a rival/spinoff of Marilyn Monroe and as a replacement for the reigning but at that point aging Rita Hayworth. At least this was the favored cover story of Columbia studio head Harry Cohn, whom *Time* magazine famously quoted in 1957 as saying, "If you wanna bring me your wife and your aunt, we'll do the same for them." It was also the treasured conceit of the American press at the time, which was all too eager to heap scorn on Novak for presuming to act — just as they were already gleefully deriding Monroe for presuming to think.

But Monroe, as we know today, was considerably smarter than most or all of the columnists who wrote about her. And Kim Novak — a major star if not a major actress — had something to offer that was a far cry from updated Hayworth or imitation Monroe (even if the latter was precisely what Columbia attempted to do with her in one of her first screen appearances, in the 1954 Judy Holliday vehicle *Phffft!*). In point of fact, Novak was more beautiful than either actress, yet paradoxically she was also less of a fantasy. Marilyn Monroe was plainly a comic-strip figure and a fantasy wish-fulfillment that simultaneously converted all the men in her orbit into both fathers and infants, whereas Hayworth apparently lived up to her own self-characterization: "Men go to bed with Gilda but they wake up with me." But Novak was real from the get-go, and it's tempting to think that her humble Midwestern origins had something to do with her reality.

Born Marilyn Pauline Novak in Chicago in 1933 — the daughter of a Slavic transit clerk for the railroad (her father) and a former teacher (her mother) — she started off in advertising, as "Miss Deepfreeze," touring the country while selling refrigerators. She became a movie star only after she started working as a model in Los Angeles, landing first an uncredited bit in *The French Line* (1954), then a full part as a gangster's moll in *Pushover* later the same year. (Her director on that film, Richard Quine, later became her fiancé, though they never married, and he wound up directing her in three more features — *Bell, Book and Candle*; *Strangers When We Meet*; and *The Notorious Landlady*. Her other most frequent director, George Sidney, projected a brassy vulgarity that was more suitable for an imperturbable powerhouse like Esther Williams than for a delicate creature like Novak, and she survived the encounter best during their first picture together, *The Eddy Duchin Story*.)

Of course it wasn't just the working-class and Midwestern aspects of Novak's background that registered in the public's mind. She was also Marjorie Oelrichs in *The Eddy Duchin Story* (1956), a well-to-do interior decorator who gets Boston pianist Duchin (Tyrone Power) his first New York gig and eventually marries him. She was Linda English from Albuquerque in Sidney's *Pal Joey* (1957), struggling to make it as a vocalist in a San Francisco nightclub. And in Quine's *Bell, Book and Candle* (1958), she was Gillian Holroyd, a classy bohemian witch in Manhattan. Furthermore, she was regally upscale as Madeleine Elster, one of the two San Francisco personas she incarnated in Alfred Hitchcock's *Vertigo* (1958).

Later on, she would play Betty Preisser in Paddy Chayefsky and Delbert Mann's *Middle of the Night* (1959), the mistress of a much older New York garment manufacturer (Fredric March); Maggie Gault in Evan Hunter and Richard Quine's *Strangers When We Meet* (1960) — a sexually and romantically frustrated Beverly Hills housewife and mother who becomes involved with a neighbor, a married architect and father (Kirk Douglas); and Polly the Pistol in Billy Wilder's *Kiss Me, Stupid* (1964), a prostitute working out of her trailer in Climax, Nevada. But in spite of such diversity in terms of class and geography, it was arguably her modest Midwestern roots — as Madge Owens (in a small town in Kansas) in *Picnic* (1955), as Molly (in the Polish slums of Chicago) in *The Man with the Golden Arm* (1955), and as the title heroine in Sidney's *Jeanne Eagels* (1957), who starts out as a Kansas City waitress — that were most operative in establishing her overall screen reality.

Even Judy Barton, the working-class character Novak plays in *Vertigo*, has the effect of making Madeleine Elster, her glitzy predecessor, seem more like a manufactured illusion — more specifically, an image that the obsessed hero (James Stewart) calls on Judy to recreate. And even though Madge in *Picnic* is middle-class, the destiny she opts for at the movie's end is distinctly downscale when she boards a bus for Tulsa — before James Wong Howe's airborne CinemaScope camera rapturously races ahead of her to connect her epic trajectory to that of Hal Carter (William Holden), her working-class beloved, on a train bound for the same destination. And even more telling than her character's class, real or adopted, in either *Vertigo* or *Picnic*, is her seeming independence as a solitary figure.

Maybe it was Novak's beauty and her acute awareness of it that made her fragile, and perhaps it was her fragility that made her real. "Mom, what good is it just to be pretty?" she says as Madge to Betty Fields in *Picnic*. This was her first big movie role, and presumably the line came from playwright William Inge. But it appeared to come from the actress as well as the character she was playing — expressing what always seemed to make Kim Novak less than wholly delighted about the burden of being a movie star and a glamorous myth, when she'd rather chow down with the rest of us. It was the kind of ambivalence that worked against the obsessive career-building of a Monroe, so that her fame peaked early on, and was already fading fairly rapidly after about a decade. Much as Novak's husky voice seemed to contradict or at least complicate the hyperbolic femininity she was supposed to project, her down-home earthiness often wound up undercutting some of her obligatory studio baggage as a glamour queen.

For all of Cohn's braggadocio, Columbia Pictures often had a confused sense of how to use her to best advantage. Perhaps its worst idea was to miscast her as a variant of *Sunset Boulevard*'s Norma Desmond in *Jeanne Eagels*, a downbeat black and white biopic about the famous 1920s stage actress who died of a drug overdose — a vehicle that was presumably meant to show off Novak's acting chops. The film begins promisingly with Eagels arriving at a Kansas City carnival to enter a beauty contest overseen by Jeff Chandler, who soon thereafter becomes her boss and lover. It's only after Eagels' driving ambition to become a stage actress transforms her into Chandler's boss that the film turns sour and its antifeminist agenda becomes fully apparent.

It's entirely to Novak's credit that she can't play hard and ruthless the way the film wants her to. Demonic divas aren't part of her repertoire — as director Robert Aldrich must have discovered to his regret when he miscast her in a double role in *The Legend of Lylah Claire* (1968), as both the deceased title diva and Elsa Brinkmann, the starlet who's hired to play her onscreen. But Novak's honorable failure in *Jeanne Eagels* still derails both the story and Sidney's leering direction (which also brutalizes her in *Pal Joey* when her masochistic character dutifully performs a nightclub strip to please Frank Sinatra's Joey); at best she can portray a tormented diva and do a few drunk scenes. The film wants to show her as a victim of her own hubris, but all she can handle is the victim part, without any clear sense of what's victimizing her — unless it's her desire to be famous. The film pretends to see her downfall as tragic, yet it almost seems to gloat over the ironic titles of some of her stage vehicles, such as *Careless Lady* and *Forever Young*.

Far more persuasive are the roles in which Novak's character comes across as loyally devoted to the movie's hero without ever sacrificing some of her spiky independence, as in her three pictures preceding *Jeanne Eagels* (*Picnic*, *The Man with the Golden Arm*, *The Eddy Duchin Story*) — and in her second and third outings with Quine, both underrated, *Bell, Book and Candle* and *Strangers When We Meet*, where her independent spirit and her libido almost seem to be running neck in neck. In all five of these movies, she's rebellious and even somewhat courageous — not quite the compliant pussycat that the mythic aura of her beauty and the sexism of '50s Hollywood sometimes make her out to be — even though Maggie Gault, her Emma Bovaryish character in *Strangers*, is sometimes in denial about her own passion. It also must be conceded that thanks to this character's repressed and sexist milieu, the only visible form of independence *or* rebellion available to her is in fact her adultery, and the only visible form of courage is the stoicism with which she faces the loss of her lover.

It's a tribute to Novak that she can make a tragic heroine rather than a pathetic victim out of Maggie, largely because she's so adept at making us experience the full fury of her blocked desires. In fact, the projection of her characters' sexual desires is a near-constant in her work. "Why don't you give me *him* for Christmas?," she purrs to her Siamese cat, Pyewacket, in the opening scene of *Bell, Book and Candle*, referring to her upstairs neighbor (James Stewart), whom she's just met for the first time. French film critic Bernard Eisenschitz aptly describes this charmed and charming movie as "the optimistic version of *Vertigo*" (made the same year, with the same costar), and James Wong Howe lights and frames her here with the same reverence that he brought to her beauty in *Picnic*. By way of contrast, her sexiness and her softness-within-firmness as "Molly-o," the Madonna-like savior of heroin addict and jazz drummer Frankie Machine (Frank Sinatra) in *The Man with the Golden Arm*, is like a triumph of neorealism in the midst of director Otto Preminger's doom-ridden, set-bound expressionism. She's trapped like Frankie, but she also comes across as more independent than anyone else in the picture, and Novak's funkiness collides with Sinatra's to create a volatile, smoky brew.

Stop Smiling, no. 27 (2006): "Ode to the Midwest"

Marilyn Monroe's Brains

This weekend the Gene Siskel Film Center launches "Merry Marilyn!," a Marilyn Monroe retrospective, starting with two pivotal Howard Hawks features, *Monkey Business* (1952) and *Gentlemen Prefer Blondes* (1953). The series will include most of her major films at Fox as well as *Some Like It Hot* (1959) and *The Misfits* (1960).

By coincidence *Playboy* this month is publishing a package of stories about her final days and death. The magazine is reviving the popular conspiracy theory that Monroe's reported suicide in August 1962 was murder, the consequence of her secret affairs with John and Bobby Kennedy. If, like me, you're less interested in how she died than in how she lived, the most interesting part of this package is an inexact transcript of the freewheeling confessional tape recordings she made for her psychiatrist, Ralph Greenson, a few weeks before her death. Greenson had asked her to free-associate during their sessions, but she found that difficult. Then she discovered that she lost her inhibitions when she was by herself speaking into a recorder. Shortly after her autopsy Greenson played these tapes — once, in his office — for Los Angeles County deputy district attorney John Miner, who like him was skeptical that Monroe had been of a mind to kill herself. The transcript is only Miner's recollection of what he heard, written hours later. It's believed that Greenson, who died in 1979, destroyed the tapes, so this imperfect record is all we have.

It may not be enough to prove that Monroe was murdered, but it's more than enough to refute the condescending claims often made by would-be experts ranging from Joseph L. Mankiewicz to Clive James that Monroe was some version of the dumb blonde she was so adept at playing. James once wrote, "She was good at being inarticulately abstracted for the same reasons that midgets are good at being short." Among the more intriguing sections of the transcript are her citations from and sophisticated discussions of Freud's *Introductory Lectures*, James Joyce's *Ulysses*, Shakespeare, and William Congreve and her persuasive critique of *The Misfits*: "Arthur [Miller] didn't know film or how to write for it. *The Misfits* was not a great film, because it wasn't a great script." There are also candid remarks about her feelings for both Kennedys, her recently acquired ability to have orgasms, a brief sexual encounter with Joan Crawford, and a preoccupation with enemas tied to her problems with constipation.

The intelligence that shines through this document can also be seen in most of her best performances, especially in the way she subtly subverted the sexist content of her material. Her brainless secretary in the otherwise brilliant *Monkey Business* — a relentless mockery of the cult of youth — is a notable exception, but it was made before she became a star. In her next film, the 1953 *Niagara* (also in the retrospective), she played her only noir heroine, and it's one of her less distinctive performances, perhaps because the script gives her so little elbow room. But then she costarred in *Gentlemen Prefer Blondes*, and it became easier for her to choose and inflect her roles.

Gentlemen Prefer Blondes — supposedly her most sexist film, and the one in which her character is supposedly the most brainless — isn't nearly as simple-minded as it may at first appear. The conniving strategies of Monroe's Lorelei Lee and her insatiable will to power as expressed through her lust for jewels — always lurking behind the dumb act and baby talk, which further infantilize her already infantile fiancé, played by Tommy Noonan — are also a parodic expose of capitalist duplicity. In this respect, Monroe's double-edged performance recalls Charlie Chaplin's Brechtian depiction of Monsieur Verdoux — based on the notorious French Bluebeard Landru — five years earlier. Like nearly all of Verdoux's female victims, the male targets of Lorelei's artillery aren't merely unattractive but grotesque — thereby implicating the spectator, who's much more likely to identify with the predator than with the victims. (The most prominent of Lorelei's victims, a bumbling, patriarchal fool played by Charles Coburn, is aptly nicknamed Piggy.) In all her films after *Gentlemen Prefer Blondes*, Monroe's Betty Boop-ish persona is similarly complicated.

Generally speaking, during the first half of the '50s Monroe concentrated on lost-little-girl figures, starting with her gangster's moll in *The Asphalt Jungle*. Variations on this role can be seen in *Clash by Night*, *Don't Bother to Knock* (in which she plays a psychotic babysitter, perhaps the part that most evokes her troubled childhood), *Monkey Business*, *Gentlemen Prefer Blondes* (in which she only pretends to be vulnerable and naive), *How to Marry a Millionaire* (in which her determination not to wear glasses makes her look literally lost much of the time), *There's No Business Like Show Business*, and *The Seven Year Itch* (in which she's still a little girl, but not so lost and much more generous). After a stint with the Actors Studio, her characters tended to become more maternal as well as more ethically grounded, as in *Bus Stop*, *Some Like It Hot*, *Let's Make Love*, and *The Misfits*. In both phases she was playing role models who represented the kind of ideal family she never had. In the underrated 1960 musical *Let's Make Love* her Greenwich Village chorine, by no means brainless, is more striking for her sense of fairness and her loyalty to her coworkers than for her gullibility.

The difficulty some people have discerning Monroe's intelligence as an actress seems rooted in the ideology of a repressive era, when superfeminine women weren't supposed to be smart. They often fail to see past the sexist clichés she used as armor, satirically and otherwise, fail to notice that she was also positing a utopian view of sex, one that was relatively guilt free and blissfully pleasure oriented — something entirely new for that period.

Like the hard-nosed Lorelei Lee — who was perfectly capable of acting like a smart grown-up when it came to her friendship with Dorothy (Jane Russell) — Monroe had discovered early on that her greatest power rested in her capacity to look and sound innocent, hapless, and helpless. A telling anecdote was recorded by a friend of hers, gossip columnist James Bacon, about the shooting of Fritz Lang's 1952 *Clash by Night*, before she became a star: "I watched Marilyn spoil 27 takes of a scene one day. She had only one line, but before she could deliver it about 20 other actors had to go through a whole series of intricate movements on a boat. Everybody was letter perfect in every take, but Marilyn could not remember that one line. . . . Finally she got it right and Fritz yelled: 'Thank God. Print it.' Later, in her dressing room, Marilyn confessed that she had muffed the line on purpose for all those takes: 'I just didn't like the way the scene was going. When I liked it, I said the line perfectly.'"

It's the kind of negative power she still seems to have been using at the very end of her career, when her absences and delays on the never-finished *Something's Got to Give* got her fired. Having seen the surviving fragments of that horrendous comedy (in the 2001 *Marilyn Monroe: The Final Days*), I can understand why she didn't want to work on it, but in the end combating the studio's tyranny with a tyranny of her own was a losing proposition. Yet she's still the best thing in this footage. Her scenes with some children tap into her maternal instincts, and she comes to life, displaying the creative intelligence and ethical grounding of her very best work.

Chicago Reader, December 2, 2005

A Free Man:
White Hunter, Black Heart

I t's the film of a free man." Roberto Rossellini's celebrated defense of Charlie
Chaplin's most despised film, *A King in New York* (1957)—a film so reviled
that it goes unmentioned in Chaplin's 1964 autobiography—is a sentence
that frequently comes to mind about some of the features directed by Clint
Eastwood, especially over the past couple of decades. Eastwood has in fact
carved out a singular niche for himself that affords him the sort of artistic and
conceptual freedom that no one else in Hollywood can claim. Starting with
the fact that he doesn't testmarket his movies and indulge in the sort of hasty
postproduction revisions that limit the range of his colleagues, he's a director
who can choose both his subjects and how he deals with them.

In some respects, of course, comparing Eastwood's freedom with Chaplin's
is highly dubious—even if one can find a few parallels that go beyond their
status as producer-director-stars, such as the fact that both have composed music for their own films. Eastwood, unlike Chaplin, isn't a writer and remains
fundamentally at the mercy of his scripts, and he doesn't own the negatives of
his own pictures. But if one compares the relative freedom of each filmmaker
in his prime with that of his commercial contemporaries, the similarities become somewhat more meaningful.

In part because of Eastwood's conservative persona, he can offer political
critiques of certain aspects of the American character, both as an actor and
as a director, that wouldn't be tolerated from anyone else in the industry. He
can seriously question the chauvinistic and propagandistic uses of a famous
Iwo Jima photograph (*Flags of Our Fathers*, 2006) and counter many popular
notions about Japanese soldiers during the same war (*Letters from Iwo Jima*,
2006), implicitly undermining some of the patriotic excuses for the recent
American occupations of Iraq and Afghanistan. And using his own persona as

a star, he can launch detailed assaults on racism in some films (most recently in last year's *Gran Torino*) and on macho behavior in certain others (including some relatively commercial projects such as the 2002 *Blood Work*) — and on both in *White Hunter, Black Heart* (1990).

The critique offered in this underrated and frequently misunderstood East-wood film goes beyond egocentric notions of masculinity to encompass certain forms of American arrogance and imperialism, even though the ostensible target in this case is a famous all-American liberal, filmmaker John Huston. Peter Viertel's 1953 novel of the same title is a transparent roman à clef about his own experience of working with Huston as a screenwriter on *The African Queen* — a job that for Huston was mainly an excuse to indulge in his obsession with becoming a big-game hunter and bagging an elephant on location, before shooting on the film even started.

Viertel — son of the famous Hollywood Jewish-émigré intellectuals Salka (Greta Garbo's best friend) and Berthold Viertel, who published his first novel when he was eighteen and later married Deborah Kerr — was already an old pal of Huston's, having worked with him on *We Were Strangers* (1949), and came on board more as a writer and friend than as someone with much taste for killing animals himself. The degree to which his friendship with Huston became tested by this encounter is one of the book's key themes, and Viertel's transparency is reflected even in the characters' names, Pete Verrill and John Wilson.

In Viertel's 1991 memoir *Dangerous Friends: Hemingway, Huston and Others* (a book that in recent years has become a pricey collectors' item), he notes that both Hemingway and Irwin Shaw told him that they regarded this transparency as a mistake and that he eventually came to agree with them: "Had I changed the names of my leading characters, my novel would probably have been judged on its own merits rather than as a scandalous 'knock piece,' which was how it was received by a majority of critics." Less critical at the time was Huston himself, who suggested the specific and devastatingly tragic, anti-imperialist ending that Viertel wound up using, after reading an incomplete version — which he praised profusely, in spite of its unflattering portrait of himself — during the shooting of *Moulin Rouge*. (He also signed a release after reading the novel's final typescript.) However, the novel goes unmentioned in Huston's own 1980 memoir, *An Open Book*, and Viertel speculates that his friend privately nursed a "long-dormant bitterness" about it.

The portrait of Huston that emerges as both a *monstre sacré* and a vain nihilist in both the novel and movie ultimately has bearing on his unevenness as a director (passing back and forth repeatedly between serious work and hack jobs), his misanthropic existentialism (often reflected in the futility of his characters' fates), and his macho pretensions as well as some of his leftist positions. By the end of the story, he's largely exposed as a destructive ugly American who poisons everything around him, in spite of his charming impudence. And his seeming lucidity about himself often comes across as simple confusion. When Pete charges Wilson with committing a crime against nature by going after elephants, Wilson counters that it's worse than a crime, it's a sin — "the only sin you can buy a license for and then go out and commit. And that's why I want to do it before I do anything else. You understand?" It's a sentiment worthy of an Ahab. But sin is a meaningless concept for an atheist, and even Wilson/Huston's cosmic pessimism and cynicism are ultimately compromised by this form of defiance. This may account for why *Wise Blood*—an atheistic take on the gallows humor of a true believer, Flannery O'Connor — seems to me the best of Huston's films, encompassing the full reach of his passionate ambivalence.

Adapting *White Hunter, Black Heart* for the screen had been a long-term project. Ray Bradbury, who also worked for Huston (on the 1956 *Moby Dick*), was commissioned to write an early screenplay in 1959, and the one that Eastwood used three decades later credits Viertel himself and directors James Bridges (*Urban Cowboy*) and Burt Kennedy (*Welcome to Hard Times*), in that order. It's an unusually faithful adaptation, and the fact that Eastwood cast himself as John Wilson appears to be the source of most of the problems many have had with the film. For me, it's one of the chief sources of its brilliance.

Auteurist issues are at the center of this debate, as they are with the no less contested *A.I. Artificial Intelligence*—which is usually read as a Steven Spielberg film and occasionally read as a Stanley Kubrick film, but is generally thought to be indigestible as both at the same time. The auteurist issues in this case, however, relate to the actorly personas of Huston and Eastwood, which are respectively hammy/rhetorical and minimalist/terse. If Eastwood as an actor has to be judged exclusively as a precise impersonator of Huston, the inadequacy of the vocal and facial equipment he brings to this task is inescapable — as inescapable, one might argue, as the inadequacy of Spielberg as a directorial impersonator of Kubrick.

But if one shifts one's expectations and evaluates Eastwood as an interpreter of and commentator on Huston's persona in relation to his own — a dialectical meditation on Huston as well as himself that is both critique and appreciation — the nature of his achievement changes. He offers in effect a Brechtian performance, especially if one thinks of Brecht's own description of how he wanted Charles Laughton to play the title role in his *Galileo* (as set down in his "Small Organum for the Theater"): "The actor appears on stage in a double role, as Laughton and as Galileo; the showman Laughton does not disappear in the Galileo he is showing; Laughton is actually there, standing on the stage and showing us what he imagines Galileo to have been."

How does this function in the film? As a running commentary on his two subjects, Huston and himself—the ruminations and questions (rather than the answers) of a free man. In many ways the centerpiece of both the novel and the movie is a scene in Entebbe, Uganda, at the Sabena Hotel's outdoor restaurant, where Wilson first verbally abuses a woman he is trying to seduce because of her blatant anti-Semitism and then picks a protracted fight with the headwaiter after observing him mistreat a black African waiter for dropping a tray. This scene derives from Huston's own account to Viertel of an hour-long drunken fistfight he started with Errol Flynn in David O. Selznick's garden in 1945 after Flynn made a scurrilous comment about a woman Huston knew. (It landed both men in separate hospitals, Huston with a broken nose and Flynn with two broken ribs, and Huston devotes over a page to the incident in *An Open Book,* describing it with obvious relish.) The novel makes this far more interesting by celebrating Huston's grandiloquence in denouncing the woman for her anti-Semitism and then making us acutely uncomfortable about the fistfight. (When Pete tries to hold him back, Wilson says, "Let go. We've fought one bout for the kikes. This is the main event . . . for the niggers.") And Eastwood improves on the novel by making his own performance at once a flashy embodiment, a scathing ridicule, and an open questioning of this kind of behavior (a potent mixture that he also employs, minus the questioning, as Walt Kowalski, the racist hero of *Gran Torino*). At the end of his hunt, ready to embark on another kind of shooting, Wilson discovers that he's an even more murderous enemy of black Africans than a racist headwaiter, and the film asks us to ponder why and how this should be so.

One Chaplinesque aspect of this kind of star performance is that it risks turning virtually everyone else in the story into a prop: Walt Kowalski's dead and unseen wife in *Gran Torino* never comes alive for us even as an absence, and we tend to ignore the functional performances of everyone else in *White Hunter, Black Heart,* including Jeff Fahey as Pete. But Eastwood turns even this limitation into a virtue by finally fusing himself and Huston/Wilson into the same figure in the film's final shot, as he starts to direct—terse and rhetorical, defeated and in control—with a single word: "Action."

Moving Image Source, December 1, 2009; www.movingimagesource.us/articles/a-free -man-20091201

Bit Actors*

Most film criticism has been hampered by the habit of dealing with narrative movies strictly and exclusively in terms of their stories. What's
overlooked by this practice is the fact that virtually all films are made up of
nonnarrative as well as narrative elements — what might be described as both
persistence and fluctuation, or nonlinearity as well as linearity. Even though
we often prefer to think we experience movies only as unfolding narratives —
which is apparently why what most people mean by "spoilers" always relate to
plot and not to formal moves — how we remember these movies is part of that
experience, and this partially consists of static images.

Consequently, it could be argued that we need more art historians writing
about movies and fewer literary critics who operate from the model of narrative fiction. And a potent suggestion of what art historians could offer us is
found in a highly original study of the B films of producer Val Lewton, practically all of which were made during World War II.

Lewton is mainly known today as a Russian-born pulp writer (the nephew
of Broadway actress Alla Nazimova) and then a story editor for David O. Selz-
nik, who became famous as a producer of cheap, arty horror films at RKO
during the '40s. Though mostly accurate, this account overlooks that Lewton
never considered himself a horror specialist and that even though nine of his
eleven RKO features were marketed as horror items, arguably only the first,
Cat People, fully belongs to the genre. And this imprecision continues to limit
our access to Lewton's films today: when Warners released a mainly excellent

Icons of Grief: Val Lewton's Home Front Pictures, by Alexander Nemerov. Berkeley:
University of California Press, 2005, 213 pp.

Lewton DVD box set last year, they omitted his two RKO features, *Mademoiselle Fifi* and *Youth Runs Wild*, that have never been labeled (or mislabeled) as horror, thereby giving the relatively clueless studio executives of that era the final say in defining Lewton's legacy.

Nemerov teaches art history at Yale, and his distinctiveness as a critic and historian goes well beyond his capacity to focus on nonnarrative aspects of films that transcend their usual genre classification. Ironically, while what he's offering is clearly an auteurist study that draws heavily on Lewton's biography — including his mostly out-of-print pulp novels, his gloomy Russianness (and with it a certain feeling of estrangement from the American mainstream), and his broad range of cultural references, which he tended to downplay in his habitual self-deprecations — it depends largely on Lewton's collaborations with other artists. And even though Nemerov is attentive to Lewton's better-known collaborators, such as director Jacques Tourneur and noir cinematographer Nicholas Musaraca, he gives most of his attention to bit actors who emerge briefly but indelibly from the busy textures of these films to compose icons of grief. He persuasively argues that these images of intense sadness express mourning for the war dead in the overseas war that was being fought, a war that goes unmentioned in virtually all the films.

Nemerov is more historian than critic, and part of his achievement is to persuade us that there's nothing at all forced or willful about his making the war's emotional impact so central to Lewton's films. Indeed, it hardly seems coincidental that Lewton thrived as a filmmaker only as long as the war continued, and that his career virtually collapsed as soon as it was over. And in order to convince us of the war's centrality and relevance, he draws substantially on the contemporary film reviews of James Agee and Manny Farber, paintings of the period by everyone from Norman Rockwell to Jackson Pollock, many other Hollywood movies (including touchstones like *Meet Me in St. Louis* and *The Palm Beach Story* as well as forgotten obscurities like *Headin' for God's Country* and *The Bamboo Blonde*). He also digs purposefully into the remaining careers of such little-known actors as Skelton Knaggs in *The Ghost Ship*, Darby Jones in *I Walked with a Zombie*, and Glenn Vernon in *Bedlam*. (Somewhat better known are Ann Carter, the little girl at the center of *The Curse of the Cat People*, and Simone Simon, the female lead of *Cat People* who reappears briefly as the ghost of her former self in the putative sequel.) In doing so, he recalls the rapturous page or two in Italo Calvino's autobiographical *The Road to San Giovanni* cataloging the supporting actors who were an essential element in his childhood moviegoing.

The poetics of Nemerov's approach seem fully compatible with the exquisite modesty of Lewton's haunting films, which typically run about seventy-five minutes or even less—though they manage to encompass more plot, atmosphere, memorable characters, and poetic inflections than current movies, which last much longer and cost many times as much. Considering how much is crowded into I Walked with a Zombie, The Leopard Man, and The Seventh Victim (three of my own favorites), including a considerable amount of tension and dread, the miracle is how quiet and still the resonance of these films is on reflection. Nemerov devotes a chapter to only the first of these, in which Darby Jones's Carré-Four—a giant black zombie standing on the crossroads of a sugarcane field at night—manages to steal the movie from the more prominent actors, and even manages to make his way into the title, despite the fact that, as Nemerov bothers to find out and inform us, Jones got paid only $225 for three days of work while Frances Dee as the heroine got $6,000.

Like the other structuring absences Nemerov finds in Lewton's films and other Hollywood features of the same period—such as the reality of a fugitive slave hunt suddenly obtruding in a rowdy slapstick sequence of Preston Sturges's The Palm Beach Story—this figures as a glimpse of a social reality too troubling to be confronted head on in films ostensibly designed to provide escapism, so it becomes artfully bracketed and strategically separated from the main story. The Sturges example occurs in the midst of the hilarious drunken revels of the Ale and Quail Club on a southbound train. To Nemerov, it

> portrays slavery with a clarity so stunning it could only have been the product of the film's complete misrecognition of its own energies. The train comes to a stop, and the Ale and Quail car is uncoupled. It is night, and we are somewhere in the South along the route from New York to Palm Beach. From the car we see the [black] bartender emerge, screaming and fleeing for his life, pursued by the gun-firing huntsmen and their baying hounds. This is the most direct representation of a fugitive slave hunt in the deep dark South in a Hollywood film of the 1940s, down to the last detail. . . . [Yet only] the certainty that all is fun-filled and innocent can produce the perfected form of an amnesia that actually remembers.

Thus "the taboo social content that brings The Palm Beach Story to a stop . . . forced the plot, like the train, to cut off a part of itself to move forward."

In other words, the detachable sliver of narrative finds some unexpected kinship with the seemingly detachable bit actor who, like Lewton himself, manages to triumph through a singular fusion of intensity with modesty. "No doubt there is an oddity to this process," Nemerov writes of his own methodology in his introduction, "to this sense of excitement as the minor player in the minor role in the forgotten or near-forgotten movie finally makes an appearance. . . . But I trust, too, that there is something promising in this strangeness, for where but in the most overlooked corners, and in the briefest moments, does one expect to find something like the past?"

A shorter version of this review appeared in *Stop Smiling*, no. 27 (2006)

Rediscovering Charlie Chaplin

Although I suspect many would dispute this characterization, I think the period we're now living through may well be the first in which scholars have finally figured out a good way of teaching film history. And significantly, this discovery isn't necessarily coming out of academic film study, even if a few academics are making major contributions to it.

I'm speaking, of course, about the didactic materials accompanying the rerelease of some classic films on DVD. Three examples that I believe illustrate my thesis especially well are: (1) the various commentaries or audiovisual essays offered by Yuri Tsivian on DVD editions of *Mad Love: The Films of Evgeni Bauer* (Milestone), Dziga Vertov's *Man with a Movie Camera* (Kino International/BFI), and Sergei Eisenstein's *Ivan the Terrible* (Criterion); (2) the commentaries offered by David Kalat on Fritz Lang's *Dr. Mabuse the Gambler* (Blackhawk Films) and *The Testament of Dr. Mabuse* (Criterion); and (3) the various documentary materials offered on "The Chaplin Collection," a twelve-box set issued jointly by MK2 and Warners and put together with the full resources and cooperation of the Charles Chaplin estate. These DVDs include not just all of Chaplin's features apart from his last, *The Countess from Hong Kong* (presumably missing due to rights issues), but historical introductions written and read aloud by Chaplin biographer David Robinson, newsreels, home movies, outtakes, production photos, relevant shorts by Chaplin and others, and twenty-six-minute episodes in a brand-new series called "Chaplin Today" devoted to historically placing each of these features as well as interviewing a contemporary filmmaker for his or her impressions about it.

The Chaplin Collection's editor, Serge Toubiana, a former editor of *Cahiers du cinéma*, has commissioned, among others, many writers from that magazine, past and present, to direct the various chapters of "Chaplin Today," each of whom has drawn materials from the plentiful Chaplin archives as well as other sources. Thus we get Alain Bergala filming (and interviewing) Abbas Kiarostami on *The Kid* (1921), Mathias Ledoux filming Liv Ullmann on *A Woman of Paris* (1923), Serge Le Péron filming Idrissa Oeudraogo on *The Gold Rush* (1925), François Ede filming Emir Kusturica on *The Circus* (1928), Serge Bromberg filming animator Peter Lord on *City Lights* (1931), Philippe Truffault filming Luc and Jean-Pierre Dardenne on *Modern Times* (1936), Bernard Eisenschitz filming Claude Chabrol on *Monsieur Verdoux* (1947), Edgardo Cozarinsky filming Bernardo Bertolucci on *Limelight* (1952), and Jérôme de Missolz filming Jim Jarmusch on *A King in New York* (1957).

The remaining DVDs, which break with this pattern, are devoted to Richard Schickel's recent documentary *Charlie: The Life and Art of Charles Chaplin; The Chaplin Revue* (consisting of *A Dog's Life, Shoulder Arms, Sunnyside, A Day's Pleasure, The Idle Class, Pay Day,* and *The Pilgrim*); and *The Great Dictator* (1940). The latter, however, gives us an excellent fifty-five-minute documentary by Kevin Brownlow and Michael Kloft called *The Tramp and the Dictator* (a virtual object lesson in how to pursue the subject of Chaplin and Hitler honestly and responsibly — in striking contrast to the capriciousness of the comparison between Orson Welles and William Randolph Hearst in the 1995 Oscar-nominated *The Battle Over Citizen Kane*), twenty-five minutes of Sydney Chaplin's color "home movie" footage of the shooting of *Dictator,* a seven-minute outtake from *Sunnyside* (1919) showing the Tramp as a barber, and even a three-minute clip from *Monsieur Verdoux.*

Although Chaplin is still the closest thing we have to a universally recognized, understood, and appreciated artist, the degree to which he needs to be reintroduced to contemporary filmgoers — and reintroduced from an international rather than American perspective — can't be underestimated. This is surely why the second volume of The Chaplin Collection garnered only a B+ from *Entertainment Weekly* (along with the headline "Film directors laud the Little Tramp's brand of camp") — in contrast to, say, *Scenes from a Marriage* (A), George A. Romero's *Dawn of the Dead* (A), and *21 Grams* (A–) in the same issue, making it tie with the "complete first session" of episodes from *The Flintstones* and the "20th anniversary edition" of *Splash,* both of which also got B pluses. After all, we're meant to conclude, Chaplin is spectacularly uneven: "*City Lights* is a classic of sentimental comedy because it gets the mix of sentiment and comedy just right. *The Kid* and *The Circus* do not. They are bathetic, and *A Woman of Paris* plays like bad Balzac." And if you're still wondering why "bad" Balzac and Chaplin are deemed inferior to "good" Bergman, Romero, and González Iñárritu, this presumably has something to do with how far back in history we have to go. (Frankly I have my own demurrals about *The Circus,* in spite of the brilliance found in certain sequences. But any dismissal that can bracket it indiscriminately with *The Kid* can't be very attentive to either.)

In other words, one can't even begin to grasp Chaplin's importance without processing sizable chunks of the twentieth century, and from a universal rather than a local perspective. For this reason, I can't say that I have a lot of patience for colleagues who still presume that it's possible to compare Chaplin and Buster Keaton in any normal fashion, either as slapstick performers or as directors. As Gilbert Adair once pointed out years ago, Chaplin doesn't simply belong to the history of cinema; he belongs to history. And for me the main problem with trying to compare him to Keaton is that such an act implicitly denies that history, which the Chaplin Collection is dedicated to explicating as clearly as possible.

Even less useful than the Chaplin versus Keaton debate is the kind of contemporary dismissal of Chaplin that writes him off as a sentimentalist, a relic of the nineteenth century, an insufferable egotist, or a technical or intellectual primitive. Not because one can't go back to certain facets of his life and work and find some evidence to support any or all of these charges, but because doing so ultimately entails a reductive reading that excludes too many other things that matter at least as much. I'm far more sympathetic to the hyperbole of Jean-Marie Straub's provocative defense of Chaplin as the greatest of all film editors — made most recently and most cogently in Pedro Costa's beautiful 2001 documentary *Où gît votre sourire enfoui?*, which documents the activity and conversation of Straub and Danièle Huillet while editing one of the versions of their *Sicilia!* Straub's justification for this extravagant claim is ingenious: because Chaplin knew precisely when a gesture begins and when it ends, he knew precisely when to cut. As an observation this is far more indicative of a close and prolonged engagement with the work than any of the curt and cavalier dismissals. And maybe because Straub is himself a lot more (radically) traditional and conservative than he's generally cracked up to be, part of what he's saying is that in spite of everything, Chaplin remains our contemporary — someone we can still learn from and converse with without condescension or apology.

Similarly, I would argue that those who reject *A King in New York* because they find Chaplin's ideas in it too obvious, simplistic, or bitter are likely to be overlooking the fact that he places many of his own most cherished leftist and anti-nationalist sentiments in the mouth of an obnoxiously self-righteous and hectoring brat (Michael Chaplin) who often won't let Chaplin's title king get in a word edgewise when he holds forth. This implies a dialectical as well as self-critical side to Chaplin — not to mention a certain intellectual depth — that few commentators are likely to concede about the man. As with Marilyn

Monroe — a charismatic figure whose parallels with Chaplin run deeper than one might initially suppose — an apparent compulsion to dismiss his intellect is so deeply ingrained and takes so many (unthinking) forms, including the premise that the lack of intelligence is self-evident, that one starts wondering about all the ideological determinations that hold this cherished premise in place. Even when faced with certain anomalies — such as Chaplin's admiration for *Ivan the Terrible* (which runs parallel to Monroe's interest in *The Brothers Karamazov*) — the usual impulse is to patronize the star with condescending "tolerance" for his or her pretensions and to try to rationalize this information out of existence.

The frequent charges waged against Chaplin's "old-fashioned" technique often seem predicated on an assumption of naïveté and/or vanity on his part. A typical anecdote that supposedly illustrates this: an assistant points out to Chaplin that some of the rails laid out for a tracking shot are visible in a camera setup, and he replies, "It doesn't matter. Whenever I'm onscreen, the public won't be looking at anything else."

I have no idea whether or not this story is apocryphal, but in the final analysis it doesn't matter. Whether or not Chaplin said such a thing, there are far too many instances in his oeuvre demonstrating the accuracy of such a remark to make either his innocence or his egotism the central point of the story. My favorite example, in fact, is probably the most famous sequence in any Chaplin film, and presumably therefore one of the most closely studied in all of cinema: the closing moments of *City Lights*, when alternating close-ups of the Tramp and the flower girl, who has recently had her sight restored, record her dawning realization that he is her benefactor, the one who paid for her operation — as well as his own dual realization that she can now see and that she knows who he is. "She recognizes who he must be by his shy, confident, shining joy as he comes silently toward her," James Agee memorably wrote in "Comedy's Greatest Era." "And he recognizes himself, for the first time, through the terrible changes in her face. The camera just exchanges a few quiet close-ups of the emotions which shift and intensify in each face. It is enough to shrivel the heart to see, and it is the greatest piece of acting and the highest moment in movies."

I wouldn't dream of disputing any of this. But how many viewers have noticed that the alternating close-ups described by Agee are flagrantly mismatched? Viewed from behind, the Tramp grasps one of the flower girl's flowers against his leg; viewed from the front, he holds the same flower in the same hand against his mouth and cheek, and this discontinuity of angle/reverse-angle even gets repeated along with the same camera setups. If we stop to wonder why almost no one seems to notice this error, I would dispute that any lapse in Chaplin's perfectionism is to blame. Indeed, it's questionable whether it even qualifies as a lapse when the emotion and ambiguity of these shots are all that finally register and matter. It's a sequence, in short, that should be shown and described to every film student who has ever believed that eyeline matches count for very much outside of routine filmmaking.

To take another approach, consider just the realm of raw experience imparted by Chaplin's films. Has there ever been another artist — not just in the history of cinema, but maybe in the history of art — who has had more to say, and in such vivid detail, about what it means to be poor? Conceivably Dickens, another artist often reproached for sentimentality, might be a contender in these sweepstakes, but surely no other figure in the twentieth century. And because there is arguably no other figure in the world during Chaplin's heyday who was more widely known and loved — not even a politician like his archenemy Hitler, much less another artist — discussing him as if he were just another writer-director or actor ultimately means shortchanging that world and that history.

The only other figure in the arts who strikes me as being even remotely comparable to Chaplin — with lots of emphasis on "remotely" — is Louis Armstrong, and only in a few characteristics: coming from the absolute bottom of society and assuming a kind of ethical elegance and nobility as well as a kind of charisma and joy informed by both wit and low comedy that were peculiarly his own; redefining the parameters of an art that was new and largely associated with America while becoming a seasoned and universally recognized world traveler and a kind of statesman.

■ ■ ■ ■ ■ ■ ■ ■ ■

If all this sounds like idolatry, it could be argued that I have plenty of company. It's hard to think of a populist mainstream figure who was more beloved by avant-garde artists on both sides of the Atlantic during the teens, '20s, and '30s. So is it any wonder that Chaplin has suffered from an almost continuous critical backlash in the seventy-odd years since then? Part of this undoubtedly comes from the ideological disturbance of attending to such a massively popular figure who was effectively forced into exile from the U.S. after the public started to turn sour on him. To understand how this radical change of heart came about entails part of the substantial history lesson offered by The Chaplin Collection, along with a prolonged and detailed look at the changes that took place in his filmmaking and in both the evolving identity of the Tramp and the subsequent parts played by Chaplin. (A comparable history lesson might undertake to explain how the persistence of Jerry Lewis as a love object in this country throughout the '50s could eventually mutate into a denial as well as an implied horror that such an infatuation could ever have existed.)

In Felice Zenoni's mainly unexceptional recent Swiss TV documentary about Chaplin in Switzerland, *Charlie Chaplin: The Forgotten Years* (2003), there's an unforgettably humanizing nugget recounted by Chaplin's daughter Geraldine about his response to discovering that his invitation to accept an honorary Oscar in the U.S. in 1972 came with a visa that only allowed him to remain in the country for a couple of weeks. Though one would expect him to have been indignant, we discover that he was in fact delighted to learn he was still regarded as being so frightening and challenging a figure to American authorities, twenty years after leaving the country. And if that sounds spiteful, it's no more so than the Tramp himself often is when faced with various enemies.

To understand the changes in Chaplin's filmmaking in any depth, we're still pretty far from having the sort of critical perspective that's needed. If we turn to the Chaplin biographies — either those in print or those on film and video (including the disappointing feature-length documentary by Schickel) — we often get continuations of the same ideological roadblocks, many of which consist of rationalizing or otherwise ratifying the critical and commercial rejections of *Monsieur Verdoux* and *A King in New York* and all that these imply.

I assume it's partly this kind of continuing backlash that held back the U.S. release of eight of the dozen features in the Warner/MK2 Chaplin box set for about half a year after they came out in Europe. The first four were *The Gold Rush*, *Modern Times*, *The Great Dictator*, and *Limelight*, and it's not surprising that the more controversial and less commercial Chaplin titles — *Verdoux*, *King*, *A Woman of Paris* — were saved for the second batch.

The packaging of the PAL and NTSC versions are different in other respects. European customers also received illustrated booklets in all dozen packages and in some cases more informative details on the boxes themselves. Furthermore, they received *A Woman of Paris* and *A King in New York* separately, while these two features are indecorously shoehorned together in the American set, presumably for no better reason than the fact that they're both regarded as awkward encumbrances, like two unwanted children. (The first is silent and doesn't star Chaplin, the second unabashedly anti-American; and both were box-office flops.)

The Masters of Cinema web site [no longer operative in the same form in 2009] maintains that "the R2 UK set from Warner/MK2 and the French MK2 set are a magnificent achievement" but that "unfortunately, the USA R1 set is a lazy PAL [to] NTSC transfer with ghosting — *extremely* disappointing." The PAL version placed third in their 2003 poll for the "DVD of the year" — after two very impressive Criterion releases, *By Brakhage: An Anthology* and Yasu-jiro Ozu's *Tokyo Story*, in the first two slots — and the ideological as well as technical differences are underlined:

> Back in 2001, the Chaplin estate wisely sought the skills of MK2 in France (after seeing their superb Truffaut boxset) and asked them to conjure up a Chaplin set. Two years later, we have this dreamlike set, with *perfect* extras. If this set had been put together in the USA we'd have extras consisting of Leonard Maltin chatting with Robin Williams, Billy Crystal and Adam Sandler. Okay, maybe Sandler would've been interesting, but what we get from MK2 raises the bar as high as it can go — Abbas Kiarostami, the Dardenne Bros, Liv Ullmann, Claude Chabrol, Jim Jarmusch, Emir Kusturica, and Bernardo Bertolucci contribute, separately, to the documentary for the film with which they have a personal affinity. It's refreshing to encounter a huge release like this with a distinctly European flavor, one that hasn't been dumbed down to the lowest common denominator to maximize dollarage. Hats off to the Chaplin estate and MK2 for doing Charlie very proud. Hats firmly left in place for Warners USA.

With all due respect to this conscientious web site, which I generally agree with and find indispensable, a couple of demurrals are in order. Having had an opportunity to compare the French PAL version of *The Kid* with the American NTSC version back to back on my multiregional DVD player and tristandard monitor, the differences in sound and image are undetectable, at least by my eyes and ears. (Nevertheless, there are plenty of other reasons for preferring the French PAL versions, including the fact that the interviews with directors that aren't in English can be seen there with English subtitles, whereas the same interviews on NTSC are saddled with English voiceovers that don't allow us to hear all of the original voices.) And while I heartily agree on principle with most of the filmmakers selected to comment on Chaplin, candor compels me to note that for all his brilliance as a filmmaker, Kiarostami seldom has anything of interest to say about his colleagues, and has very little to offer on this occasion, either about Chaplin in general or *The Kid* in particular. (Significantly, when he recently decided to subtitle his *Five* — a collection of five short and rather beautiful digital videos concentrating on relatively uneventful patches of the natural world found on a beach — *Five Takes Dedicated to Yasujiro Ozu*, this was a clever way of alerting his audience to what they should and shouldn't expect, even though the actual resemblance of these videos to anything by Ozu is highly questionable.)

On the other hand, the various comments offered by the Dardenne brothers about *Modern Times* comprise the most insightful criticism about the film

I've encountered anywhere. Starting with the observation that the famous early shot of the Tramp moving literally like a cog through the factory machinery is an image that recalls a film running through a projector, they proceed to speculate why, in relation to an entire commercial cinema predicated on success stories, the Chaplin Tramp essentially remains a tramp — even though this time he's identified in the credits as a factory worker. They also discuss the importance of hunger in his work ("Food is everything in his films"), the degree to which the film serves as a documentary on the period, and how the women in the film "aren't very nice" until we get to Paulette Goddard.

With a similar commonsensical bent, Jarmusch on *A King in New York* speaks about how the title city becomes "representational" of "America as an empire," money, and thievery, with a great deal of prescience about what America would become over the next several decades (and an apt observation that the film's depiction of "rock and roll" is in fact a phony commercialized version of that music — not simply a misperception of it, as some commentators would have it), how Dawn Addams' eerie eye contact with the camera while taking a bath anticipates her activity as a TV huckster, how the film's overall technique is wholly subsumed to the storytelling, and how the film's tragic ending completely avoids sentimentality. More generally, what makes Jarmusch a good commentator on the film isn't just his own status as a political maverick but his special feeling for Chaplin's independence: "He's maybe the first truly independent master of cinema, because he has control over everything in his films." In a way, this is a variation on Roberto Rossellini's celebrated defense of *A King in New York* — "It's the film of a free man" — and it highlights the degree to which Chaplin's absolute independence had aesthetic as well as ideological consequences. (Indeed, part of what continues to make the film indispensable historically is the degree to which it deals with all the major issues missing from the Hollywood features of the same period — including Tashlin's *Will Success Spoil Rock Hunter?*, its only true satiric competitor.)

In other parts of the Truffault documentary on *Modern Times*, we see newsreel footage of Chaplin meeting Gandhi in London, detailed production information on *Modern Times*, an exploration of the issues involving Chaplin's development of the Tramp in this film, a more general discussion of Chaplin's evolving relationship to sound — including a newsreel clip of him briefly recording his voice on film for the first time during a 1931 visit to Vienna, a clip of the jabbering speeches we hear in the opening scene of dialogue in *City Lights*, the original plans for spoken dialogue in *Modern Times*, and a fascinating montage of three of its slapstick sequences, including the famous dance on roller skates, shown successively at eighteen and then twenty-four frames per second. One fascinating piece of information that we don't get here — but which is imparted in the Schickel documentary — is the fact that the famous malfunctioning feeding machine was secretly operated manually by Chaplin himself under the table it was on. (Similarly, there's a fascinating piece of information imparted by the 1975 *Oxford Companion to Film* that's lamentably missing from *The Tramp and the Dictator*: that *The Great Dictator* was originally banned in Chicago, reportedly to avoid offending the sizable German population there.)

De Missolz's "Chaplin Today" episode on *A King in New York* begins with the detail in the film that feels most contemporary today — the fingerprinting of King Shahdov upon his arrival in the U.S. — and proceeds from there to such matters as newsreel footage about Ethel and Julius Rosenberg, Chaplin's move to Switzerland in 1952, United Artists' refusal to distribute Chaplin's film (and the fact that the film was shortened by ten minutes when it finally opened in the U.S. fifteen years later — although we aren't told what was removed), and the film's rapid shoot (only ten weeks) in London and its editing in Paris. But perhaps the most touching sections concern Michael Chaplin — starting with an anecdote about the consternation he caused at the age of seven in his father's office in Switzerland when he entered one day in a homesick mood singing "God Bless America." Elsewhere we see him watching his own spouting of political oratory in the film and then speaking about the whole experience in French, implying that the experience of acting was the time when he was able to be closest to his workaholic father. A particularly poignant "bonus" in this already poignant interview is the background music used — Chaplin singing his heretofore unheard lyrics to a song he wrote that is used in the film as Michael's theme.

The highlights in Eisenschitz's *Verdoux* documentary include Chabrol's celebration of the audacity of the film's unapologetic atheism and of the fact that all the women Verdoux kills "are ugly and unbearable," thereby putting the audience as much as possible on Verdoux's side, and his stressing of the fact that all of Chaplin's work is about survival. Chabrol also offers a fascinating extended commentary on a shot showing professional tango dancers in a restaurant, the sort of detail that few other critics would even notice. We also get material about Chaplin's public defense of Hanns Eisler (with a fascinating clip of Eisler's angry HUAC testimony, and an account of Chaplin's unsuccessful effort to gain Picasso's support against Eisler's threatened deportation), details involving Hays office objections to the script, a generous sampling of production storyboards as well as some rushes, interesting analyses of the characters played by Martha Raye (as an American shrew transferred to a French context) and Marilyn Nash (as a figure who alters Verdoux's destiny), and some interesting remarks about the film's final shot (including the fact that

Chaplin shot it before anything else in the film), by Chabrol as well as by André Bazin.

To show his own contempt for Chaplin's FBI file, Cozarinsky on the *Limelight* DVD has his offscreen narrator quote copiously from it before we see a pair of hands (actually Cozarinsky's) tear the document into shreds and toss it into a river. The high point of Bernardo Bertolucci's commentary about the film is his observation that when the young dancer (Claire Bloom) declares her undying love for Calvero, "She is lying, and deep inside she knows she is. He [Calvero] knows Terry is lying, and we know he knows. It's all sort of staged." (This shows the limitation of Pauline Kael's 1953 hatchet job — her first published film review, recently reprinted in *Artforum* — which assumes a complete absence of ambiguity or irony about this matter.) By contrast, I would call the low point of Bertolucci's commentary his labored effort to persuade us that when Calvero dies, the sheet draped over his body is supposed to make us think of a movie screen. Far more interesting on this DVD is a troubling scene with Calvero conversing with a former colleague with one arm that Chaplin decided to cut from the film.

Among the other treasures to be found in this set, I would cite in particular, apropos of *The Gold Rush* — and apart from the fact that we get both the 1925 original and the 1942 retooling with Chaplin's offscreen narration — Ouedraogo's hypothesis that the Tramp's crazed image of a gigantic chicken is so large because it "becomes proportionate" to the size of his hunger (which leads logically to both a quote from art historian Élie Faure and an earlier hunger gag from *A Dog's Life*); images of children in Ouedraogo's village watching Chaplin for the first time in a video of *The Gold Rush*; a clip of Fatty Arbuckle in the 1917 *The Rough House,* which shows us the source of the dance with the rolls; and portions of an audio interview with Mary Pickford about the source of Chaplin's interest in the Klondike.

And apropos of *A Woman of Paris*, I would cite in particular the sensitivity of Ullmann's observations, eleven minutes of outtakes, ten minutes of footage documenting Paris in the '20s, and an extraordinary film document of 1926: a thirty-three-minute version of *Camille* by Ralph Barton in which the cast of celebrity cameos includes not only Chaplin, but also, to cite less than a third of the remaining lineup, Sherwood Anderson, Ethel Barrymore, Richard Barthelmess, Paul Claudel, Clarence Darrow, Theodore Dreiser, John Emerson, Dorothy Gish, Sacha Guitry, Rex Ingram, Sinclair Lewis, Anita Loos, H. L. Mencken, George Jean Nathan, Max Reinhardt, and Paul Robeson.

To keep track of all these appearances, a program listing who plays whom is obviously essential. This information is part of the booklet included in the French PAL version but not something that anyone has bothered to make available on the American NTSC version. If there's any lesson to be gleaned from this, this is surely that the same team of French people who lavished so much care on this box set obviously cared more about making it user-friendly than the American team devoted to distributing it. And this difference in concern for historical value suggests another key lesson, for both the present and the foreseeable future: that one of the crucial qualifications of an educated and cosmopolitan DVD watcher is owning a multiregional player.

Cineaste 29, no. 4 (September 2004)

Second Thoughts on Stroheim

Preface

Total object, complete with missing parts, instead of partial object. Question of degree.
—Samuel Beckett, "Three Dialogues"

Two temptations present themselves to any modern reappraisal of Erich von Stroheim's work; one of them is fatal, the other all but impossible to act upon. The fatal temptation would be to concentrate on the offscreen image and legend of Stroheim to the point of ignoring central facts about the films themselves — an approach that has unhappily characterized most critical work on Stroheim to date. On the other hand, one is tempted to look at nothing but the films — to suppress biography, anecdotes, newspaper reviews, reminiscences, and everything else that isn't plainly visible on the screen.

Submitting Stroheim's work to a purely formal analysis and strict textural reading of what is there — as opposed to what isn't, or might, or would or could or should have been there — may sound like an obvious and sensible project; but apparently no one has ever tried it, and there is some reason to doubt whether anyone ever will. Over the past fifty-odd years, the legend of Stroheim has cast so distinctive a shadow over the commercial cinema in general and his own work in particular that the removal of that shadow would amount to nothing less than a total skin graft; above all, it would mean eliminating the grid through which his films were seen in their own time — a time that, in many crucial respects, remains our own.

From one point of view, Stroheim's films only dramatize problems of directorial control and intention that are relevant to most Hollywood films. They dramatize these problems, however, in a particularly revealing way: we re-member his best works (*Foolish Wives*, *Greed*, *The Wedding March*, *Queen Kelly*) not merely because of their power — which is considerable — but also because of their will to power, which is always even more considerable. We are constantly brought up against the problem of considering his films as in-dications and abbreviations of projected meta-films that were either reduced and reedited by the studios or, in the case of *Queen Kelly*, never completed in any form.

It is central to Stroheim's reputation that he is valued today more for the unseen forty-two-reel version of *Greed* than the ten-reel version that we do have. And if history and legend have conspired to install Stroheim as an ex-emplary figure in cinema — virtually the patron saint of all directors who have suffered at the hands of producers — it is precisely because of this discrepancy, the gap between the power and control that was sought and the amount that was visibly achieved.

How are we made aware of this discrepancy? Certainly we sense it almost as much in Stroheim's acting in the films of others as in his own projects — not simply because of all the dictatorial parts, from Prussian officers to assorted lunatics, but in the very style of his delivery, the very manner of his presence. Consider the sublime and all-but-hallucinatory tedium of his first role in a sound film, James Cruze's *The Great Gabbo*, when he seems to speak each line at roughly half the speed of everyone else in the cast; here one can witness the will to power in a strictly temporal arena — the apparent desire to remain on the screen as long as possible — lending to the part of the mad ventriloquist an intolerable tension and demonic mulishness that go well beyond the melo-dramatic demands of the plot, as though he were pulling at his character like taffy to see how far it could stretch before breaking. Insofar as a single perfor-mance can be compared to an entire film, it is likely that the duration of the original version of *Greed* was motivated along similar lines.

The opening credits of *Greed*, *The Merry Widow*, and *The Wedding March* alert us to Stroheim's aspirations before anything else appears on the screen: the first two are said to be "personally directed by Erich von Stroheim," the third is labeled "in its entirety an Erich von Stroheim creation." But if accept-ing Stroheim's legend means submitting to a fiction — a supplement, in many cases, to the fictions that he filmed — denying it is tantamount to imposing another, alternate fiction. (However much we may ever learn about Stroheim, it's highly unlikely that we'll know enough to do away with fictions entirely.) Bearing this in mind, an attempt will be made here to isolate his legend when-ever possible, but not to dismantle it.

1

It is bad for man to believe he is more almighty than mountains.
—Sepp (Gibson Gowland) in *Blind Husbands*

Some favorite devices, recurring frequently throughout Stroheim's work: a long shot dissolving into a medium shot of the same character, a camera movement that turns a medium shot into a close-up, and an upward or downward pan taking in the whole body of a character. Each represents a different way of taking a closer look at someone—the first usually introduces characters, the second permits an increasing concentration of dramatic focus and detail (like the extraordinary track up to the face of Dale Fuller, the exploited maid in *Foolish Wives*, where we're enabled to see revenge being hatched in her eyes), and the third is more in the nature of an inventory.

Eyes have an unusual authority in Stroheim's films, and what is frequently meant by his "control of detail" is his uncanny gift for conveying information through an actor's eye movements. How someone looks and sees is always a central character trait, and the story of each film is partially told in glances.

A memorable example occurs as one of the privileged camera movements in *The Wedding March*, when Mitzi (Fay Wray), standing in a crowd, looks up at Prince Niki (Stroheim) sitting on a horse, and an upward pan gives us her exalted estimation of him. We can trace this shot all the way back to *Blind Husbands*, Stroheim's first film (1918), when Erich von Steuban (Stroheim) first encounters "Silent Sepp," the local Tyrolean mountain guide. Each sizes up the other in a separate pan: Steuban looks at Sepp, a slow pan from feet to head; Sepp looks at Steuban, a slow pan from head to feet. The central metaphysical conceit of the plot is hung on these two camera movements. Significantly, they are repeated in different but related contexts near the end: a slow pan all the way up the mountain on which the climactic struggle will take place, introduced as "The Pinnacle" (Stroheim's own original title for *Blind Husbands*) and which Dr. Armstrong (Sam de Grasse) and Steuban are about to ascend; and in the midst of this struggle, while Armstrong stands over Steuban, clenching him by the throat—a slow pan from Steuban down the mountain to the rescue party of soldiers and others, including Sepp, making their way up.

From top to bottom, from bottom to top: thematically and dramatically, all of Stroheim's films refer to this basic pattern. *Blind Husbands* provides at best only a rough sketch of what is to follow, but the essential lines are already there. Sepp is the pinnacle, the higher aspiration, and also something of a dumb-ox innocent, earthy and inert, who prevents Steuban from seducing

Mrs. Armstrong (Francelina Billington) by appearing in the hotel corridor at just the right moment. (A cryptic monk appearing out of a rain storm in *Foolish Wives* functions identically.) Steuban is the depths, the lower aspiration, the grim, deadly, and well-dressed seducer, full of bluff and pretension. In between stand the Armstrongs, an American couple, naïve without being simple or wise (like Sepp), adventurous without being irresponsible or pretentious (like Steuban) — two freefloating characters who are, by extension, ourselves: likable zeros susceptible to the influences of a Sepp or a Steuban.

These and several other characters in *Blind Husbands* represent archetypes traceable back to the nineteenth-century novel. The credits indirectly acknowledge this heritage by claiming that the film is derived "from the book *The Pinnacle* by Erich von Stroheim," an apparently imaginary work that no visible research has ever uncovered — much like the book *Foolish Wives* that the heroine of that film is shown reading. If the "realist" tag assigned to Stroheim often seems today like an outdated literary category — and one that might make Stroheim seem more outdated than he actually is — this is equally the case with his first literary models, Zola and Norris. The fictional worlds of all three are so charged with metaphysical forces and intimations of fatality that the "realism" they project is not one in which free will predominates; characters are usually doomed to be what they are by class and social position, heredity, mysterious turns of fate, or some malign combination of all three.

Steuban and the Armstrong couple can easily be seen as first drafts of Karamzin and the Hughes couple in *Foolish Wives* — an elaborated remake in many respects. (*The Devil's Passkey*, made during the interval between the two, is a lost film today, but existing synopses indicate it to be another version of the same plot, which remained with Stroheim for years: Stroheim completed a new script based on *Blind Husbands* in 1930, which he planned to film in sound and color.) But the distance traversed between Stroheim's first and third film is cosmic, even though only three years separate them. Vaguely sketched essences of character and locale became "three-dimensional" embodiments — not merely ideas expressed, but ideas incarnated — and we leap from an apprentice work to something closely approximating a mature style.

2

They are showing only the skeleton of my dead child.
— Stroheim after the release of *Foolish Wives*

Comparing the Italian and American prints of *Foolish Wives* in *Cahiers du cinéma* no.79, Jacques Rivette observed that they differ not only by length, order of sequences, and editing within scenes, but also by the fact that they don't always have identical takes of the same shots. He offers the very plausible hypothesis that the longer Italian version corresponds much more closely to Stroheim's, while the American print is the version recut by Universal after the film's New York premiere. It seems quite possible — I haven't seen the American print in a few years — that the remarkable close-up of Dale Fuller's storytelling eyes and the fire/firetruck montage, as described here, exist only in the Italian version.

A particularly troubling problem with both versions is the absence of what must be considered the film's climactic sequences: the rape of Ventucci's half-witted daughter (Malvine Polo) by Karamzin — or "Karamazin," according to Thomas Quinn Curtiss — resulting in the murder of Karamzin by Ventucci (Cesare Gravina); and after Ventucci's depositing of Karamzin's body in a sewer (visible in both versions), the corpse shown at dawn in the midst of garbage floating out to sea; and Mrs. Hughes giving premature birth to a child, which brings about a reconciliation with her husband. (These scenes are all indicated in Stroheim's synopsis.)

Lacking these scenes, our understanding of Karamzin's function in the film remains incomplete. Unless we can see the contrast between his magisterial first appearance by the Mediterranean and his exit as "rubbish" in the same setting, the trajectory of his scurrilous career is not fully articulated. And without the birth of the Hughes's child — apparently suggesting a quasi-mystical resurgence of life out of the ashes of corruption — his death fails to achieve the proper resonance. But despite these and other regrettable lacunae, Karamzin remains Stroheim's most complex and fascinating character outside of *Greed*, and provides the occasion for his definitive performance.

The differences between Karamzin and Erich von Steuban are so closely related to the differences between Stroheim's authority as a director in each film that it is difficult not to see both characters as partial autobiographical counterparts. Karamzin displays all the low traits of Steuban, from vanity to cowardice, but two crucial characteristics are added: he is an impostor; and he is mainly out for money. Moreover, he is something of a professional con man while Steuban is at best a promising novice in the arts of deception, too often a fumbler to convince us that he is truly malignant. Both characters are identified with an "artistic" sensibility: one of Steuban's ploys with Mrs. Armstrong is to play soulfully on the violin along with her piano, while *Foolish Wives* invites us to relish Karamzin's more subtle methods of enticement, delight in his grander fabrications.

A classic instance of Stroheim as trickster: the episode of the armless veteran. Already, in contrast to *Blind Husbands*, he is firmly establishing a very specific milieu and period in which to locate his story — Monte Carlo just after the war, where veterans on crutches and kids playing soldiers (some of whom seem to mock and "see through" Karamzin's postures) form an essential part of the background. Because we don't realize that the stolid man who, early in the film, neglects to pick up Mrs. Hughes's gloves is armless, we assume that he's around merely to indicate the kind of courtesy that she's accustomed to receiving, and to provide Karamzin with an opportunity to display his own gallantry. The second time the man appears, exhibiting similar behavior in an elevator, we might imagine him to represent some sort of running gag. Then, when we discover he is armless, we are brought up short, and moved to pity: a strong ironic point has been scored. But Stroheim refuses to stop there. As Mrs. Hughes proceeds to fondle and caress one of the veteran's armless sleeves, pity quickly turns into disquieting morbidity, and what we've previously been led to ignore we're now obliged to dwell upon. In a brief instant that illuminates the rest of the film, comedy turns into tragedy and the tragedy becomes a fetish. It is a remarkable transformation of tone, created throughout by a series of false narrative expectations. . . . If *Blind Husbands* squats somewhere uncomfortably between a "symbolic" play and a cheap novella, *Foolish Wives* all but invents the novelistic cinema.

How does *Foolish Wives* resemble a nineteenth-century novel? By turning the spectacle of Griffith into an analysis of social and psychological textures — Monte Carlo was his *Intolerance* set — Stroheim asks us to move around in his frames and episodes in a way that grants us some of the freedom and leisure of a reader's experience. Griffith's suspense montage has enough Kuleshovian (and Pavlovian) effects to deny the spectator the opportunity to use much of his intelligence. This creates momentum, to be sure, but Stroheim usually sweeps the spectator along with a different kind of persuasion. Griffith either lulls or harasses you into the role of just plain folks; Stroheim starts with the assumption that you're witty, discerning, and twice as sophisticated as the fellow sitting next to you. Karamzin may be a sneak fooling that American ambassador and his wife with his phony credentials, but he doesn't fool us.

We hate him because he is evil; we love him because we know him: that's probably why we love to hate him. Stroheim loves to hate him too; it is something he is sharing with us as much as showing us. It is a very strange process: what the actor creates, the filmmaker annihilates, and the portrait is as merciless as the character. He is confidential about what he shows us, like a novelist; he tells us the kind of things that are going on behind closed doors, when certain people are out of earshot. He wins our confidence by telling us secrets.

I had graduated from the D. W. Griffith school of filmmaking and intended to go the Master one better as regards film realism. In real cities, not corners of them designed by Cedric Gibbons or Richard Days, but in real tree-bordered boulevards, with real streetcars, buses and automobiles, through real winding alleys, with real dirt and foulness, in the gutters as well as in real castles and palaces. . . . I believed audiences were ready to witness real drama and real tragedy; as it happens every day in every land; real love and real hatred of real men and women who were proud of their passions.

—Stroheim, date unknown

It is witty for Godard to suggest that Méliès made documentaries, and rewarding to look at Feuillade's films under that aspect; but Stroheim turned the fiction film into the documentary in a much more central and decisive way. He did this above all in *Greed*, and not so much through "stripping away artifice" as by reformulating the nature that his artifice was to take.

This was not simply a matter of shooting *Greed* on locations. More crucially, it was a direct confrontation with the challenge of adapting a literary work. *McTeague* is a work of fiction that impressed Stroheim and his contemporaries for its "realism"; by attempting to arrive at an equivalent to this literary mode, Stroheim wound up having to deal exhaustively with all of the essential problems inherent in adapting any fictional prose work. There was certainly no filmmaker prior to Stroheim who attacked these problems in quite so comprehensive a manner, and it is arguable whether there has been anyone else since. For this reason alone, *Greed* remains a laboratory experiment of the first importance — valuable for its failures as well as its successes, and comprising a virtual textbook on some of the formal issues that it raises.

When Stroheim filmed *Greed*, Kenneth Rexroth tells us in the Signet edition of Norris's novel, "he is said to have followed *McTeague* page by page, never missing a paragraph. We'll never know because the uncut *Greed*, greatest of all movies, is lost forever." To understand the important aspects of Stroheim's adaptation, the first step is to dismiss hyperbole of this sort and work with the materials available: the novel, Stroheim's screenplay,[1] the version of *Greed* that we do have, and the existing stills of scenes that were cut from the film.

The first thing that the published script tells us is that an enormous amount of material has been added to the novel, particularly in the opening scenes. About sixty pages — nearly one-fifth of the screenplay — pass before we reach McTeague eating his Sunday dinner at the car conductors' coffee joint, the subject of Norris's first sentence. Mac's life prior to his arrival in San Francisco is conveyed by Norris in a brief resume of two paragraphs; in the script it consumes twenty-five pages. A brilliantly designed sequence that runs even longer, and is completely missing from the final version of the film, introduces us to all of the major characters on a "typical" Saturday afternoon that precedes the novel's opening.

Interestingly, this sequence is largely constructed around cross-cutting between characters whose interrelations in the plot have not yet become clarified and, in the case of Mac and Trina, between characters who have not yet even met—so that the juxtapositions are unusually abstract, even from a thematic point of view. As an approach to narrative that was already common to prose fiction but far from being a convention in cinema, this is probably the most "advanced" and experimental departure in the script: nearly everything that takes place is descriptive and inconsequential as plot, and each character is linked into an overall pattern of significance that nothing in the story has yet justified. Harry Carr, one of the only people who saw *Greed* in its complete form, may have had this sequence partially in mind when he compared the film to *Les Miserables* and remarked that "Episodes come along that you think have no bearing on the story, then twelve or fourteen reels later, it hits you with a crash" (*Motion Picture Magazine*, April 1924).

Undoubtedly the most problematical element in Stroheim's adaptation is its use of repeated symbolic motifs—shots of gold, greedy hands, animals and other emblems—which seem to be a direct misapplication of literary principles to cinematic structures. The recurrent image in *McTeague* of Mac's canary "chittering in its little gilt prison"—a phrase repeated with slight variations in many contexts, before it appears as the final words in the novel—works symbolically and "musically" because it is laced smoothly into the thread of the narrative, with no breaks in discourse or syntax. But in *Greed*, the repeated images have the disadvantage of interrupting the narrative, usually without adding any useful perspectives to it: they are like footnotes that mainly say "Ibid." In their limited use in the film that we have and their implied use in the script, they tend to seem like dead wood clinging to the rest of the film.

The script further leads us to suspect that many of the motifs are repeated without variation—like the mother rocking the cradle in *Intolerance*—and occasionally without any naturalistic explanation, like the shot of wood being sawed, which recurs no less than eight times during the wedding sequence. Such a shot is a purely abstract intrusion, but not one that serves to expand the narrative; like Tolstoy's historical arguments in *War and Peace*, it seeks to contract the total picture into a graspable, didactic design. And it fails, one can argue, for roughly the same reason that Tolstoy fails — because Stroheim has more to show than he has to say. The world he creates in the wedding sequence alone overwhelms anything he has to say about it: it is too rich to accommodate supplementary lessons.

Which brings us back to the "realism," the documentary aspect of *Greed*. Clearly one of its most extraordinary aspects remains the unusual conviction of the performances, which is apparent even in the random instants offered by stills. Look at any frame enlargement from *Greed* showing ZaSu Pitts, Gibson Gowland, or Jean Hersholt and you'll see not a familiar actor "playing a part," but a fully rounded character existing — existing, as it were, between shots and sequences as well as within them (or such is the illusion). How many films in the history of acted cinema would pass this elementary litmus test? Certainly not *Citizen Kane*; perhaps *The Magnificent Ambersons*, a film whose achievement (and mutilation) parallels that of *Greed* in many important respects.[2]

One recalls André Bazin's famous remark about Stroheim: "In his films reality lays itself bare like a suspect confessing under the relentless examination of the commissioner of police. He has one simple rule for direction. Take a close look at the world, keep on doing so, and in the end it will lay bare for you all its cruelty and its ugliness. One could easily imagine as a matter of fact a film by Stroheim composed of a single shot as long-lasting and as closeup as you like."

This is the spirit of documentary — a tendency that is equally present in Stroheim's introduction of outside chance elements into his fictions. It's not so much a matter of letting random accidents creep into the staged actions (as in Léonce Perret's 1913 melodrama *L'enfant de Paris*, when a friendly dog wanders into a shot at the heels of an actor) as a sort of semi-organized psychodrama, exemplified in a scene missing from current prints of *Greed*: When Trina discovers Maria Macapa with her throat slit, she runs out of Zerkow's junk house and hysterically reports the murder to the first people she sees. Stroheim shot this sequence with hidden cameras, and the responses came from passersby who were not aware that a film was being made. When Samuel Fuller used a similar technique at the beginning of *The Crimson Kimono* (1959) and Godard followed the hero of *Le petit soldat* (1960) down the streets of Geneva holding a gun, they were drawing on a common principle that Stroheim had already made extensive use of thirty-five years before.

4

O Love — without thee marriage is a savage mockery.
— opening title of *The Wedding March*

Greed stands at roughly the halfway point in Stroheim's fifteen-year career as a director, constituting both a caesura and a change of direction in his oeuvre. Four features precede *Greed* and four follow it, and beneath the continuity of certain undeniable stylistic and thematic traits, Stroheim's preoccupation with realism, his concern with narrative, and the nature of his ambition all undergo important transformations.

The first thing to be said about *The Merry Widow*, the film immediately following *Greed*, is that it represents a nearly total inversion of the former's approach: after filming his least compromised, most "realistic" work, he promptly made a film that was his most compromised and least "realistic." At its best, *The Merry Widow* has a lightness of touch and a grace of movement suggesting a presound musical, with an idealized fairy-tale landscape (clearly established in the opening shots) that necessitates a very different kind of discourse. The most striking offbeat elements in this Hollywood dream bubble, Prince Mirko (Roy D'Arcy) and Baron Sadoja (Tully Marshall), figure in the overall scheme in a way that is analogous to the "marginal notations" of irreverence that characterize most of Buñuel's films in the fifties: they offer ironic swipes at the conventional aspects of the material without ever seriously threatening the root assumptions of these conventions.

Prince Mirko is an obvious derivation of Erich von Steuban and Count Karamzin, but his role here is not as central: as a foil to the romantic figure of Prince Danilo (John Gilbert), he can not wield the same kind of lethal authority. Similarly, the more grotesque part of Baron Sadoja — a "first draft," as it were, of the even more monstrous Jan Vooyheid, incarnated by Tully Marshall in *Queen Kelly* — is allowed to function as a grim commentary on the action and an intrusion on the central love story, but at no point is he really permitted to dominate the film.

Regarding *The Merry Widow* as a transitional work, one can perhaps best understand Mirko and Sadoja not as "'realistic" intrusions — they are anything but that — but as rebellious counterfantasies provoked by the more conventional fantasies embodied by Danilo and Sally O'Hara (Mae Murray). If the earlier films were an attempt to subvert Hollywood from an outsider's position — eliminating the characteristically romantic leads and, in the case of *Greed*, literally moving out of the studios to locations — *The Merry Widow* announces the counterstrategy of boring from within. There is more than one prefiguration of this procedure in *The Merry Widow*. The most celebrated instance occurs in the theater, when Sadoja, Mirko, and Danilo each look at the dancing heroine through opera glasses: the first concentrates on her feet, the second on her body, the third on her face.

Another noticeable shift in Stroheim's style is a somewhat different use of durations in relation to narrative. In the silent films after *Greed*, despite Stroheim's continued interest in making long films, the novelistic aspect becomes less important, and the ritualistic, ceremonial aspects of duration gradually come to the fore—the obsessive desire to keep looking at something not in order to "understand" or "decode" it, but in order to become totally absorbed in it, transfixed by it; not to penetrate the surfaces of things, but to revel in these surfaces. As suggested earlier, the aggressivess of Stroheim's camera eye ultimately leads to a kind of passivity. In the films after *Greed*, this change becomes much more explicit. The belligerent eye of the skeptic gradually turns into the passive eye of the voyeur.

This generalization tends to oversimplify a great deal of Stroheim's work, and probably shouldn't be taken as literally as it is stated above; but it does help to account for the peculiarly dreamlike elongations of actions and scenes in *The Merry Widow*, *The Wedding March*, and *Queen Kelly*. A simple comparison might help to clarify the difference: when the camera slowly approaches Dale Fuller's face in *Foolish Wives* to reveal the revenge plans being formed in her eyes, the lingering effect has a purely narrative function, permitting us to watch a process more clearly than we could otherwise. But when the camera slowly tracks up to the face of Mae Murray in her wedding dress, and then recedes a bit to frame her entire figure as she proceeds to tear up the dress, we are being asked to concentrate on her primarily as an object; the "process" at work is chiefly the camera movement itself. We can intuit that the character's visible distress leads to her act of violence, but the steps leading from A to B are implied more than chronicled. They are the scene's justification, but not its major focus.

Nor is it just a question of the relative lack of virtuosity in Murray's performance. Gloria Swanson's performance in *Queen Kelly* is quite adept in its development and exposition of motives. But this is no longer the camera's primary subject: virtually all of the characters in Stroheim's last silent films exist as essences, fixed points of reference—"static essentials," to borrow Cesare Pavese's phrase. That Stroheim intended to show Kelly undergoing a complete transformation—from innocent to brothel madam to queen—must be acknowledged, but the evidence of this change was not recorded on film; it isn't until *Walking Down Broadway* that we find a visible (if partial) throwback to a "narrative performance" in the part of ZaSu Pitts as Millie.

The Merry Widow announces a more static view of action and character;

The Wedding March and *Queen Kelly*, both epics of slow motion, expand and sustain it. It is hardly accidental that religious and military ceremonies figure so importantly in these films — they, too, are "static essentials." The "realistic" impulse goes through no less pronounced a change: the European countries of *The Merry Widow* and *Queen Kelly* are fantasy kingdoms, and even the celebrated accuracy of detail in the Vienna of *The Wedding March* is subject to fanciful additions and idealizations. "I am through with black cats and sewers," Stroheim is reported to have said while making the film. "I am going to throw perfumed apple blossoms at the public until it chokes on them. If people won't look upon life as it is, we must give them a gilded version."

And a gilded version is what *The Wedding March* supplies. Even though the villain Schani (Matthew Betz), a pigsty, and a slaughterhouse are all clearly intended to offset the apple blossoms, these supposedly "realistic" elements are just as idealized as the romantic ones. Next to Stroheim's other villains, Schani is a crude cardboard cutout who is never allowed to expand beyond a few basic mannerisms (mainly spitting); and the other major characters — Prince Nicki (Stroheim), Mitzi (Fay Wray), and Cecelia (ZaSu Pitts) — are unusually simplistic creations for Stroheim.

One could be charitable (and many critics have been) by regarding the figures and themes of *The Wedding March* as mythic distillations of their counterparts in previous Stroheim films; or one can be less charitable and regard them as inert calcifications — rigid prototypes whose original *raison d'être* is lacking. *The Wedding March* is generally accorded a high place in the Stroheim canon, and it must be admitted that it has a magisterial, "definitive" quality that is missing from most of his other work. But speaking from a minority viewpoint, I might argue that a certain price has to be paid for this rather self-conscious classicism. Apart from rare scenes — like the remarkably subtle exchange of looks and gestures between Nicki and Mitzi during the Corpus Christi procession — the action, characters, and symbolic motifs (e.g., the Iron Man) are so schematically laid out that they assume a certain thinness; investigation is consistently bypassed for the sake of a polished presentation, and the eighth time that we see Schani spit could just as functionally be the second time or the ninth.

Seen purely on its own terms, *The Wedding March*[3] is undeniably an impressive work. Offering us spectacle more than drama, it is a stunning display of lavishness and an ironic commentary on a particular kind of royal decay lurking underneath. It is only when we place it alongside *Foolish Wives*, *Greed*, and *Queen Kelly* that we can understand its limitations. What these films (and even the others, to lesser degrees) possess that *The Wedding March* lacks is an acute sense of transgression. And it is precisely this sense that makes *Queen*

Kelly, for all its own limitations, a more pungent and exciting work. If *The Wedding March* converts many of the familiar Stroheim themes into a series of dry homilies and mottoes, all suitable for immediate framing, *Queen Kelly* converts many of these same themes into a species of delirium — a possessed work of hypnotic, almost hallucinatory intensity. In contrast to the icy elegance of *The Wedding March*, *Queen Kelly* breathes fire.

It is trashy, yes; but in the best sense, like Matthew G. Lewis's *The Monk* and Faulkner's *Sanctuary*. And at certain moments it achieves an elegance of its own, an elegance recalling that of a Nathanael West or a Georges Bataille, at least in stylistic control and continuity.

Which is not to praise *Queen Kelly* for its literary qualities: it has none, or at least no more than Stroheim's novels like *Paprika* do. On the contrary, *Greed* and location work aside, it is the most "cinematic" of his films, the one most alive to the medium's formal possibilities. The lighting is his most richly orchestrated, the camera moves about with an unprecedented freedom (assuming the hero's angle of vision, for instance, as it scans the doors in the convent for Kelly's room), and the use of duration has never been quite as operative as it becomes here. *Queen Kelly* is Stroheim uncensored — which is to say, more kinky, due to the effect and implications of the durations, than he ever intended it to be.

The unnatural protraction of the fireside seduction scene and (most particularly) the marriage of Kelly to Jan Vooyheid over the figurative and literal corpse of her aunt, would probably seem more sentimental and less carnal if they were trimmed down to conventional lengths. As they stand, they tend to create an emotional detachment in the spectator by making the actors and settings into purely aesthetic objects, delectable or abhorrent surfaces arranged in such a way that the possibilities of identifying with them or sentimentalizing them are decreased. Considering the increase in sentimentality in all of Stroheim's films after *Greed*, this is rather a throwback to the dryer, more "scientific" style of his earlier period, but here it is exercised on a fictional world that is substantially more metaphysical and dreamlike, and less concerned with sociological and psychological matters. *Queen Kelly* is probably the closest thing in the Stroheim canon to an abstract work, a self-enclosed film that secretes its own laws. The sense of transgression that we experience in the previous films is always grounded in morality; here it seems to come to life as a direct expression of the id — as when Queen Regina (Seena Owen) beats Kelly with a whip across an enormous hall, down a grand flight of steps, and out the door of the palace — and morality mainly seems to figure in the action like the memory of a bad dream.

Unconsummated lust, a sustaining leitmotif throughout Stroheim's work —

a stalemated struggle reflected in the pull between the nineteenth- and twentieth-century aspects of his art — is finally stretched out into a slow-motion reverie that is studied as if it were taking place under a microscope. Vooyheid is even literally seen as an insect, when he appears in the final marriage-and-death sequence comprising the recently discovered "African" footage: a scarred preying mantis on crutches, with a cigar in his teeth (or fist) and various objects sticking out of his pockets like additional legs, and a tongue that moves over his lips like a feeler.

He and Kelly stand on opposite sides of the aunt's deathbed; a wedding veil is fashioned out of a bed awning by some local prostitutes. Intercut with close-ups of Kelly in tears are shots of the black priest (who, like her, is dressed in white) from her viewpoint, blurring (to suggest tears) and then turning into an image of Prince Wolfram in white robes; another blur, and the Prince is in a black uniform; still another blur, and we return to the black priest in white. When her aunt expires, Kelly throws herself down on the body; the priest kneels; and then Vooyheid, who is kneeling, slowly raises himself on his crutches until he is the only figure standing.

As far as the silent cinema is concerned, this Manichaean spectacle constitutes Stroheim's last rites: an arbitrary ending, perhaps — it was certainly not the one he had in mind for *Queen Kelly* — but an appropriately emblematic conclusion nevertheless. With the death of the aunt, we arrive at the imminent loss of innocence and the ascension to power of pure evil — a lurid ellipsis and a suspension of possibilities that were already rather explicit in *Blind Husbands*. But the "message" is no longer "Watch out for him!" It has become, simply, "Look at him!" And were it not for the somewhat problematical footnote provided by *Hello, Sister!*, one might say that Stroheim's career as a director ends at roughly the same time that virtually all remaining pretense of free will vanishes from his imaginary kingdom.

Epilogue

Do you like funerals? I saw the cutest one last Saturday. . . . I'm just a fool about funerals!
—Millie (ZaSu Pitts) in *Hello, Sister!*

Even in its mutilated, garbled, and partially reshot form, *Hello, Sister!*, the release version of *Walking Down Broadway*, is recognizably Stroheim for a substantial part of its running time.[4] The "final shooting script" of *Walking Down Broadway* — dated August 9, 1932, assigning story and continuity to Stroheim, and dialogue to Stroheim, Leonard Spigelgass, and Geraldine Nomis —

helps us to understand some of the original intentions, but also suggests that even in its original state it would have been a minor Stroheim work. The absence of certain audacities and eccentricities in the release version — which include Mac (Terrance Ray) on a dance floor "[holding] up his middle finger at Jimmy," jokes about Prohibition, and various things relating to Millie (such as her pet turtle Lady Godiva and her dialogue with Miss Platt, a middle-aged hunchback) — are somewhat offset by various banalities that are also missing. The ending of the film that we have is a standard Hollywood clincher; but it is hardly much worse than the one prefigured in the script, in which "Peggy and Jimmy walk close to show window and look. Wax baby in Nurses' arms — as before — except window is dressed for Easter." Peggy says "(Motherly): Isn't it cute?" Jimmy says "(Fatherly): Sure is!" And "They draw close together and look at each other admiringly."

Much of the interest in *Hello, Sister!* today derives from the opportunity to see Stroheim recasting many of his most familiar procedures in the context of sound. The repetitious character trait that would have been expressed visually in *The Wedding March* — e.g., Schani spitting — is conveyed here in the dialogue: Mac uses the phrase "Catch on?" nearly two dozen times in the script, much as Veronica (Françoise Lebrun) continually makes use of "*un maximum*" in Jean Eustache's recent *The Mother and the Whore*. Elsewhere the dialogue often becomes less functional and tends to distract from the visuals. The Southern and New York accents of Peggy (Boots Mallory) and Jimmy (James Dunn) are important aspects of the characters, but their narrative function is not controlled in the way that the actors' visual presences are. When Jimmy provokes Millie's sexual jealousy in a scene near the end by refusing her help ("You're all right, Millie — but you wouldn't understand"), the extraordinary expressiveness of ZaSu Pitts's reaction — the way her eyes flare up at his casual dismissal — is as striking as the close-up of Dale Fuller already alluded to in *Foolish Wives*. (The relationship doesn't stop there: both characters suffer from sexual rejection, and take revenge by starting fires which provoke the grand finales of both films.) But Pitts's acting in this case becomes the subtext of the dialogue rather than vice versa, a classic instance of the way that sound films often teach spectators not to see; the mystery inherent in her character tends to be minimized by the "explicating" power of the dialogue, and what might have been twice as powerful in a silent context can easily escape attention here.

To some degree, the dialogue in *Hello, Sister!* only makes more explicit some of the schematic simplifications of character and situation that are constants in Stroheim's work, negating some of the openness and the demands on the spectator's imagination imposed by silence. In every silent Stroheim film but *Greed*, the sound of English or American voices invading the continental kingdoms would surely have worked as an alienating factor. *Hello, Sister!*, which relates back to *Greed* in many respects (Mac and Jimmy are derived from Mac and Marcus, and even a lottery figures comparably in the *Walking Down Broadway* script), is set in New York, and doesn't have to deal with this problem — indeed, the accents and inflections here are aids to verisimilitude — but at the same time, the screen is no longer quite the *tabula rasa* that it was, and the characteristic Stroheim Stare (the trained concentration of the camera on his fictional world) recedes somewhat under the verbiage, which frees us partially from the responsibility of looking.

The major stylistic developments in Stroheim's career took place between *Blind Husbands* and *Foolish Wives*. One can speak of additional developments up through *Greed*, but after that one can principally refer only to certain simplifications and refinements. This is surely characteristic of Hollywood cinema in general, where Howard Hawks can devote a lifetime to refining *Fig Leaves* and *A Girl in Every Port*, and even a director as "experimental" as Hitchcock is periodically forced to retreat to the formulas of earlier successes. In the case of a maverick like Stroheim, the miracle — apart from his remarkable early development — is not that he wasn't able to develop his style after *Greed*, but that he was able to make further films at all.

And in order to do so, he clearly had to pay a price. Whether or not future work in sound films would have led to other stylistic developments is impossible to determine; at best, all that *Hello, Sister!* suggests is the desire to accommodate his style to sound rather than to expand its basic options. Considering its relatively small budget, *Blind Husbands* can be seen as another sort of accommodation; and in a sense the evidence of the best in *Hello, Sister!* is comparable. It marks Stroheim as a promising director.

Film Comment, May–June 1974 (adapted from an entry originally written for *Cinema: A Critical Dictionary — The Major Filmmakers*, vol. 1, edited by Richard Roud [New York: Viking Press, 1980])

Notes

1. Originally published by the Cinémathèque de Belgique in 1958; a somewhat copyedited version has recently been brought out by Lorrimer, edited by Joel W. Finler. Finler, who has kindly assisted me on much of my research, has informed me that he has subsequently seen another, presumably later version of the script at the Cinémathèque de Belgique; on the basis of a quick examination, Finler estimates that if this was the draft used by Stroheim as a shooting script, the film would have been roughly an hour shorter than the version prefigured in the published script. [2009 postscript:

For a much more detailed comparison of the novel, screenplay, and film, see my *Greed* (London: BFI Publishing, 1993).]

2. Consider the close relationship between Mac's and Trina's loss of the Dental Parlors and the ultimate fate of the Amberson mansion (and the accompanying scenes in each film); consider the use of a closing iris to seal off an era when the Sieppes depart on the train at the end of part I of *Greed,* with the retreating horseless carriage in *Ambersons.* Even the "real" explosion of anger between Gowland and Hersholt in the last reel of *Greed* is matched by Agnes Moorehead's "real" hysteria as Aunt Fanny in a climactic scene. Indeed, the primary contrast between these films (apart from the nearly two decades that separate them — a period that corresponds quite precisely, eighteen years, to the time that passed between the first appearances of *McTeague* and the Tarkington novel) is in the respective economic and social classes they depict.

3. Regrettably, the only portion of the film that can be considered here is the first part, as edited by Stroheim for the Cinémathèque Française in 1954; the second part, *The Honeymoon,* was destroyed in a Cinémathèque fire, and apparently no other copies survive today.

4. Cf. the factual/speculative reports of Richard Koszarski (*Sight and Sound,* Autumn 1970) and Michel Ciment (*Positif* 131 [octobre 1971]).

Sweet and Sour: Lubitsch and Wilder in Old Hollywood

The camera cranes around the grand façade of a palace, a chateau, or a luxurious grand hotel, peering obliquely through the windows at the various doings inside. Or it stays perched in a hallway, outside a bedroom or a suite inside one of these buildings, while servants, musicians, or cigarette girls enter or leave, encouraging us to imagine what romantic shenanigans might be taking place on the other side of the door.

These are the two main signature shots of the great Hollywood filmmaker Ernst Lubitsch — especially during his Hollywood heyday, the '30s — and one can also find variations of the second kind, the outside-the-door interiors, in the more romantic movies of Billy Wilder, Lubitsch's major disciple, whose own Hollywood heyday was the '50s. In Lubitsch's *Ninotchka* (1939), which Wilder and his frequent writing partner Charles Brackett helped to script, we're made to understand how much three Russians in Paris (Sig Ruman, Felix Bressart, Alexander Granach) on a government mission are enjoying themselves in their hotel suite when they order up cigarettes, meaning three cigarette girls. And in Wilder's *Love in the Afternoon* (1957) — the most obvious and explicit and also, arguably, the clunkiest of his tributes to Lubitsch, partially inspired by Lubitsch's 1938 *Bluebeard's Eighth Wife* (which Wilder and Brackett also helped to script, and which also starred Gary Cooper, again playing a womanizing American millionaire in France) — the camera periodically returns to its favorite spot, outside the millionaire's suite at the Ritz, whenever the Gypsy musicians he hires arrive to help him pull off his various seductions with their soulful rendition of "Fascination."

Despite their reputations, I'm afraid that neither *Ninotchka* nor *Love in the Afternoon* qualifies as a favorite of mine. Among other things, they're both limited by the fact that Cary Grant refused to play their male leads. (In *Ninotchka*,

Melvyn Douglas took that part, opposite Greta Garbo; and in *Love in the Afternoon*, where Audrey Hepburn plays the daughter of Paris detective Maurice Chevalier, it would have been more interesting if Cooper had played her father and Chevalier had played her lover.) But I'm beginning with these examples because they offer the simplest and clearest illustrations of what "the Lubitsch touch" consists of.

As counterexamples, I'd like to propose the tributes to Lubitsch offered by two French New Wave directors, Jean-Luc Godard and Alain Resnais, both of whom allude to the exterior, horizontal crane shots around façades that can be found in many of Lubitsch's musicals with Chevalier and Jeannette MacDonald as well his supreme comedy of the '30s, *Trouble in Paradise*. Both examples, I should add, are readily available, because the two French films in question (along with *Trouble in Paradise*) are now accessible in excellent DVD transfers.

In Godard's *A Woman Is a Woman* (1962), one of the leads, Jean-Paul Belmondo, plays a character named Alfred Lubitsch, and the first time we hear his surname, he's being called to the phone. We then cut to a curious long shot of an apartment house façade where a neighbor on the top floor climbs out his window onto a catwalk and then walks around the side of the building to Alfred Lubitsch's window. There's no camera movement; but this is a low-budget comedy and Godard clearly couldn't afford a crane, so he merely suggests the movement with the neighbor's trajectory.

By contrast, in Resnais's relatively big-budget *Stavisky . . .* (1974) — which also stars Belmondo (in the title role), and is set in 1933 — there's a breathtaking piece of mise en scène crafted in and around a palatial resort hotel in Biarritz that actually looks even more opulent and elegant than anything to be found in Lubitsch. It's all part of a flashback away from Stavisky and his friend Baron Raoul (Charles Boyer) in Paris, narrated by the latter as he describes his recent visit to Biarritz, where he saw Stavisky's wife Arlette (Anny Duperet). As the Baron in this flashback enters the super-deluxe hotel where Arlette is staying, to the haunting strains of Stephen Sondheim's first movie score, and takes the elevator, there's a crane outside the building charting his progress through French windows as he crosses her sumptuous suite, a flurry of crisscrossing maids marking his path, until we see, through the last of the many windows, Arlette getting dressed in her bedroom. Then there's a startling, very un-Lubitsch-like cut from the Baron knocking on her door to a closeup of her swiftly turning her head in response to his knock. It's a bit like waking from a swank, Lubitschian dream — an apt effect, because back in the present, Stavisky is asking the Baron about a nightmare that Arlette had, a seeming premonition of his own downfall.

Based on these affectionate tributes, one might ask more generally, what did the famous "Lubitsch touch" consist of, exactly? "It was the elegant use of the superjoke," said Billy Wilder, Lubitsch's most famous and enduring Hollywood disciple, to the much younger writer-director Cameron Crowe in the interview book that they did together (*Conversations with Wilder* [New York: Knopf, 1999]). According to Wilder, it was a kind of extra spin on a comic situation — the sort of thing that once prompted Wilder as a screenwriter to place a sign on the wall of his office saying, "How would Lubitsch do it?" Wilder, a Viennese Jew, used Lubitsch, a Jew born in Berlin, as a major reference point throughout his filmmaking career, and to what degree he succeeded as well as failed in emulating his master is the main issue I'd like to address here. Both filmmakers tended to use little-known European stage farces, often French or Hungarian, as springboards for their own comic inventions, and both had a singular way of juxtaposing European and American customs and styles of behavior as a subtle way of critiquing as well as appreciating both.

Wilder's best example of what he meant by "the Lubitsch touch" was a suggestion Lubitsch made during the scripting of *Bluebeard's Eighth Wife*: "Gary Cooper goes down the street in Nice, and what he's looking for is maybe in a shop, a big, big shop like Macy's. In the store window was information written out, FRENCH SPOKEN . . . DUTCH SPOKEN . . . ITALIAN SPOKEN . . . CZECHOSLOVAKIAN SPOKEN . . . and the last one was ENGLISH SPOKEN. The kind of thing you see in Nice. Then underneath that — this was [Lubitsch's] idea — he added one more line: AMERICAN *UNDERSTOOD*. That was Lubitsch. [*Laughs.*] We had no joke there before."

Wilder himself insisted that Lubitsch was inimitable, recalling a famous exchange between himself and fellow director William Wyler when they were both pallbearers at Lubitsch's funeral in 1947. "No more Lubitsch," Wilder sadly noted, to which Wyler added, "And worse, no more Lubitsch pictures."

But for all his admiration for Lubitsch, Wilder was no film historian. He claimed to Crowe that Lubitsch "didn't do any comedies in Germany, he did great big expensive historical pictures" — an account that omits two of the funniest German comedies ever made, Lubitsch's *Die Puppe* (*The Doll*) and *The Oyster Princess*, both made in 1919 — and other Lubitsch silents that were "historical" (i.e., costume) pictures but also comedies, such as *Romeo and Juliet in the Snow* (1920) and *The Wildcat* (1921). (Incidentally, excellent restorations of both *The Oyster Princess* and *The Wildcat* are available on DVD.) Wilder also claimed that after *The Marriage Circle* in 1924 — Lubitsch's second Hollywood picture, after *Rosita* (1923), a comedy set in 1840s Spain — the master stuck exclusively to comedies, which is almost but not quite true: the exception was the underrated and sincere but commercially disastrous antiwar drama with a post–World War I setting, *The Man I Killed* (1932), also known as *Broken Lullaby*—which also proved to be Lubitsch's first collaboration with the man who became his best screenwriter, Samson Raphaelson, the author of *The Jazz Singer* who also worked on all three of Lubitsch's supreme masterpieces: *Trouble in Paradise* (1932), *The Shop Around the Corner* (1940), and *Heaven Can Wait* (1943), all fortunately available in excellent DVD editions.

I'd like to propose a somewhat different definition of "the Lubitsch touch"—one that helps to account for why Wilder was able to adopt some of its aspects on his best pictures while other aspects eluded him. It's a definition that comes in three parts. Part one, as I've already suggested, is a specifically Eastern European capacity to represent the cosmopolitan sophistication of continental Europeans to Americans—and with a double edge, as becomes clear in the "American understood" gag. Lubitsch himself was well aware of the ironies involved in his role as a cultural translator: "I've been to Paris, France and I've been to Paris, Paramount," he once famously remarked. "Paris, Paramount is better." This was arguably one of his few immodest claims, because "Paris, Paramount," was practically his own invention. And he differed from his silent Viennese predecessor Erich von Stroheim in the way he packaged his expertise for the public. As Stroheim once said, "Lubitsch shows you first the king on his throne, then as he is in his bedroom. I show you the king first in his bedroom so you'll know what he is when you see him on his throne."

Part two of "the Lubitsch touch" wasn't so much a touch as a kind of guarded embrace. It was actually a vision—a way of regarding his characters that could be described as a critical affection for flawed individuals who operate according to double standards. This probably doesn't take in Lubitsch's entire Hollywood oeuvre, but it does seem to apply to all the American comedies mentioned above, as well as such other gems as—sticking only to sound films—*The Love Parade* (1930), *Monte Carlo* (1931), *The Smiling Lieutenant* (1932), and *To Be or Not To Be* (1942).

Two of the three leading characters in *Trouble in Paradise*, played by Herbert Marshall and Miriam Hopkins, are jewel thieves in Venice and Paris who double as consummate con artists, plying their trade on each other as well as on other victims, such as an heiress played by Kay Francis. These breezy crooks are romantic hypocrites who can't be simply condemned or simply applauded, and one might describe the Lubitsch touch here as a rare capacity to view their romantic and hypocritical sides with equal amounts of nuanced attention and moral complexity without succumbing to any sentimentality about them. Similarly, the very different romantic leads of *The Shop Around the Corner*—two repressed and lonely clerks employed at a Budapest notions shop, played by James Stewart and Margaret Sullavan, who snap at each other at work without realizing that they're also passionate penpals who believe they haven't yet met. By giving so much attention to their cranky peevishness with one another, Lubitsch makes their secret amorous sides even more touching. And the rakish hero played by Don Ameche in *Heaven Can Wait* is another version of the same kind of duplicity — a man who clearly loves his wife (Gene Tierney) yet periodically cheats on her throughout his life.

The third and simplest part of my own definition of The Lubitsch Touch would be a graceful way of handling music as an integral part of a film's construction. This talent, I would submit, is the one clear way in which Wilder even surpassed his master: in his supreme late masterpieces *The Private Life of Sherlock Holmes* (1970) and *Avanti!* (1972), it is largely his exquisite uses of music — a score by Miklós Rózsa in the first, a collection of Italian pop songs in the second — that makes these movies as memorable as they are.

■ ■ ■ ■ ■ ■ ■ ■ ■

Wilder, who also started out as a Paramount director, eventually left the studio after some executives there tried to persuade him to change the German villains in *Stalag 17* (1953) — a World War II comedy-drama set in a concentration camp — into Poles, in order not to interfere with the film's potential German market. (As someone who'd lost much of his family in the Holocaust, Wilder was understandably offended.) The fact that he started out as a journalist may have been the most significant of the differences in background between him and Lubitsch, for it might be argued that one of the strongest aspects of his work is a kind of quasi-documentary realism that places him in a world that's very different from that of Lubitsch. Think of the documentary aspects of Wilder's greatest noncomic films, such as *Double Indemnity* (1944), *Sunset Boulevard* (1950), and *Ace in the Hole* (1951), with their indelible portraits of Los Angeles, Hollywood, and New Mexico, and you can already see part of what would make such later comedies as *One, Two, Three* (1961), *Kiss Me, Stupid* (1964), *The Private Life of Sherlock Holmes*, and *Avanti!* distinctive — namely, their canny uses of locations in Berlin, Nevada, London and Inverness, and southern Italy, conveying a sense of actuality that no studio simulations could approximate.

If he had a comic theme of its own that made him more cynical than Lubitsch — even at times a sour misanthrope — this might be described as the double standard that drives his characters into elaborate and often tortured deceptions. The classic example would be Tony Curtis and Jack Lemmon as jazz musicians on the run from Prohibition gangsters who wind up in drag, playing in an all-girl band at a plush resort hotel, in *Some Like It Hot* (1959), Wilder's most popular comedy. But one can also cite *The Seven Year Itch* (1955); *Love in the Afternoon*; *One, Two, Three*; *Kiss Me Stupid*; and *The Fortune Cookie* (1966), among many other examples.

Both Lubitsch and Wilder had reputations of being "naughty" as comic directors. But it's worth noting that in some ways the topics of capitalism and class are even more taboo as topics of discussion in American culture than sex, and from this standpoint, part of the naughtiness of both directors had to do with their treatment of these topics, especially from the perspectives of their respective eras. There are few '30s comedies that have a more morally complex view of capitalism than *Trouble in Paradise*, and few comedies of the '50s, '60s, and '70s that expose the potential ugliness of capitalism more directly than *Ace in the Hole*; *Sabrina* (1954); *The Apartment* (1960); *One, Two, Three*; *Kiss Me, Stupid*; *The Fortune Cookie*; and *Avanti!* (In Lubitsch's films, by contrast, in keeping with '30s fantasies about wealth, we most often get royalty and military pomp instead of capitalism — which is in part why Maurice Chevalier wound up as his standby actor, much as Jack Lemmon would subsequently become the favorite actor of Wilder.)

In keeping with this topic, Wilder is often drawn to characters whose strongest suit is a certain vulgar vitality: think of Kirk Douglas's ruthless journalist in *Ace in the Hole*, or James Cagney's Pepsi Cola executive in *One, Two, Three*. In this respect he is quite unlike Lubitsch, who ridicules both actors and Nazis in *To Be or Not To Be* for their vanity and childishness but would never dream of celebrating anyone's coarseness the way Wilder would. And on the matter of sex, one should note that male homosexuality and crossdressing crop up repeatedly in Wilder's work as comic standbys, but they hardly appear at all in Lubitsch's. Think of how much comic mileage is wrested out of men dressed as women in *Stalag 17* or *Some Like It Hot*, or out of suggestions of gay behavior in the opening sequences of both *The Private Life of Sherlock Holmes* and *Avanti!*

■ ■ ■ ■ ■ ■ ■ ■ ■

Was Lubitsch really inimitable? I bring this matter up because there are some characteristic "Lubitsch pictures" that he oversaw as Paramount's production chief that were mainly or exclusively directed by other people, such as *Love Me Tonight* (1932, directed by Rouben Mamoulian), *One Hour with You* (1932, codirected by George Cukor), and *Desire* (1936, directed by Frank Borzage). A few critics even plausibly maintain that *Love Me Tonight* — starring Maurice Chevalier and Jeanette MacDonald, the romantic leads in Lubitsch's *The Love Parade*, *The Smiling Lieutenant*, and *The Merry Widow* (1934) — is superior to the musicals Lubitsch directed.

On the other hand, one could argue that Wilder's greatest applications of "the Lubitsch touch" are those that get beyond the master's surface tics and in some ways might even be said to beat the master at his own game in sympathetically critiquing his characters while satirizing certain national traits. (Interestingly enough, this never happened during his excursions to Paris: in *Love in the Afternoon*, the cliché observations about the city, like those about the French in general, feel like secondhand derivations from Lubitsch, while the French caricatures in the blowsy 1963 *Irma la Douce* are strident as well as phony.)

For me, Wilder's most profound treatments of Europeans occur in two of his late masterworks, made back to back, both of which tanked at the box office — *The Private Life of Sherlock Holmes* and *Avanti!*, movies which register as definitive statements about English repression and Italian sensuality (in addition to Italian bureaucracy in the latter movie). In the case of the Holmes film, it's the whole Victorian era, including Queen Victoria herself, that's submitted to Wilder's critical scrutiny, and the sensuality of a Continental heroine played by Genevieve Page figures centrally in throwing the hero's inhibitions into relief. In both films, working with his favorite and perhaps best collaborator, cowriter I. A. L. Diamond, Wilder uses material derived from others (characters in the former, a play in the latter) to create a story that is highly personal.

It's a pity that Wilder himself didn't value these films more. In his interview book with Crowe, he confesses that he essentially abandoned *The Private Life of Sherlock Holmes* after it had an unsuccessful preview, allowing it to be extensively cut by others, and he's mainly disparaging about *Avanti!*, in part because of what might be regarded as one of its greatest strengths: "It smelled that it was shot in Italy," he complained — as if a studio-created artificial Italy would have been better, matching Lubitsch's own preference for Paris, Paramount, over Paris, France. But the journalist in Wilder turns out to be a lot more relevant than the more celebrated confectioner, and in some respects the filmmaker's images, which are usually overlooked, are allowed to supersede his words: both films essentially begin with pungent sequences without dialogue that bring us back to the expressiveness of silent cinema. (*Avanti!* is also exceptional in Wilder's work for its profanity and nudity — not to mention the degree to which it actually qualifies as an Italian film because of the number of Italians who worked on it, and the amount of unsubtitled Italian dialogue it employs, without ever allowing viewers who don't understand the language to lose the narrative thread.)

Both films have rather inhibited heroes — the brilliant but withdrawn and emotionally armored Holmes (Robert Stephens) in the first, a brash but inexperienced and prudish American businessman from Baltimore named Wendell Armbruster Jr. (Jack Lemmon) in the second — with consequences that are respectively tragic and comic. Holmes, the ultimate sophisticate and cosmopolitan, turns out to be an extremely vulnerable innocent when it comes to women and affairs of the heart, periodically driving him back into the solace of his cocaine addiction. And even though there are no American characters in *The Private Life of Sherlock Holmes*, I think it could be argued that Dr. Watson (Colin Blakely) as Holmes's incredulous comic foil functions here in the same way that an American character among Europeans would in a Lubitsch movie. (He's the supposedly commonsensical character whom Holmes periodically has to explain the plot to when it's actually us, the Yankee rubes, who have to be clued in.)

All of Wilder's ambivalences about both Europe and the U.S. are held in exquisite balance in *Avanti!* (1972), perhaps the least known but surely the most achieved of all his Lubitsch-style comedies, which over the years has gradually become my favorite of all his pictures. It describes the very brief romance that ensues between the aforementioned Armbruster and a working-class English woman named Pamela Piggott (Juliet Mills) when they meet at a health resort and luxury hotel not far from the bay of Naples. They've arrived at this particular spot because his father and her mother, who've just died together in a car accident, had been carrying on a secret affair at this hotel for a month every summer over the past decade — something Piggott knew about that was completely unknown to Armbruster Jr. As they discover and essentially recapitulate various details about their parents' amorous past at the same hotel, the quintessential German appreciation for Italian culture (equally apparent in such literary classics as *Death in Venice*), which also encompasses here a lot of satirical observation, becomes the main bill of fare. (Curiously, one reason why Wilder was himself disappointed with the way this film turned out was that he originally wanted Armbruster Sr.'s longterm affair to have been with a male hotel bellhop, until studio executives dissuaded him.)

Both Wendell Armbruster Jr. and Pamela Piggott are flawed individuals, to say the least: he's brash and shallow, the ugliest of "ugly" Americans in confronting Italian customs, and she's a neurotic obsessed with being overweight. Yet as with Cervantes's pairing of Don Quixote with Sancho Panza, the pairing of their separate faults makes the two of them irresistible, and far greater than the sum of their parts. It's characteristic of Wilder's mastery of this romantic material — which he adapted with Diamond from a play by Samuel A. Taylor, the author of *Sabrina* — that (a) a full two hours of the movie's 144 minutes pass before the couple finally arrive at a kiss and that (b) it's well worth the wait. Thanks to Wilder and Diamond's careful script construction, this happens at precisely the same moment that an American who's even more boorish, insensitive, and clueless than Armbruster suddenly arrives on the scene—a yahoo government bureaucrat named Blodgett, astutely played by Edward Andrews—who makes Armbruster seem like a civilized role model by comparison.

Is it possible to speak of a Wilder touch? I think so, especially if one thinks about the writer-director's subtle and delicate way of charting the emotional lives of Sherlock Holmes and Wendell Armbruster Jr. in these late masterpieces. Come to think of it, I think even Lubitsch might have been envious.

Stop Smiling, no. 32 (2007): "Hollywood Lost and Found"

Ritwik Ghatak:
Reinventing the Cinema

I have no way of knowing if Ghatak ever saw Jacques Tati's 1953 master-piece *Mr. Hulot's Holiday,* but when I look at his second feature, *Ajantrik* (1958), it's hard not to be reminded of it. Tati discovered with that film — while introducing his most famous character, Hulot, who went on to appear in his next three features (*Mon Oncle, Playtime,* and *Trafic*) — that he didn't even have to appear onscreen every time he wanted Hulot to be evoked. All he had to do was duplicate the sound of Hulot's car — a rattling antique and an embarrassment that very early on in the picture becomes closely associated with him, identifying him from the outset as the odd man out among vacationers at a summertime beach resort.

There's a similar association made between Bimal (Kali Banerjee), the cab-driver hero of *Ajantrik,* and his own broken-down car. The fact that this car has a name, Jagaddhal, and is even included in some rundowns of the film's cast, also seems emblematic of this special symbiosis. And it's interesting that Ghatak also uses some artificial-sounding noises on the film's soundtrack that oddly evoke science fiction, as if to express his fascination, his bemusement and amusement, with Bimal talking to and more generally treating his 1920 Chevrolet as if it were both a living creature and an extension of his own personality. (In interviews, Ghatak stated that he spent many years thinking about the philosophical implications of this relation between man and machine — a relation that seems especially pertinent to the technology of film itself.) And offscreen as well as onscreen, the various sounds that Ghatak uses to characterize this vehicle through various stages of health and fitness are a major aspect of this film's tragicomic tone — as important as the music, or the sound of Bimal's weeping when Jagaddal finally and irrevocably breaks down. The sound of this wreck being pulled away in the final scene is especially harsh and poignant, yet the sound of the detached car horn still wheezing and honking when an infant squeezes it allows the hero some sense of triumph and joy in the film's final shot.

In short, we have to acknowledge that the sound of this picture is far more than a neutral accompaniment to and counterpart of the images. And more generally, when we consider the soundtracks of some of Ghatak's other features, such as *The Cloud-Capped Star* (1960), it is tempting to imagine that Ghatak in effect created these features at least twice — once when he shot them, and then once again when he created their soundtracks.

On the British Film Institute's DVD of this film, there is a detailed introduction by the former *Guardian* film critic Derek Malcolm that puts much emphasis on its sound. Although Malcolm speaks of the film having an innovative use of "natural sound," which I rightly or wrongly interpret as "direct sound," I've been told by Ghatak's son Ritaban that none of his father's films employ direct sound and that all of them, by technical necessity, are post-dubbed. But this latter fact only emphasizes the degree to which Ghatak's soundtracks are composed, and what I find most striking about his highly unorthodox methods of sound composition are the ways that they essentially "rethink" the dramaturgy of the visuals and affect the ways that we look at these visuals by drawing our attention towards certain details and away from certain others.

This principle is facilitated by the way that Ghatak seems to compose both his visual mise en scène and his aural mise en scène in discrete layers. He frequently employs deep-focus cinematography, permitting a certain counterpoint between background and foreground details that on occasion reminds me of the early films of Orson Welles. (The last time I saw *The Cloud-Capped Star*, at the Ghatak retrospective held at the Jeonju International Film Festival in South Korea, I was especially struck by certain similarities to Welles's second feature, *The Magnificent Ambersons* — another tragic portrayal of the shifting fortunes of a family set against a larger backdrop of a culture in relentless decline, with a great deal of emphasis placed on the sacrifices made by some of the family members.) And Ghatak's sound is often layered between music, dialogue, and sound effects that can be naturalistic (such as the sound of food cooking on a grill, which Malcolm mentions) or expressionistic (such as the recurring sound of a cracked whip, which Malcolm also mentions). Much as our visual attention can shift in certain shots from foreground to background and back again because of the construction of the layered images, our aural attention might shift at times between music, dialogue, and sound effects, which might in turn affect the direction of our gaze in relation to those images.

■ ■ ■ ■ ■ ■ ■ ■ ■

There are two basic ways that a filmmaker can relate to film history: to work within an existing tradition or to proceed more radically as if no one else has ever made a film before. I think it would be safe to say that at least 99 percent of the films we see in theaters are made according to the first way. The Danish narrative filmmaker Carl Dreyer and the American experimental filmmaker Stan Brakhage are two of the rare exceptions who might be said to have followed the second way. Even though they too both worked to some extent in existing traditions, their principles of editing and camera movement and tempo and visual texture are sufficiently different to require viewers to move beyond some of their own habits as spectators in order to appreciate fully what these filmmakers are doing artistically. Without making such an effort at adjustment, one's encounters with the films of Brakhage and Dreyer are likely to be somewhat brutal in their potentiality for disorientation.

Ghatak, I believe, is another rare exception who followed the second route I have described, and one who provides comparable challenges of his own. And his methods of composing soundtracks for his films as well as his ways of interrelating his sounds and images are among the things I would point to first in order to describe his uniqueness as a filmmaker. One might conclude, in other words, that he reinvented the cinema for his own purposes both conceptually, in terms of his overall working methods, and practically, by rethinking the nature of certain shots he had already filmed — specifically, by starting and/or stopping certain kinds of sounds at unexpected moments, sometimes creating highly unorthodox ruptures in mood and tone.

It might be argued that these ruptures were not necessarily intentional. At least I've found no acknowledgment of them or of many of Ghatak's other eccentric filmmaking practices in his lectures and essays such as "Experimental Cinema," "Experimental Cinema and I," and "Sound in Cinema," all collected in *Rows and Rows of Fences: Ritwik Ghatak on Cinema* (Calcutta: Seagull, 2000). But by the same token, I find little if any acknowledgment by Carl Dreyer of his unorthodox editing practices in his own writings. And the issue of artistic intentionality remains a worrisome one in any case, because artists aren't invariably the best people to consult about their own practices, and it can be argued that what artists *do* is far more important (at least in most cases) than what they say they do. The radical *effect* of Ghatak's ruptures in his soundtracks strike me as being far better illustrations of his manner of reinventing cinema than any of his theoretical statements. To put it as succinctly as possible, they reinvent cinema precisely by reinventing us as spectators, on a moment-to-moment basis, keeping us far more alert than any conventional soundtrack would. And this makes them moments of creation in the purest sense.

Rouge 10 (2007), available at www.rouge.com.au

Introducing Pere Portabella

The first North American retrospective of Catalan filmmaker Pere Portabella started last week at the Gene Siskel Film Center, and it's one of the year's biggest cultural events. None of his films has ever been screened in Chicago, and none has ever been released anywhere on DVD or VHS. All five of his features are showing here (though none of his ten shorts), and if you don't see them now, chances are you never will.

Most of Portabella's films can be classified as experimental, though they have little in common with the films usually given that label, which tend to be nonnarrative and shot in 8- or 16-millimeter or on video. All of his features are in 35-millimeter and use narrative, though they never tell a complete story. They all have rich soundtracks that go in and out of sync with the images, sometimes reinforcing what we see, sometimes contradicting it. They all drift smoothly, often unexpectedly, from narrative to reverie and from fiction to documentary, interjecting rude shocks along the way. They're full of comic incongruities as well as creepy interludes, and they're all intensely physical experiences — sounds and images that assault or caress. Their formal brilliance reflects Portabella's long involvement with painting and music, and their intellectual and political themes are almost always implicit.

My favorite Portabella film, screening this week, is *Vampir-Cuadecuc* (1970), a black-and-white silent documentary about the shooting of a Dracula film with Christopher Lee (*Count Dracula* by celebrated hack Jesus Franco) that becomes much more than a documentary. It glides effortlessly between telling parts of the Dracula story (with Dracula as an implicit stand-in for General Francisco Franco) in a dank period location to providing a personal and ironic commentary on *Count Dracula*'s production by focusing on stray details: a fan blowing confetti over a corpse, a ghoulishly made-up actress making a face at someone between takes,[1] a bag of unspecified something crawling across a floor. Meanwhile, periodic sounds of jet planes, drills, operatic arias, syrupy Muzak, and sinister electronic droning ingeniously locate Dracula and our perceptions of him in the contemporary world — until the end, in the film's only use of sync sound, when Lee reads a climactic passage from Bram Stoker's novel. Recalling without imitating such classics as *Nosferatu* and *Vampyr*, the film uses high-contrast cinematography to evoke the dissolution and decay that strikes viewers who see those films today in fading prints. It all adds up to a kind of poetic alchemy in which Portabella converts one of the world's worst horror films into one of the most beautiful movies ever made about anything. (It's characteristic of his artistic integrity that he refused to allow *Vampir-Cuadecuc* to be used as an extra on a *Count Dracula* DVD.)

I first encountered this masterpiece at Cannes a little over thirty-five years ago, and I've been a sucker for Portabella's work ever since. (A year later at Cannes, I saw his even wilder *Umbracle*.) Portabella wasn't at either festival because his passport had been taken away. He was one of the Spanish producers of the first feature Luis Buñuel ever made in his native Spain, *Viridiana* (1961). Denounced by the Vatican after it won the top prize at Cannes, the film created such a scandal that the Franco government confiscated or destroyed all of the official papers that identified it as a Spanish film and punished Portabella by taking away his passport for several years.

Born into a family of wealthy industrialists in Barcelona in 1929, Portabella has been closely tied to the city's art scene for most of his life and has been a major patron of Catalan artists, including Joan Miró, the focus of three of his shorts. (One of his major collaborators is the prolific Catalan poet and playwright Joan Brossa, cowriter on the first three features.) He also served for many years as a senator in the post-Franco parliament. He started working in film in 1960, when he produced the first full-length feature of Carlos Saura (*Los Golfos*) and an early feature by Marco Ferreri (*El Cochecito*), followed by *Viridiana*.

The first feature he directed was the 1968 *Nocturno 29*, which inhabits a space somewhere between art cinema and experimental cinema. It stars Lucia Bosé — an Italian actress associated with such art-house directors as Michelangelo Antonioni, Juan Antonio Bardem, and Buñuel — and exploits many of the tropes and ritzy settings associated with them and with Alain Resnais' *Last Year at Marienbad*. It's my least favorite Portabella feature, more provocative than achieved, but insofar as its dissimilar parts add up to something, it can be read as a kind of first draft of *Umbracle* — which itself was a kind of first draft of the 1990 *Warsaw Bridge*.[2]

Like *Vampir-Cuadecuc* and *Umbracle*, *Nocturno 29* was made completely outside commercial channels and for the most part was shown clandestinely. Its anti-Franco stance is implied in the film's title — it was made during Franco's twenty-ninth year in power. That stance is even more apparent in the formally more adventurous *Umbracle*, which uses some Catalan at a time when speaking the language was forbidden. This opposition became more overt in the 1977 *Informe General* (*General Report*), a relatively conventional 158-minute documentary made after Franco's death that attempts to deal with the enormity for Spaniards of his nearly forty years in power.

Umbracle belongs to an international avant-garde subgenre of films made in the late '6os and early '7os that juxtapose disparate materials to spark a radical combustion. (Other examples include Jean-Luc Godard's *Sympathy for the Devil* and Dusan Makavejev's WR: *Mysteries of the Organism*.) The film adds up to a scream, expressing the frustration of living under Franco through the combination of widely diverse materials: statements by a Spanish intellectual about censorship, a Buñuelian tour of a shoe store, a traditional clown act, clips from a kitschy 1948 Spanish propaganda feature and silent American slapstick comedies, a parade of plucked chickens in an automated slaughterhouse, Christopher Lee taking hallucinatory trips around Barcelona. In the penultimate sequence a woman puts on a recording of Beethoven's Pastoral Symphony and moves toward a telephone, then both the record and the image become "stuck": the same four notes keep repeating, while the same fingers are seen from different angles, poised above the dial they will never reach.

While radical discontinuity is the main fare in *Umbracle*, a kind of radical continuity underlies the often bewildering and audacious shifts in locations and styles in *Warsaw Bridge*. It's Portabella's first color feature (there's a brief patch of color in *Nocturno 29*), and his first feature in which the "enemy" isn't Franco. If anything has replaced him, it's probably the complacencies of commercial narrative cinema.

In commercial movies the standard logical flow is produced by style as well as content — a set of links composed of music cues and other continuities of sound and image that carry us smoothly across shot changes. Portabella highlights this process in *Warsaw Bridge* by retaining the links while sabotaging the narrative logic that usually justifies them. (One of its cowriters, Carles Santos, has created the music or sound tracks for all of Portabella's features since *Vampir-Cuadecuc*.) The film also appears to be an anthology of his passions and interests and a somewhat ironic and funny portrait of his milieu.

At the center of *Warsaw Bridge* is a romantic triangle between a prizewinning novelist, a symphony conductor, and a university marine-biology lecturer, but the narrative crisscrosses more than follows these characters. In between it offers, among other things, meditations on Spanish architecture and landscapes, an outdoor concert where the conductor is on an elevated platform in a shopping arcade and the musicians are on nearby balconies, a lavish state party thrown for the novelist, a verbal chess match at the party, a credit sequence twenty-odd minutes into the film, a concert inside a cathedral, extended love-making, a recitation of part of the novelist's book, an opera performed at a gigantic fish market, a university lecture on algae, another opera set (though not staged) in a Turkish bath, a TV interview, a meal prepared and eaten by the three lovers, a film screening, and a plane trying to extinguish a forest fire. The images of operas and at least one of the concerts move gracefully in and out of sync with the music, and the opera in the fish market includes some spectacular bits with sharks and blocks of ice. Some of the dialogue and action segues into non sequiturs and nonsense. And whatever it all means, the whole thing is gorgeous.

Chicago Reader, November 10, 2006

Notes

1. Alas, this shot, which I recall vividly from the several times I saw the film in 1971, is no longer part of the film. Presumably Portabella had second thoughts about it. [2009]

2. In my capsule review for the *Reader* of *The Silence Before Bach* (2007) — Portabella's subsequent feature, in Spanish, Italian, and German — I described it as "his most pleasurable and accessible film to date, above all for its diverse performances of the title composer's work. Gracefully leapfrogging between fact and fiction in at least two centuries and several countries, it recalls some playful aspects of his *Warsaw Bridge* while juxtaposing past and present as if they were separate attractions in a theme park." [2009]

Portabella and Continuity

Filmmakers who reinvent the cinema for their own purposes generally operate under certain distinct handicaps. In a few privileged cases (Griffith, Feuillade, Chaplin, Hitchcock) it's the cinema itself, as art form and global institution, that winds up readjusting to the reinvention. But what happens more often is either a prolonged banishment of the filmmaker's work from public awareness or a protracted series of misunderstandings until (or unless) the new rules are recognized, understood, and assimilated.

In the case of Pere Portabella, where some of the principles of production, distribution, and exhibition have been reinvented along with some concepts of reception, the frequent time lags between completed projects have only exacerbated some of the difficulties posed to uninitiated viewers. Interestingly, these difficulties have relatively little to do with an audience's receptivity to the films themselves and a great deal to do with an audience discovering the very fact of their existence.

In my own case, I was fortunate in having my first acquaintance with Portabella's cinema at a relatively early stage, in May 1971 and May 1972, when, as a Paris-based American expatriate in Cannes, I encountered *Vampir Cuadecuc* and then *Umbracle* in the Directors Fortnight, and briefly reviewed each of them for the *Village Voice* as part of my festival coverage. At that time, the familiarity I had with Spain and Catalan culture under Franco was so minimal that I could only respond to these films as if they had arrived from Mars — suggesting not only what Santos Zunzunegui has called an "extraterritorial Portabella" but also an extraterrestrial Portabella in the bargain. One example of what I mean was my incapacity to notice, process, or even acknowledge "Cuadecuc" as part of the first film's title in my review, and a comparable lack of assurance the following year that I had any clear notion of what "Umbracle" meant, even after Carles Santos once tried to explain it to me in Paris. All I knew was that these films were being shown clandestinely, if at all, inside Spain.

Even after attending the San Sebastian Film Festival in July 1972, the insights I had into Franco Spain remained cursory, apart from such oddities as specific articles having been scissored out of some of the individual copies of the *International Herald-Tribune* that I purchased there, and a few glimpses of the local police station after my passport was stolen, on the final day of the festival — a lucky occurrence, as it turned out, because most of what I discovered over the next twenty-four hours, including a bus trip the next morning to the American Embassy in Bilbao, was precisely what the festival's superb hospitality had contrived for me not to notice. I knew, of course, that Portabella had been unable to travel with his own films to Cannes because, as punishment for having been one of the Spanish producers of *Viridiana*, his own passport had been confiscated. But the only other thing I knew about his Spanish profile, apart from whatever I could glean from *Vampir Cuadecuc* and *Umbracle*, was that *Variety*'s Spanish correspondent, an American, had responded to my bringing up Portabella's name in San Sebastian with dismissive hostility. Although I was able to see *Nocturno 29* a little later in London, where I wrote a brief article about Portabella for *Time Out* to accompany a minimal retrospective at the National Film Theatre, three more decades would pass before I was able to see any other Portabella films, and the only one of these I'd even heard about was *Informe General*. My renewed acquaintance, moreover, came about only through the initiative of Portabella himself, corresponding with me in Chicago. (More recently, I would only begin to understand the special function of Poland as a generic foreign country vis-à-vis Spanish fantasy, in both *Warsaw Bridge* and Calderón's *La vida es sueño*, through the help of a friend with Catalan parents.)

Eventually, I would receive in the mail homemade video or DVD copies of *No Compteu Amb El Dits* (1967), *Nocturno 29* (1968), *Miró l'Altre* (1969), *Miró 37* (*Aidez l'Espagne*) (1969), *Vampir Cuadecuc* (1970), *Umbracle* (1972), *El Sopar* (1974), *Informe general sobre unas cuestiones de interés para una proyección pública* (1977), and *Pont de Varsòvia* (1990), eventually to be followed by *Die Stille vor Bach* (2007). And in the meantime, an old filmmaker friend who now works as a producer for public television, Peter Bull, had emailed me asking if I'd ever heard of *Warsaw Bridge*, which he'd just seen at a screening in New York's Westchester county hosted by Jonathan Demme, describing it to me as "a fascinating blend of Tati and Buñuel" — a shrewd comment considering that he was then unaware of Portabella's role as coproducer of *Viridiana*. In fact, Peter, whom I'd met in San Diego in 1978 when he was a graduate student, knew nothing about my reviews of Portabella films in the *Village Voice* or *Time Out*. As someone who had once made an experimental film I was privileged to star in (playing myself being interviewed as a film critic about an imaginary, nonexistent film that Peter then proceeded to shoot, based on my description, which he then intercut with the interview), he assumed that I would be interested if I'd never heard of Portabella and possibly helpful in furnishing him with more information if I had.

I wrote back to Portabella that even though *Vampir Cuadecuc* remained my favorite of his films, the "very exciting and beautiful" *Pont de Varsòvia* was "the biggest revelation." "I'm especially struck by the remarkable continuity of your work over at least two decades — work that for me is in many ways largely concerned with issues of continuity, in almost every meaning of that term (historical, thematic, narrative, poetic, musical, stylistic, formal)."

I should have added "political" to my list of adjectives, because the continuity between Portabella's political and aesthetic concerns has indeed provided the basis for most of the other links I had in mind. But there is a continuity between Portabella's separate works that also rewards close scrutiny — not just the way, for instance, that most of them occupy some netherworld between fiction and nonfiction, but also the way that Francisco Franco and his own forms of fiction and narrative link *Nocturno 29*, the Miró shorts of 1969, *Vampir Cuadacuc*, *Umbracle*, *El Sopar*, and the opening sequence of *Informe general*, while other forms of narrative dominance relating to Hollywood and other western models of continuity, including the Common Market, seem to figure more prominently afterwards. Indeed, the end of *Informe general*'s lengthy title, *una proyección pública*, inevitably calls to mind all the preceding *proyecciones privadas*. Clearly Portabella's second career as senator, starting in 1977, which included his participation in writing the new Spanish Constitution, helping to abolish the death penalty, and assisting Spain's entry into the Common Market, has redirected the focus of his filmmaking, even though the larger and the smaller concerns of continuity between the two parts of his career have been more lasting.

Provocative forms of continuity and discontinuity within as well as between his films abound. The stuttering, staccato rhythms of *Miró l'Altre* that chronicle the making and unmaking of a Miró painting are succeeded by the making and unmaking of Spain in the mid-1930s via newsreel footage that is also made to stutter in *Miró 37 (Aidez l'Espagne)*; and this is succeeded in turn by the legato camera movements of *Vampir Cuadecuc*, which in a different way chart the making and unmaking of a Count Dracula story by another Franco. Meanwhile, the continuity and discontinuity formed by Portabella's collaborations with Carles Santos in this work so that sound either amplifies or contradicts image (creating especially brutal and aggressive combinations of the two in the aforementioned Miró shorts and *Umbracle*) provides another form of persistence.

Or consider the continuity of the camera movements in *Vampir Cuadecuc*, which typically proceed from the Count Dracula story being filmed by Jesús Franco to surrounding details pertaining to the actors, crew, and locations, thereby traversing centuries as well as the space between fiction and documentary. These disconcerting shifts of syntax within single shots bears some similarity to the effects obtained by William S. Burroughs in switching syntax within individual sentences in *Naked Lunch* and *Nova Express*, often achieved through "cutups," which allow the formal shapes of expressive units (shots, sentences) to overtake their narrative meanings and thus highlight some of the means by which those meanings get produced.

Many portions of *No compteu amb el dits*, *Nocturno 29*, *Vampir Cuadecuc*, *Umbracle*, *Pont de Varsòvia*, and even *Die Stille vor Bach* evoke certain aspects of the Surrealist universe — especially ones associated with the Buñuel of such films as *Un chien andalou*, *L'age d'or*, *El*, *Viridiana*, *El Ángel exterminador*, *Belle de jour*, *Tristana*, and *Le Charme discret de la bourgeoisie*, and partly consisting of decorous people in decorous clothes and decorous surroundings doing indecorous things. Sometimes these indecorous things are merely evoked (as in *El Sopar*) rather than shown, and sometimes they are only suggested by implication (e.g., the extreme close-ups of a priest being shaved in *Don't Count on Your Fingers*). But since Surrealism already testifies to the power of one's imagination, this distinction should probably be regarded as secondary. ("Is that true?" asks a woman's offscreen voice in *Don't Count on Your Fingers*. "No, it's not true, replies a man's offscreen voice. "But if you repeat it often enough, a falsehood becomes an affirmation" — thereby affirming what amounts to a Surrealist manifesto.) Even more evocative of early Buñuel are the odd juxtapositions suggesting poetic metaphors: the menace and torment located in a Pepsi Cola bottling factory in *Don't Count on Your Fingers*, or the shift from the unseeing "glass eye" of a TV screen in *Nocturno 29* to the literal unseeing glass eye of the man who was just watching it, or the painfully silent drop of a piano into a river in *The Silence Before Bach*. Portabella's avowed method of composing the script of *Warsaw Bridge* — "taking a short article from a newspaper about the body of a diver found in a burnt forest" and then expanding "in all directions" from there — certainly suggests a Surrealist procedure comparable to that of "Data Toward the Irrational Enlargement of a Film: *Shanghai Gesture*," with the pertinent distinction that in this case, the game involves an enlargement/expansion based on establishing continuities of characters, locations, themes (such as the crossing of class boundaries involving culture during a verbal chess match in a kitchen, a brief discussion of verse forms at an adjacent party, and an opera staged in a fish market), stray motifs (such as "Constantinople" and algae), visual patterns (such as cutting from adjacent buildings to a row of ties, or from one airplane to another airplane), and camera movements, all of which ultimately supersede conventional narrative continuities.

But it would be misleading to limit Portabella's references to Buñuel, or to Murnau and Dreyer (in *Vampir Cuadecuc*), or to Antonioni and Resnais (despite echoes of *La notte* and *L'année dernière à Marienbad* in both *Nocturno 29* and *Warsaw Bridge*) or to Welles (even if *Informe general* begins rather like *Citizen Kane* as it hovers creepily around Franco's tomb—before mutating into something closer to the car ride in *Vampir Cuadecuc*, albeit one arriving this time at "Barcelona 1976"), or to Straub-Huillet when it comes to discovering both the materiality and the persistence of Bach. We also have to consider all the references that precede cinema, ranging all the way from Bach himself to Bram Stoker.

If the overall movement of *Warsaw Bridge* is towards enlargement and expansion, the overall movement of *The Silence Before Bach* tends more towards contraction and convergence. It's the music, mainly Bach's, that provides the continuity and the convergence, spatial as well as temporal, crossing boundaries of class and language, modes of representation, musical instruments, forms of both spirituality and food preparation, and several centuries, not to mention musical staffs. Meanwhile, vehicles predominate—truck, train, boats, subway, and an almost continually moving camera traversing roads and rooms, streets and rivers, countries and centuries with a fluidity that matches the flow of musical notes. Starting as well as ending in a neutral white space, *The Silence Before Bach* presupposes an "after" as well as "before"—that is to say, another new beginning.

Written for the Pere Portabella DVD box set, 2009

Two Neglected Filmmakers: Eduardo de Gregorio and Sara Driver

The texts below were both written for the catalogue of the fifth edition of the Buenos Aires Festival of Independent Film in 2004. Both are about neglected filmmakers who are also longtime friends of mine, although neither, to the best of my knowledge, has ever seen any films by the other, and they met for the first time at the festival, where complete retrospectives of both filmmakers were being presented. (I first met Eduardo in Paris in 1973, shortly after he'd finished working as a screenwriter on Jacques Rivette's Céline et Julie vont en bateau, *and I first met Sara about ten years later in New York, shortly before I saw her first major film,* You Are Not I, *and decided to devote a chapter to her in my book* Film: The Front Line 1983.*)*

When I was asked to write these two pieces for the BAFICI catalogue, I opted to make them each exactly the same length and to make them rhyme with one another in various other ways.

Eduardo de Gregorio's Dream Door

It must be a bummer to be an Argentinian writer and/or filmmaker and constantly get linked to Jorge Luis Borges. It must be especially hard if you're Eduardo de Gregorio, whose first major screen credit is on an adaptation of "Theme of the Traitor and the Hero" for Bernardo Bertolucci's 1970 feature *The Spider's Strategem*.

I don't mean to question the credentials of de Gregorio as a onetime student of Borges — just the appropriateness of a too-narrow understanding to impose on a singular body of work that owes as much to cinematic references as to literary ones, and one that indeed juxtaposes the two almost as freely as it juxtaposes different languages and historical periods (while including all the cultural baggage that comes with each of them). For if we agree with historian Eric Hobsbawm that the overall development from the nineteenth century to the twentieth and then to the twenty-first is a gradual slide from civilization to barbarism, I believe we've arguably accepted not only an operating hypothesis of Argentinian culture in general and of Borges' work in particular, both steeped in a particular kind of cultural nostalgia, but one of the most precious legacies of both. And considering how roomy the nineteenth century is, it's obviously a resource that can be put to radically different uses.

In the case of de Gregorio's features and his participation as a writer in the elaboration of a few others, the literary tradition most in play is probably the Gothic — and especially one of the principal sites of that tradition, the Old Dark House, which crops up directly in *The Spider's Strategem* (where it's also known as Tara), Rivette's *Céline et Julie vont en bateau* (1974), *Sérail* (1976), *Aspern* (1984), *Corps perdus* (1989), and, more metaphorically, in my two favorites of de Gregorio's own features, *La mémoire courte* (1979) and *Tangos volés* (2001). (In the heavy Langian menace of the former, it's the tainted history of Nazism, functioning like an active form of decay inside a film noir in color; in the light, Renoiresque affection and swarming activity of the latter — appropriately overseen by a character named Octave, recalling Renoir's own character in *La règle du jeu* — it's the "old bright house" of a film studio.)

From another point of view, these houses in de Gregorio's films function in much the same way as manuscripts, paintings, and films — as time machines that are also thresholds into alternate realities, which in Borgesian terms might be described as alternate fictions. For it's important to recognize that what we call "reality" in de Gregorio's universe is most often a matter of dialectical fictions: two scheming sexpots (Bulle Ogier and Marie France Pisier — whether they're competing in *Céline et Julie's* film-within-a-film or working in tandem in *Sérail*); the separate interests of art and commerce (in *Sérail*, *Aspern*, and *Corps perdus*); juxtapositions of the Anglo-American nineteenth century (via references to Collins, James, Poe, Stevenson, et al.) with the continental European or South American twentieth — indeed, nearly always two or more separate national cultures interfacing and interacting across separate time frames and historical periods.

Basically a filmmaker of the *fantastique* — even when he's rummaging around in a reasonable facsimile of real history in *Aspern* and an even more persuasive (if chilling) version of real history and politics in *La mémoire courte* — de Gregorio also participated in generating the other-worldly fantasies of Rivette's *Céline and Julie*, *Duelle*, *Noroît*, and *Merry-Go-Round* (as well as the history of Jean-Louis Comolli's 1975 *La Cecilia*), only the first of which is playing in this retrospective. All of these share with most of de Gregorio's own features a universe where women, many of them divas, are often the ones in control. What they don't share is the conniving and cynical men who try to deceive and outwit them — i.e., the heroes of *Sérail*, *Aspern*, and *Corps perdus*, played respectively by Corin Redgrave, Jean Sorel, and Tchéky Karyo. One thing that's especially likable about *Tangos volés* — a film whose conscious influences include *Hellzapoppin'* and *The Secret Life of Walter Mitty* — is the relative lack of malice in the male characters (played by, among others, Liberto Rabal, grandson of Franciso; Guy Marchand; Juan Echanove as Octave; and a little boy who irresistibly recalls Michael Chaplin in A *King in New York*) — although de Gregorio's caustic wit is not entirely absent from his treatment of tangomania.

I'd like to conclude by citing a few other insufficiently recognized treasures in his work. There's the only real performance as an actor (as opposed to cameo appearance) of Jacques Rivette, in *La mémoire courte* — which, combined with William Lubtchansky's ravishing color cinematography and the paranoic intensity of the multinational script, makes this film, along with early Robert Kramer, one of the only true successors of *Paris nous appartient* (even if it gets cited as infrequently in Rivette's filmographies as de Gregorio's own performance in Straub-Huillet's *Othon* gets cited in his). There are the interesting and varied ways of representing and evoking de Gregorio's native Buenos Aires in absentia (in *La mémoire courte*, where it's present only in documentary footage borrowed from coscreenwriter Edgardo Cozarinsky's . . . ; and in *Tangos volés*, where it's entirely a matter of memory and pastiche) and perversely and dialectically shutting out most evidences of the city while actually filming there (in *Corps perdus*). There are three of Bulle Ogier's most delicate and beautifully shaped performances, in *Sérail*, *La mémoire courte*, and *Aspern*. And finally, there's the exhilaration as well as the heady vertigo of shuttling between eras and continents via what *Tangos volés* calls "la porte des songes" — a handy device for a nostalgic expatriate.

Sara Driver's Dream Dog

It must be a bummer to be a woman surrealist — a tradition that is rarely acknowledged to exist, at least among American and European writers and filmmakers. In Mexican painting, there's Frida Kahlo and Remedios Varo. But when it comes to fiction writers like Shirley Jackson or Flannery O'Connor, other affiliations such as "gothic" or "Southern" always take precedence, much as "feminist" does when it comes to Jane Campion, Chantal Akerman, or Leslie Thornton. Possibly all of this is due to the abiding sexism of André Breton, Luis Buñuel, Salvador Dali, and other talented, macho Latin ideologues, but it seems in any case that David Lynch and Raúl Ruiz are automatically deemed honorary members of the club while Sara Driver is usually deprived of any tradition at all, except maybe "weird" and "independent."

I have to admit, though, that she makes things difficult—and difficult in the best sense—by being so contrary, even when it comes to only three extended narrative films to date. While we can readily speak about the surrealist "worlds" of a Buñuel, a Lynch, or even an Akerman (at least if we think of Belgian surrealism), the three films of Driver, even if we can easily call them all surrealist as well as "Driveresque," clearly take place in three distinctly different worlds. That doesn't mean that there aren't various stylistic, thematic, and temperamental connections between them going well beyond the recurrence of various collaborators. Think of the dense and hyperactive soundtracks of all three, the downscale milieus, the trancelike rhythms, the layered relation of distant past to present (bringing to mind the fact that Driver spent her junior year in college abroad, studying archeology in Athens), the depictions of bullying power-mongers and solitary children, the dreamy passivity of seemingly hapless protagonists and the prominent attention given to their dreams, and chaotic eruptions of various kinds occurring in the midst of their compulsive routines, leading to the major plot developments in all three cases.

Perhaps an even more singular common trait in *You Are Not I* (1982), *Sleepwalk* (1986), and *When Pigs Fly* (1993) is the simultaneous urge to follow characters conceived in unabashed fantasy terms—a schizophrenic (Suzanne Fletcher) who can think herself into the social identity of her sane sister (Melody Schneider), a Caucasian mother with a Chinese son (Dexter Lee), two ghosts (Marianne Faithfull and Rachel Bella) who move around with a rocking chair and its owners (Maggie O'Neill and Alfred Molina)—while charting their various interrelations with the world and each other with a great deal of plausibility. Put another way, she knows how to get the poetic and the prosaic, the supernatural and the mundane, to rub shoulders with one another. (Two perfect performances—Fletcher's poetic fixity in *You Are Not I*, Molina's mundane nonchalance in *When Pigs Fly*—form the center of each film.)

Still, the differences between Driver's three films are huge, each one confounding many of the expectations set up by its predecessor. (The same is true of her 1994 short video documentary *The Bowery*—a fond, factual tribute to her own Manhattan neighborhood, narrated by local historian Luc Sante, that also manages to encompass a morbid, surrealist "Oddatorium" and references to "ghosts," "a magic place," and a "wonderland.") Even though it begins like the way that *Psycho* ends, and is never entirely removed from mainstream horror, *You Are Not I*—an adaptation of a Paul Bowles story, made for a masters thesis in film school, that is surprisingly faithful (aside from the fact that a highway accident replaces a train wreck) — registers unapologetically like an art film, and so, in a very different way, does *Sleepwalk* (this time working closer to Jacques Rivette than to Georges Franju, integrating choreography rather than literary narration into the *mise en scène*). Yet *When Pigs Fly* is informed at every turn by the character types of popular commercial cinema, Hollywood romantic comedy in particular; even the principal avowed influence is *Topper*.

Another significant distinction: the fantasy elements in *You Are Not I* can ultimately be traced back to the American tradition of Poe, which associates them with mental derangement, and the fantasy elements in *When Pigs Fly* can apparently be related to Irish folk tales as well as the generic staples of *Topper*. But even though *Sleepwalk* is set in its entirety in the neighborhood of lower Manhattan where Driver lives, the film belongs more to the free-wheeling trappings of what the French call *"fantastique"* — which includes surrealism without being limited to it — than to any particular national or ethnic tradition. Could this be because the Bowery is itself a cultural melting pot, like much of New York? Significantly, the Chinese text being translated by the heroine derives from four separate fairy tales: one Chinese, one African, one by the Brothers Grimm, and one made up by Driver herself.

There's also a shift from unbridled ferocity in the Bowles adaptation to a kind of fairy-tale malice (such as the loss of fingers and hair) on the edges of the much gentler *Sleepwalk* to a juxtaposition of wife-beating and murder with slapstick in the still gentler *When Pigs Fly*. Meanwhile, the same irreverence that can virtually start the latter film off with a dog's giddy musical dream to match his master's, and can later use a performance of Thelonious Monk's "Misterioso" as a pretext for a lyrical themepark ride (and Marianne Faithful as a pretext for a lovely rendition of "Danny Boy"), can also, in the earlier *Sleepwalk*, use the Chinese Year of the Dog as a good excuse for making a passing executive bark in the street.

Buenos Aires Festival of Independent Film catalogue, 2004

Vietnam in Fragments: William Klein in 1967-68: A Radical Reevaluation

Out of all the items selected for a recently concluded course and weekly film series in Chicago devoted to world cinema in the 1960s, William Klein's *Mr. Freedom*, the most obscure by far of the fourteen features I picked, was the one I was most worried about in terms of its likely reception. What worried me could be summed up in my capsule review for the *Chicago Reader*:

> William Klein's over-the-top fantasy-satire (1968) is conceivably the most anti-American movie ever made, but only an American (albeit an expatriate living in France) could have made it. Despite Klein's well-deserved international reputation as a still photographer, his films are almost unknown in the U.S., so this spirited and hilarious second feature offers an ideal introduction to his volatile talent. Filmed in slam-bang comic-book style, it describes the exploits of a heroic, myopic, and knuckleheaded free-world agent (*Playtime*'s John Abbey) who arrives in Paris to do battle against the Russian and Chinese communists, embodied by Moujik Man (a colossal Cossack padded out with foam rubber) and the inflatable Red China Man (a dragon that fills an entire métro station). Donald Pleasence is the hero's sinister, LBJ-like boss, and Delphine Seyrig at her giddiest plays the sexy, duplicitous double agent who shows him the ropes. Done in a Punch and Judy manner that occasionally suggests Godard or Kubrick, and combining guerrilla-style documentary with expressionism, this feisty political cartoon remains a singular expression of '60s irreverence.

In short, to paraphrase George S. Kaufman, just the sort of thing you'd expect to close in New Haven — even though it was just about to appear on DVD for the first time with two other Klein features, in Criterion's invaluable Eclipse series.

As one indication of how easy it is to forget a film that received scant attention everywhere when it came out, consider the passing thumbnail description given to it by Gilbert Adair, one of my favorite contemporary writers (and an old friend), in a recent article in the *Guardian* about 1968 and its recent anniversary celebrations. Discussing a small retrospective at the BFI Southbank, Adair expresses some warranted dismay about a remark in the programme booklet regarding *The Bride Wore Black*: "Truffaut used this Hitchcock homage as an argument against the use of guns." Yet a paragraph later, Adair himself offers the following: "Among the several other films featured, William Klein's *Who Are You, Polly Maggoo?* and *Mr. Freedom* are enjoyable, exasperatingly scattershot satires on, respectively, the fashion industry and the anti-war movement."

The anti-war movement? This sounds like Adair must have been thinking of some other movie. But considering that *Mr. Freedom*, shot in 1967 and early 1968, was released in 1969 only after the French government banned it for six months, it's never come close to being a familiar reference point — unlike, say, *Polly Maggoo* (which a Paris student bar that survives to this day was named after). Speaking for myself, I only caught up with this marginalized item in London in the early '70s, some time before I wound up working briefly for Klein in Paris — translating a script of his from French to English, for a project that would eventually mutate into *The Model Couple*.

So *Mr. Freedom* was a film that had clearly fallen by the wayside. And yet it was the only film shown in my '60s world cinema course that sold out every ticket. I even suspect that this may have happened because of its being described as "conceivably the most anti-American movie ever made," though it's hard to imagine that this would have attracted much of a crowd three or four years ago. And the fifty or so enrolled students and 150 others who came to the screening seemed to take to it like ice cream. Could it be that almost forty years after its original, unheralded release, Klein's movie has finally found its audience — meaning that we've finally caught up with it? "As far as I'm concerned we can never go *beyond* expressionism," Alain Resnais remarked in a 1969 interview, referring specifically to Klein's film. And maybe it took a George W. Bush — a full, real-life embodiment of Klein's ridiculous antihero — to drive home the satiric point.

Sometimes what we call expressionism is a matter of content as well as style. Klein's wide-angle photography and its propensity for caricature, which is also fully evident in his still photography, crops up as well in some of the documentary footage he shot in the U.S. for *Loin de Vietnam* (*Far from Vietnam*) shortly before *Mr. Freedom* — an agitprop feature he and Resnais made collectively, along with Jean-Luc Godard, Agnès Varda, Claude Lelouch, Joris Ivens, and

Chris Marker. I saw *Far from Vietnam* in the fall of 1967, when it concluded the New York Film Festival, and, contrary to *Mr. Freedom*, it created more angry debates than anything else I saw that year. (Paradoxically and lamentably, unlike *Who Are You, Polly Maggoo?* and *Mr. Freedom*, this feature is almost impossible to access today; my own VHS copy was purchased in Tokyo roughly a decade ago.)

In the *Village Voice*, for instance, Andrew Sarris denounced it, in a review later reprinted in his first collection, *Confessions of a Cultist*:

> Zero as art. Some polite applause for Jean-Luc Godard, Alain Resnais, Joris Ivens. They at least tried to make a personal statement. But where was Chris Marker's "unifying" editing? I haven't seen such a patchwork quilt since *Mondo Cane*. The English-language commentary sounds like a parody of the thirties' Stalinist sermon. As for the footage on the big parades in New York earlier this year, the point being made is unclear. The "peace" marches are presented as grotesquely as the "loyalty" marchers, as if all Americans of every political persuasion had gone mad over Vietnam. By contrast, the Vietnamese peasants are neat, alert, and dedicated. It struck me that the film was intended for neither Paris nor New York but for Hanoi.

This attack irritated Sarris's fellow *Voice* columnist Jonas Mekas so much that the following week, Mekas's entire column consisted of a drawn cartoon of a disdainful Sarris watching the film on television. Interestingly enough, the footage of prowar and antiwar marches in New York described as grotesque by Sarris were both shot by Klein, and ironically I assume it was Klein's "personal" use of wide-angle lenses that led to much of Sarris's irritation. (Similar grotesquerie can be found in the faces and wide-angle photographic styles of both Louis Malle's 1960 *Zazie dans le métro*, on which Klein is credited as artistic consultant, and Stanley Kubrick's 1964 *Dr. Strangelove*.) Reviewing the film myself at the time in a student newspaper (as a graduate student at the State University of New York at Stony Brook), I defended it then — and would defend it today — as one of the most powerful documentary statements about the opposition to the U.S. involvement in Vietnam. (In fact, I would cite Emile de Antonio's *In the Year of the Pig* and Joris Ivens and Marceline Loridan's *17th Parallel: Vietnam in War*, both 1968, and the collectively made 1972 *Winter Soldier* as its only real competitors.)

Although I didn't know who Klein was at the time — and it appears that Sarris didn't either — it was his documentary footage in *Far from Vietnam*, comprising roughly a fourth of this two-hour film, that affected me the most. It had far more to say to me than Resnais's uncharacteristic and mannered episode (in which Bernard Fresson pontificates at length in a Paris flat about Hermann

Kahn's *On Escalation* to his wife or girlfriend — a bit that already looked dated in 1967, and was briefly ridiculed by Manny Farber in *Negative Space*), or even Godard's very characteristic monologue from behind a camera, interspersed with clips, about not being able to shoot a film in Vietnam.

Klein's footage appears in two separate parts of the film. The first part — about six minutes long, appearing twenty minutes into the film — deals successively with a 1967 march in New York down 5th Avenue supporting the war and an antiwar demonstration on or near Wall Street that provokes many hecklers, many of whom are seen jeering "Bomb Hanoi!" (This is the only stretch of the film in which the wide-angle distortions are very pronounced, and a few snippets of this march footage are actually recycled in *Mr. Freedom*.) The second part, which comes almost ninety-one minutes into the film — which is far more powerful, and runs for about twenty-three minutes — comes in two sections separated by an intertitle, "Vertigo" (the latter strongly suggesting the intervention of Chris Marker, the film's editor). The first part, dated 1965, is about Norman Morrison, the thirty-one-year-old American Quaker who, following the example of several South Vietnamese Buddhist monks, protested the war by pouring kerosene on himself, lighting a match, and burning himself alive — an act he performed outside Robert McNamara's office at the Pentagon, taking along his one-year-old daughter Emily. This section intercuts a young woman named Ann Uyen serving watermelon to her three children in a Paris garden and calmly explaining the importance of Morrison's act in North Vietnam (where even a street in Hanoi was named after him) and Anne Welsh, Morrison's widow and her own three children, having a meal with others in Baltimore and playing with her kids while she no less calmly explains her own support of her late husband's drastic act. The second part documents the 1967 antiwar march in New York in which close to half a million people participated. In this segment, we also see many concurrent arguments and debates about the war on the street; most memorably, we see a bearded man with a small child, chanting, growling, and screaming the word "napalm" in different intonations, apparently mad as a hatter — until someone in the crowd asks him what the word means, and he abruptly switches gears and proceeds to define it calmly and precisely ("It's a form of jellied gasoline . . ."), in a normal and even tone of voice.

It was probably the episode about Norman Morrison that had the strongest impact — not only in 1967, when I first saw *Far from Vietnam*, but also late last March, when I screened nearly all of this Klein footage with Japanese subtitles for the same audience who had just seen *Mr. Freedom*. Back in 1967, I'd already known about Morrison and what he'd done, but all I'd heard about his act from friends and colleagues and in the press and on television was that he was obviously a madman whose suicide had accomplished nothing.

His act was seen, in short, as an alienating and alienated gesture that epitomized the affectless violence of the period, which is more or less how the same sort of act registered when Jean-Pierre Léaud encountered it on the street in Godard's *Masculine Feminine* (1966). But, like the supposed madman on the street during the antiwar march, Klein's footage challenged me to accept another meaning—and even more remarkably, it did this without any signs of special pleading or tortured rationalization. And late last March, seeing this with my students, it carried a related message: that the true legacy of 1968 wasn't what succeeded or failed politically at the time—it was how much it mattered, and what some people were willing to do in order to achieve it.

The importance of this information wasn't part of the media as I understood it back then, but part of something else. It was like receiving a letter from a friend who lived far away but knew exactly what I was thinking. That's still what matters the most to me in current movies, and the major legacy of 1967–68 for me is the certainty that there are still friends of this kind scattered in various groups across the globe, regardless of the state of our postal delivery.

Moving Image Source (www.movingimagesource.us), posted June 4, 2008; see also www.jonathanrosenbaum.com/?p=7487

Movie Heaven:
Defending Your Life

From the very titles of his four comedy features, we know that Albert Brooks is both a serious and an honest filmmaker, because each one is a precise and accurate indication of what the movie is about: *Real Life, Modern Romance, Lost in America*, and *Defending Your Life*. But what makes Brooks funny is much harder to get at or agree on.

You can't demonstrate how funny Albert Brooks is by quoting any of his one-liners, the way you can the vastly more popular and respected Woody Allen. And you can't say that Brooks is funnier than Allen if you're measuring by the average number of laughs produced. (I find most of *Modern Romance* too painfully accurate to laugh at, although the comic conception remains flawless; and even though the laughs come more readily in Brooks's other pictures, the degree of emotional pain being seriously dealt with is well beyond Allen's range.) Nevertheless, I think Brooks is the best comic writer-director-actor we have in this country at the moment — certainly the most original and thoughtful, and the one who has the most to tell us about who we are.

At his best, Woody Allen excels at eliciting (and soliciting) surface responses, whether he's working in comedy or drama. But despite his flair for intellectual name-dropping, fashionable literary themes, and stylishly derivative mise en scène, none of his movies offers as much genuine and original substance as any of Brooks's in subject, conception, style, feeling, or execution. Yet Brooks, whose original name was Albert Einstein, doesn't wear his brain on his sleeve; his intelligence is so integral to his conceptions and their realizations that one can't reduce it to simple markers — although one could cite his avoidance of close-ups and reaction shots (both Woody staples) and his taste for long takes as emblematic of his more analytical vantage point.

Brooks acknowledges a certain complicity with — as well as distance from —

his somewhat obnoxious heroes. Like Woody Allen, as well as such earlier verbally based comics as Jack Benny and Fred Allen, he sculpts his comic vision around his own persona, and partially invites the audience to identify with that persona; he differs most crucially from Woody Allen in the rigorous critical distance he is able to sustain in relation to that identification. While Brooks's heroes tend to be every bit as regional as Allen's — as tied to the cultural limitations of southern California as Allen's heroes are to the cultural limitations of New York — the worlds they inhabit are not at all comparable. When Allen uncharacteristically turns up in Los Angeles in *Annie Hall*, the city we see is a New Yorker's Los Angeles; but when Brooks turns up in Phoenix, Arizona, in *Real Life* or in Las Vegas and less urban parts of the southwest in *Lost in America*, these areas are not depicted exclusively from a southern California perspective.

In short, Brooks as an artist is able to break away from his roots and see the world outside with some degree of detachment and lucidity, while Allen's artistry, like his persona, is virtually defined by his inability or disinclination to do that. It's theoretically possible to imagine and even visualize the comic grotesqueness of one of Brooks's malcontent heroes actually going to India and working with Mother Teresa;[1] when Allen postulates the heroine of *Alice* doing precisely that, he simply borrows a clip from a Louis Malle documentary to fill in the blanks. At the very least Brooks would explore the idea; at most Allen can only entertain it.

For all their obvious, fascinating differences, all four of Brooks's features are contemporary satires, philosophical parables, and highly realistic comedies about self-defeating behavior. And all of them have something to do with the role played by movies in messing up people's heads and lives. Brooks is the flawed, image-conscious West-coast hero in each one — a filmmaker and comic in *Real Life* (1979), a film editor in *Modern Romance* (1981), and advertising executives in *Lost in America* (1985) and *Defending Your Life*. Acute self-consciousness is a problem that all four of these heroes either engender or encounter.

Interestingly enough, the brassy show-biz type Brooks plays in *Real Life* — so close to Brooks's own public persona that he's called Albert Brooks in the movie — professes to be impervious to all this. Shooting an extended documentary about the life of a "typical" family in the style of the 1973 PBS series *An American Family*, he claims that anything the family does in front of the camera is "right," without admitting that the acute self-consciousness created by his film and camera crew ultimately has more to do with reel life than real life. A related but different sort of obsessive neurosis plagues the self-absorbed editor in *Modern Romance*, who is consumed by alternating bouts of jealousy and romantic fantasy that make him incapable of either ending or revitalizing a longterm relationship. Like the director, he never seems to know when to leave well enough alone; and while his girlfriend (Kathryn Harrold) ultimately seems as trapped in their unresolved relationship as he is, she's the main one dealing with the self-consciousness and embarrassment his behavior creates.

The *Real Life* director ultimately goes berserk when he loses control over both the family being filmed and his picture. By contrast, the *Modern Romance* editor may act like an infant with his girlfriend, but he never loses his professional cool — which he needs in servicing the demands of the director of a routine, low-budget SF picture (played by James L. Brooks) who is every bit as obsessive about his silly picture as the editor is about his silly relationship. (Both characters are compulsive revisers of mundane, imperfect "material" that seems impossible to redeem, much less improve.)

The yuppie admen played by Brooks in *Lost in America* and *Defending Your Life* may seem slightly less demented, but they're equally victims of impulses that belong to their profession. They're constantly trying to sell themselves (and others) concepts that might redeem their inadequate lives. Blowing his top and thereby losing his job when he is offered a New York transfer instead of an expected promotion, the hero of *Lost in America* seizes on his nostalgic '60s memories of *Easy Rider* and sets out with his wife in a fancy mobile home to rediscover America; acute self-consciousness sets in only when he begins to discover how different his dreams are from the reality he encounters.

Daniel Miller, the blinkered hero of *Defending Your Life*, loses his life in the precredits sequence by driving his brand-new $39,000 BMW straight into a bus, after being distracted by the CD albums he has just been given as a birthday present. He finds himself in a secular new-age version of purgatory known as Judgment City, a bland, cheerful holiday resort with themepark trimmings designed especially for recently deceased former inhabitants of the western part of the United States. Daniel gradually discovers that he, like the others, is there to face an examination of his entire life — complete with defender and prosecutor — before he can either proceed to a higher form of existence (if he wins) or return to earth in a fresh reincarnation (if he loses). Only when faced with selected scenes from his life, screened in the form of film clips before a skeletal tribunal, does Daniel acquire the debilitating self-consciousness experienced by Brooks's other heroes. Around the same time — between the first and second of his four sessions with the tribunal — he meets the recently deceased Julia (Meryl Streep), who has led a far more exemplary life than he has. She is one of the few younger arrivals like him, and the two fall deeply in love.

One can say that each of Brooks's movies is structured around a key concept—reality (*Real Life*), romance (*Modern Romance*), "dropping out" (*Lost in America*), and fear (*Defending Your Life*). The ruling principle in Judgment City is that you keep returning to earth in various incarnations until you finally get it right and learn to overcome your fears, at which point you graduate and go on to a higher realm.

We're told early on that most human beings like Daniel use only about 5 percent of their brains, while those who eventually overcome their fears during their various incarnations on earth—including the Judgment City staffers—use closer to half. We're also told early on that Judgment City itself is designed to minimize the fears of the recently deceased who are being examined. By extension we can also say that *Defending Your Life* is designed in order to minimize our fears: this serious examination of the successes and failures of our lives is presented in the form of a lighthearted and fanciful Hollywood cream puff, complete with an improbable happy ending. So the significance of movies in Judgment City isn't merely that Daniel's examination takes place in a windowless chamber that resembles a Hollywood screening room—with Daniel seated in a comfortable revolving chair directly in front of the screen, and with occasional beeps given on the sound track at the beginning of film sequences being reviewed (a standard signal in the film industry used for synching up rushes)—but also that Judgment City itself is constructed and experienced like a Hollywood movie.

This general principle even extends to some of Judgment City's dietary codes: visitors can eat as much as they want without gaining weight. Real people who fill up on popcorn, candy, and pop at the movies obviously gain weight as a result, though many of them are more careful about their diets in the world outside; part of the attraction of movies—and the obvious selling point behind concession counters—is that they encourage one to suspend the usual rules and restrictions that pertain in "normal" life.

A few stray aspects of *Defending Your Life* recall Ernst Lubitsch's *Heaven Can Wait* (a questionable life is reviewed to determine where the deceased should proceed next), Fritz Lang's *Liliom* (an afterlife screening-room tribunal), and Alfred Hitchcock's *North by Northwest* (a flashy, superficial adman gets stripped of his identity and rediscovers it with the help of an ethereal blond; the film's closing shot). But no one can accuse Brooks of cloning this movie from some previous model, as Woody Allen nearly always does; this is a fresh and distinctive work that generates its own rules and bylaws, not a familiar trip down memory lane.

Indeed, much of the comic richness of *Defending Your Life* derives from the thoroughness with which it has mapped out the specifics of Judgment

City. We see billboards and placards heralding the resort's various events and attractions ("Welcome Kiwanis Dead," says one); get glimpses of three coffee-table books in a reception lounge and all the TV channels available in the hotel rooms (including a soap-opera, a game-show, a talk-show, and a "perfect weather" channel); visit four restaurants, two hotel lobbies, a nightclub, and a miniature golf course; and are told about the recently built mini-malls on the outskirts of town. We learn about the quality of the hot dogs at the Past Lives Pavilion (where viewers can sit in individual booths and glimpse some of their previous incarnations, introduced by a Shirley MacLaine hologram) and even find out about some of the minor perks that favored guests receive. (Julia, Daniel discovers, is staying in a plusher hotel, has a Jacuzzi in her bathroom, and finds chocolate cream-filled swans on her pillow; he only gets breath mints.) The dreamlike, slightly overlit cinematography is by Allen Daviau, a longtime associate of Steven Spielberg, and the bleach-bland look of Judgment City may remind us slightly of Spielbergland. But what Brooks does with that resemblance ultimately turns Spielberg on his head: we become aware not only of the pastel-pretty, racially and ethnically homogenized white-bread fantasy — Los Angeles's Century City sprinkled with gold dust by Tinker Bell — but of the fears that call this vision into being.

It's a city modeled, of course, on the world the guests already know — down to their individual defenders, prosecutors, and judges. Daniel's defender, played with juice and gusto by Rip Torn, is an affable salesman type who unctuously slides over information that he assumes Daniel won't understand, while his prosecutor (Lee Grant) is a no-nonsense professional and "Dragon Lady." When Daniel's defender doesn't make it to one of the examining sessions ("I was trapped near the inner circle of thought," he later offers by way of explanation), he is replaced by the glib and reticent Mr. Stanley — a nice comic turn by Buck Henry, who manages to satirize most of the irritating lawyer traits left untouched by Torn and Grant.

During the examination periods, which occupy a fair amount of the movie, we see scenes from Daniel's entire life, and most scenes are given contrasting interpretations by the defender and prosecutor (each of whom selects half the scenes to be reviewed), followed by comments from Daniel himself. (When the defender shows a scene with Daniel in his crib cutting short an argument between his parents with a brief, tearful cry, it's to counter the prosecutor's clip of Daniel at eleven letting himself get creamed by a playground bully. The defender's gloss on the earlier incident is "At this moment, he learned restraint." Daniel's comment is "I feel very good about the restraint idea.")

Most of these scenes are hilarious — there's an especially riotous montage offering excerpts from "164 misjudgments over a twelve-year period" selected by the prosecutor, a wonderful short compendium of sight gags — but it's part of Brooks's special slant on things to make some of the pro and con arguments about the clips even funnier. Taken as a whole, these tribunal sessions ultimately add up to an internal debate on Daniel's part that runs parallel to — and alternates with — his nightly meetings with Julia and their developing relationship. The examinations and the love story increasingly illuminate one another and finally merge to become the same story.

According to the movie's metaphysics, fear and stupidity are virtually the same thing. And nearly all of us in the world today are plagued by the resulting inhibitions — a problem illustrated with particular poignance when the possibility of sex between Daniel and Julia arises. Without a trace of pretension or posturing, Brooks expands this comic perception into a kind of testament about what we go to movies to find and what we do with our lives. It's one sign of his achievement that his fourth brilliant movie is actually the first that ends without a three-part printed epilogue that explains what happened to the characters afterward. Thanks to the fulfillment that we and the characters share by then, nobody even has to ask.

Chicago Reader, April 5, 1991

Note

1. In fact, Brooks, playing some version of himself, wound up going to New Delhi in *Looking for Comedy in the Muslim World* (2005), his most recent feature; see www .jonathanrosenbaum.com/?p=5887. Brooks's two intervening features were *Mother* (1996) and *The Muse* (1999); see www.jonathanrosenbaum.com/?p=6684 and www .jonathanrosenbaum.com/?p–6458. [2009]

The World as a Circus:
Tati's *Parade*

1   Jacques Tati's last feature, *Parade* (1973), is about as unpretentious as a film can get. One of the first films to have been shot mostly in video (on a shoestring budget for Swedish TV), it's a music-hall and circus show featuring juggling, music, gags, pantomime, minor acrobatics, and various forms of audience participation. Though it might seem a natural for TV—and in fact has been shown on TV, as well as theatrically, in Europe—it has never been broadcast in this country. Most critics who have seen it, including many passionate Tati fans, regard it as minor and inconsequential. (A striking and valuable exception is Kristin Thompson, whose article on it appeared in the film journal the *Velvet Light Trap* three years ago.) When, in 1984, a severely mutilated version—missing at least fifteen minutes, including the crucial and sublime epilogue—was released in England, London reviewers who scream bloody murder if slasher films are slightly trimmed couldn't be bothered to raise even a minor protest.

When the uncut movie ran briefly at Facets Multimedia Center three years ago—the only theatrical run it has ever received in the U.S.—practically no one went to see it. Since Tati's movie seems to have joined the legion of the damned, one might well wonder why I am going to the trouble of making a big deal out of it.

I don't wish to argue that *Parade* is a work of undiscovered depths, any more than Tati's other half dozen features are. The paradoxical thing about all of his films is that what you see (and hear) is what you get; like Poe's purloined letter, it's all there, right on the surface—if we are alert enough to observe what is happening right in front of us. But thanks to a lifetime of bad training in watching movies and TV, we often can't be that alert. *Parade* is devoted to showing us how we could be.

2   Sometimes the most radical and profound ideas turn out to be very simple. Some of the most radical and profound ideas in *Parade* are at least as old as Brueghel, although they're a good deal fresher and considerably more advanced than those in any of the commercial features released this year. A few of these ideas can be represented in simple sentences, all of them having to do with the nature of spectacle, and all of them saying pretty much the same thing:

> *There is no such thing as an interruption.*
> *There is no such thing as "backstage."*
> *At no point does life end and "the show" begin — or vice versa.*
> *Amateurs and nobodies — that is to say, ordinary people — are every bit as important, as interesting, and as entertaining as professionals and stars.*
> *Poetry always takes root in mundane yet unlikely places, and it is taking place all around us, at every moment.*

3   Simple ideas, and in the film they're all expressed exclusively in terms of light entertainment; yet sixteen years after *Parade*'s release, they remain elusive, difficult, complex, and highly subversive in relation to most notions about the art of spectacle that circulate today. Worse yet, they are often expressed in terms that are unfashionable, in relation to either 1973 or the present.

When a European rock band performs in the film, for instance, it is the unhippest hippie band imaginable, at least by our own standards, and when we see some of the youths in the bleachers clap and dance to the music, we become painfully aware of Tati's remoteness from that segment of his audience (he was in his mid-sixties when he made *Parade*). Even in *Playtime* (1967), Tati's supreme masterpiece, the gaucheness and lack of stylishness of the leading female character, a young American tourist, represents a stumbling block for many viewers.

Still another potential problem is represented by the visual quality of the video in *Parade*, which is fairly muddy by contemporary standards. Tati was probably the first major filmmaker to shoot in videotape, and he approached it with the same artisanal craft and innovative daring that he brought to cinema; but the technical options available in video in 1973 were far from what they are today. To the best of my knowledge, the only previous theatrical color feature shot mainly or wholly in video was Frank Zappa and Tony Palmer's dreadful *200 Motels* (1971); the visual clarity of *Parade* is light years ahead of the quality of that film, but it is still a far cry from the overall definition available in video transfers today. There are certainly positive and even exciting aspects of witnessing the birth of a new medium (an experience afforded in similar ways by some of the earliest films, made around the turn of the century) — but for a contemporary audience it is also liable to be somewhat disconcerting, or, even worse, disheartening.

4   One of our besetting limitations in relation to art is that we tend to distrust pretension, yet at the same time we're wary of taking entertainment seriously if it doesn't wear art with a capital A on its sleeve. A look at the career of Woody Allen offers distressing evidence of what it takes to be taken seriously as a film artist in this culture: not original uses of image or sound (in fact, the more like secondhand Bergman or Fellini the better), not a unique vision of the world or how to deal with it; all it takes is an array of cultural references and the proper amount of gloom and doom to register true artistic intentions.

Tati's refusal — or inability — to make movies that were fashionable or conventionally slick didn't prevent his first three features — *Jour de fête* (1949), *Mr. Hulot's Holiday* (1953), and *Mon oncle* (1958) — from becoming worldwide hits, each bigger than the last. All three films were highly original and eccentric expressions — in their loose and unconventional attitude toward narrative, in their peculiar handling of humor, in their satirical comments on the periods and milieus in which they were made, in the sorts of characters and behavior they focused on, and in their unique employments of sound, pacing, editing, and framing. Yet the truth of Tati's observations was so immediately recognizable to the general public that none of these idiosyncrasies stood in the way of commercial success.

But when Tati made his most ambitious, accomplished, and expensive movie, *Playtime*, building and expanding upon everything he knew, the public wasn't ready for it. In *Playtime* the five maxims about spectacle cited above — particularly the idea about stars and ordinary people, already integral in many ways to both the conceptions of the previous films and the experiences they offered — were pushed to even more radical and innovative extremes.

In an attempt to sabotage the centrality of Hulot, the character Tati had created and played in his two previous features, Tati in *Playtime* created a series of false Hulots — characters who resembled Hulot from a distance — which deliberately and productively confused both on-screen characters and the audience. (In the final sequence, when Hulot buys a farewell gift for the American tourist, it is significantly one of the false Hulots who winds up delivering it.) But the public only wanted more of their hero Hulot, not a mechanism demonstrating that everyone else — on the screen and in the audience — was equally funny and important.

From then on, Tati's career operated under a shadow that persists to this day—not merely because of the box-office failure of *Playtime*, which landed him in bankruptcy, but also because it had become painfully clear that Tati's vision threatened the politics of spectacle as we know it. The democratic, non-elitist idea that three dozen characters can all be on-screen at once and can all be equally worthy of interest—which is central to the hour-long climactic sequence in *Playtime* devoted to the opening of a restaurant, conceivably the most richly orchestrated piece of mise en scène in the history of cinema—sabotages not only the star system, but principles of story telling, dramaturgy, composition, foreground and background, and moral and social hierarchies central to other movies. And indeed, the immediate consequence of this crisis was that Tati was forced to make a conscious regression in his next film (*Trafic*)—bringing back Hulot as a more central character in a simpler and more conventional story—in order to continue making movies at all. (*Trafic*, one should add, has plenty of beauties and wonders of its own—Tati was incapable of making an indifferent film—but it is significantly the only one of his features that betrays any bitterness. This comes to the surface most noticeably in the treatment of its leading female character—a flashy, phony, and superficial public-relations officer who embodies the pressures of commerce.)

5   I can speak of Tati's intentions with some confidence because I was privileged to have worked for him on an unrealized feature called *Confusion* in 1972, the year after *Trafic* was released. Tati was trapped in the paradox of being loved all over the world for his creation, a character he had grown to detest; it was Hulot who stood in the way of Tati's desire to grow as a filmmaker. This is not to say that Tati had ceased to be a performer; our four- and five-hour work sessions were dominated by his impromptu performances (and my so-called job as "script consultant" consisted of responding to those performances). But it is equally important to note that, for him, the role of performer and the role of spectator were inseparably linked.

He had started out as an athlete and amateur comic whose routines, based on what he saw and heard, led to an extended stint in music halls, and all his movies were vast frescoes of observations that became inventions only when he tried to duplicate and/or develop them. Having lunch with Tati in a bistro mainly consisted of sitting next to him in front of the spectacle of everyday life, which he was constantly reacting to and mimicking; "scripting" a film sequence, for him, mainly consisted of remembering such moments and translating them into shots—duplicating with his body and voice everything that one would see and hear. A purely intuitive rather than intellectual process, based less on words than on sounds and images, it equated acting with watching and watching with acting to such a degree that it dissolved the usual distinctions between the two.

6   *Parade*'s title appears over a drumroll, in the form of a multicolored marquee in the night sky above a circus building, and the camera pulls back from this building before cutting to a closer shot of people filing in. Then the first "gag" occurs — a detail so slight that by conventional standards it hardly qualifies as a gag at all, although it is quintessential Tati: a teenager in line picks up a striped, cone-shaped road marker on the pavement and dons it like a dunce cap; his date laughs, finds another road marker, and does the same thing.

At least three basic Tatiesque principles are set forth in this passing detail. There is the notion of *bricolage*, or the appropriation of impersonal objects for personal use that enables people to reshape and reclaim their environment, an idea central to Tati's work (the restaurant sequence in *Playtime* formulates it on an epic scale), which reaches its distilled essence throughout *Parade*, both offstage and on. (Tati, one should note, directed all the stage acts himself, altering in some instances the performers' usual props, costumes, and gestures, such as getting the jugglers to juggle with paintbrushes — another good example of *bricolage*.)

Then there is the offhand inflection and punctuation of the gag, making it a slightly disorienting moment of strangeness in the midst of normality rather than the conventional setup followed by a payoff. (Critic Jean-André Fieschi has aptly noted that Tati's gags "are not placed in salient positions, as are the *bon mots* in boulevard theater. Every remarkable idea seems clogged, every flash of wit annulled in a kind of imperturbable equalization.") As a consequence, the dunce-cap gag is more likely to make us smile than laugh; but the cumulative effect of dozens of such underplayed gags is to make reality itself seem both slightly off-kilter and alive with comic possibilities — every moment brims with potential gags that often require an audience's alert participation in order to be noticed at all.

Finally, one should note that at the very outset, Tati is placing spectators rather than performers in the primary creative role. The "parade" begins before the audience even enters the theater, as is fully apparent in the brightly colored, festive, and flamboyant clothes worn by the hippies in the audience as well as the props carried by many of the younger kids. The implication of this principle, along with the preceding two, is that Tati's democratic aesthetics are more than just a matter of everything and everyone in a shot being worthy of close attention. They also function on a temporal plane — every shot and moment is worthy of close attention, and a moment without a fully articulated gag is not necessarily inferior to a moment with one, because the spectator's imagination is unleashed by the mere possibility that one might occur.

One of the kids, a little girl wearing a gun and holster, stops briefly inside the lobby to adjust her gear, and briefly makes eye contact with a little boy before each of them is dragged off in opposite directions by his or her respective parent (her mother and his father). These are the same two children who will literally take over the movie in the epilogue, entering the empty stage and playing with various props as they try to reproduce the acts they have seen. They are also seen periodically in the bleachers throughout the show — the girl in the front row, the boy behind her — and their responses to the show and each other are accorded at least as much attention as any of the acts.

7   The movie lingers over a good many other preliminaries before the circus actually begins: people drifting to their seats, musicians tuning up, carpenters and painters (who later prove to be performers) working on props. The fact that these activities are as important as what follows dawns on us only gradually, in part because it becomes difficult to determine when and where the show *does* begin. When the opening trumpet fanfare is played by two clowns in the bleachers, many spectators are still arriving, and the camera seems so distracted by such details that we come to accept the fanfare, the following introduction of performers, and a subsequent drum fanfare as part of the preliminaries, too. Even when Tati himself strolls onstage in a top hat and is greeted by applause, the camera abruptly sweeps past him to settle on the front rows in the bleachers, where the little boy is clearly bored out of his wits, and the little girl, while applauding (along with her mother) in the row ahead, is looking at the boy, not at Tati.

When Tati, the official master of ceremonies, begins to speak, it is in a multilingual, semi-nonsensical patter that goes something like this: "We have the pleasure of presentera a show where everybody can, for I may, I am pleased to include you, me, we are all together around *ménage* called parade —" But then the camera cuts away from him again to focus on the drifting trajectories of a wandering toddler, proceeds out into the lobby to linger on a latecomer checking his motorcycle helmet at the cloakroom (which makes a loud clunk when it hits the counter), remains with the befuddled female attendant surrounded by a sea of other helmets, then proceeds down a hallway to the comic entrances and exits of a hockey player and a violinist. When the camera finally returns to the auditorium, it is to the bleachers, where another motorcyclist is asked by the woman seated behind him to remove his helmet so she can see better — but his decompressed hair creates even more of an obstruction.

Finally we get to see the musicians playing onstage, but from an oblique over-head angle that includes the stage rigging.

Even when the camera spends more time on the stage, the physical borders of spectacle and audience are broken down through a variety of means. The painters and carpenters working on props are frequently visible and even prominent as spectators during some of the acts. (Only much later, when a painter starts competing with an onstage magician in performing card tricks, and when several of the painters start juggling with their paintbrushes, does it become fully apparent that these characters are "performers" rather than "extras.") An onstage row of fake bleachers containing black-and-white cutouts of spectators is integrated into some of the acts; this effect is undermined in turn when real spectators are later glimpsed in the same spot, or when fake spectators are glimpsed in the actual bleachers. Time and space often become mutable (as they are in Raúl Ruiz's dance film *Mammame*), but the premise as well as the illusion of a show taking place in real time and on a single stage is rigorously maintained.

8   Among the acts included—tumblers, musical novelties, a singer (Pia Colombo) introduced from the audience, and an audience-participation inter-lude involving an obstreperous mule—are many of Tati's most famous music-hall pantomimes, depicting a football game, a fisherman, a tennis match, a tennis player circa 1900, and a horseback rider. The continuity between these solo routines and Tati's directorial style is that both appeal to a spectator's imagination through a panoply of subtle suggestions. (Reviewing one of Tati's mime performances in 1936, Colette wrote, "He has created at the same time the player, the ball and the racket; the boxer and his opponent; the bicycle and its rider. His powers of suggestion are those of a great artist.")

While it might seem from the foregoing description that Tati somehow undercuts the performers (himself included) in order to glorify the spectators, he actually treats them all with respect. His directorial sleight of hand keeps bringing the audience into the act, but never in such a way that it betrays or impugns the talents of the performers. It is the ideology of spectacle and its attendant hierarchies that he is out to dismantle—not the pleasures of spectacle itself, which he is in fact inclined to spread around liberally and democratically, emphasizing their continuities with everyday life.

9   A central aspect of *Parade* that makes it more contemporary and more in tune with advanced filmmaking than all its other qualities is complex interaction between nonfiction and fiction, chance and programming—a dialectical approach followed with comparable fruitfulness in such films as Jacques

Rivette's *Out 1: Spectre*, Orson Welles's *F for Fake*, Chris Marker's *Sans soleil*, Françoise Romand's *Mix-Up*, Claude Lanzmann's *Shoah*, Joris Ivens and Marceline Loridan's *A Story of the Wind*, and the most recent works of Peter Thompson and Leslie Thornton.

Tati began by shooting with an audience in the circus building for three days, using four video cameras. Then he spent twelve days in a studio reshooting portions of the stage acts in 35-millimeter. Thus he wound up with a film that combines spontaneous and planned material on video with planned material on film, and although the visual definition in the studio-filmed portions is noticeably sharper, the mixture of materials is so deft in other respects that it is generally impossible to separate the documentary segments from the fictional details. The sole exception to this is the film's epilogue and *pièce de résistance*, in which the boy and girl are left alone with the stage props after the show has ended. Tati shot two hours of their improvised play with several video cameras, then extracted the few minutes that are used in the film.

The studio shooting of *Playtime*, which entailed the construction of an entire city set, precluded such experimentation — the only real location used in the film is the exterior of Orly airport — but some early forays into documentary can be found in certain sequences of *Trafic*, detailing the behavior and habits of various drivers, which are so gracefully threaded into the rest that they register as a continuation of the fiction rather than a departure from it.

10   Expanding this technique considerably, *Parade* creates a privileged zone of its own in which the free play between fiction and nonfiction becomes an open space to breathe in. It is a utopian space where equality reigns between spectators and performers, children and adults, foreground and background, entertainment and everyday life, reality and imagination — an evening's light diversion that, if taken seriously, as it was meant to be, could profitably crumble the very ground beneath our feet.

Chicago Reader, December 1, 1989; see also www.thefanzine.com/articles/film/256/jacques_tati%27s_trafic_on_criterion_dvd

The Sun Also Sets:
The Films of Nagisa Oshima

No major figure in postwar Japanese cinema eludes classification more thoroughly than Nagisa Oshima. The director of twenty-three stylistically diverse feature films since his directorial debut in 1958, at the age of twenty-six, Oshima is, arguably, the best-known but least understood proponent of the Japanese New Wave that came to international prominence in the 1960s and '70s (though it is a label Oshima himself rejects and despises). Given the size of his oeuvre and the portions that remain virtually unknown in the West—including roughly a quarter of his features and most of his twenty-odd documentaries for television—the temptation to generalize about his work must be firmly resisted.

But to grasp at least how Oshima situates himself, 100 Years of Japanese Cinema, the fifty-two-minute documentary he made for the British Film Institute in 1994, provides a helpful start. That he was offered this assignment at all is comical, given his oft-expressed and unyielding hatred of Japanese cinema as a whole, including his own films. He expressed this aversion in his first major interview in Cahiers du cinéma in March 1970, when he told his interlocutors that Europeans who praised Japanese cinema for its formal beauty should speak more about its content. At the time, one should note, these critics had only recently learned how to love Kurosawa in addition to Mizoguchi (whom they had championed since the '50s), without having yet discovered Ozu or Naruse. Oshima detested all four. A quarter of a century later, offering a leftist and almost exclusively content-driven survey of his subject in 100 Years, he chose to mind his manners—even if he restricted Ozu, Mizoguchi, and Kurosawa to I Was Born, But . . . (1932), Osaka Elegy (1936), and No Regrets for Our Youth (1946), respectively, and omitted Naruse entirely.[1] In covering the period that encompasses his own career, he obligingly switches from third to first per-

son in his narration, and the eight titles he cites from his own filmography—
Cruel Story of Youth (1960), *Night and Fog in Japan* (1960), *Death by Hanging*
(1968), *Boy* (1969), *The Ceremony* (1971), *In the Realm of the Senses* (1976),
Merry Christmas, Mr. Lawrence (1983), and *Max, Mon Amour* (1986)—constitute (apart from the last item) a credible rundown of his greatest directorial
achievements. (Since then, he has made one more feature, arguably another
aesthetic high point—1999's *Taboo*, a haunting and dreamlike tale center-
ing on a beautiful, androgynous, and narcissistic merchant's son recruited to
become a samurai warrior in the Shinsengumi militia, a nationalist legion
assigned to protect the shogun.)[2] In *100 Years of Japanese Cinema*, Oshima
claims that his principal contribution was to introduce new kinds of subject
matter relating to politics, war, and sex into the national cinema.

Oshima suggests in the documentary that *Max, Mon Amour*, shot in Paris
with a European cast, may not even be Japanese. Cowritten with Jean-Claude
Carrière and produced by Serge Silberman (the two had together famously
teamed with Luis Buñuel on his French and Spanish films of the '60s and
'70s), this comic tale about a British diplomat's wife (Charlotte Rampling) having a fling with a chimpanzee mostly registers as a failed attempt at Buñuelian
whimsy. But the film's internationalism relates to Oshima's point: The last line
in his commentary equates the future "blossoming" of Japanese cinema with
its capacity to "free itself from the spell of Japanese-ness." And considering
how preoccupied with Japan he remains—his ambitious work *The Ceremony*
is virtually an attempt to psychoanalyze the country over a quarter of a century,
as Maureen Turim, his most astute American commentator, has implied[3]—
this sounds like a classic case of a filmmaker turned against himself. He often
comes across as a man who hates Japan almost as much as he hates Japanese
cinema yet is hard put to come up with any other sustaining topic.

Born in 1932 to an aristocratic Kyoto family with samurai ancestors, Oshima
studied law at Kyoto University and became deeply engaged there in the leftist
student movement that would become increasingly anti-American and anti-
Communist. (The bloody demonstrations against the US-Japanese Security
Treaty of 1960 and the internal struggles of the student movement are the
primary focus of *Night and Fog in Japan*.) By the time Oshima turned to filmmaking, in his twenties, he had already come to regard cinema chiefly as a
means to political ends.

Starting out as a contract director for Shochiku Studios—albeit one who
quickly acquired auteurist credentials, as suggested by his brief appearances
in some trailers for his first features—he went independent after the political
and formal provocations of *Night and Fog in Japan* prompted the studio to suppress it a few days into its initial run. (His actress wife, Akiko Koyama, who has

played in many of his independent films, also started out at Shochiku, though he found most of his other recurring collaborators, such as writer Tamura Tsutomu and cinematographer Akira Takada, only after leaving the studio.) Shochiku went on to distribute some of his independent features, however, and Oshima eventually returned to that studio to make *Taboo*.

On a Japan Foundation visitor's fellowship in 1999, I was able to view some of *Taboo*'s sets shortly after the film was completed and had been screened for the Japanese press, mostly to favorable reactions. In the mid-nineties, while Oshima was on a speaking tour of the United Kingdom, he had suffered a stroke, leaving the right side of his body paralyzed and delaying the start of shooting. He directed from a wheelchair, and given his failing health, it seems unlikely that he will direct another feature. The filming of *Taboo* was done in Kyoto, using a few temples for some of the exteriors and the Shochiku studio specializing in period films for everything else. (The studio was the same one where Mizoguchi shot *The Story of the Last Chrysanthemums* in 1939.) Accordinging to a film scholar who followed the shooting, Oshima's direction focused on the placement and moves of the camera rather than on the actors — many of whom, such as Takeshi Kitano, were among the most popular in Japan and were accorded a fair amount of autonomy.

Ironically and surprisingly, Oshima is perhaps best known in Japan today as a television talk-show host and guest. I saw him once on TV during my visit, and he came across as something like a Japanese Oprah Winfrey. When I later asked leftist film critic Tadao Sato if being on TV had forced Oshima to compromise his politics, he replied that, on the contrary, it had enabled him to express his political positions to a wider audience.

Oshima's cinema consists of particular interventions in Japan's internal political debates, and freely draws on forms as well as styles that seem to come from everywhere, including Japan. Some would call this disconcertingly voracious trait "very Japanese," and it helps to account for the truism that no two Oshima films are alike. Each new feature critiques its predecessors: After vowing to abolish green from his palette in his first foray into color, *Cruel Story of Youth*, as a way of refusing any trace of domestic tranquility, he used green frequently and effectively two features later (without suggesting much domestic tranquility), in his first truly personal work, *Night and Fog in Japan*, meanwhile countering the earlier film's neorealist locations and handheldcamera movements with artificially lit theatrical spaces and smooth if restless pans between characters at a wedding party. Both films are steeped in the dark pessimism characteristic of Oshima's films of the '60s.

The focus on aggressive or outlaw eroticism in the director's five most recent features — *In the Realm of the Senses*; *Empire of Passion* (1978); *Merry*

Christmas, Mr. Lawrence; Max, Mon Amour; and *Taboo*—could be seen as a function of his growing political despair, an overall shift in his explorations of freedom from public to private spheres. But this is an inadequate way of summing up these odd films, especially the first and third, which can be described respectively as thoughtful and provocative hard-core porn (which has yet to show in Japan in undoctored form), and a bold foray into bilingual, crosscultural filmmaking that has often been compared to David Lean's *The Bridge on the River Kwai* (1957) but might now be viewed more interestingly as an anticipation of Clint Eastwood's recent World War II diptych (though Oshima is more critical of Japan). *Merry Christmas* could likewise be described as a broaching of a certain politically incorrect homoeroticism, which eventually gets reconfigured in *Taboo*. Although *In the Realm of the Senses*—based on the true 1936 story of renegade prostitute Sada Abe, who erotically asphyxiated her lover Kichizo Ishida with his seeming complicity, then severed his penis and testicles and carried them around in her purse for several days—cannot be said to contradict the tragic vision of twentieth-century Japan that underlies Oshima's work, it may nevertheless qualify as his most celebratory feature, in its emphasis on the pleasure and rapture of sex. By contrast, *Merry Christmas, Mr. Lawrence*—conceived as a kind of ideological and macho/erotic duel between pop stars David Bowie and Ryuichi Sakamoto in a Japanese POW camp during World War II—more typically views sex in terms that are mainly punitive.

Where Oshima differs most strikingly from an antisentimental, leftist provocateur like Buñuel is in the relative absence of humanism in his work. (*Boy*, a mainly sympathetic look at a lonely ten-year-old con artist, is a rare exception.) If *The Sun's Burial* (1960)—an early shocker about rival street gangs in an Osaka slum—was partly inspired by Buñuel's *Los Olvidados* (1950), as the British DVD's liner notes maintain, the notion of Oshima showing any tenderness toward his doomed punks, as Buñuel does toward Jaibo, is unthinkable—even if Oshima is no less outraged by corpses being dumped like garbage. And the repeated occurrences of sexual assault (mainly rape) in *Cruel Story of Youth, The Sun's Burial, Violence at Noon* (1966), *Sing a Song of Sex* (1967), *Death by Hanging, Diary of a Shinjuku Thief* (1968), *The Man Who Left His Will on Film* (1970), *Empire of Passion*, and *Merry Christmas, Mr. Lawrence*—usually committed by his protagonists and often seen as acts of rebellion against the Japanese state (a view at least contested in *Death by Hanging*)—suggest that, with the possible exception of *In the Realm of the Senses*, feminism and nonviolence are not exactly hallmarks of his leftist positions.

Oshima's preoccupation with Japan, central to most of his films, has many formal consequences. The most striking of these is a graphic obsession with the national flag that gets applied quite differently — though most often ironically or tragically — from film to film. This fixation, neither as abstract nor as playful as it might first appear, usually reveals profound intellectual and emotional conflicts about his subject matter.

Sometimes his employments are mainly anecdotal — as when, for example, near the beginning of *In the Realm of the Senses*, a little girl exposes an old male beggar's genitals with the tip of her tiny Japanese flag. And sometimes they are simply emblematic or metaphoric and proliferate in every direction, as in the black-and-white *Death by Hanging*. The film begins like a documentary about capital punishment (evocative of Alain Resnais's 1955 *Night and Fog* in both its exploratory camera movements and the narration's focus on banal details) before gravitating into a didactic, deconstructive comedy-satire, complete with Brechtian section headings, about the philosophical, existential, ethical, social, racist, and bureaucratic assumptions underlying the attempted execution of a twenty-three-year-old Korean named R for raping and killing two Japanese schoolgirls. The scenario was inspired by the 1958 real-life case of Ri Chin'u, and it is surprising how hilarious Oshima manages to make much of it; the plot and theme development intermittently and improbably call to mind a slapstick version of *Native Son*. After R strangely refuses to die and undergoes a form of amnesia, state dignitaries and functionaries proceed frantically to reenact his crime to refresh his memory. The execution chamber is at one point theatrically converted into R's family home, the walls covered by newspaper pages. In a small section of one of these walls, inside what resembles a fairground booth, the public prosecutor and a security guard, with a huge Japanese flag directly behind them, preside over these reenactments. (No less pointedly, an unfurled American flag can also be seen inside this boxed-in space.) Later, R and his sister are discovered jointly using a still bigger Japanese flag as a bedsheet. And in the final sequence, R's face in close-up as seen through an empty hangman's noose is made to rhyme eerily with the sizable wall flags that frame all the major concluding speeches.

Thematically and plastically, Oshima's flag obsession goes far beyond Jean-Luc Godard's ironic uses of tricolored compositions suggested by the French and American flags in some of his more politically oriented pre-1968 color films. In *The Sun's Burial*, where the flag is even implicit in the title, we get many apocalyptic images of the setting sun punctuating the grim narrative. In *The Ceremony*, the obsession arguably has something to do with the film's compulsive center framing, suggesting a kind of ongoing critique both of rituals (mainly weddings and funerals) and of symmetry within the orderly CinemaScope compositions that frame them — rituals and symmetry that are moreover constantly on the verge of capsizing in various perverse and grotesque ways.

In *Boy*, which uses 'Scope even more brilliantly, the flag figures in everything from the abstract design behind the credits — a variation on the credits of *Sing a Song of Sex* (a film featuring an alternate version of the national standard, with a black sun instead of a red one at the center of a white field) — to strategically placed Japanese flags and many rhyming images, such as the splatter of blood on a snow-covered ground and the title hero's planting of a red boot in the center of a snowman.

In this film, moreover, Oshima creates a potent dialectic between the center framing suggested by the flag and a reverse compositional strategy. The film is based on a famous news story from 1966 about parents who taught their ten-year-old boy to pretend to be hit by cars so they could then collect damages from the drivers via guilt-tripping or threatening to go to the police, the family of four meanwhile moving constantly across the country to stay ahead of the law. So *Boy* is conceived as a kind of travelogue of perpetual estrangement, frequently locating its characters at the far edges of the frames in order to articulate their profound separation from wherever they happen to be. And the significance of the red boot in the snowman is that it belonged to a little girl accidentally killed in one of the staged accidents.

However one slices up Oshima's career, it is still hard to reconcile his profile as a mainstream television personality with his commitment to radical politics and with the avant-garde moves of some of his films. But it is important to stress that his avant-garde gestures, even when they yield the throwaway, anything-goes construction of *Diary of a Shinjuku Thief* or the opaqueness of *The Man Who Left His Will on Film*, are seldom dilettantish. Tadao Sato has argued that the stripped-down, neotheatrical settings of both *Night and Fog in Japan* and *Death by Hanging* partly derived from constraints of time and budget, and one might add that Oshima's more radical representational strategies, including his diverse uses of the flag, are generally dictated by intellectual content. Maureen Turim aptly notes that R in *Death by Hanging* evokes X, A, and M, the central characters of Resnais's *Last Year at Marienbad*; she could have added that Oshima's deconstructive methodology throughout the film often suggests a highly politicized retooling of some of *Marienbad*'s procedures involving memory and persuasion.

Deeply marked by their sense of historical moment, regardless of whether they happen to be contemporary or period films, Oshima's most potent works — *Death by Hanging*, *Boy*, and, more debatably, *In the Realm of the Senses* — are significantly all inspired by newspaper stories. Whether one winds up regarding their flamboyance as sincere or opportunistic, their mastery in alternating silence with imaginative employments of sound, mobile mise en scène with the sudden insertions of stills, and subjective fantasies with social reality is irrefutable. It is characteristic of Oshima's flexibility (or fickleness) that he can cheerfully jettison his own carefully established codes of realism at the drop of a hat, such as when he allows David Bowie in *Merry Christmas, Mr. Lawrence*, Oshima's most mainstream picture, to survive a firing squad without explanation. If we are still puzzling over the logic and fractured unity of this iconoclast's work, it is entirely to his credit that he invites and shares our curiosity.

Artforum, October 2008

Notes

1. In fact, though Oshima has never been any sort of cinephile, even when he functioned as a film critic, at least two of these filmmakers have marked him, in very different ways. He once admitted that seeing the aforementioned Kurosawa film at the age of fourteen was what persuaded him to attend Kyoto University. And much of *Taboo* registers as a multifaceted tribute to Mizoguchi—the long takes, the nearly constant camera movements, the Kabuki-like ostentation, and the ghostly and atmospheric studio expressionism. There is even a direct allusion in the dialogue to the eighteenth-century literary source of Mizoguchi's *Ugetsu*, Akinari Ueda's classic *Tales of the Moonlight and Rain*.

2. "Taboo" is not an accurate translation of the original title, *Gohatto*—a somewhat old-fashioned term meaning "against the law" or "against the laws." (One fascinating aspect of the Japanese language from a Western perspective is its lack of distinction between singular and plural nouns, which injects ambiguity into many titles.)

3. See Maureen Turim, *The Films of Oshima Nagisa: Images of a Japanese Iconoclast* (Berkeley: University of California Press, 1998), 117–23.

Part 3

Films

Inside the Vault [on *Spione*]

If Fritz Lang's *Die Nibelungen* (1924) anticipates the pop mythologies of everything from *Fantasia* to *Batman* to *Star Wars*, his master spy thriller of four years later seems to usher in some of the romantic intrigues of Graham Greene, not to mention much of the paraphernalia of Ian Fleming, especially in their movie versions. No less suggestively, the employments of paranoia and conspiracy by less mainstream artists such as Jacques Rivette (*Out 1*) and Thomas Pynchon (*Gravity's Rainbow*) seem rooted in the seductively coded messages, erotic intrigues, and multiple counterplots of *Spione*.

One is also tempted to speak of Alfred Hitchcock, who certainly learned a trick or two from Lang—though in this case the conceptual and stylistic differences may be more pertinent than the similarities. One could generalize by saying that Hitchcock is more interested in his heroes while Lang is more interested in his villains, and the different approaches of each director in soliciting or discouraging the viewer's identification with his characters are equally striking, especially if one contrasts the German films of Lang with the American films of Hitchcock.

Comparing Giorgio Moroder's reedit of *Metropolis* with Lang's original, film scholar Thomas Elsaesser has theorized that "much of 20s German cinema was based on a visual grammar different from what we have come to accept as the norm, namely Hollywood-type continuity editing. Moroder gives the narrative a unilinear direction, via establishing shot, scene-dissection, close-up, by the simple expedient of relying on reverse-field editing, and point-of-view shots to generate continuity, cutting out most of the inserts which in Lang's version had separated — in time and in space — the characters' looks from their objects." For Elsaesser, "the hallmark of Lang's style" that's missing in Moroder's *Metropolis*—and, by implication, in most Hollywood movies, including Hitchcock's — "is precisely the interpolation of disorienting or disrupting visuals into the classic match-cut sequence, making what is represented seem ambiguously motivated and always happening at one remove."[1]

Paradoxically, the results of this style can be described as more objective and distanced yet also more abstract and dreamlike, because the continuities established are more metaphysical than physical, and sometimes more irrational than rational in the bargain. For related reasons, including its voluptuous performances, *Spione* is easily the most erotic of Lang's German films, and perhaps the only one (discounting a few mad moments in *Metropolis*) that borders on the pornographic.

Significantly, the villain, Haghi (Rudolf Klein-Rogge — who had already played both the title role in *Dr Mabuse der Spieler* and Rotwang, the villain in *Metropolis*) — is more central and prominent than the hero (Willy Fritsch), who's identified in the credits only as "No. 326." It is Haghi, after all, who is the first and last character of any importance that we see in the film. Architecturally, he's the principal support of Lang's house of fiction, holding up the entire structure, because every narrative path leads either up to him or away from him; like a telephone switchboard, he's plugged into everyone and everything. In this respect, he clearly functions as Lang's surrogate — an all-knowing puppetmaster who not only creates and animates the plot but also ultimately terminates it when he finds himself cornered in the final sequence. Disguised as an onstage clown, he shoots himself in the head as part of his act, soliciting a round of applause from the onscreen audience and thereby ending the film itself as the curtain falls. (The fact that Klein-Rogge was the first husband of Lang's wife and co-writer Thea von Harbou only enhances his role as Lang's *doppelgänger*.)

Lang shares with Orson Welles a taste for using powerful authoritarian figures to forge a kind of autocritique of his own artistic practice and its will to power. He differs in using actors other than himself to play these roles and in his emphasis on sadomasochism — as well as his curious interest in tyrants figuring as pimps and erotic matchmakers, which is particularly pronounced here.

■ ■ ■ ■ ■ ■ ■ ■ ■

The first film to have been made by Lang's own production company, *Spione* economized in time and money after the outsized expenditures of both on *Metropolis*, his previous film. However, given Lang's clout and preeminence during this period — even after *Metropolis* failed to make back its budget — one shouldn't conclude from this that his resources were any less lavish. The shooting of *Metropolis* consumed 310 days; though the shooting of *Spione* only took about a third as long — fifteen weeks, or about a hundred days — this was still, according to Lang in a 1969 interview, over twice as much time as he was allowed on any of his Hollywood films, where he "never had more than 42 or 45 days."[2]

Immensely popular with the German public, *Spione* was the first film ever carried to the U.S. by plane, where it was released by MGM in a substantially shorter version — fifty-odd minutes less than the original 143. This reedited version, with No. 326 renamed "Donald Tremaine" — presumably as a concession to the Anglo-American audience — has been the main version available until this new restoration. As far as I'm aware, it hasn't been proven that Lang oversaw the abridgement of the export version, but it seems likely he did given how much of the film's original conception and editing was retained, in contrast to the relative butchery carried out on *Metropolis* after its own initial release. Even the most glaring difference in the editing is highly instructive in the way it highlights the film's overall Lego-like construction of almost interchangeable parts — a facet that seems to be one of Lang's main preoccupations throughout. This is a scene in a post office in which the hero writes to his headquarters a message whose contents are intercepted by the villain's lackeys through the carefully prepared-for ruse of reading the message's impressions on a blotter. In the original, this event occurs about ninety minutes into the film, but in the export version it was moved up to a position near the beginning, shortly after the hero makes his first appearance. Thanks to this radical shift, the country where the scene takes place isn't the same and the message isn't the same, yet the function of the scene is almost identical.[3]

One might argue that *Spione* was in some respects a more personal project for Lang than its gargantuan predecessor — even though, ironically, one of its most personal touches is in fact a cluster of posters for *Metropolis* seen on a city street at night, surely one of the first in-jokes of its kind. Superficially, this entertaining movie might appear to be a simple yielding to public taste in its emphasis on straight-ahead action and sexy intrigue, but it's actually a return to Lang's sources — a kind of compression and refinement of his 1922 *Dr Mabuse der Spieler* (with its villain made into even more of an abstraction by virtue of the sheer unmotivated gratuitousness of his schemes) as well as the even more lurid 1919 *Die Spinnen* before it. (It's also a brilliant forecast of the *découpage* of *M* that links together diverse social forces in a montage pattern structured around a central figure who goads these forces into action and eventually becomes their victim).

There seems to be general agreement now that the most seminal of Lang's early influences was Louis Feuillade serials like *Fantômas* (1914), *Les vampires* (1916), *Judex* (1917), and *Tih Minh* (1919) — paranoid crime thrillers that were often drawn from newspaper serials or *feuilltons*, mainly filmed in natural locations and sometimes improvised, following the mysterious adventures of high-tech, conspiratorial gangs that preyed on the rich. (The comic servants in *Les vampires* and *Tih Minh* who are more resourceful than their masters are recalled in No. 326's valet cleaning up after his employer when the hero turns up in his deluxe hotel suite in his sooty tramp disguise.) Though Lang was more prone to shoot in studios and plot out his stories in advance, he had an unapologetic taste for the same sort of pulp fiction derived from both newspaper stories and current events as the criminal exploits celebrated by Feuillade, and *Spione* can be regarded as the apotheosis of that tendency in Lang's work. In films of this kind, he remarked to Jean Domarchi and Jacques Rivette in 1959, citing specifically *Dr Mabuse der Spieler* and *Spione*, "there is only pure sensation, character development doesn't exist."[4] Neither does social analysis in the case of *Spione*, at least in any ordinary sense — though arguably the social implications of Lang's formal patterning remain relevant on a more subterranean level, as a kind of dream material.

Spione was directly inspired by a story in the London *Times* during the mid-1920s about the so-called Arcos raid. A special branch of Scotland Yard raided a Russian trade company called the All Russian Co-operative Society, or Arcos for short, under the suspicion that it was a spy ring. To be sure, Lang's desire to exploit newspaper headlines and public fears would achieve a different kind of fruition when he combined it with overt social analysis a few years later in *M* — something he had already done to some extent in *Dr Mabuse der Spieler*.

However, the more disreputable fantasy-based elements of this impulse in *Spione* are a bit harder to separate from Lang's social conscience and his analytical impulses than one might initially suppose. Indeed, critic Tom Gunning persuasively argues that Lang himself would subsequently confuse *Spione* with *Dr Mabuse* in his memory while describing the latter's relevance to contemporary events.[5] Norbert Jacques, whose novel provided the source of *Mabuse*, was more culturally respectable than Pierre Souvestre and Marcel Allain (the latter two co-authored the original *Fantômas feuilleton*), at least to the extent that he was viewed by some as a social commentator and not merely a spinner of tales. Yet a desire to exploit the irrationality of certain contemporary public fears could surely be found in both sources. At least part of the difference in cultural prestige between, say, *Fantômas* and *Dr Mabuse*, or between *Mabuse* and *Spione*, was attributable to fashion. Even the French Surrealists provocatively defended a Feuillade serial in 1928 (the year of *Spione*'s release) without mentioning its director by name: a character in a play written by Louis Aragon and André Breton declares, "It's in *Les vampires* that one must look for the great realities of this century."

German intellectuals of the period such as Rudolf Arnheim and Siegfried Kracauer who would later be respectful of *M* regarded *Spione* with a certain amount of scorn. (Both seemed especially irritated by the elaborate ballyhoo surrounding the publication of von Harbou's spinoff novel of the same title, as if it were a literary classic.) Comparing *Spione* to *Mabuse*, Kracauer argued that both films "refrained from conferring moral superiority upon the representatives of the law. Espionage and counterespionage were on the same level — two gangs fighting each other in a chaotic world. Yet there was one important difference: while Dr. Mabuse had incarnated the tyrant who takes advantage of the chaos around him, the master spy [Haghi] indulged in the spy business for the sole purpose, it seemed, of spying. He was a formalized Mabuse devoted to meaningless activities."[6]

Insofar as the treaty in *Spione* stolen by Haghi's agents from Matsumoto (Lupu Pick), a Japanese diplomat, is important only because it's stolen, not because of its contents, it's easy enough to see Kracauer's point. Arnheim arrived at a similar conclusion, but gave more prominence to the film's validation of technology. For him, Lang "fabricates castles in the air from telephones, telegraphs, neon signs, microphones, switches, and signal lamps. . . . The utensils of technology serve the artisan's purpose solely, the formulas are only for decoration. . . . The personages in this film seem to have been engaged less for espionage purposes than for the operation of the technical instruments."[7]

It's difficult to refute these charges of formalism and technological fetishism (the latter of which would return in force with the James Bond films). Strangest of all, the patches of the film that carry the most emotional charge, all having to do with sex or honor — the manipulation of Sonja (Gerda Maurus) by Haghi; the seduction of Matsumoto by Kitty (Lien Deyers), the ghosts of his slain emissaries returning to haunt him, his eventual hari-kari — register like subplots, detaching themselves from the main lines of action as if they were afterthoughts.

Yet it's also possible to argue that Lang's emphasis on process over everything else is precisely what remains so fascinating and compelling about *Spione*. He strips the spy-thriller form down to its basics and reveals in the course of this purification the underlying mechanisms of that form. And he does this above all by making his plot as abstractly generic as possible — set in an unnamed country where an unmotivated villain assuming various disguises and enlisting many spies and emissaries, mainly through coercion, contrives to steal unspecified government documents and intercept an equally undescribed treaty. Even when Lang resorts to oblique social commentary — such as the fat capitalist saved from a fatal bullet by the wad of fat bills in his pocket — the jokey concept doesn't rebound on the villain, who supposedly runs a bank (and whose only comment about his wealth is "I'm richer than Ford, even though I pay less taxes"). And Kracauer's implicit charge that the forces of good and the forces of evil are virtually made equivalent seems borne out by many of the formal rhymes, e.g., No. 326's face lathered with shaving cream echoed by Haghi's clown make-up.

■ ■ ■ ■ ■ ■ ■ ■ ■

There are two key recurring shots in the film that function as narrative pivots while also providing both questions and answers regarding the plot's machinations, thereby pretending to explain the inexplicable. (*Spione*'s opening intertitle: "Throughout the world . . . strange events transpire.") One of these shots is a close-up of Haghi's face, sometimes wreathed in cigarette smoke; the other is a network of crisscrossing iron stairways and four tiered balconies that are apparently just outside his secret headquarters. (This is more a felt proximity than a demonstrated one — implied by the editing and the absence of any exterior shots as people proceed from these stairways and balconies into Haghi's office.) Each of these images simultaneously explains everything and explains nothing, functioning repeatedly as a spatial and narrative transition between blocks of material that otherwise seem disconnected. In this respect they suggest a kind of narrative-based recasting of the famous Kuleshov experiment whereby unrelated shots create a fusion of meaning through the viewer's imagination.

The close-up of Haghi first appears immediately after a government official asks himself, "Almighty God — what power is at play here?" It's a rhetorical question, asked when a messenger has just dashed into his office to disclose the identity of a culprit involved in the theft of state documents and the assassination of a trade minister — events that are breathlessly depicted in the film's opening moments — and is shot through the glass window pane by an unseen assailant before he can pronounce the name. And the rhetorical answer to this rhetorical question is Haghi's close-up, concluding the film's prologue with the equivalent of another question mark.

The second key image occurs much later, after we've been introduced to No. 326 — a government spy disguised as a tramp who's summoned to his chief's office, where he promptly exposes the miniature hidden camera of a counterspy posing as an office assistant (the first of many James Bond gadgets *avant la lettre*). Then we return to Haghi, this time seen from behind at his desk, being presented by lackeys with photographs of No. 326 in his tramp attire taken by another miniature camera. When we return to Haghi again a little later (introduced by the intertitle "The Enemy . . ."), smoking a cigarette and barking out orders over an intercom, another intertitle introduces us to

"His Headquarters," which proves to be a prison, and three shots later we have our first glimpse of the crisscrossing stairways and balconies — a complex of pathways made even more intricate by the people walking up, down, or across each of them. Like the animated shot in the prologue of radio towers sending out widening signals, this image forms a kind of dialectic with the glowering close-ups of Haghi by offering multidirectional movements instead of stasis, suggesting the tentacles of an octopus.

The irrationality of this image is that it's a prison block yet we're also informed that Haghi runs a bank bearing his name and that his office is inside that bank. The dreamlike logic according to which Haghi works inside both a prison and a bank, doubling as prison warden and bank president, is only compounded by the fact that Haghi sits in a wheelchair (shades of Dr. Strangelove) and is attended to by an elderly nurse, suggesting that he may even be a patient inside a hospital — a hospital that he also runs.

Like Mabuse before him, Haghi can rule and manipulate the diverse sectors of society without leaving home. But in this case the home itself becomes an image of that society — an enclosed city that evokes the one in *Metropolis*, full of hidden, windowless chambers that might be prison cells, bank vaults, and/or hospital rooms. And, again as in *Metropolis*, Freud plays a more significant role than Marx in determining the schema of this bizarre layout — despite the fact that Haghi is deliberately made up to resemble Lenin.

Or is it Trotsky? As with Lang's subsequent confusion of *Spione* with *Mabuse*, film historian Nicole Brenez has teased out another layer of ambiguity regarding Lang's subsequent memories: "In *Spione*, Rudolf Klein-Rogge reproduces trait for trait the face of Lenin. But this figural candor engenders critical confusion since, as an exegete of his own work, Lang effects a splendid referential transference thanks to which Lenin (political boss) serves to mask Trotsky (military boss): 'the invented super-spy Haghi was played by the actor Klein-Rogge in the make-up of the political master-mind Trotsky.'"[8] All of which is anticipated by the main villain in Feuillade's *Tih Minh*, concentrating the serial's anti-German and anti-Bolshevik sentiments in a single figure — a German spy suggestively named Marx. For Lang and the reflexes of his own audience almost a decade later, conflating Lenin and Trotsky in the figure of Haghi seems to serve pretty much the same function.

Yet the fact that communism plays no role at all in either film apart from vaguely signifying a generic evil threat is equally relevant, no doubt helping to account for Arnheim and Kracauer's scorn for *Spione*. Indeed, it's hard to avoid the fact that this is Lang's most politically incorrect film as well as his sexiest and most sensual, perhaps for related reasons.

In what other thriller does the act of taking a hot bath, alone, seem more monumental? The elliptical editing here and at the very beginning of the film invites the viewer's imagination to take flight, and so do countless dreamlike images, many bordering on narrative illogic or a sense of the uncanny: the disembodied hands of Haghi's nurse entering the frame (a motif that recurs with other characters); Haghi glimpsed at a nightclub just after Sonja has been slipped a message summoning her to his office; her dismantled house, gradually exposed under the glare of No. 326's flashlight; Haghi offering her a glass of champagne with a string of pearls wrapped around it; Matsumoto's hallucinatory vision of his three dead agents returning with their three fake treaties amidst falling sheets of paper and a superimposed Japanese flag; Haghi/Nemo's strange clown act utilizing musical notes and instruments. Yet thanks to the film's centripetal structure, these and other details take their place with the masterful suspense sequences in the train and bank as functional parts of an internal design no less encompassing than Haghi's. Like those recurring shots of his face and his passageways, which function as both deceptive tokens of meaning and agents of transition, these uncanny images lock the machinations of an incoherent, malevolent universe precisely into position.

Essay in booklet accompanying DVD of *Spione*, issued in the U.K. by Masters of Cinema (Eureka Entertainment) in April 2005; see also www.jonathanrosenbaum.com/?p=6204

Notes

1. Thomas Elsaesser, *Metropolis* (London: BFI Publishing, 2000), 39–40.
2. Charles Higham and Joel Greenberg, "Interview with Fritz Lang," 1969, reprinted in *Fritz Lang Interviews*, edited by Barry Keith Grant (Jackson: University Press of Mississippi), 103.
3. This anticipates the separate coded messages received by Colin (Jean-Pierre Léaud) in the two versions of Rivette's *Out 1*, composed in each case by Rivette himself. [2009]
4. Jean Domarchi and Jacques Rivette, "Interview with Fritz Lang," 1959, reprinted in *Fritz Lang Interviews*, op. cit., 16–17 (translation modified).
5. Tom Gunning, *The Films of Fritz Lang: Allegories of Vision and Modernity* (London: BFI Publishing, 2000), 117–18.
6. Siegfried Kracauer, *From Caligari to Hitler: A Psychological History of the German Film* (New York: Farrar, Straus & Cudahy, 1959), 150.
7. Rudolf Arnheim, *Film Essays and Criticism*, translated by Brenda Benthein (Madison: University of Wisconsin Press, 1997), 134–35.
8. Nicole Brenez, *De la figure en général et du corps en particulier: L'invention figurative au cinéma* (Paris/Bruxelles: DeBoeck Université, 1998), 120. (My translation. The quote from Lang is taken from Lotte H. Eisner, *Fritz Lang* [London: Secker & Warburg, 1976], 96.)

Family Plot

"Everything's perverted in a different way," Hitchcock has noted; and perhaps no other filmmaker has illustrated this postulate better, by starting from precisely the opposite premise. Without a well-established sense of the normal, the abnormal doesn't even stand a chance of being recognized, and the director has always made it his business to offer all the right signposts and comforts to guarantee complacency before proceeding to unhinge it. Yet one of the rules of the game is deception, and if the Master's artistry has been identified more with rude shocks than with the subtler conditioning which makes them possible, one can be certain that this too plays a role in his overall strategies. Since *Psycho* in 1960, his public image has largely been construed as a relish for nastiness that invariably associates violent death with the stylish flourish, the director's "touch" with the grandstanding set-piece — a tendency culminating in the rape-murders and potato-sack maneuvers in *Frenzy*.

If in fact the public equation of Hitchcock with mayhem has established its own form of complacency, one of the triumphs of *Family Plot* is to turn this cherished notion — along with several others — squarely on its head. A marvelously fluid light comedy with scarcely a slack moment, it blithely omits murder entirely, and its only death — of a secondary villain — pointedly occurs off-screen. In striking contrast to the sour distaste expressed for food, sex, and practically all the characters in *Frenzy*, the mood could hardly be more benign; and with explicitness systematically transposed from a visual to a verbal plane, practically every relationship in the film carries a pronounced erotic undercurrent.

Grasping after precedents, even most of the film's champions have labeled it only a minor achievement, commonly tracing its virtues back to *The Trouble with Harry* and regarding it as a kind of septuagenarian's garden sport. But apart from a certain echo of Shirley MacLaine's delicious kookiness in Barbara Harris' performance, and an uncharacteristic excellence in the acting throughout, it could be argued that the earlier comedy (one of Hitchcock's personal favorites) has more importance in his work than is usually admitted, as an oblique commentary on—and critique of—his more "official" classics. And within this context, *Family Plot* can be seen as a veritable testament—a measured assessment by the director of his methods that, by evaluating which is and isn't essential to them, clarifies everything in his career preceding it. A central clue to this enterprise is offered by the film's working title, *Deceit*; its climactic expression is Barbara Harris' wink to the audience in the final shot.

The main title credits grow out of shimmering green shapes in a crystal ball while strings and a heavenly choir are heard off-screen; then the face of Blanche (Harris) appears inside the ball, and we find ourselves present at a fake séance—Blanche intermittently speaking in the male voice of her other-worldly "control," Henry, while catering to the needs of Julia Rainbird (Cathleen Nesbitt), a dowager of seventy-eight. A brief cut to Blanche peeking between her fingers instantly alerts us to the deception—a dramatic form of illusion-making not unrelated to Hitchcock's—and we soon discover that Rainbird is offering her $10,000 to find her dead sister's illegitimate son, on whom she wishes to bestow the family fortune. Leaving the house, Blanche steps into a cab driven by her shaggy boyfriend George (Bruce Dern), a self-professed "actor" reduced to hacking who scoffs at her references to Henry as though he were real—reminding her of the sleuthing he does to furnish her séances with facts—before she mentions the $10,000, and alludes to his future "performance" that night on the waterbed. "Tonight," he promises, "you're gonna see a standing ovation"—and there is an abrupt cut to a mysterious blonde in black crossing the street in front of them, literally slicing into the plot at a right angle and thereby preempting the narrative.

The second plot features another couple, another deception: the blonde is Fran, a brunette Karen Black in disguise, collecting a huge diamond as payment for the return of the kidnapped Mr. Constantine, then returning by car with her own boyfriend Arthur (William Devane) to their upper-class house, where they clean up the secret basement chamber recently vacated by Constantine. Sexual references run through their own dialogue: clearly more at ease with crime and violence, Arthur gloatingly remarks that initially danger makes you sick, "then it makes you very, very loving." As they start upstairs to bed, he coyly alludes to the diamond he's just hidden, stressing that she'll have to torture him to find out its location; and as the camera moves into a large closeup of the jewel, hanging from the chandelier, she says that she intends to do just that.

This comprises only the first movement of the film, with a great deal of plot yet to come, including the discovery that Arthur, a jeweler who long ago murdered his foster parents, is Rainbird's long-lost nephew. But already an intriguing double structure is well underway, with diamond echoing crystal ball, each couple counterpointing the other in terms of class and behavior, and allusions to off-screen sex implying in both cases some of the contrasting power relations, with Blanche and Arthur in the dominant roles. (Significantly, the bedrooms of both couples are never even glimpsed.) Further developing a visual/narrative rhyming structure first noted by Truffaut and Godard in *Shadow of a Doubt* and *The Wrong Man* respectively, and more recently appropriated by Rivette in the giddy construction of *Céline et Julie vont en bateau*, Hitchcock creates a rigorous framework for demonstrating that deception and seduction are opposite sides of the same coin, and that every piece of exposition regarding one couple immediately affects our perception of the other. And whether it's Arthur picking lint off a policeman's jacket, Fran fixing gourmet meals for the kidnapped victims, or Blanche and George quickly devouring a hamburger supper, the behavioral charm of all four runs agreeably thick.

Thanks to the precision of Ernest Lehman's script, the movie proceeds like an immaculately polished mechanism that continually bears witness to the fact and wit of its own operations. Eliminating not only murder from his formula (and from the pedestrian Victor Canning novel *The Rainbird Pattern*, which served as his starting point), Hitchcock has pared down his devices to the point where whole areas of his expertise can be covered in single, functional, shorthand notations. The hilarious gag of a headstone being carved to loud pop music is also an establishing shot into a scene at the caretaker's office; and just as the ringing of a doorbell at a crucial juncture registers as a terse summary of all his experiments with sound, a few inches of a bishop's red habit "leaking" out under a car door suffice as a recapitulation of his inventive uses of color. Best of all is a hair-raising sequence with Blanche and George in a car without brakes barreling down a steep mountain road. An ultimate expression of Hitchcock's storyboard technique — clearly devised at a desk rather than during shooting or editing — its suspense derives from algebraic essentials, where the purest kind of "musical" variations can be played on the threats of passing cars, culminating in a wonderfully timed procession of motorcyclists.

At the same time, it defines a pivotal moment in relation to our feelings for the heroic couple: a team of dotty bumblers in contrast to the suave elegance of Arthur and Fran — perpetually embroiled in domestic spats, and usually figuring like seedy, not very bright opportunists as they clumsily follow the trail left by the missing heir — their absurdities are brought to a head in this moment of crisis, with Blanche nearly strangling George in hysterical efforts to hold her balance and George howling his irritation as he struggles to guide the runaway car. But it is precisely amidst all this low comedy and frenzy that we realize how little we want this crazy, lovable pair to die. When they subsequently emerge undamaged from the wrecked car and he lifts her into his arms, for once the old-fashioned Hollywood cliché has been proudly earned: the romantic couple from such earlier films as *The 39 Steps* has improbably been resurrected before our very eyes.

And where does Hitchcock himself figure in all this? We glimpse him earlier on, chatting with a woman in his familiar TV silhouette at the Registry of Births and Deaths, in a rural courthouse where George goes to collect a clue; and it might not be too far-fetched to identify him directly with Henry, Blanche's alleged "control." Who else is it, after all, who leads Blanche in a mysterious trance up the stairs in Fran and Arthur's house after the villainous couple have been safely locked away at the end, tracing a bee-line in a long dolly-and-crane shot to the hidden diamond on the chandelier? The films ads declare: "You must see it twice!," and sure enough, an earlier clue is dropped in the adjacent garage as to how she theoretically *might* have discovered the jewel's whereabouts. Yet the issue of her psychic powers is deliberately left open, and perhaps a more apposite clue is offered by the strings and voices accompanying her trance-like walk — the same music heard during each of her former séances, and the epitome of that Hollywood "mood" music justly famous for its fostering of illusions. But this time we become another one of her clients, along with George. Concluding this sunny tale of sex, money, and death with her wink at the camera, Hitchcock cheerfully acknowledges his full hand and his trump card in the same play, slyly suggesting that the real question isn't whether we've been deceived but whether we'd like to have been. Either way, his luminous crystal ball provides all the answers.

Sight and Sound, Summer 1976; slightly revised, August 2009

"The Doddering Relics of a Lost Cause": John Ford's *The Sun Shines Bright*

My father helped to run a small chain of movie theaters in northwestern Alabama that were owned by my grandfather while I was growing up in the '40s and '50s. He and my mother weren't cinephiles, but on two separate occasions they took the trouble to travel to cities in different states to attend world premieres in the South. One was for a big Southern film from a big studio (M-G-M), *Gone with the Wind*, held in 1939 in Atlanta. The other was for a small Southern film from a small studio (Republic Pictures), *The Sun Shines Bright*, held in 1953 in what I believe was a city in Tennessee — most likely Nashville or Chattanooga, possibly Memphis or Knoxville. The film is set in a town called Fairfield, Kentucky, so one may well ask why its premiere was held in Tennessee. I don't know the answer to this question, but expect it had something to do with some form of expedience on the part of Republic Pictures.

I was ten years old when my parents saw the latter film, and although I was keeping a diary for much of that year that contained many references to movies, I never wrote down anything in this diary about *The Sun Shines Bright*—not even when it showed at one of my family's theaters a few weeks or months after the premiere. I can vividly remember seeing it, however, and, just after I did, asking my father about the famous people he met at a dinner he attended at the movie's premiere and what each one of them was like. At the age of ten, I already knew who John Ford was — along with Alfred Hitchcock, Cecil B. DeMille, and Walt Disney, he was one of the only auteurs I knew about, and I had already seen a few of his westerns by then, such as *She Wore a Yellow Ribbon*—and to this day I can remember being told that Ford wasn't at the premiere but that several of the leading actors were: at the very least Charles Winninger (Judge William Pittman Priest) and John Russell (Ashby

Corwin), since I clearly remember my father speaking about these two; most likely Stepin Fetchit (Jeff Poindexter) and Arleen Wheeler (Lucy Lee Lake); and probably some others as well. I should add that by the age of ten, I was already well aware of the difference in market power between *Gone with the Wind* and *The Sun Shines Bright*, but I still didn't realize that the stars of the latter film weren't famous.

Today *The Sun Shines Bright* is my favorite Ford film, and I suspect that part of what makes me love it as much as I do is that it's the opposite of *Gone with the Wind* in almost every way, especially in relation to the power associated with stars and money. Although I'm also extremely fond of *Judge Priest*, a 1934 Ford film derived from some of the same Irvin S. Cobb stories, the fact that it has a big-time Hollywood star of the period, Will Rogers, is probably the greatest single difference, and even though I love both Rogers and his performance in *Judge Priest*, I love *The Sun Shines Bright* even more because of the greater intimacy and modesty of its own scale. Apparently Ford did as well, because, along with *Wagon Master* — which it resembles in its low budget, its lack of stars, and its focus on community — I believe this is the film of his that he cited most often as a personal favorite.

Let me attempt to sketch a synopsis of the film — which is no easy matter, because it's cluttered with events and characters in spite of the fact that it's quite leisurely in its pacing. Around the turn of the century, soon after Ashby Corwin returns by riverboat to his home town in Kentucky and starts courting Lucy Lee Lake, Judge Priest, an alcoholic judge who's up for reelection, cared for by his black servant Jeff Poindexter, goes to court and defends U.S. Grant Woodford (Elzie Emanuel), a teenage black banjo player, and Mallie Cramp, the town madam, against the charges of his stuffy opponent Horace K. Maydew. That night, he attends a regular meeting of Confederate veterans, borrowing an American flag for the occasion from the Union veterans, and announces that he'll take home the Confederates' portrait of General Fairfield and his late wife. (For the past eighteen years, Fairfield, whose banished daughter — Lucy Lee's mother — became a prostitute, has refused to attend the Confederate meetings, and Priest is afraid that Lucy Lee will discover that she's his granddaughter if she sees the painting and notices that she looks exactly like his late wife.)

Meanwhile, Lucy Lee's prostitute mother (Dorothy Jordan) arrives in town, heading for Mallie Cramp's bordello, and collapses. She's taken to the home of Dr. Lake (Russell Simpson) for treatment, where she glimpses Lucy Lee, his niece, just before she dies. Rushing over to Priest's house, Lucy Lee sees the family portrait and discovers her true identity. Meanwhile, a local girl has been raped and U.S. Grant Woodford, tracked down by bloodhounds, has been arrested as the rapist.

The next day, Priest stands outside the prisoner's cell and with a gun prevents a lynching from taking place.[1] That night, Mallie conveys to Priest the dying wish of Lucy Lee's mother that she receive a proper local funeral. Ashby takes Lucy Lee to a local dance, where disapproving looks compel her to leave around the same time that Buck, a romantic rival of Ashby who led the lynch mob, is identified as the true rapist, and shot while trying to escape with a captive Lucy Lee.

On the following day, Election Day is interrupted by the appearance of a white hearse, a carriage full of prostitutes, and Priest, gradually joined by about a hundred more local people, who all wind up at a black church for the funeral. There Lucy Lee is joined by General Fairfield and Priest delivers a sermon.

The men who wanted to lynch U.S. Grant turn up to vote for Priest, making the election an even tie that Priest breaks by voting for himself. That evening, practically the whole town parades past Priest's house, paying him tribute — first the white people, and then many of the black people, who serenade him, along with Jeff, as he retreats into his empty house.

At the age of ten, I had some trouble following certain parts of the movie's plot. Some of this was because of the Production Code, which made Mallie Cramp's status as a prostitute completely unclear to me, and some was because of the movie's sheer fancifulness. The early scene in the courtroom combines those two problems by having Mallie Cramp brought to court for unexplained reasons and U.S. Grant Woodford charged by Maydew for refusing to support his uncle — a charge that we immediately learn is baseless and which also seems to be a highly improbable reason for Maydew going to court, even in postbellum Kentucky. (As we quickly discover, it's really nothing more than an excuse for Judge Priest and the movie's audience to hear the boy's banjo-playing — providing yet another echo of *Judge Priest*, which had many more courtroom scenes, as well as the comic idea of American courtroom justice making room for a certain kind of musical entertainment with specific political and historical overtones, e.g., "Marching through Georgia" and "Dixie.")

Still another reason why I had some trouble following the plot was some fairly arbitrary and apparently vindictive cuts to the film made or at least ordered by Herbert J. Yates, the head of Republic Pictures, totaling about ten minutes. According to Joseph McBride in *Searching for John Ford* (New York: St. Martin's Press, 2001), "The full hundred-minute version, which played theatrically overseas, was rediscovered when Republic inadvertently used it as a master for the 1990 videotape release." Lamentably, this full version doesn't appear to be available on film today, but the video does make the plot much easier to follow.

■ ■ ■ ■ ■ ■ ■ ■ ■

The Sun Shines Bright had a particular significance in the Deep South because of its Southern details. But so did other films by other important directors during this era, sometimes for less direct reasons. I don't think anyone in my neck of the woods had a clear idea of who Howard Hawks was during the early '50s, but three of his films — *The Thing, The Big Sky,* and *Land of the Pharaohs* — had a particular significance in my home town, Florence, Alabama, because the actor Dewey Martin, who had important roles in all three, was said to have come from there. I can even dimly recall a local newspaper ad referring to "Florence's own Dewey Martin." Yet now that I've tried to research this detail — which is no easy matter, because Martin's career as a prominent actor was short-lived — I'm unable to come up with any corroboration. The only biographical information I can find says that he was born in Katemcy, Texas, in 1923 and made his first film appearance, uncredited, in Nicholas Ray's 1949 *Knock on Any Door,* so if he wound up in Florence at any point in between those two dates, this is a fact that's now apparently lost in the sands of time, at least outside of Florence.

I'm bringing this up only because I'm interested in trying to determine how certain films registered in my home town when they first appeared. I know that my friends and I felt a special relation to *The Thing, The Big Sky,* and *Land of the Pharaohs* because Dewey Martin was felt to be "one of us," and I believe this had particular significance in *The Big Sky,* where Martin plays an uneducated rural character consumed by racial hatred and a desire for revenge, both of which made him seem familiar to us.

Apart from the fact that my parents attended the premiere, *The Sun Shines Bright,* another period film, felt somewhat more remote to us, even though it was more closely tied to Southern issues, because it was less a film for kids — less "fun" and more serious. I should stress, however, that there are also uneducated rural characters in this film — notably those played by Francis Ford (in his final film performance) and Slim Pickins (in his first film performance), two hillbillies who are principally around as comic relief — as well as characters consumed by racial hatred and a desire for revenge, specifically a group known as the voters of the Tornado district, who come very close to lynching an innocent black boy for the rape of a white woman until stopped by Priest, who threatens them with a gun. Later, when the guilty white rapist is killed while trying to flee, it is the older of these two hillbillies who shoots him, and

Priest congratulates him for this by saying, "Good shootin', comrade," adding that this saves everyone the trouble of holding a trial — meaning, in other words, that this is a politically correct form of lynching. And still later, all the vengeful bigots who wanted to lynch U.S. Grant Woodford turn up at the polls to vote for Judge Priest, assuring his reelection, and then join the parade of well-wishers who pay tribute to this patriarch in front of his house, carrying a banner which reads, "He saved us from ourselves."

This is no doubt Ford's view of his own ideal epitaph, which could be spoken at his own funeral. It reminds me of the way my grandfather once cussed out a black male servant who worked for him when he discovered that he'd been duped by a loan shark — treating him in the most demeaning way possible, as if he were a stupid child, and then calling up the loan shark with threats and more abuse in order to extricate the servant from his highly exploitative debts. This is the closest I can come in my personal memory to summoning up the way Judge Priest treats U.S. Grant Woodford in his courtroom. Jeff Poindexter, on the other hand — who plays dumb in order to honor Judge Priest's various quirks, including his paternalism, a trait that's clear in Stepin Fetchit's performances in both *Judge Priest* and *The Sun Shines Bright* — is quite another matter, and I'm sorry to say that the only echoes of his obsequious manner in my memories are blurred by the racially informed confusions of my own childhood. Making things even more difficult for me is the fact that, in spite of my having grown up in the Deep South and being around many black servants, I've never been able to understand large portions of what this actor says because of his heavy dialect. (Whether or not this makes his dialect inauthentic is impossible for me to judge.)

I should add that in between Judge Priest's stopping of a lynching and his triumphant reelection brought about in part by the potential lynchers is the act that Ford regards as his key act of moral and civil virtue — arguably far more important in certain ways, at least in this film's terms, than his prevention of the lynching. I'm speaking, of course, of his joining a funeral procession for a fallen woman on election day, thereby fulfilling her dying request that she be given a proper burial in her own home town. Once Billy Priest joins this procession, he is followed by almost every other sympathetic member of the community, starting with the local bordello madam and her fellow prostitutes, and continuing with the commander of the Union veterans of the Civil War, the local blacksmith, the German-American who owns the department store, Amora Ratchitt (Jane Darwell), Lucy Lee, Ashby, Dr. Lake, and finally — after the procession arrives at its destination, a black church — General Fairfield, Lucy's grandfather, who has up until now refused to recognized his daughter under any circumstances.

There are actually two protracted and highly ceremonial processions in the film, occurring quite close to one another—the funeral procession for Lucy Lee's mother and the parade of tribute to Judge Priest—and the fact that these two remarkable sequences are allowed by Ford to take over the film as a whole is part of what's so extraordinary about them. Retroactively one might even say that they almost blend together in our memory as a single procession—despite the fact that the first is an act of mourning and the second is an act of celebration—and this undoubtedly contributes to the feeling of pathos in the film in spite of its overdetermined happy ending.

■■■■■■■■■

In order to explain some of the reasons why I consider *The Sun Shines Bright* to be Ford's greatest film, I'd like to compare it to a few of my other favorite films. Let me begin by citing a film that would seem to be at the opposite end of the spectrum from Ford's in many obvious respects: Jacques Tati's *Playtime* (1967). The two-part structure of *The Sun Shines Bright* is, I believe, very close to that of *Playtime* insofar as the first half is devoted to introducing various members of a large community who are profoundly and painfully separated and estranged from one another, lost in frustration and loneliness, and the second half is devoted to bringing all these characters together in mutual appreciation and celebration. In both cases, one fairly modest and lone individual helps to bring about this change—deliberately in the case of Billy Priest, accidentally in the case of Monsieur Hulot. In this respect, the continuous carousel of traffic that we see towards the end of *Playtime* might have as much of a bittersweet edge as the two lengthy processions towards the end of *The Sun Shines Bright* because in both cases the triumph of community is accompanied by a certain loss of individual identity. In very different ways, Lucy Lee's mother and Judge Priest become the occasions for communal affirmations that in some ways have more to do with the communities involved than with them as individuals. Lucy Lee's mother may be little more than a shadow while Judge Priest is the film's hero, but both are ultimately effaced by the town that honors them, because the town becomes an image of interactive togetherness while these individuals are ultimately isolated and alone.

Another favorite film of mine, Carl Dreyer's *Gertrud*, resembles Ford's in other ways—and not merely because they're set in the same period (apparently 1905[2] in Ford's film, 1906 in Dreyer's), and tinged with melancholy nostalgia and yearning for still earlier periods. More strangely and paradoxically, I think both films are tragic in feeling despite—or is it because?—they both have what could be described as overdetermined happy endings. Moreover, both films concentrate at great length on highly ceremonial tributes paid to old men for their life's work. And both virtually end with figures retreating through doorways (two doorways in Ford's film), in eerie images that strongly suggest mortality and the ultimate isolation of death.

Although both of these endings can be summarized by the Fordian formula "victory in defeat," they're nonetheless quite different. Gertrud's victory and her defeat both remain offscreen in the minimalist severity of Dreyer's final shot of a closed door, whereas both Judge Priest's victory and the extreme pathos of his isolation, which implies a kind of defeat, are spelled out directly in Ford's conclusion—albeit made more complex and ambiguous by Ford intercutting between Priest and Ashby with Lucy Lee at Priest's front gate, the latter silently restraining the former from going to Priest. Ford then records their offscreen exit in long shot as they walk pass Jeff in profile in front of Priest's mansion, playing his harmonica on the front steps. In other words, both victory and defeat are represented but not shown in our interminable view of the door that closes behind Gertrud after she waves goodbye to her friend, whereas intimations of both defeat and victory are expressed successively in Ford's final shots: Judge Priest in his apotheosis as a paternal hero, being celebrated by his entire community, whites and blacks alike, says, "Jeff—I gotta take my medicine, I gotta get my heart started" (a running gag which means that he must once again retreat to his bottle, like a helpless infant), and, turning his back on his community, which also, in the gesture of Lucy Lee, chooses to leave him in his isolation, marches stoically towards his lonely death (a kind of defeat), while his loyal servant, also alone yet facing the same community, celebrates his master's apotheosis (a kind of victory).

■ ■ ■ ■ ■ ■ ■ ■ ■

Ultimately, what the film may be expressing is neither celebration nor lament, perhaps just simply affection for cantankerous individuals who exude a certain sweet pathos because history has somehow passed them by—as someone says in the film, I believe in reference to the Confederate veterans, "the doddering relics of a lost cause," which also suggests The Southerner as Everyman. This implicitly suggests a certain darkness as well as lightness—which is why the local blacks serenade the judge with "My Old Kentucky Home," the first line of which is "The sun shines bright"—and yet this is a film bathed mainly in the melancholy of twilight. For to emphasize and focus on lost causes as opposed to causes that still might be won assumes a certain abstention from politics associated with defeatism—one reason among others, perhaps, why the Civil War plays such a central role in American history as well as in Ford's work. (In a way, the fact that Judge Priest is a Confederate veteran who is also friendly with many Union veterans nearly sums up his overall relationship to Fairfield as a community.)

■ ■ ■ ■ ■ ■ ■ ■ ■

Although Ford has with some justice been called both Brechtian and dialectical, he has also more debatably been called a liberal and leftist filmmaker. However appropriate this description might be to the impact of his films during the 1930s, I'd like to argue that in *The Sun Shines Bright* Ford is better described as conservative or a reactionary, albeit one with certain progressive convictions. This is also true of the orientations of some of the cinephiles who value him the most — a list that would include, among others, Tag Gallagher, Gilberto Perez, Maurice Pialat, Jean-Marie Straub and Danièle Huillet, and Michael Wilmington. For what I'm describing as conservative and reactionary in this context means devoted to a certain idea of tradition; it also entails a certain view of human nature that is relatively pessimistic.

I think this can be seen more easily if one compares *The Sun Shines Bright* to two other low-budget Hollywood black-and-white pictures of the same period that I would describe as authentically liberal. One of these, Jacques Tourneur's *Stars in My Crown* (1950), is commonly viewed as liberal, and the other, Samuel Fuller's *Pickup on South Street* (1953), released the same year as *The Sun Shines Bright*, is commonly viewed as right-wing — some would even say fascist because of its treatment of communist spies as standard-issue gangsters and its sympathy for an uneducated woman who expresses unreasoning hatred for them. But I should stress that my definitions of ideology throughout this essay are dependent almost entirely on what I believe their ideological significance was in America when they first appeared, not on what they meant or mean in a European context. And from this vantage point, it's important to recognize that J. Edgar Hoover's objections to *Pickup on South Street* (provoked in part by Richard Widmark's sarcastic remark to a policeman in the film, "Are you waving the flag at me?") were — and are — far more pertinent than Georges Sadoul's. And both of these films are, in my opinion, radically liberal, whereas *The Sun Shines Bright* qualifies as either conservatively liberal or (more apt, I think) as liberally conservative.

On the level of plot, the most striking similarity between *The Sun Shines Bright* and *Pickup on South Street* is the issue of where a disreputable woman will be buried and whether or not her own wish to be buried somewhere respectable will be honored. There's a certain amount of pathos and irony that we feel about the expression of this wish in both films, but this is more keenly felt, I believe, in Fuller's film than in Ford's. One reason for this is that Thelma

Ritter's Moe — a professional informer in Fuller's film who makes her living by giving information to the police — is one of the most touching and authentic characters in all his work, and an interesting test case for his radical humanism. So the issue of how someone like Moe is treated in the wider world, even as a corpse — felt especially (and, within the film, uniquely) by Widmark's character, Skip — is arguably an Old Testament issue, profoundly Jewish in both its sense of exclusion and its sense of justice, while the issue of how Lucy Lee's mother is treated posthumously is a Christian issue, underlined by Judge Priest's sermon about adultery and forgiveness. In this case, holding a proper funeral is the community's way of doing penance for its own sins in ostracizing this woman while she was alive, thereby revising its somewhat tarnished view of itself. This issue never comes up with Fuller's Moe, not only because she never even has a funeral — the only issue is whether or not she gets buried in Potter's Field — but also because no one apart from Skip cares enough about her to bury her elsewhere. By contrast, Lucy Lee's mother, who lacks even a name, is, as I've already stated, scarcely more than a shadow. (Maybe she's something more than that for Lucy Lee, but from all that we see, the portrait of her grandmother plays a more significant role in defining her identity than the life of her mother.) The moral importance of where and how a discarded woman is buried is clear in both films, but *Pickup on South Street* has a more radical expression of loyalty by one pariah for another because Skip and Moe are more culturally estranged and socially isolated than any prostitute could be in Ford's film. Perhaps one could go even further and argue that there is more sensitivity towards the issue as a class issue in Fuller's film.

The most interesting parallel between *Stars in My Crown* and *The Sun Shines Bright* is the prevention of a lynching by the film's leading character — a minister in Tourneur's film, a judge in Ford's, although, as the judge's name suggests and his climactic sermon confirms, the latter is in some ways a lay member of the clergy. By the same token, Josiah Doziah Gray (Joel McCrea), a minister, becomes a man of law on many separate occasions in *Stars in My Crown*, and his successful effort to discourage a band of the Ku Klux Klan from lynching Uncle Famous Prill (Juan Hernandez) has many things in common with delivering a legal brief. In fact, it's an action which apes that of a lawyer — the recitation of an imaginary will by Uncle Famous that Gray is pretending to read, using a blank sheet of paper — which ultimately shames the mob into retreating. Significantly, we only learn that this will is Gray's own invention after he succeeds in disbanding the group of men, once the film's narrator, John Kenyon (Dean Stockwell), a foster child of Gray and his wife, looks at the discarded sheet of paper.

Just as Ford clearly identifies his own practice with that of Judge Priest, I believe that Gray's ruse on this particular occasion is a perfect illustration of Tourneur's own aesthetic of mise en scène, predicated on both a pronounced feeling for absence and a profound trust in and respect for the imagination of the spectator to fill that absence. In a way this ruse on Tourneur's part, a bit like a magician's trick, is as radical as Fuller's sympathy for Moe because it implicitly places the audience on the same plane as an unsympathetic lynch mob and then trusts this mob's good nature as well as its imagination to pacify its own violent impulses. Judge Priest, by contrast — an armed crusader more than a magician — starts off by trying to reason with the crowd but ultimately has to depend on the threat of violence by pulling out his revolver to stop the lynching. Even if the potential lynchers wind up improbably celebrating him a day later by carrying the banner "He saved us from ourselves" — another example of religious terminology, like "priest" — this act of saving implicitly comes out of the barrel of a gun.

■■■■■■■■■

As a Southerner, it's very hard for me to reconcile all my contradictory feelings about Ford in *The Sun Shines Bright*, but I'm not sure that there's any necessity for me to do so. Recalling *Gertrud* again, I think that some works are great because of the challenges they offer to our beliefs. William Faulkner — who of course was a Southerner himself, unlike Ford — has just as many contradictions as Dreyer and Ford, and we don't value him any less because of them.

In a memorable lecture about Ford at the Buenos Aires Festival of Independent Film — given last spring by Kent Jones, with interjections by Gerald Peary — the point was made that for every celebration of war and battle in Ford one could counter with examples that sow serious doubts on these celebrations. Similarly, alongside the instances of racism — most noticeable, I would argue, in the indifference shown towards the casting of Native Americans and the languages they speak, which is not an issue in *The Sun Shines Bright*, and in the absence of any assumption of Native American spectators[3] — are many expressions of antiracist sentiments regarding Native Americans, blacks, and other minorities (or majorities, perhaps, if one considers the black Africans in *Mogambo* or the Asian characters in *Seven Women*).

Most of Ford's films, perhaps all of them, qualify as fantasies of one kind or another, and few are as unabashedly brazen about this as *The Sun Shines Bright*. I'm not sure how relevant this is to its social effect, because it was such a modest film in terms of its public reception that I can't imagine it doing either much harm or much good. (Its anti-lynching "message" was completely uncontroversial, even for Alabama in 1953 — and its nostalgia for master-servant relationships, though informed by a great deal of humor and irony, was equally unremarkable for its period.)

Thinking back to *She Wore a Yellow Ribbon*—which is possibly the first film of his I saw, and which I would argue is one of Ford's less Brechtian and dialectical efforts—it's hard for me to overlook the possibility that some boys who grew up with me in Alabama may have enlisted to fight in Vietnam partly because of the heroic and idealized image of John Wayne, which this film among others contributed to, even if it shows him as more vulnerable than he is in some of the others. I should add that Fuller refused to cast Wayne in *The Big Red One*, despite Wayne's own interest in starring in the film, because he thought the image of Wayne in relation to war was false. But Fuller was someone who grew up as a newspaperman and as a soldier, not as a filmmaker, and it might be argued that fantasy played a very different kind of role in his work because of this difference.

"Ford is very interesting as an object for psychoanalysis," the film critic Shigehiko Hasumi once said to me, going on to suggest that "there's something traumatic in Ford's films; I don't know what it is, but it's there." Assuming that this observation is true, it's another common point between Ford and Faulkner—not to mention Yasujiro Ozu—and I suspect it has something to do with leaving home.

The author's thanks to Alexander Horwath and Regina Schlagnitweit for their advice and encouragement.

Rouge 7 (2005), available at www.rouge.com.au; originally published in *Die Früchte des Zorns und der Zärtlichkeit* (Viennale, 2004)

Notes

1. Reportedly a scene very much like this one was cut by Fox from *Judge Priest*, with Stepin Fetchit playing the prisoner—who was known as Jeff Poindexter—and this became the prime motivation for Ford doing a loose remake, even though much of the remaining plot in *The Sun Shines Bright* is quite different. The only other actor who's in both films is Francis Ford, and the only other secondary character is Horace K. Maydew—in this case a senator, played by a different actor.

2. This is the approximate date given by Tag Gallagher in his Ford biography, though Joseph McBride in his much more recent biography estimates the setting to be around 1896. Not knowing the reasoning used by either writer, I wouldn't know how to choose between these dates.

3. In my book on *Dead Man* (London: BFI, 2nd ed., 2001), I argue that this is a key ethical and ideological distinction to be made between Jim Jarmusch's film and other westerns.

Prisoners of War:
Bitter Victory

Jane (Ruth Roman): What can I say to him?

Leith (Richard Burton): Tell him all the things that women have always said to the men before they go to the wars. Tell him he's a hero. Tell him he's a good man. Tell him you'll be waiting for him when he comes back. Tell him he'll be making history.

— *Bitter Victory*

This week, the Gene Siskel Film Center continues the first part of its series devoted to the war film, which will continue in August. I don't know if the recent overlapping of this series with the Chicago Palestine Film Festival is deliberate or coincidental, but it has already yielded some provocative juxtapositions. And this Friday and Monday the Film Center is showing a restored version of one of the least well-known masterpieces of Nicholas Ray — a powerful (albeit flawed) black-and-white CinemaScope feature set mainly in Libya during World War II that offers one of the most radical reflections on war that I know.

For me, its pertinence to the current war in Iraq goes far beyond desert settings and references to antiquity. But in order to explain this pertinence, I first have to offer my own particular reading of this disquieting movie. Though it's always been rightly regarded as an antiwar film, that describes a good many pictures, including ones that proceed from antithetical premises. (In the '60s, for instance, a popular revival house in Manhattan used to favor a double bill of *Grand Illusion* and *Paths of Glory*.)

Ray's critique — parts of which could probably be traced back to his past as a radical activist during the Depression, before he turned to movies — is only deceptively simple. The story appears on the surface to be one with a courageous hero (Captain James Leith, quoted above) and a cowardly villain (Major David Brand, his superior, played by Curt Jürgens—the "him" and husband Jane is referring to). Both men are assigned to a special unit sent on a dangerous mission from Cairo to Benghazi to steal important documents from Rommel's Nazi headquarters. Leith, a Welsh archeologist who has previously lived in Libya, has had little military experience—unlike Brand, who has spent most of the war behind a desk—and significantly both men want the assignment in spite of its enormous dangers. Leith and Jane were lovers before the war until he departed without warning for Libya; then—shades of *Casablanca*—she married Brand while secretly continuing to be in love with Leith. Brand becomes aware only of Jane's current attraction to Leith when he sees them dancing together in a restaurant and becomes sick with jealousy, shortly before he and Leith both leave for Benghazi.

Disguised as Arabs, they stand outside the Nazi headquarters, and when Brand can't bring himself to stab a sentry with a dagger, Leith does the job for him, launching a series of recriminations and accusations over the remainder of the mission. They successfully seize the documents, but their return trek across the desert becomes an agonizing series of ordeals and disasters in which their mutual enmity predominates.

■ ■ ■ ■ ■ ■ ■ ■ ■

Judging by the accounts of Bernard Eisenschitz's biography of Ray and a recent memoir of screenwriter Gavin Lambert, *Bitter Victory*—Ray's first effort to break away from Hollywood, made during his mid-fifties—had an extremely troubled production, resulting in what may well be his most ambiguous and disquieting work. (Its only competitor in Ray's oeuvre is the similarly pessimistic *Bigger Than Life* [1956], which makes ordinary American middle-class life look almost as deranged as war does here.) In California Ray began adapting a French novel by René Hardy, in collaboration with the author as well as Lambert—the former editor of the English film magazine *Sight and Sound* whom Ray had brought to Hollywood as both a screenwriter (on *Bigger Than Life* and *The True Story of Jesse James*) and lover. Their relationship was already on the wane when Lambert accompanied Ray to North Africa (to scout locations) and Paris, where, on the sly, Ray hired the blacklisted writer Vladimir Pozner for script revisions without the knowledge of producer Paul Graetz—who would himself later insist on rewrites by Paul Gallico that Ray would either ignore or alter in turn. And to complicate matters further, Hardy had final script approval.

The casting imposed by Graetz was even more of a tragicomedy of crosspurposes: Ray wanted to cast Burton, but as Brand rather than as Leith (for whom he wanted Montgomery Clift or Paul Newman); his own choice for Jane was Moira Shearer; and he approved German actor Jürgens—but as a captured German officer, not as Brand. (To rationalize Brand's distracting German accent, Graetz insisted on adding an early line of dialogue identifying him as a South African Boer; and it seems he hired Gallico in deference to Jürgens's complaints that his character wasn't sufficiently sympathetic.)

Things only got more chaotic from there: Lambert was fired by Graetz after refusing to serve as his spy in Libya who would report back on Ray's drinking (already a problem), although Ray continued to phone him in Paris at regular intervals. After Ray shifted to studio shooting in Nice and Paris, already behind schedule, he spent his evenings gambling compulsively—losing $60,000 one night in Monte Carlo—and then, in Paris, became involved with an eighteen-year-old Moroccan girl who was a heroin addict. By the time he completed the film's sound mixing, he had to be hospitalized for exhaustion.

What relevance does all this have to the finished film? A great deal, I think. On all the occasions when I met Ray in Paris and New York during the '70s, he seemed a victim of his own macho poses, as I suspect Ernest Hemingway often was, and which these subsequent biographical accounts only confirm. (When I once found him stranded in the rain at St-Germain-des-Près around ten one morning and invited him to a nearby café for a drink, he promptly ordered, with an obvious touch of bravado, tequila with a beer chaser.)

In *Bitter Victory*—a ruthless and relentless autocritique that is periodically confused or at least complicated by the casting—one finds him repeatedly exposing the childish vanity of such behavior. (An earlier foray in the same general direction was his semiautobiographical noir masterpiece of 1950, *In a Lonely Place*.) It's possible that Ray's bisexuality helped give him certain insights into macho attitudes. For what he's exposing isn't only the self-absorption and self-deception of Brand, which are painfully obvious. He's also less obviously exposing the same traits in Leith—and not simply despite the fact but also because the character (a) is played by Burton in his most suave, romantic Welsh-literary manner, (b) has all the best lines and most quotable rejoinders, and (c) is regarded by everyone else in the film as heroic—especially alongside Brand, whom everyone despises as a hypocrite.

Yet the film's overall architecture—especially its story and dialogue, which is full of ambiguities regarding motives and behavior, and its opening and closing scenes with the hanging figures of stuffed dummies that are used for bayonet practice in combat training—ultimately implies that Leith is nonetheless a smug poseur. He's determined to have the last word on every subject, dishonest about his feelings for Jane, and narcissistically smitten with his own cynical nihilism and suicidal despair (which we're also expected to relish). Meanwhile, hapless Brand, much less successful in hiding his feelings — and simply played by Jürgens as a classic cuckold figure whose most expressive feature is his plaintive cocker spaniel eyes — is treated by everyone as a scapegoat.

If Ray had had his own way with the casting, the antagonists would surely have been more evenly matched in terms of audience sympathies; but even so, the better acquainted I've become with this film over the years, the more questionable Leith's overdetermined charisma becomes. Even when Brand actually shows real courage by being the first to drink from a well that may have been poisoned, this is immediately dismissed by Leith as merely another attempt to cover up his shame for his former cowardice, implying that there's no possible way he could ever redeem himself. Yet if we recall Leith's own earlier behavior with the two dying soldiers he's ordered by Brand to stay with — finding the courage to shoot the German, then losing the courage to put one of his own men out of his misery, even after the man begs to be shot — we realize that both men are ultimately condemned by the rhetoric of war to assume absurdist positions. (As Leith puts it, more articulately than Brand ever could, "I kill the living and I save the dead.") And as the English critic Geoff Andrew has pointed out, Leith is more generally a coward in his own way "since he fears life itself."

In both cases, you're damned if you do and damned if you don't; any form of self-testing becomes a futile macho pose — an infantile form of acting out encouraged by "war" and the license it provides. Even more drastically, according to this theoretical mix of psychoanalysis and existentialism, it's implied that bravery and cowardice can be viewed as alternate versions of the same cheap impulse — the "positive" and "negative" sides of the same dubious mythology. The issue, finally, isn't whether wars accomplish good things or bad things — we never get a clue about why those captured documents are important — but why some men seek them out or welcome them regardless of their meaning or consequences.

This isn't the only Ray film that postulates male antagonists as mystic equals. Consider *Wind Across the Everglades* (1958), which he directed just afterwards, set around the turn of the century, in which an Audubon society game warden (Christopher Plummer) and a renegade bird trapper (Burl Ives) in the swamps wind up as temporary drinking buddies and fellow celebrators of "protest." Or consider Jim Stark (James Dean) and Buzz Gunderson (Corey Allen) in *Rebel Without a Cause* (1955), teenage boys arriving at an unexpected rapport and moment of mutual recognition immediately before competing in the absurdist macho ritual of a "chickie run." But *Bitter Victory* takes this premise further by postulating neither friendship nor common understanding between the rivals but an eerie fusion of identities — like Jekyll turning into Hyde or vice versa.

The film's final scene makes this idea inescapable—a scene missing from the truncated original release version in the U.K., which must have made nonsense of the rest. (That version was 90 minutes; it originally ran for 82 in the U.S. and 87 dubbed into French—though the restored version at the Film Center runs for 103.) Prisoners of the rhetoric of war, both men are literal as well as figurative dummies; Leith simply has the classier cover story, making him even worse in some ways than his honestly bumbling and universally scorned rival. On a more mystical level, the two men become morally and existentially equivalent: Leith, who loves Jane, has consistently lied or been evasive about his feelings for her, but Brand, lying to her about what he thought Leith's final words for her might have been, imagines them as a declaration of love, which he tells her would have been his last words as well—and which we know in his case would have been the truth.

"Basically [Nick] was both of them," Lambert is quoted as saying of Ray in Eisenschitz's book. "And I think that was the mainspring of the film for him. . . . I liked the idea that the outcome of the mission [really had] nothing to do with how they performed it, but with what they felt about each other. That, in a way, said something about war. That it was an example of people's neuroses coming out. And that if people could discover how neurotic they were in a war . . . it might never have happened."

■ ■ ■ ■ ■ ■ ■ ■ ■

As luck would have it, I was able to attend a special screening of *Bitter Victory* a dozen years ago in Rotterdam, as part of a symposium about the previous gulf war, which was then in progress and being widely celebrated in the U.S. This second gulf war hasn't been celebrated nearly as much—at least not since the infamous "mission accomplished" banner flew behind Bush as he spoke on an aircraft carrier—and the increasing relevance of this film to our queasiness about it starts with the film's title.

To understand the rhetorical power of "war" as an abstract concept, one should consider the degree to which Bush's employment of the word shortly after September 11 almost immediately transformed him from an unpopular president who seemed unsure of himself into a popular one who exuded confidence and purpose, switching at once from a Brand to a Leith. Just as I doubt that we'd fetishize *Casablanca* today and the nostalgia for wartime unity and certainty it embodies in the same way if it had starred Ronald Reagan and Ann Sheridan, as was originally planned—even though the media has been posthumously fetishizing Reagan himself as if he were an intimate family member—I suspect that Bush would never have enjoyed his sudden upsurge in the polls after September 11 if he hadn't uttered that magic word, thereby transforming the terrifying and unfathomable singularity of the terrorist attacks into something far easier to process.

All of a sudden, we were back on familiar ground. And if the death of Reagan could summon up warm evocations of Lincoln, FDR, Nixon, Princess Di, and maybe even Frank Sinatra and O. J. Simpson—not because Reagan had anything in common with them but because the media treated him almost identically—September 11 was miraculously made to rhyme with Pearl Harbor (one size fits all). The fearful image became domesticated; even if "war on terror" was grammatically a non sequitur, conjuring up a military engagement with no conceivable end—and maybe also a euphemism for invading a couple of relatively defenseless countries—it somehow felt right because it put us all on automatic pilot, nostalgically brought back to the patriotism of previous military campaigns, including the cold war. And then, once the Iraqi war seemed to resume after we were told it was virtually over, the possibility that we might be witnessing a war of independence fought by citizens who didn't like being occupied couldn't be readily adapted to "war" in the sense that Bush and the media were employing the term.

Crucially, that sense was an abstraction making all sorts of other things possible. When one heard from Red Cross estimates that 70 to 90 percent of the Arabs tortured in Abu Ghraib were innocent of any wrongdoing—which provides a significant clue about why American efforts to win over Iraqi hearts and minds haven't been more successful—it becomes easier to comprehend how this could have happened, and why a few Fox News pundits can even continue to defend such procedures, if what's being conducted is called a war on terror or terrorism and not a war on terrorists. If you're targeting terrorists, you know you've made a mistake in a majority of cases, even if you think you can justify the torture morally or even practically. But if you're targeting terrorism, it becomes a lot easier to rationalize the indefensible. In other words, part of the rhetorical function of "war"—less as an activity than as an emotional and mythological button to push—is to give whoever's using the term a wider, freer, and simpler playing field, eliding in some cases the need for other arguments or explanations.

I should confess I have little problem in agreeing with Bush when he classifies Osama bin Laden and Saddam Hussein as evil—even if the latter is better described as an evil despot than as an evil terrorist. It's only when I have to consider that both men are former U.S. allies who were once empowered by our government that I feel excluded from his rhetoric, which seems addressed only to people who don't know or don't care to acknowledge such facts. Theoretically, if Bush were addressing me and all the others he's currently excluding, he'd have to put some spin on this information—that these men weren't evil when the U.S. supported them, or were less evil at that time than Communists or Iranians, or that the U.S. was wrong then but is right today. Maybe there are even better explanations he could come up with, but any of them would necessitate a somewhat weaker resolve as well as a greater depth of understanding in admitting that the world is never as simple as we like to think, even when it comes to evil. And without such depth, we get the equivalent of a Leith without a Brand — an employment of "war" as a piece of unexamined rhetoric, turning dummies into heroes and vice versa.

Chicago Reader, June 18, 2004

Art of Darkness:
Wichita

One reason why Jacques Tourneur (1904–1977) remains a major but neglected Hollywood filmmaker is that elusiveness is at the core of his art.
A director of disquiet, absence, and unsettling nocturnal atmospheres whose
characters tend to be mysteries to themselves as well as to us, he dwells in un-
certainties and ambiguities even when he appears to be studiously following
genre conventions. In other words, his brilliance isn't often apparent because
he tends to stay in the shadows. As with Carl Dreyer, it took me years to fully
appreciate the textures of his work, but now I can't get enough of his films.

A case in point is *Wichita* (1955), Tourneur's first film in CinemaScope and
possibly the most traditional of all his westerns, showing in LaSalle Bank's classic film series this Saturday. It's full of actors associated with other westerns, including Joel McCrea, Vera Miles, Lloyd Bridges, Edgar Buchanan, Jack Elam,
Walter Sande, Robert Wilke, and even a barely recognizable Sam Peckinpah
in a bit part as a bank teller. The lead character is Wyatt Earp (McCrea) in the
mid-1870s, before he became famous in Dodge City. (The real Earp served
only as a policeman in Wichita, where he lived from 1874 to '76, before moving to Dodge City and working for three years as assistant city marshal.) He's
a wholly virtuous man who reluctantly accepts the job of marshal in Wichita
to stop drunken cattlemen from terrorizing the locals, after being goaded into
action by the accidental shooting of a five-year-old boy. Bat Masterson, a standard character in the Earp story, also figures in the action as a cub reporter. But
despite these generic staples, there are plenty of times when the story seems to
be taking place on Mars.

After the opening credits, for instance. They're accompanied by Tex Ritter
belting out the hokey title tune, which seems to recount the entire plot in
advance — as good a way as any of making us feel we're in familiar territory.

Then we're out on the range with the cattlemen, whom we have no reason yet to see as villains. The first glimpse we get of Earp is as a tiny speck on the horizon, immediately seen by them (and therefore us) as an eerie potential menace. But they wind up inviting him to join them for dinner, and later two of the cattlemen — brothers named Gyp (Lloyd Bridges) and Hal (Rayford Barnes) — try to steal his money when they think he's asleep.

Gyp, Hal, and the other cattlemen seem to be the bad guys from this point on, and soon Earp seems to be not only a law-and-order man but an implacable killing machine and angel of death. Jacques Lourcelles describes the setup succinctly in his excellent *Dictionnaire du Cinéma*: "In Wichita, a city without law and without 'values' in the midst of a full economic boom, Wyatt Earp, the incarnation of these absent values, appears like a being from elsewhere, a sort of extraterrestrial."

A goody two-shoes who's also a little creepy because he's an outsider, Earp seems solid only in comparison with the cattlemen, all-too-human louts who can't help themselves, and with the local businessmen, who change their positions so often we can't be sure what side they're on. They're confused in part because as soon as Earp gives up the idea of starting his own business and becomes marshal, he outlaws all guns in town except his own. This strikes most of the businessmen as too much of a good thing, because they fear the ban on firearms will be bad for trade (one of many details that feel up-to-the-minute). In the end no one's really in control — not even Earp, who seems trapped in a destiny he'd rather avoid. To confuse matters further, Earp turns out to have a couple of brothers, who enter the film as potential villains before we realize who they are and why they've come to town. They create a disturbing rhyme with Gyp and Hal as we gradually discover that the main difference between "good" and "bad" is the direction in which the guns are pointed.

Two shocking accidental deaths from the cattlemen's gunfire represent turning points in the plot, yet Tourneur's staging of them is so quick, so de-dramatized, and so peculiar that we can't view them as ordinary climaxes. Instead they come across as incongruous quirks of fate, throwing both us and the characters off balance. This prompted whoever wrote LaSalle Bank's blurb to remark, "The scene where the kid gets shot in the window could've used a retake." That's certainly true in terms of conventional dramaturgy: the boy immediately crumples and slides out of frame without any visual evidence that he's been struck by a bullet. The staging might provoke derisive laughter, yet it also helps make us more queasy about the boy's senseless death — something we might not feel if the action were more legible and pointed, the way John Ford might have filmed it. This death and a later one reminded me of the messy, absurdist deaths from gunfire in Jim Jarmusch's 1996 antiwestern *Dead Man*, which also tend to provoke uneasy titters.

In the second part of the video documentary *A Personal Journey with Martin Scorsese Through American Movies* (1995) is a nine-minute stretch devoted to Tourneur that focuses on the first two horror films he directed for producer Val Lewton, the 1942 *Cat People* (made for only $134,000) and the 1943 *I Walked with a Zombie*. "In its own way," Scorsese says, "*Cat People* was as important as *Citizen Kane* in the development of a more mature American cinema." It seems an extreme statement, but it's actually reasonable, because Tourneur and Lewton brought subtlety and poetic suggestion to B movies, while Welles brought a kind of intelligent bombast to A pictures. Both movies startled audiences — *Cat People* ran longer at some venues than *Citizen Kane* — but only *Citizen Kane* gained cultural prestige.

A short list of Tourneur's best films would have to include those two pictures as well as the 1943 *The Leopard Man* (his final picture for Lewton and, in spite of a flawed ending, his most frightening), *Out of the Past* (1947), *Stars in My Crown* (1950), and *Night of the Demon* (1957 — cut and retitled *Curse of the Demon* for its U.S. release) — all black-and-white chamber pieces. My second tier of favorites, mainly in color, would include the westerns *Canyon Passage* (1946) and *Wichita*.

All eight of these films have some noir elements, and the literal as well as metaphysical darkness helps define Tourneur's stamp. (Chris Fujiwara's definitive 1998 critical study, one of the best pieces of auteurist criticism I know, is aptly called *Jacques Tourneur: The Cinema of Nightfall*, with reference to the expertly made 1957 thriller *Nightfall*.) Other defining traits include an insistence on showing realistic light sources in interior scenes; a slightly surreal manner of lighting and filming exteriors that makes them feel like interiors; an emphasis on doorways, windows, and other thresholds in sets that are thoughtfully constructed and furnished; direction of actors that encourages underplaying and generally reflects the nuanced sensibility of an unostentatious humanist; and, more elusively, a preoccupation with death and a general sense that the universe is ruled by irrational elements. Tourneur believed to some extent in the supernatural and the paranormal but was too intelligent to come across as a crank; his interviews suggest he was more interested in the notion of parallel universes than in ghosts.

In short, what identifies a Tourneur picture isn't strictly speaking a style, a manner, or a group of themes, but rather a way of perceiving the world — one that perpetually finds ambiguities and leaves troubled impressions. This sensibility often works wonders in his genre films — suspense, horror, fantasy —

and even when he focuses on spirituality, as in *Stars in My Crown*, with its small-town, late-nineteenth-century preacher. But it may have hurt some of his other films commercially, even if they linger longer in our memories as a consequence.

Tourneur was the son of one of the most distinguished and cultivated film-makers of the early silent era, Maurice Tourneur (1876–1961), who made films in France and the U.S. after working as an assistant to sculptor Auguste Rodin and as an actor. The son, by most accounts, had a difficult and somewhat lonely childhood in both countries, serving a protracted apprenticeship as a script boy, actor, editor, production assistant, and second-unit director, and throughout his career he regarded his own work with self-effacement — though he was proud of his unusually respectful treatment of nonwhite characters.

Another thing that differentiates Tourneur from directorial grandstanders like Hitchcock and Welles is that he almost never chose his own material. He was notorious for almost never turning down an assignment, and his thoughtful rationale was that directors can't be sure in advance whether they have something to bring to a project. He did fight to make *Stars in My Crown*, his first film with McCrea and understandably one of his favorites. He wanted to make it so badly he finally agreed to direct it for a pittance — inadvertently lowering his salary for the remainder of his career. Apparently the only other time he took an active role in deciding what to direct was at the same studio, MGM, the same year, 1950, when he rejected *Devil's Doorway*, saying the script was awful.

Tourneur is one of the few important American directors of the '50s who welcomed CinemaScope, arguing that "it reproduces approximately our field of vision," "obliges the director to work harder," "makes it possible to create interesting relationships between characters in the foreground and those in the background," and "makes it necessary to compose." *Wichita*, his first film in CinemaScope, is also, as Fujiwara points out, his major work in Cinema-Scope, though lamentably it's almost impossible to see the film in that format. Turner Classic Movies, which generally letterboxes all widescreen films, cropped it horribly when screening it in 1999. I've been told that LaSalle Bank is screening a 16-millimeter 'Scope print, but I don't know how much of the original format will be visible and undistorted. [2009 postscript: Gabe Klinger, who attended that screening, reported back that it was a "reduction print."][1]

This format matters, partly because *Wichita* is about the relationship between an individual and a community, and both the community and the setting (as well as their interplay) get reduced and simplified whenever the image is cropped. Here peripheral details count as much as empty space and off-center compositions — all of which get obscured when the image is mutilated to fit TV screens. I should add that Tourneur's superb taste as a colorist would undoubtedly be enhanced by the full rectangular glimpses of the town, where some of the buildings are painted yellow, green, orange, and brown in striking juxtapositions.

Wichita superficially resembles some John Ford westerns because of Earp (a character in Ford's *My Darling Clementine* and *Cheyenne Autumn*), because the romantic interest is played by Vera Miles (who would later turn up in *The Searchers* and *The Man Who Shot Liberty Valance*), and because the town has a newspaper run by an idealistic but ineffectual drunk (like Edmond O'Brien in *The Man Who Shot Liberty Valance*). But this shouldn't lead one to suppose that the characters in Tourneur's films belong to the same universe. The world of Ford is ruled by community, and everyone has a place. The world of Tourneur is ruled mainly by fear and terror, and nothing and no one remains fixed.

As Earp first approaches and then enters the town, we see three times in succession a placard and banner that reads, "Everything Goes in Wichita." The slogan suggests freewheeling capitalism, raucous boozing, and womanizing — all implicitly equated — but it eventually takes on an apocalyptic meaning, as in "Everything Goes to Hell in Wichita." Bringing law and order to such a place is surely a noble activity, yet bringing it through one death after another may not be. Earp says he's sorry before he dispatches the final villain, and because of Tourneur's delicacy, we're sorry too. "He shot it out with the worst men in Wichita," sings Ritter at the beginning, "made every man lay his pistol down. No one fooled with the marshal of Wichita, and today it's a very nice town." Maybe, but thanks to Tourneur, I don't quite believe it.

Chicago Reader, December 5, 2003

Note

1. Since this was written, the film has become available on DVD, in the correct format. [2009]

Cinema of the Future:
Still Lives: The Films of Pedro Costa

Gene Siskel Film Center, November 17–December 4, 2007

The cinema of Portuguese filmmaker Pedro Costa is populated not so much by characters in the literary sense as by raw essences — souls, if you will. This is a trait he shares with other masters of portraiture, including Robert Bresson, Charlie Chaplin, Jacques Demy, Alexander Dovzhenko, Carl Dreyer, Kenji Mizoguchi, Yasujiro Ozu, and Jacques Tourneur. It's not a religious predilection but rather a humanist, spiritual, and aesthetic tendency. What carries these mysterious souls, and us along with them, isn't stories — though untold or partially told stories pervade all six of Costa's features. It's fully realized moments, secular epiphanies.

Born in Lisbon in 1959, by his own account Costa grew up without much of a family, and family life — actual or simulated — is central to his work. All his films are about the dispossessed in one way or another. As the Argentine film critic Quintín puts it, he's "a cool guy — very rock 'n' roll" (in fact he was a rock guitarist before he turned to filmmaking). "At the same time," Quintín continues, he is "quietly telling whoever will listen that cinema is exactly the opposite of what 99% of the film world thinks, and he is getting more radical every day."

One can't claim Costa is critically unrecognized. His films have been discussed very perceptively by Thom Andersen, Tag Gallagher, Shigehiko Hasumi, James Quandt, Mark Peranson, and Jeff Wall, among others. (Look online for fine essays by Costa and Hasumi in *Rouge* and by Gallagher in *Senses of Cinema*.) But, like Kira Muratova and Pere Portabella, he's never had a feature in the Chicago or New York film festivals,[1] and he's been ignored or scorned by most of the mainstream critics at Cannes. Now the Gene Siskel Film Center is offering a retrospective of all his features (though lamentably none of his shorts).

Despite his rigor and his attachment to avant-garde filmmakers Jean-Marie Straub and Danièle Huillet—the subjects of his fifth and most accessible feature, *Where Lies Your Hidden Smile?* (2001)—many of Costa's cinematic reference points are Hollywood auteurs. You could even say that he's been consciously remaking some of the movies of John Ford, Howard Hawks, Fritz Lang, and Tourneur on his own terms—in Portuguese slums, most recently in digital video, with nonprofessional actors, some of them exiles from the former Portuguese colony of Cape Verde or junkies. Though this makes the films sound crude, the dialogue is scripted, the scenes are rehearsed and shot several times, and visual beauty is a constant. *Colossal Youth* (2006) can be seen as a remake of Ford's theatrically lit *Sergeant Rutledge* (1960), with the traumatized Cape Verdean patriarch Ventura standing in for Woody Strode. And Costa's frequently dazzling color palettes derive in part, he says, from having watched Ford's *She Wore a Yellow Ribbon* (1949) "very, very stoned."

Costa's films have the reputation of being difficult, but I would argue that three of them are relatively accessible. I had no trouble diving headfirst into his first color feature, *Casa de Lava* (1994, stupidly translated as *Down to Earth*), a voluptuous remake of Tourneur's 1943 film *I Walked with a Zombie*; the zombie here is Isaach de Bankolé, playing a construction worker in a protracted coma. And Costa's black-and-white first feature, *The Blood* (1989), was gripping even though I couldn't follow all of the plot, its fairy-tale poetics evoking Charles Laughton's *The Night of the Hunter* (1955) and its milky whites, inky blacks, and delicate balances of light and shadow suggesting Lang's *The Big Heat* (1953) and Bresson's *Pickpocket* (1959). *Where Lies Your Hidden Smile?* shows Straub and Huillet editing their 1999 feature *Sicilia!*, making only five cuts per day and quarreling endlessly over each one; it reveals the difference a single frame can make and how much the two need each other. Aptly described as a romantic comedy, it's the only Costa feature that isn't sad and the best film ever made about filmmaking.

But teasing out the narrative in the other three features—all shot in Lisbon slums and hovels, many being audibly and visibly razed—is no easy matter. And getting used to their idiosyncrasies is a challenge because, as Quintín suggests, you have to accept Costa's terms, which means rethinking the way you watch movies. *Bones* (1997), *In Vanda's Room* (2000), and *Colossal Youth* focus on some of the same people and places. *Bones* was shot on film with a conventional crew and has a conventional running time (ninety-four minutes); the actors, though mostly nonprofessionals, play characters with different names. But Costa himself shot the latter two on DV over several years, using crews of just two or three people. They're both about three hours long, the camera never moves, and the performers, all nonprofessionals, play themselves.

The most common complaint about Costa is that he aestheticizes poverty. But the same complaint could be made against many novelists — Nelson Algren, for instance — and countless visual artists. None of Costa's aestheticizing makes abject poverty look attractive, and much of it confounds the very notion that neorealism opens a door onto the world. Costa himself describes what he creates as "a closed door that leaves us guessing" — the title of a lecture he gave in Tokyo, presented on the *Rouge* site. Given how obsessed he is with doors and windows in his films, it's a literal as well as figurative description of his work. "Fiction is always a door that we want to open or not — it's not a script," he said. "We've got to learn that a door is for coming and going. I believe that today, in the cinema, when we open a door, it's always quite false, because it says to the spectator: 'Enter this film and you're going to be fine, you're going to have a good time,' and finally what you see in this genre of film is nothing other than yourself, a projection of yourself."

There's no way you can project yourself into *Casa de Lava, Bones, In Vanda's Room* (Costa's toughest film), or *Colossal Youth*. Costa even discourages identification by refusing to shoot reverse angles, Hollywood's conventional way of drawing us into the characters' space. But it's hard to be indifferent toward these characters and what they do (or don't do). Costa combines Straub and Huillet's fanatical belief in capturing material reality with a more disembodied search for spiritual essence found in some chamber works by Tourneur and Dreyer. What emerges from this apparent contradiction is a passageway designed for coming and going, not a simple portal that opens onto "the truth." Rather than charge onto the premises, we go back and forth to get our bearings, and Costa's beautifully constructed sounds and images are our guide and not a destination. For all their difficulty, and despite the fact they build on older work, Costa's films are the cinema of the future, partly because of their intimate scale. As we get to know them better, they steadily grow in stature.

Chicago Reader, November 15, 2007

Note

1. As this book was going to press, the New York Film Festival was preparing to show Costa's music documentary, *Ne change rien*. [2009]

A Few Eruptions in the
House of Lava

I know I'd go from rags to riches
If you would only say you care
And though my pocket may be empty
I'd be a millionaire.

My clothes may still be torn and tattered
But in my heart I'd be a king
Your love is all that ever mattered
It's everything.

[. . .] Must I forever be a beggar
Whose golden dreams will not come true?
Or will I go from rags to riches?
My fate is up to you.

—"Rags to Riches" (by Richard Adler and Jerry Ross; sung by Tony Bennett)

In my mind, there isn't as much of a distinction between documentary and fiction as
there is between a good movie and a bad one.
—Abbas Kiarostami in an interview

The living are as scary as the dead.
—Tina in *Casa de Lava*

1   Let me preface my remarks with an embarrassing personal confession,
which also could be interpreted as a very long-winded apology. After encountering both Pedro Costa and his work for the first time in Rotterdam in early

2002, when I first saw his amazing *Où gît votre sourire enfoui?* (2001), I had an opportunity to hang out with him a little at the Buenos Aires Festival of Independent Film three months later. And soon after I returned to Chicago, Pedro kindly sent me subtitled VHS copies of that film and three others — *Casa de Lava* (1994), *Ossos* (1997), and *In Vanda's Room* (2000).

Rather than succumb to my first temptation and look at these right away, I decided to wait, for what then seemed like sound professional reasons. It's one of the terrible aspects of regular film reviewing that whatever films you happen to see, sometimes including the ones that affect you the most, tend to be forgotten once you have to see dozens or hundreds of other films, most of them terrible, afterwards. And because I knew it was only a matter of time before all of Pedro's films made it to Chicago and that I'd want to write about them all when they arrived, I decided it was better to wait and then see all or at least most of them at the same time.

Then a few glitches came along to complicate this grand scheme. I hadn't realized that it would take more than five years for a Costa retrospective to make it to Chicago. Even worse, while enjoying the unparalleled luxury of having unlimited length at my disposal in all the longer pieces I wrote for the *Chicago Reader* for at least fifteen years, I hadn't foreseen that a decrease in the paper's ads due to the growth of the Internet might have led to a curtailment of that freedom, which is precisely what happened before I was finally able to write my piece in November 2007. During the five long years that I waited, my assigned length went from unlimited to 1,200 words — an absurdly tight space in which to consider all six of Pedro's features. And to make matters worse, Ricardo Matos Cabo, the editor of this collection,[1] had meanwhile contacted me half a year earlier, inviting me to contribute something of about twice that length, but not having seen most of the films, I felt I was unable to accept.

Finally, by the time a Chicago Costa retrospective was scheduled, I'd seen *Juventude em marca* (2006) in Toronto, but not yet *O sangue* (1989) or the three features that followed it. So I wound up discovering most of his oeuvre backwards and in a hurry, long after many friends and colleagues had written eloquently about it. And while doing so, I found that, even though I simultaneously loved and had to struggle in diverse ways with all of Costa's films, *Casa de Lava*, his only landscape film, was the one that blew me away the most. So when Ricardo emailed me again in early January 2008, inviting me specifically to write about this film as a last-minute entry for his collection — even though neither of us had much time to spare — I had to say yes. Nevertheless, I hope I can be forgiven for imitating this movie a little by letting improvisation, fragmentation, and somewhat disconnected notes overtake any firm position, sustained argument, or conclusion.

2   I don't know whether the Tony Bennett song quoted above is the un-acknowledged (or perhaps unrecognized) source of the lovely melody played repeatedly by Bassoé (Raul Andrade) on his violin in *Casa de Lava* or if the re-semblance is coincidental. Either way, and whatever the intentionality might be on the part of Andrade or Costa or anyone else, the relation of one to the other reminds me of the relation of *Casa de Lava* to *I Walked with a Zombie* and other Hollywood and non-Hollywood films. Some people, unlike me, feel that as a reference point, *I Walked with a Zombie* provides an obstacle or distraction when it comes to appreciating *Casa de Lava* rather than a useful key that unlocks some of the film's treasures. Others feel that *Stromboli* is a more helpful reference point, whereas for me it is the Rossellini film, with its very different and less politicized form of mysticism, that provides a distraction and an obstacle, whatever its own merits.

There are at least four other Andrades listed in the cast of *Casa de Lava*, all of them playing children of Bassoé—one of many factors that suggests that the film, like all of Costa's other films, is an intricate mixture of fact and fic-tion. Costa told Mark Peranson in *Cinema Scope* (issue no. 22) that the film was originally scripted, but "at one point I just left the script behind, because I thought that if I'm going to try to shoot this girl in this new place that's foreign and dangerous, then I have to shoot it from her point of view" and "There was a lot of improvisation each day"—one indication among many that Mariana (Inês Medeiros), the lead character, largely functions as Costa's surrogate in the film. Nearly all the ethical questions and ambiguities posed about her involvement with the islands' residents are those raised by Costa's involve-ment—that is to say, his filmmaking—as well. And improvisation is perhaps the most obvious way of raising the existential stakes of these issues. As Costa notes, he and Isaach De Bankolé even came to blows over the latter's objec-tions as a professional actor to his character Leao having to remain in a coma for most or all of the film. (It's also my impression—gleaned from the account of a friend who attended Costa's discussion of the film in Los Angeles—that Leao, like his rough counterpart in *I Walked with a Zombie*, never would have come out of his coma at all if it hadn't been for Bankolé's objections.)

In the same interview, speaking about *O sangue*, Costa admits a personal as-pect in his concentration on "the three boys, the family" in that film, "because I never really had a family. My mother died early, then I went to live with my father, who then went away. From the age of 14, I was alone . . ." And I've noted elsewhere my impression that all of Costa's films seem to be about outsiders and improvised families. So it seems to me that the passionate struggle of out-siders to find and maintain makeshift families provide much of the meaning as well as the methodology of his work. Existentially speaking, if one combines this struggle with Costa's uncanny and always evolving talent for composition and color, the overall aspiration resembles both what Godard has called "the definitive by chance" and the fusion of fiction and documentary sought and found by Kiarostami (especially in *Life and Nothing More*, *Through the Olive Trees*, and *The Wind Will Carry Us*, whose plots also feature strained interactions between big-city protagonists and the impoverished yet exotic villagers they're visiting).

It also suggests that *Casa de Lava* may be the film of Costa's that poses the most constant and furious tug of war between Hollywood narrative and the portraiture of both places and people, staging an almost epic battle between the two. These warring modes become almost magically fused whenever there is a landscape shot with one or more human figures; every time this happens, the film moves into high gear.[2]

The film begins with stark island portraits, evocative of films by both Straub-Huillet (their fiery Etna and their actors, sometimes glimpsed from behind or in fragments) and Dovzhenko (brooding and heroic still-lifes), only to shift from there to the shards of a Lisbon narrative. Typically, in the latter stretches, we're either told too little about what's happening in order to be able to follow the story or everything we could possibly want to know — in both cases in a rather mannerist fashion. First we get quizzical fragments and a very oblique narrative, served up almost as directly as the island portraits were — the sounds and images of a Lisbon construction site, anticipating later Costa films, and then Leao and other construction workers seen before Leao's accident — including a bit of seemingly choreographed, playful sparring between two of them as they hustle through a doorway, returning to work — and just afterwards as well. (The accident itself is elided, but we glimpse a coworker reporting it.) Then, shortly after we're introduced to Mariana, a nurse, with a coworker at the hospital, we get enormous chunks of exposition, dumped unceremoniously into our laps. A doctor speaking to Mariana over Leao's body concludes, "They say he was sad. His name is Leao. He's been two months in a coma. Oddly, he's been discharged. The ticket's bought. Leao's going home. A check and a letter from his village, both anonymous. A woman's letter. Sad."

Much later in the film, the son (Pedro Hestnes) of a white islander, Edite (Edith Scob), gives a similarly telegraphic account of his mother, himself, and the allotment of funds, again to Mariana, over his father's grave: "She came after him. She was twenty years old. She was half his age. I never met him. He was a political prisoner. Afterwards, she never went home. She's been here for years with me. People help her. She likes them, they like her. We live here. Now we get a check every month, his pension, to pay everyone back. They know, they all wait. They all want to leave."

3   Although I can't hear Bassoé's song without thinking of Tony Bennett's, just as I can't watch *Casa de Lava* without thinking of *I Walked with a Zombie*, each transposition — if that's what it is in both cases — is so radical that there's a recasting of basic elements and presuppositions. The unhinged and bereft lack of definition of Bassoé, the old violinist — except perhaps for his melancholy "Music is a bitch. I worship her" — makes a mockery of Tony Bennett's wistful lyrics. And whatever else the man in the coma might be, he isn't a zombie, much less Tourneur's more mythical and statuesque zombie, Carrefour. As far as we can tell, Leao's an illiterate Cape Verdean construction worker in Lisbon who has an accident, winds up in a coma, and then, after being taken back to Cape Verde, takes his time coming out of it because even if he has a home to come back to, everyone else is leaving there and no one wants to stay — except, perhaps, for Mariana (if only by default) and Edite and her son. And at least the latter two speak Creole.

Whenever Mariana repeats the phrase "Speak Portuguese" to someone on the island, I'm reminded of Arthur Hunnicutt in Hawks' *The Big Sky* trying to relate to his French partners as they trek across the wilderness: "Speak English, hoss." But Mariana has no partners, and consciously or not, she remains a colonialist, perhaps even more than Edite and her son are colonialists, because she hardly gives anything to the islanders. And Costa can't interrogate her motives for remaining on the island without interrogating his own.

Is the film itself his own patient? And if so, what can Costa do once the film wakes up on its own, without his help or input? Answer: The same thing we can do. He can watch.

4   The film is a suite of denials, one after the other. Bassoé refuses to acknowledge directly that he's the father of Leao, and other locals refuse to respond when Mariana asks them if Leao is a relative. But Mariana is no less in denial when people ask her directly or indirectly why she isn't back in Lisbon. Edite's son puts it the plainest: "Why are you here?" And, like Bassoé, she never answers the question of whom she belongs to and who belongs to her.

Worst of all, she can't seem to go native as Edite, her doppelgänger, does, maybe because her own self-appointed function on the island is merely to be the caregiver of Leao, who has no clear place of his own on the island, and who can't even figure out what her exact function is even after he wakes up. Maybe she likes boys, as she puts it to Edite's son, but unlike Edite, who likes girls as well as boys, she's pretty much in denial about her sexuality whenever it has to rub shoulders with any sort of emotional commitment. The only emotional commitment she seems to have is to Leao, and this has nothing to do with Hawksian professionalism. In fact, there are no professionals in this movie —

apart from the soldiers, who never come back from whatever war they're servicing, or the doctor in the medical compound, who seems to evaporate about
halfway through the picture, or Edite, at least if she qualifies as a professional
colonialist. The other characters, so far as we can tell, are all lost children.

5　　Leao regains consciousness almost exactly halfway through the movie,
although it takes Mariana much longer than that to become aware of this.
Even some of the lost children, such as Tina, know it sooner. It would be
interesting to know what Costa's original scenario would have consisted of if
Leao had remained in a coma for the remainder of the movie. As things stand,
and no doubt because of the improvisation, the film breaks up and gradually
atrophies into fragments and miniplots, a little bit like *Muriel* or *Petulia*. But,
come to think of it, *I Walked with a Zombie* also winds up subverting the very
notion of a consecutive, coherent plot. Here one could almost say that each
beautiful composition — that is to say, each shot — tells a separate story. Put
them all together and they might seem to resemble the lengthy tracking shot
that follows Mariana's stride through the village, at once purposeful and aimless, as various obstructions pass and periodically block our vision. Now we
see her, now we don't — and neither we nor she seems to know where she's
headed.

Written for a collection of essays about Pedro Costa edited by Ricardo Matos Cabo

Notes

1. This collection finally appeared in Portuguese only, in Fall 2009, in a very handsome volume, *Cem Mil Cigarros: Os Filmes de Pedro Costa*, published jointly (in Lisbon) by Orfeu Negro and Midas Filmes.
2. In November 2008, when I was in Lisbon (serving on the DocLisboa jury), I asked
Costa at one point why he hadn't made any more landscape films. "It's too easy," he
said.

Unsatisfied Men:
Beau travail

Maybe freedom begins with remorse. [*Pause.*]
Maybe freedom begins with remorse. I heard that somewhere.
—from the narration of *Beau travail*

I know it sounds fancy to say this, but the difference between Claire Denis's early work and *Beau travail* is quite simply the difference between making movies and making cinema. By analogy, Charlie Parker went from playing jazz with Jay McShann to making music with his own groups, and that quantum leap included content and substance as well as technique — matter and manner became indistinguishable. Denis too has developed a new kind of mastery while tackling a new kind of material.

The predominant mode of this material is reverie — poetic rumination that pointedly doesn't discriminate between major and minor events, intertwining both into a kind of endless magical tapestry. A gorgeous early image superimposing emerald blue water in motion over a hand writing in a diary evokes the magic to come. At times the movie suggests Terrence Malick's *The Thin Red Line* without the warfare; Denis works in a wonderfully spare and beautiful style that allows mountains, plains, deserts, and bodies of water to speak eloquently for themselves, and she lets a tone of plaintive lament in the offscreen narration run across these diverse settings and textures without ever becoming self-pitying. (Literally, "beau travail" means "beautiful work," and idiomatically, it might be translated as "good work" or "fine craftsmanship"; all three meanings are apt.)

In interfacing everyday banality with tragedy and violence, the film bears an indirect relationship to two important French New Wave features of the early '60s, Jean-Luc Godard's *Le petit soldat* and Alain Resnais's *Muriel*, both of which dealt with the contemporary — and then-taboo — subject of the Algerian war. (Initially the Godard film was banned in France and the Resnais film widely attacked; both were commercial flops just about everywhere they were shown.) In different ways, both of these controversial and courageous films examined the impossibility of dealing with torture and violence in Algeria in relation to daily life in Europe at the time; *Beau travail* — set in contemporary Marseilles and peacetime Djibouti, where an interracial group of legionnaires is camped — is explicitly postcolonial. (It alludes specifically to Godard's film by casting that film's lead actor, Michel Subor, as a character with the same name, Bruno Forestier; the relation to *Muriel* is more tenuous, seen in the mood of lonely reflection and regret.)

Beau travail uses these New Wave touchstones in much the same way it uses Herman Melville's *Billy Budd* and two of his late poems, passages from Benjamin Britten's opera *Billy Budd*, and Djibouti itself: they're not so much works to be adapted or sites to be explored as they are personal talismans, aesthetic aphrodisiacs, inspirational reference points, incantations. Significantly, *Le petit soldat* made similar use of some of its art references, though that made its political positions somewhat dandyish: Forestier was modeled after Michael O'Hara, the hero of Orson Welles's *The Lady from Shanghai*, and his torture at the hands of the Algerian National Liberation Front was based on an episode in Dashiell Hammett's *The Glass Key*. His narration in the film begins, "For me, the time of action is over. I've grown older. The time for reflection has begun." And it ends, "I was happy, because I had a lot of time ahead of me." The offscreen narration of *Beau travail* — spoken by Chief Master Sergeant Galoup (Denis Lavant) — begins, "Marseilles, late February. I have a lot of time ahead of me." The difference between the Algerian war in the '50s and '60s and the relatively aimless futility of the Foreign Legion today may make the implied link seem anomalous. But other details support it: for example, Forestier in *Le petit soldat* was a French army deserter, and Denis's foreign legionnaires are figurative or literal orphans — Galoup being the most painfully romantic loner of them all, styling himself as the perfect legionnaire, which reminds one of Melville as well as Godard.

The eldest daughter of a French civil servant, Denis spent nearly all of her preteen years in Africa, including Djibouti, and part of what's so striking about her tale of the French foreign legion is that most of it doesn't proceed like a tale at all. It grew out of a French TV commission to explore the theme of "foreignness," and central to what makes it different from her earlier works is that she hired a choreographer, Bernardo Montet (who also plays one of the legionnaires), to help her stage some of the training exercises and maneuvers, which at times register like luminous and mysterious rituals. These are among the most alive and electric moments in the film — moments that improve on comparable passages in Kubrick's *Full Metal Jacket* and at times even recall certain exalted passages in Eisenstein's *Alexander Nevsky* when the sweep of sculptural male torsos in formation perfectly matches the ecstatic cadences of Prokofiev's music. It's also central to Denis's achievement that, with or without the astute musical choices — which also include a song by Neil Young, Afro-pop, Corona's "Rhythm of the Night," and legionnaire songs — one can't always tell which of the scenes Montet worked on. The whole film unfolds like a continuous dance, and there's as much choreography in the movements between shots as there is in the movements of the actors or the placement of the landscapes. (The notion of a military theater has seldom been so pronounced, even if it usually registers as avant-garde theater; how much this inflects the postcolonial meaning of the story, which pivots around the idea of existential futility, is one of the film's key ambiguities.)

Lavant, the lead actor, is familiar to American audiences from his lead performances in the first three features of Leos Carax — *Boy Meets Girl* (1984), *Bad Blood* (1986), and *Lovers on the Bridge* (1992) — in which he plays essentially the same character, a guy named Alex, Carax's own real first name. Trained as an acrobat and used like an actor in silent cinema for his sheer physicality, Lavant is almost a decade older than he was in *Lovers on the Bridge*, but he still seems like a switchblade ready to spring open. His contained intensity cuts loose in a solitary disco dance he performs at the end of *Beau travail*, in which he moves to "Rhythm of the Night" like a dervish, recalling one of his manic cadenzas in *Bad Blood*. His identity as Galoup is a far cry from his previous incarnations as Alex, yet Denis is clearly superimposing Galoup on Alex, just as she's superimposing Subor's Forestier on his Forestier in Godard's film; Grégoire Colin's Gilles Sentain might also remind one of his previous roles in *Oliver, Oliver*; *Queen Margot*; *Before the Rain*; *The Son of Gascogne*; Denis's *Nenette and Boni*; *Secret défense*; and *The Dreamlife of Angels*. All three of these characters are also designed to echo, respectively, Master-at-Arms Claggart, Captain Vere, and Billy Budd in Melville's novella.

The plot, also suggested by the novella, consists of Galoup, alone in Marseilles and toying with the possibility of suicide, recalling his life in Djibouti before he was dishonorably discharged by Forestier, and selected memories of what led to his dismissal: developing an irrational and obsessive hatred for Sentain, a new recruit everyone else liked, and eventually dropping him off a truck in the middle of a desert with a faulty compass. Sentain almost dies but is found by African civilians and nursed back to health by a woman we see with him on a bus; the final glimpses we have of him are practically the only scenes that don't include Galoup, and for all we know, they could be transpiring in Galoup's imagination.

None of this is meant to imply that you need to have Denis's cinematic, literary, or musical background to appreciate this movie. No more necessary are the two late Melville poems she cites as direct inspirations, "The Night March" and "Gold in the Mountain," which suggest that raw feelings are what really count, not intellectual associations. The first poem reads:

> With banners furled, and clarions mute,
> An army passes in the night;
> And beaming spears and helms salute
> The dark with bright.
>
> In silence deep the legions stream,
> With open ranks, in order true;
> Over boundless plains they stream and gleam —
> No chief in view!
>
> Afar, in twinkling distance lost,
> (So legends tell) he lonely wends
> And back through all that shining host
> His mandate sends.

The second reads:

> Gold in the mountain,
> And gold in the glen,
> And greed in the heart,
> Heaven having no part,
> And unsatisfied men.

Machismo isn't what I generally go to movies hoping to find, nor is the homoeroticism of military imagery. I suspect it was my lack of taste for the macho in general and Denis's dark vision in particular that led me to write of her semiautobiographical *Chocolat* (1988) when it came out, "As a first feature, this is respectable enough work, though the intelligence here seems at times closer to Louis Malle (for better and for worse) than to any of Denis's former employers"—i.e., Eduardo de Gregorio, Jim Jarmusch, Dusan Makavejev, Jacques Rivette, and Wim Wenders, all of whom she'd worked for as an assistant director. Since I didn't like Malle as much as the other five directors — I thought his pessimistic view of humanity bordered on sadism — I suppose I meant mainly "for worse."

The same bias also led me to choose adjectives such as "grim," "sordid," and "depressing" two years later when I reviewed Denis's *No Fear, No Die*, a well-acted, noirish B-film about cockfighters in the Paris suburbs. And even though I liked her extended documentary *Jacques Rivette, le veilleur* (1990) and found more and more things to like in *I Can't Sleep* (1994) and *Nenette and Boni* (1996), the most I could say for her until recently was that she was a talented filmmaker who didn't speak to me. *I Can't Sleep*, a serial-killer movie, offered an interesting portrait of a Paris neighborhood, but it seemed to wallow in a kind of professional morbidity; *Nenette and Boni*, an even more troubling — and more interesting — sicko story about two teenage siblings in Marseilles, irritated me by coyly suggesting incestuous abuse without being explicit.

Did previous Denis films have a poetry I didn't notice or appreciate, or did she make a quantum leap as an artist in *Beau travail*? Probably some of both. In any case, I now think she's capable of poetry well beyond the range of someone like Malle. And it isn't as if the homoeroticism here makes her a soul sister to Jean Genet, even if some of her imagery — perhaps most notably a patch of lyricism about legionnaires ironing trouser creases — calls him to mind. In fact, "homoerotic" might superficially describe a few strains of the polytonality Denis is working with (Kent Jones aptly cites Ornette Coleman in the May–June 2000 *Film Comment*), but it isn't an adequate label for her new material.

Part of what fascinates me so much about *Beau travail* is how unmistakably it qualifies as a film directed and cowritten by a woman (and, incidentally, shot by another woman, Agnès Godard), even though it doesn't conform to any platitudes about women filmmakers' films. For instance, I can't for the life of me think of another film by a woman that reminds me of Eisenstein. *Beau travail* evokes him not only in the aforementioned encounters between sculptural bodies and heroic music, but in its musically inflected montages and its beautifully ordered compositions devoted to various maneuvers: crawling under barbed wire, vaulting over bars, occupying the shell of a half-constructed building, walking across parallel wires like tightrope artists imitating flurries of notes on a musical staff. (Leni Riefenstahl gave us only kitsch Eisenstein at best, and she was much more conventionally homoerotic in both *Triumph of the Will* and *Olympia*.)

Maybe what most marks *Beau travail* as a film by a woman is the way Denis uses African women to subtly impose an ironic frame around the story; from beginning to end, they figure implicitly and unobtrusively as a kind of mainly mute Greek chorus — whether they're dancing in the disco, speaking in the market, appearing briefly as the girlfriends of some legionnaires (including Galoup), or serving as witnesses to portions of the action. They're clearly outside the plot, yet they're by no means absent, either physically or morally — and their noble function is underscored by the contrast between the splashy colors of their apparel and the green rot of the military uniforms. In an early scene, when the women briefly observe the meaningless occupation of the construction site and begin laughing, the choral function of the perpetually amused black characters in Elia Kazan and Tennessee Williams's *Baby Doll* is what sprang to my mind. The film virtually opens with women dancing to Afro-pop in the same disco lounge where Galoup explodes at the end, punctuating the tune they're dancing to with what Stuart Klawans in the *Nation* calls air kisses. These playful, pecking riffs, which are like little laughs as well as kisses, mock the very notion of a mating ritual, which in effect means mocking in advance Galoup's melodramatic-romantic obsession with Sentain and all the turmoil it produces. And implicitly they mock his doomed and equally absurd love affair with the French foreign legion.

Chicago Reader, May 26, 2000; slightly revised, August 2009

Viridiana on DVD

Spoilers ahead: The title heroine (Silvia Pinal) of Luis Buñuel's master-piece, a Spanish novice about to take her final vows, is ordered by her mother superior to visit her rich uncle (Fernando Rey), Don Jaime, who's been supporting her over the years but whom she barely knows. A necrophiliac foot fetishist, he's preoccupied with how closely his beautiful niece resembles his late wife, who died tragically on their wedding night, and somehow man-ages to persuade Viridiana to put on her wedding dress, which he's faithfully preserved. With the help of his servant Ramona (Margarita Lozano), he then drugs her with the intention of raping her, but, deeply mortified by his behav-ior, ultimately holds back and hangs himself instead, using the skipping rope he previously gave to Ramona's little girl.

If this opening strongly evokes the horror of a Gothic novel — a form of literature Luis Buñuel was especially drawn to — it takes on further dimensions just after this suicide, an outcome already complicated by the fact that Don Jaime, no simple villain and highly principled, is shown rather sympatheti-cally. Believing herself to have been ravaged, Viridiana renounces her vows without losing any of her faith and piety, and, inheriting Don Jaime's estate, decides to take in local beggars as an act of charity. Their responses to her generosity are mainly venal, and they immediately start treating one another with scorn and envy. One of them takes over the skipping rope as a belt to hold up his trousers — an emblematic example of how Buñuel imbues his universe with a sense of ironic relativity.

Meanwhile, Don Jaime's illegitimate son, Jorge (Francisco Rabal), arrives as co-heir, hoping to improve the neglected property and meanwhile sharing the house with Viridiana and the beggars. He has a mistress in tow, but she quickly departs after deciding he's more interested in his cousin. Then, when

Viridiana and Jorge go off on a day trip, the beggars throw a raucous party and have an orgiastic feast, at one point briefly duplicating in their stances and gestures the figures in Leonardo da Vinci's *Last Supper*. When Viridiana and Jorge return, another attempt to rape her by one of the beggars is only averted by Jorge's offer of a bribe. In a teasingly ambiguous finale, Viridiana is later seen participating in a three-way card game with Jorge and Ramona.

■■■■■■■■■

It's seldom recognized that *Viridiana* (1961) is the first feature Buñuel ever directed in his native Spain — and only the second film he directed there after his half-hour documentary *Las Hurdes* almost three decades earlier. Given all his years of exile in the U.S. and Mexico, this reestablishing of his roots is an important aspect of what enabled him to reinvent himself afterwards as an international arthouse icon. "For us," said Pedro Portabella, one of the film's two Spanish executive producers, in a 1999 interview, "Buñuel was the only solid reference point in our cinema." And insofar as he was the most Spanish of Spanish filmmakers, this particular context is worth stressing.

It isn't stressed on Criterion's otherwise excellent DVD of *Viridiana*, which doesn't mention Portabella — in my view, another important Spanish film-maker, quite apart from his producing — either in the extras or in the accompanying booklet. (By contrast, he was mentioned twice in a brief production story about *Viridiana* in the Spring 1961 issue of *Sight and Sound*, which also cited his then-recent work with Carlos Saura and Marco Ferreri.) But then again our overall sense of Buñuel's history tends to be rather spotty, and our sense of Spanish cinema under Franco is almost nonexistent. A dictatorship which caused time to freeze and a closed society to remain insulated helped to sustain our ignorance about the country for decades, and Buñuel's fractured career has also been subject to certain capitalist forms of censorship. Most readers of his autobiography in English translation — titled *My Last Sigh* when "My Last Gasp" would be more appropriate — are unaware that unacknowledged excisions in the text have been made on practically every page, apparently on the assumption that us Yanks wouldn't care or be interested. (I once went to the trouble of photocopying the French version so I could start to glean all I'd been missing.)

Spanish cinema under Franco has become such a closed book to us that notable acts of witness as well as resistance to its repressions have often been ignored or misread, with Buñuel sometimes perversely used as an instrument of — or alibi for — our own repression. Having recently made a belated discovery of two remarkable (if currently unfashionable) features by Juan Antonio Bardem (1922–2002), *Death of a Cyclist* (1955) and *Calle Mayor* (1956) — both forthright antifascist films that, in the tradition of Clouzot's *Le Corbeau* (1943), take the shape of displaced allegories out of necessity, exposing the ugliness, cruelty, and brutality of fascism's social effects as reflected in male-female relationships — I was shocked to find them both dismissed in David Thomson's *A Biographical Dictionary of the Cinema* as simple realist melodramas. (*Calle Mayor* — which evokes *I Vitelloni* to the same degree that *Cyclist* evokes *Cronaca di un amore* — is even misdescribed as an adaptation of Sinclair Lewis's *Main Street*, apparently on the basis of its English title, when a more accurate reference point would be Neil LaBute's *In the Company of Men*, which arguably bears the same relation to capitalism that *Calle Mayor* bears to fascism.) But to get some inkling of the difficulties Bardem faced while making it, check out Betsy Blair's *The Memory of All That*. Worst of all, Bardem — whose films have far more to tell us about Franco Spain than *Viridiana* — is chastised by Thomson for not being Buñuel; only one anti-Franco vision is permitted. Clearly some kinds of fascist prohibition are contagious. But it would be bracing to see Criterion defy them long enough to bring out a Bardem film or two on DVD. [2009 postscript: It has subsequently brought out *Death of a Cyclist* — but not, alas, *Calle Mayor*, which I find far superior.]

In other words, the limitations in Criterion's grasp of *Viridiana*'s Spanish context are basically inherited ones — the outgrowths of long-term and fairly widespread lazy habits. And they're both offset and to some extent underlined by the DVD's extras: fine interviews with *Viridiana*'s Mexican star Pinal (whose husband became the film's Mexican producer) and *Cineaste* editor Richard Porton, and an equally informative 1964 documentary on Buñuel for the French TV series *Cinéastes de notre temps*. (The menu claims that the latter is only "edited excerpts," though a comparison of running times suggests that the only likely missing pieces are a few odd clips due to clearance problems.) Porton usefully links what he calls *Viridiana*'s religious masochism with Buñuel's earlier *Nazarin* and his subsequent *Simon of the Desert*, thus opting for a certain thematic continuity that downplays the distinction between the Mexico of these two films and the Spain of *Viridiana*. (To be fair, however, he's also attentive to Buñuel's links to Spanish Communists and the way in which Spain offered him a way of redefining his Surrealism in more realistic terms.)

Pinal, of course, offers a Mexican view of Buñuel while the documentary offers an explicitly French one, with Georges Sadoul among the interviewees. What seems missing from all three of these approaches is a sense of how the seemingly "timeless" medievalism of Franco Spain — encompassing the same sort of Quixotic nostalgia for feudalism that presumably led Orson Welles to overlook his political scruples when he chose to live and work there during the '50s and '60s — may have provided Buñuel with a more "universal" canvas for his ironic parables than anything he could find in Mexico. (Arguably, Robert Bresson profited from a similar medieval ambience in rural France in *Au Hasard Balthazar* and *Mouchette* a few years later.)

Admittedly, a helpful interview with Buñuel in Criterion's booklet is headlined "The Return to Spain," and Michael Wood's notes, even if they don't mention *Las Hurdes*, say that *Viridiana* "did cause a tremendous stir" after winning the Palme d'or at Cannes and that the film was banned in Spain until 1977. (In 1961, the heads of at least two Franco government officials rolled — apparently the one who approved the film getting made, whom Wood vaguely mentions, and the one who accepted the award while Buñuel craftily remained in Paris, whom Wood doesn't mention. But, citing Buñuel, Wood adds that Franco himself, when he finally came to see the film, reportedly found little to object to.) What the notes don't say is to my mind far more telling: that the film was denied Spanish nationality by the Franco government after the Cannes prize and that all its official papers were confiscated and/or destroyed. "*Viridiana* simply did not exist," Portabella remarked in the 1999 interview. "They did not prohibit it, they simply erased it. . . . Eight years later, the [censors], at a meeting on January 30, 1969, prohibited the exhibition of a Mexican film entitled *Viridiana*. It was classified as: 'Blasphemous, antireligious. Cruel and contemptuous of the poor. Also morbid and brutal. A poisonous film, caustic in its cinematographic ability to combine images, references, and music.'"

I'm far from being a specialist in these matters, and should confess that some aspects of my slant on *Viridiana* derive from recent correspondence with Portabella. Furthermore, I don't speak Spanish, but a Cuban playwright friend who recently resaw *Viridiana* told me he was amazed by the absolute accuracy of all the dialects and accents given to each of the characters in terms of class, profession, cultural background, and region — a kind of precision that he found unmatched in Buñuel's subsequent *Tristana*, after his encroaching deafness became worse, as well as in his Mexican pictures, most of which were made earlier.

Some of this exactness gets conveyed even to those of us who don't know the language (although I'm told it helps to understand the double entendres involving the "threesome" in the final card-playing scene — Buñuel's clever and suggestive way of replacing a more obviously carnal finale of Viridiana forsaking her chastity after the censors objected.) It's part of the film's overall triumph of combining simplicity and directness with so much moral ambiguity that no character is ever being set up for simple scorn or admiration. This includes Viridiana, Don Jaime, Ramona (the most ambiguous figure of all in terms of her shifting alliances), Jorge, and even the beggars.

While Buñuel, possibly the cinema's key master of political incorrectness, is certainly interested in challenging his heroine's sense of virtue with the beggars' orgy, he never stoops to scorn or ridicule. When Robert Altman in *M*A*S*H* copied Buñuel's *Last Supper* gag, there's some form of mockery that seemingly got added to the mix, but it's absent from the original, where nothing's ever that simple, even when it feels fairly elemental. And it's no less characteristic of Buñuel, an equal-employment humanist, to assign a humane protest against the mistreatment of a dog not to Viridiana but to the acerbic Jorge.

Cineaste 31, no. 4 (September 2006)

Doing the *California Split*

"Trusting to luck means listening to voices," Jean-Luc Godard reportedly said at some point in the mid-sixties. This has always struck me as one of his more obscure aphorisms, and one that even seems to border on the mystical. Yet the minute one starts to apply it to Robert Altman's *California Split*, released in 1974 — a free-form comedy about the friendship that develops and then plays itself out between two compulsive gamblers, Charlie (Elliott Gould) and Bill (George Segal), and the first movie ever to use an 8-Track mixer — it starts to make some weird kind of sense.

What's an 8-track mixer? According to the maestro of overlapping dialogue himself, speaking in David Thompson's *Altman on Altman* (Faber and Faber, 2006), this is a system developed by Jim Webb known as Lion's Gate 8-Tracks, and it grew directly out of Altman's ongoing efforts to make onscreen dialogue sound more real. Sound mixers would frequently complain that some actors wouldn't speak loudly enough and Altman would counter that this was a re-cording problem, not a performance problem involving the actors' deliveries. Plant enough microphones around the set or on the location — in this case, eight — and one could always adjust the volume later, when the separate chan-nels were being mixed together and one could decide which channels should predominate, and in which proportion. In other words, assuming that you had a certain amount of scripted dialogue and a certain amount of "background" improvs being delivered at the same time — the modus operandi of many Alt-man movies, especially this one — trusting to luck was a matter of recording all this dialogue on eight separate tracks. And listening to voices was what you did afterward — shoot first and ask questions later, working out a hierarchy of what should have the most clarity after the fact. If an improv was funnier or more relevant than a scripted line delivered at the same moment, allow the former to overtake the latter.

Even before the title sequence starts, over the familiar Columbia Pictures logo, *California Split* has already started to chatter. A steady rush of talk — telegraphed, overheard, sometimes barely audible — spills into the opening scenes like a scatter of loose change from a slot machine, meeting or eluding our grasp in imitation of a strictly chance operation. Admittedly, the overall odds of the game are somewhat fixed because the movie has a script (by Joseph Walsh, a gambler himself), two box-office favorites, and hard Hollywood money behind it. But the improvisatory spirit is unmistakable, if only because an alert audience is obliged to ad-lib in order to keep up, compelled to shift its attention as often as the characters.

So using Lion's Gate 8-Tracks was putting into practice a certain dialectic of chance and control, one of the cornerstones of Altman's filmmaking style. And this would become even more systematic in the movie Altman made next, *Nashville*, where instead of having just two main characters, Altman opted, at least in theory, to feature two dozen. (Some of them proved to be much more prominent than others.) And when he made *A Wedding* in 1978, he arbitrarily decided to double that number to forty-eight.

But in fact, the most apt cross-reference to *California Split* in the Altman canon isn't either of those films but his lesser-known *Jazz '34: Remembrances of Kansas City Swing* (1977) — a feature-length adjunct to *Kansas City* that featured real jazz musicians in period costume casually performing after hours in a 1934 Kansas City club. This culminates in a friendly but frenetic cutting contest between two tenor sax players trading solos, not unlike some of the riffs developed in *California Split* between Gould and Segal. More generally, this simultaneously relaxed and lively swing-fest, a celebration of collective euphoria, shows how deeply akin Altman's style is to the aesthetics of improvised jazz, which at its best tends to thrive not so much through competition as through the kind of sudden inspiration that fellow players can spark in one another.

A compulsive casino gambler, Altman once boasted, "At one time I could stand at a craps table for two days." And he inherited "by chance" a film project scripted by another compulsive gambler, Joseph Walsh, who had been developing his script with Steven Spielberg, of all people, during his pre-*Jaws* phase. (Walsh was a child actor in the fifties and sixties, prominently featured as Joey Walsh in such films as *Hans Christian Andersen* and *The Juggler* and countless TV shows; in *California Split* he plays Sparkie, a bookie owed a fortune by Bill.)

Of course Walsh was taking a gamble himself by trusting his script to a master doodler like Altman who favored improvs. Nevertheless, figuring out what's prearranged or not in this movie isn't always a simple matter, and it's often the spirit and climate of improvisation that counts more here than anything else. The opening sequence, where Charlie and Bill first encounter one another at a poker table in a gambling hall, certainly looks and sounds authentic, but it was shot on a set designed by Altman regular Leon Ericksen, who redressed a dance hall. Most of the extras were hired from the drug rehabilitation center Synanon, although a few real gamblers were included as well, and some of the background dialogue was loosely plotted if not precisely scripted by Walsh (whose own brother Edward plays a pivotal role as another poker player — a sore loser who accuses Charlie of cheating, and later beats him up). So the mix between real and semi-real, simulated and actual, is pretty intricate, and it's only because of the DVD commentary by Altman, Walsh, Gould, and Segal that we know that Charlie and Bill's drunken efforts to reel off the names of all the seven dwarfs were invented by the two actors.

We also know that the house Charlie shares with two hookers (Ann Prentiss and Gwen Welles) is a real house and not a set, that most of the film was shot in continuity (allowing the seven dwarfs gag to get reprised at the house), and that Altman staged both the horse race and the prizefight that the heroes attend, but also used plenty of extras at those locations who qualified as authentic. Most importantly, the mix between fiction and documentary throughout is so fully entangled that each winds up educating the other, while the multiple sound levels lead to periodic eruptions, especially in bar scenes, where peripheral characters briefly upstage and overtake the two leads, background becoming foreground and vice versa. One example among many is actually set in a paint store, where Bill looks up his old friend Harvey and gets an impromptu and irrelevant monologue from him about his alleged ESP and why he thinks Bill has tracked him down. Like a minor character in a painting by Brueghel or a comedy by Preston Sturges, he momentarily takes over the movie, then drops out of sight.

Needless to say, this resembles gambling in the number of risks and unforeseeable outcomes that are involved, and there are naturally some losses in this kind of game as well as a few winning streaks. As Altman pointed out, *California Split* has less plot and more concentration on character than most of his other movies; and when the story is supposed to build to a climax — after Bill rushes off to Reno to gamble his way out of debt, with Charlie in tow — it arguably dribbles off into random shtick, or at least a dramatic diminuendo as it shows the hollowness of Bill's victory. (We also learn on the DVD that the final scene in the movie isn't the one Walsh scripted.)

Some of the chance encounters in the movie are between the dialogue and various gritty songs that are sung offscreen by Phyllis Shotwell — encounters "staged" during postproduction by the film's editor, Lou Lombardo. Shotwell eventually appears onscreen in the movie at the Reno casino, belting out her numbers to her own piano accompaniment, but the fact that we start to hear her music much earlier in the movie, long before Reno is even mentioned, suggests an eerie kind of predestination, as if she were gradually pulling the two heroes toward her establishment like a magnet.

Her lyrics usually have only the broadest relation to the action, but sometimes they draw closer in witty surprises — or at least they once did. Unhappily, two of the most magical conjunctions between her songs and the onscreen action vanished from the movie on its way to DVD, due to problems with music rights: "Goin' to Kansas City" was originally heard over the trip to Reno, and after the heroes arrived there, Gould's and Shotwell's seemingly independent raps, hers heard offscreen while Charlie and Bill crossed the street toward the casino, suddenly converged on the word "nobody," pronounced by the two voices simultaneously. But on the DVD, Shotwell's performance in this sequence is replaced by simple instrumental music, and thanks to yet another glitch, the DVD's commentary still alludes to the magical convergence of the two voices saying "nobody" as if this were still in the movie. (Win a few, lose a few.)

In what might be his best performance to date, Gould is a perpetual live wire. His verbal cadenzas embody his character's freewheeling spirit throughout the picture, for Charlie is an aggressive loudmouth forced to justify his vulgarity with invention and virtuosity, whereas Segal plays, as it were, a sort of inner-fire Miles Davis to Gould's Charlie Parker, smoldering with brooding intensity. A similar contrast is afforded by the respective "hard" and "soft" styles of Prentiss and Welles as Charlie's affable housemates, demonstrating a comparable kind of creative teamwork.

In both cases, you might say that feeling ultimately counts for more than thought. ("I can never think and play at the same time," the great jazz pianist Lennie Tristano once maintained. "It's emotionally impossible.") And one might also argue that it's the ensemble that matters — which in this movie extends even to the energy and vibes provided by the minor characters, whether they're bit players or extras, especially in all the scenes set in bars and gambling joints. Like the listeners and dancers in *Jazz '34: Remembrances of Kansas City Swing*, they prove there's an art to being a spectator or a participant that's just as important in a way as the art of being a performer. And if watching an Altman movie like *California Split* makes you a bit of an artist and a bit of a gambler, feeling your way into what remains imponderable and unforesee-able, that's part of what's being celebrated.

Stop Smiling 35 (June 2008): "Gambling" (with a few elements borrowed from my review of *California Split* in *Monthly Film Bulletin*, no. 291 [December 1974])

Mise en Scène as Miracle
in Dreyer's *Ordet*

Ordet (*The Word*, 1955) was the first film by Carl Dreyer I ever saw. And the first time I saw it, at age eighteen, it infuriated me, possibly more than any other film has, before or since. Be forewarned that spoilers are forthcoming if you want to know why.

'The setting and circumstances were unusual. I saw a 16-millimeter print at a radical, integrated co-ed camp for activists in Monteagle, Tennessee — partially staffed by Freedom Riders, during the late summer of 1961, when we were all singing "We Shall Overcome" repeatedly every day. So the fact that *Ordet* has a lot to do with what looked like a primitive form of Christianity — combined with the particular inflections brought by the black church to the Civil Rights Movement, including one of its appropriated hymns — had a great deal to do with my rage. I was an atheist who'd grown up attending a Reform Jewish temple in northwestern Alabama, surrounded by white Christians in the segregated schools I'd attended. The fact that *Ordet*, based on a celebrated play by the Lutheran pastor Kaj Munk — a famous martyr of the Danish resistance who received a bullet in the head for his denunciation of the Nazis — ends with a Christian miracle after very persuasively sowing religious doubts and skepticism for roughly its first two hours seemed like an ultimate gesture of hypocrisy and deceit. And maybe because I'd been sufficiently moved and even devastated by the preceding tragic story, in which a remote family of Christian farmers in Jutland loses its only mother, Inger, the story's most vibrant and generous character, after she gives birth to a son who also dies, I was especially ill-prepared for the *coup de théâtre* and miracle of her sudden resurrection. Worst of all, it was brought about by her brother-in-law Johannes, who up until this final scene has been a crazed religious fanatic calling himself Jesus Christ. As far as I could tell, this was as crass an about-face as a film could make — a cynical reversal whereby everything the film had been carefully propounding about the futile despair that often derives from faith and religious belief was instantaneously and inexplicably refuted.

Almost half a century later, it's easier for me to see that the film poses an irresolvable challenge to believers and unbelievers alike — and that what drove me nuts as a teenager is far from unconnected to what makes me consider *Ordet* one of the greatest of all films today. The experience of the film demands a certain struggle, regardless of one's beliefs, and the fact that it can't be easily processed or rationalized or filed away is surely connected to what keeps it alive and worrying (though try telling that to an irate eighteen-year-old). And it obviously bears some relation to what makes, in Dreyer's preceding and following masterpieces, medieval witch-hunts and executions a deadly game in which the accused parties are every bit as gullible, as superstitious, and as complicitous as their accusers (in the 1943 *Day of Wrath*) or makes a beautiful singer who renounces all her romantic relationships in turn because of her impossible ideals about love both an absolute monster and a martyred saint, not even alternately but simultaneously (in the 1964 *Gertrud*).

It's surely a tragedy that Dreyer managed to make only five sound features. Discounting his 1944 Swedish film *Two People* — which he understandably disowned after he lost control of its casting, and which is, indeed, a paltry thing alongside his 1932 *Vampyr*, *Day of Wrath*, *Ordet*, and *Gertrud*, all incontestable masterpieces — this amounted to only one feature per decade, none of them including his dream project about Jesus, which occupied him for most of his later years. And out of these four sublime features, *Ordet* is understandably the one he was happiest with, both because it had the largest public success and because the experience of making it was, from all indications, far more relaxed than the others had been (or, in the case of *Gertrud*, would be). It was also conceivably, with the possible exception of *Gertrud*, the most personal of his sound films, for reasons that can perhaps be understood only if one considers Dreyer's biographical origins.

But before getting to the project's personal aspects, let's take a look at what made the production of *Ordet* relatively relaxed and untroubled for Dreyer. For one thing, he started work on the project not long after he received a special, prestigious grant from the Danish government in 1952 that consisted of a free license to operate a prominent film theater in Copenhagen, the Dagmar, and which gave him economic security for the remainder of his life. (Built as a legitimate theater in the late nineteenth century and converted into a cinema in 1939, the building also housed a suite of offices, and ironically had been used by the Germans as Gestapo headquarters during the war. Dreyer happily ran it as a commercial theater and not simply as an art cinema — some of its more successful crowd-pleasers included *Carmen Jones, East of Eden, Baby Doll,* and a revival of *Gone with the Wind,* although it also premiered *Ordet.*)

Dreyer also had the advantage of working with a very harmonious and skillful cast — including, as Johannes Borgen, Preben Lerdorff-Rye, who had previously played Martin, a major role in *Day of Wrath.* (The two parts and performances are so dissimilar that many people familiar with both films are unaware that the same actor plays in both, unless they look at the respective cast lists.) Birgitte Federspiel, in the major role of Inger, was the daughter of Einar Federspiel, who played Peder Skraedder, a tailor and a member of the Inner Mission (a rival and more fundamentalist faction of the Danish Lutheran Church than the more popular and liberal Grundtvigian faction subscribed to by the Borgen family); but in the original stage production of *Ordet,* Einar Federspiel had played the tailor's rival, old Morten Borgen. Meanwhile, the actor originally intended to play Morten Borgen on the stage, Henrik Malberg, who'd been unable to take the role because of his contract with the Royal Theater at the time, finally got to play him in the film at the age of eighty-one. (The parts of both Anders, the youngest son in the Borgen family, and Anne, the daughter of the tailor whom he falls in love with, were played by nonprofessionals.)

It also appears that Dreyer had all the time and budget he needed to make the film. Not only was someone hired to train all the actors to speak with the proper Jutland accents in a way that could be understood by the general Danish public, but Dreyer even managed to purchase a farm there and then transport it piece by piece to a studio soundstage in Copenhagen — before stripping it down to essentials. (Most famously, he reportedly outfitted the Borgen kitchen in the studio with over a hundred implements and then carefully removed most of them, one at a time, until arriving at what he regarded as the essentials which wouldn't distract the viewer.) And he also remained in Jutland long enough to shoot most or all of the exteriors. More generally, he had enough time to rehearse each scene for a few days while the elaborate tracks for the camera movements would be laid out and the extremely difficult and subtle lighting schemes were plotted with Henning Bendtsen, the same gifted cinematographer who would later also shoot *Gertrud.* (What made the lighting especially tricky is the fact that each character is lit separately and in a somewhat different way from the others — which is made even more difficult when the camera and the characters that are followed are in almost perpetual motion. Johannes, to take one extreme example, mainly moves about in relative darkness, and becomes fully lit only in the final sequence.) It seems characteristic of the relaxed quality of the shooting that the final scene, associated closely in our minds with daylight, was actually shot exclusively at night in order to escape from the distractions that might have been posed by others working at the same studio. And the execution of all the film's long takes proved to be so focused and satisfactory that Dreyer managed to edit the entire film in only five days — the same length of time, according to Jean and Dale D. Drum,[1] that it took Kaj Munk to write the original play.

■ ■ ■ ■ ■ ■ ■ ■ ■

How was *Ordet* a personal project for Dreyer? According to his major biographer — the late Maurice Drouzy, whose groundbreaking 1982 *Carl Th. Dreyer né Nilsson* has been published in French and in Danish but lamentably not in English — and contrary to most would-be reference works, Dreyer's upbringing was neither strict nor Lutheran, and he was born a Swede, even if he grew up in Denmark. He was born illegitimately in 1889 to Josefine Bernhardine Nilsson, an unmarried thirty-three-year-old Swedish servant living and working in a large country estate — a woman who died horribly a year and a half later trying to abort a second child in her seventh month of another pregnancy by taking a box and a half of matches, cutting off their heads, and swallowing them, which led to a painful and hideous death from sulfur poisoning. (The father or fathers responsible for the two pregnancies are unknown.) It appears that Dreyer himself eventually learned about the fate of his mother as a young man, and for Drouzy this became the key determining factor in his work; the second and longest part of his biography, covering all of Dreyer's career as a filmmaker, is entitled "The Monument to the Mother." And clearly much of the cinema of Dreyer is preoccupied with the extreme suffering of women. So the fact that Inger in *Ordet* dies from childbirth after her baby is aborted and cut into four pieces by the doctor, and then becomes miraculously brought back to life again, surely must have had a deep and complex personal resonance for the filmmaker. Existentially speaking, Dreyer himself could have been aborted by his mother, and the fact that she inadvertently killed herself while desperately trying to abort a second child surely must have given him a lot to brood over.

Returning to his infancy, after brief periods with foster parents, in an orphanage, and then with another family, the baby was adopted by the Dreyers in Copenhagen — a typographer named (as his adopted son would be) Carl Theodor Dreyer and his wife, Marie, who already had an illegitimate daughter named Valborg. Marie, who felt cheated that the infant Carl's real mother hadn't lived long enough to pay child support, reportedly made a habit of complaining to her adopted son about it, and often punished him by locking him in a closet. He grew up despising her, and when she died many years later, he refused even to attend her funeral.

According to Drouzy—whose biography of Dreyer was initially written as a dissertation in Denmark and refused as one, most likely because his meticulously researched account of Dreyer's autobiographical obsessions is itself so obsessive—Dreyer worshiped his real mother and hated his adopted one, and good as well as bad mother figures subsequently abound in his films.

Although at the age of two he was christened in a Lutheran church, Dreyer the future filmmaker was essentially brought up nonreligiously. When he later went to Sunday school at a French Reformed church, this was reportedly mainly done in order to sharpen his French, though it's possible—and this is my hypothesis, not necessarily Drouzy's—that the French Huguenot concept of arbitrary grace, the belief (which might be said to underline most of the action unfolding in *Ordet*, before the miracle) that God's will is not manifested in response to prayer or good deeds, left a certain mark on him.

In any event, what I and many others had originally taken to be deep-seated and rigid religious beliefs on the part of Dreyer were actually calculated challenges to belief and nonbelief, believers and nonbelievers alike. And according to what Dreyer's friend Ib Monty once told me, he wasn't especially religious at all. Indeed, Dreyer even made sure to direct Lerdorff-Rye's performance as Johannes in order to make the character as irritating and as creepy as possible, patterning his high-pitched intonation specifically after that of someone in a mental asylum whom Dreyer took his actor to meet. (This intonation disappears when Johannes regains his sanity in the final scene, but as Lerdorff-Rye pointed out in later interviews, his performance was widely criticized even by some critics who loved the film—Tom Milne in his book on Dreyer is a case in point—simply because he followed Dreyer's instructions precisely.)

Dreyer's own way of accounting for or at least rationalizing the miracle at the end of *Ordet* is a rather curious and convoluted one that deserves to be examined in some detail. In a letter written to *Film Culture* the year after *Ordet* was released (1957, no. 7), he responded to the charge of critic Guido Aristarco that "it is disconcerting to find Dreyer, in this atomic age synthesized by Einstein's equations, rejecting science for the miracles of religion." To refute this charge, Dreyer twice quoted from a September 1954 interview that he gave on Danish State Radio before the film was completed. First he recalled attending the very first performance of the play at the Betty Nansen Theater in 1932: "I was deeply moved by the play and overwhelmed by the audacity with which Kaj Munk presented the problems in relation to each other. I could not but admire the perfect ease with which the author put forth his paradoxical thoughts. When I left the theater, I felt convinced that the play had wonderful possibilities as a film." And in fact, Dreyer published a major essay the following year, "The Real Talking Film" (1933), in which he outlined what some of those possibilities were — which he realized precisely when he finally was able to make the film:

> Characteristic of all good film is a certain rhythm-bound restlessness, which is created partly through the actors' movements in the pictures and partly through a more or less rapid interchange of the pictures themselves. A live, mobile camera, which even in close-ups adjusts flexibly and follows the persons so that the background is constantly shifted (just as for the eye, when we follow a person with our eyes), is important for the first type of restlessness. As for the interchange of images, it is important when the manuscript is adapted from the play that the play provide as much "offstage" as "onstage" action. This creates possibilities for new rhythm-making elements. Example: the third act of Kai Munk's *Ordet* takes place in the drawing room of the Borgen family's farm.
>
> Through the conversation of those present, we learn that the young woman who is to give birth has become ill suddenly and put in bed and that the doctor who has arrived in haste fears for her life and the baby's life. Later, we learn first of the baby's death and after that of her death. If *Ordet* were to be filmed, all these scenes in the sickroom, which the theatre audience gets to know only through conversation, would have to be included in the film. The actors going to and from the sickbed would contribute to creating the two kinds of restlessness or excitement that condition the rhythm of the film to an essential degree.

Returning to Dreyer's letter to *Film Culture*, his second quote from his interview on Danish radio was a response to the question of when he wrote his script for *Ordet*:

> It did not happen until nearly twenty years later. Then I saw Kaj Munk's ideas in a different light, for so much had happened in the meantime. The new science that followed Einstein's theory of relativity had supplied that outside the three-dimensional world which we can grasp with our senses, there is a fourth dimension — the dimension of time — as well as a fifth dimension — the dimension of the psychic that proves that it is possible to live events that have not yet happened. New perspectives are opened up that make one realize an intimate connection between exact science and intuitive religion. The new science brings us toward a more intimate understanding of the divine power and is even beginning to give us a natural explanation to things of the supernatural. The Johannes figure of Kaj Munk's can now be seen from another angle. Kaj Munk felt this already, in 1925 when he wrote

his play, and intimated that the mad Johannes may have been closer to God than the Christians surrounding him.

Finally, Dreyer concludes his letter by citing "recent psychic research, represented by pioneers like Rhine, Ouspensky, Dunne, Aldous Huxley, and so forth," which he links to "the paradoxical thoughts and ideas expressed in the play"—a sort of early invocation of "new age" beliefs that reconcile or at least claim to reconcile the separate claims of science and religion.

■ ■ ■ ■ ■ ■ ■ ■ ■ ■

The key word in all this is "paradoxical," because *Ordet* as a both a play and as a film is founded on a central paradox, essentially arguing and reinforcing the principals of rational skepticism only to overturn them in the story's closing moments. Dreyer himself was unabashed about stating that his intentions were to deceive the audience, yet paradoxically a certain amount of fudging also extends even to some of his explanations about these intentions. For instance, Munk's intimation, which Dreyer cites with approval, "that the mad Johannes may have been closer to God than the Christians surrounding him," is not exactly verified by the film's conclusion when it is clearly a sane Johannes and not a mad one — a character who has visibly and audibly recovered his sanity, backed by the innocent faith and belief of Inger's little girl, Maren (Elisabeth Groth) — who brings Inger back to life. (Maren, one should add, believes utterly in the power of Johannes to resurrect her mother, and regardless of whether he's sane or insane, since she gives no indication of knowing what the difference is.)

The best analysis of *Ordet* I've encountered is by P. Adams Sitney,[2] and in it he describes the sickbed scene, "a model of 'rhythm-bound restlessness,'" that Dreyer already evoked in his 1933 essay. Apart from cutaways to Borgen, Inger's father-in-law, rushing home on his horse-drawn wagon, the scene concentrates mainly on the movements of the doctor while Mikkel, Inger's husband, tries to comfort her and holds a lamp to help the doctor while the midwife and another woman also lend some assistance. The second part of this sequence, Sitney adds, "is in fact the most brutal scene I know in the history of the art. The scene, which in Dreyer's words 'would have to be included in the film,' is the abortion of Inger's baby." (As Sitney notes, the possibility of sacrificing Inger's life to save the baby is never raised or discussed in either the play or the film.)

Although we don't view any of this action directly — the camera remains close to Mikkel, where we can view only the doctor's face and arms while most of Inger's body is blocked by her upraised knees under a sheet — we hear her cries of pain as the doctor performs offscreen an episiotomy with a small pair of scissors and then, with a large pair of forceps, makes four successive cuts with a great deal of effort while we hear Inger scream. (In fact, Birgitte Federspiel, who plays Inger, was herself pregnant when she played this role. She finally gave birth after the shooting, and Dreyer brought a tape recorder to the hospital on that occasion to capture the audible signs of her labor pains, which he later mixed into the soundtrack.) The doctor also asks for Mikkel to fetch a pail, and afterwards, to confirm the grim finality of what has happened, when Borgen, who has by now arrived, asks Mikkel, "Was it a boy, as Inger promised me?" — a patriarchal issue of much concern during the play's preceding action, because Borgen's only other grandchildren, both the offspring of Mikkel and Inger, are little girls — Mikkel replies that it is. But then can only add, bitterly, "It's lying in there — in the pail — in four pieces."

Sitney is also very helpful in describing some of the changes Dreyer made to the play — which on the whole are modest, especially compared to the changes he made in the plays that both *Day of Wrath* and *Gertrud* were based on, and mainly consist of reducing certain sections, such as the theological debates between the priest and the doctor. In the Munk play, the insanity of Johannes, a former divinity student, is principally motivated by the death of his fiancée, which occurred after they emerged from the performance of *Beyond Our Power* — a play by Bjørnstjerne Bjørnson (a friend and rival of Ibsen and a Nobel prizewinner) in which an incurable character becomes miraculously cured. Johannes was so carried away by the play that he stepped in front of a car; his fiancée pushed him to safety, and was killed herself as a result. So the cause of his insanity, according to his older brother Mikkel, an atheist, speaking to the new priest in the play, is "Bjørnson and Kierkegaard." But there's no reference to a fiancée in the film, so when the priest (Ove Rud) similarly asks Mikkel (Emil Hass Christensen) if love was the cause, the response is now, "No, no — it was Søren Kierkegaard."

Deliberately or not, this may the closest thing in the film to an outright gag — although as Sitney points out, the early stretches of the story often register as a comedy that is occasionally interrupted by the disquieting interjections and prophecies of Johannes. Even here, Dreyer is playing with our expectations so that we assume the stubborn resistance of Old Borgen to his youngest son Anders marrying the daughter of the Inner Mission tailor is only a temporary problem that will eventually be overcome. This eventually proves to be the case, although by the time it does, the harrowing tragedy of Inger's death has so overwhelmed everything else that it no longer seems nearly as important.

One important addition to the play is signaled by Sitney: when Johannes disappears after trying and failing to raise Inger from the dead, he leaves behind a note that we first see him writing, and which proves to be a quote from the New Testament, John 8:21 ("I go my way, and ye shall seek me. Whither I go, ye cannot come."). And as Sitney points out, Johannes for the first time is quoting his namesake ("Johannes" is the Danish form of John) rather than Jesus, which subtly suggests that he is already beginning to overcome his delusion that he is Christ by quoting from His evangelist.

But perhaps the most pivotal moment in both the plot and the mise en scène comes somewhat earlier, when Inger's life is still hanging in the balance. Maren, at night, comes to Johannes to ask both if her mother will die and, if she does, whether he will raise her from the dead. For once, Johannes appears somewhat less delusional and self-absorbed while responding to her, although he does reply to her second question, "I dare say it will come to nothing [because] the others won't let me." This plants a notion suggesting, like the survival of Tinker Bell in the play *Peter Pan* (which is said to depend on the audience's capacity to believe in fairies), that the capacity of the characters to believe in miracles may be related to the capacity of the audience watching *Ordet* to believe in such things as well. (This notion of a shared belief raises the issue that the meaning and impact of a miracle in a play necessarily becomes somewhat different from the meaning and impact of a miracle in a film — if only because the conventions in each that rule illusion and deception are different.) Thematically, in any case, Dreyer is preparing us for accepting Johannes differently in the final scene, as he subsequently does when he has him quote from John.

What happens over the course of this scene between Maren and Johannes constitutes, however subtly, a miracle of its own, expressed through an "impossible" mise en scène. As Johannes remains seated at screen center, Maren approaches him from behind, and after a cut to a closer shot of both of them in profile, from a very different angle, the camera appears to move very slowly around them in almost a full circle while the scenery in the room appears to glide correspondingly around them. And yet the camera never frames these characters from behind at any point in its nearly 360-degree rotation. They remain positioned either frontally or in profile, with Maren lit more brightly than Johannes throughout the scene.

Is this because the camera is tracking and panning in opposite directions at the same time, or is it, more likely, because the actors are seated on a rotating surface while the camera is also moving? I don't have the technical knowledge to explain or account for what happens, but I think what matters far more than how it was done is the fact that we become so entranced by the actors and their delivery as well as by the camera's movement that in effect we become hypnotized, and are not even aware that we're watching a miracle unless we're noticing what's happening and not merely following it. So Dreyer essentially gulls us into accepting one kind of miracle as a way of preparing us to accept another kind somewhat later.

What emerges from all this is a sense of the uncanny that's clearly related to what we experience in Dreyer's only "obvious" fantasy film, *Vampyr* (1932), as well as in the evocations of witchcraft in *Day of Wrath* and predestination in *Gertrud*. In fact, our memory of *Vampyr* returns irresistibly during the final shot of *Ordet*, when the plainly carnal desire of the resurrected Inger for Mikkel recalls the no less lustful desire of a female vampire for another woman in a bedroom.

■ ■ ■ ■ ■ ■ ■ ■ ■

I've long believed that the two summits of mise en scène in the history of cinema are Carl Dreyer's *Ordet* and Jacques Tati's *Playtime*, so it's interesting to note one striking thing regarding their respective productions that they have in common. In both cases, the mise en scène was extremely complicated and plotted by the director so thoroughly and so far in advance of the actual shooting that, in both cases, the director would arrive each day at the studio soundstage without his script, because by that time he knew it all by heart.

For all their profound differences, *Ordet* and *Playtime* are also alike in the way that the extreme and unorthodox style of the mise en scène in each case exists to articulate a radical vision, and that part of the supreme achievement of the director in each case is to delineate a particular transition over the stretch of two hours that we creatively participate in without necessarily realizing that we're doing so. This is a transition that moves us steadily yet invisibly towards a miracle, though the miracle in each case is of a very different kind: a spiritual epiphany in *Ordet* and a social utopia in *Playtime*, even though the experience in each case is undoubtedly a collective one — which makes the prospect of watching either film alone or on a small screen, without the reinforcement of a surrounding community, incomplete. But let us nonetheless celebrate Dreyer's deceptive form of enlightenment and his enlightening form of deception whenever and however we can, even as we continue to quarrel with it. There is surely no other experience in cinema that comes close to it.

Essay in booklet accompanying Australian DVD of *Ordet*, issued by Madman in 2008; see also www.jonathanrosenbaum.com/?p=14604 and *"Gertrud* as Nonnarrative: The Desire for the Image," in *Placing Movies: The Practice of Film Criticism* (Berkeley: University of California Press, 1995) and at www.jonathanrosenbaum.com/?p=15649

Notes

1. Jean Drum and Dale D. Drum, *My Only Great Passion: The Life and Films of Carl Th. Dreyer* (Lanham, MD/London: Scarecrow Press, 2000), 240–41.

2. P. Adams Sitney, "Moments of Revelation: Dreyer's Anachronistic Modernity," in *Modernist Montage: The Obscurity of Vision in Cinema and Literature* (New York: Columbia University Press, 1990), 55–73.

David Holzman's Diary/
My Girlfriend's Wedding:
Historical Artifacts of the Past
and Present

In my mind, there isn't as much of a distinction between documentary and fiction as there is between a good movie and a bad one.
—Abbas Kiarostami

Artifact #1: A softcover book, *The Film Director as Superstar*, by Joseph Gelmis (Garden City, NY: Doubleday & Co., 1970)—a collection of sixteen interviews in three parts, each of which has two subsections: "The Outsiders" ("Beyond the Underground," "Their Own Money, Their Own Scene"), "The European Experience" ("The Underemployed Independent," "The Socialist Film Schools"), and "Free Agents within the System" ("Transitional Directors," "Independents with Muscle").

Offering a good sense of what was seen as edgy filmmaking thirty-five years ago, Gelmis singled out Arthur Penn, Richard Lester, Mike Nichols, and Stanley Kubrick as his muscular independents and Roger Corman and Francis Ford Coppola as his transitional figures. Milos Forman and Roman Polanski were his two graduates of the socialist film schools, Lindsay Anderson and Bernardo Bertolucci his two underemployed independents. The three with their own money were Norman Mailer, Andy Warhol, and John Cassavetes (the latter was seen on the book's cover, camera in hand). And the three who were beyond the underground? Jim McBride, Brian De Palma, and Robert Downey. All three eventually wound up in Hollywood—like virtually everyone else in Gelmis's lineup, apart from Mailer and Warhol—though it seems sadly emblematic that Downey is best known today for his actor son with the same name while McBride is perhaps best known for his 1983 U.S. remake of Jean-Luc Godard's *Breathless*.

One reason for citing all these strange bedfellows now is to convey some sense of where McBride stood at the time, on the basis of the two legendary films, his first two, included on this DVD—neither of which has ever had a normal theatrical distribution anywhere, apart from a limited release of *David Holzman's Diary* in Paris. Yet in spite of this limited exposure, the interview with McBride is not only the first in Gelmis's book, but one of the most substantial.

In a way, this shouldn't be too surprising, because when we speak about the impact of influential works in art cinema, whether it's *Citizen Kane* or the original *Breathless*, we're speaking more about the quality of the response than about the quantity of respondents. However personal some of its origins might be, *David Holzman's Diary* is in fact a great work of synthesis summarizing the very notions of the film director as subject (and therefore as superstar) and the camera as tool of self-scrutiny that the '60s film explosion inspired. And its ambiguities about the various crossovers between documentary and fiction remain as up to date as the films of Kiarostami.

Artifact #2: Another softcover book from the same year, *David Holzman's Diary: A Screenplay by L. M. Kit Carson from a Film by Jim McBride* (New York: Farrar, Straus and Giroux, 1970). This is an even more flagrant case of relatively unseen "underground" work being heralded by a mainstream publisher. The title's a bit confusing, because in fact the film was made without a screenplay and Carson is crediting himself with an after-the-fact transcription and description. Its dialogue was basically written (when it was written) on a scene-by-scene basis, by McBride working with either Carson, the lead actor playing David Holzman, or Lorenzo Mans aka Pepe, in the latter's own extended dialogue. (Shot in front of Mans's own Cuban mural, this is in many ways the most provocative scene in the film, as well as the funniest. Given that Mans's own apartment at the time was serving as David Holzman's, his influence and impact on the film probably shouldn't be restricted to this sequence; he later served as the main screenwriter on McBride's first relatively big-budget feature, the 1971 *Glen and Randa*.) But the frank sexual talk from the lady in the Thunderbird—actually a transsexual who'd recently undergone a sex-change operation—was 100 percent impromptu, including the offscreen questions and comments from David, who at this point was being impersonated by the film's cameraman, Michael Wadley. (Incidentally, during the same year that artifacts 1 and 2 were published, Wadley—who also shot Martin Scorsese's first feature the same year as *David Holzman*, and *My Girlfriend's Wedding* two years later—released his own first film, *Woodstock*, now spelling his surname Wadleigh.)

Artifact #3: *David Holzman's Diary* (the film, 1967). One of the first and best of the great pseudo-documentaries, sometimes known nowadays as mockumentaries—and certainly one of the cleverest to be made in the '60s after Peter Watkins's *Culloden* (1964) and *The War Game* (1965)—McBride's first film is still quite capable of fooling unsuspecting viewers almost forty years later, in part through the effectiveness of Carson's performance, and despite a contradictory ending which logically should (yet in fact generally doesn't) give the whole fictional game away, just before the final credits. (The story ends with Holzman losing his Éclair and Nagra, reduced to recording his face and voice in a penny arcade—though how these abject substitutes are still conveyed to us on film is left unexplained.)

The film shares an important trait with the early French New Wave features of Godard, François Truffaut, and Jacques Rivette that helped to inspire it by growing out of cinephilia and film criticism. Specifically, it drew part of its stimulus from a never-completed book that McBride and Carson were researching for the Museum of Modern Art about cinéma-vérité by interviewing such figures as Robert Drew, Richard Leacock, and D. A. Pennebaker, while the more personal and experimental filmmaker Andrew Noren was also providing them with much food for thought. Prior to this, McBride had started a similar film in 1965 with actor Alan Rachins—who two decades later became a mainstay on the TV show *L.A. Law*—that was aborted when the unedited rushes were stolen. So in fact *David Holzman* grew out of two unfinished projects, and undoubtedly benefited from the many second thoughts that resulted.

Playing with the form of cinéma-vérité while subverting much of the content by making extended portions of it fictional, McBride was emulating the practice of his French models, filming his theory rather than just writing about it. Of course, a good bit of the film *is* documentary, especially when the camera is roaming around Manhattan in the west 70s. And even when the narrative premises and performances are fictional, the film qualifies as documentary in quite another way—by bearing witness to the mood, preoccupations, and lifestyles of its own epoch. In a similar spirit, Rivette once remarked that D. W. Griffith's *Intolerance* today has more to say about 1916 than about any of the historical periods it depicts.

But more generally, *David Holzman* is an extended meditation on the metaphysical underpinnings of cinéma-vérité and other notions of the camera as a probing instrument, especially in relation to voyeurism and other forms of aggressive sexual appropriation as well as self-scrutiny. (*Rear Window* and *Peeping Tom* are both repeatedly evoked—along with the sense of duration and the accompanying sense of existential dread found in many of Warhol's films.)

Artifact #4: *My Girlfriend's Wedding* (1969). In many respects, the best "critique" of *David Holzman's Diary* that I know is McBride's sixty-three-minute follow-up to it. Initially conceived as an accompanying short, the film wound up with a running time of only ten minutes shorter, and the distributor of both films promptly went bankrupt, so this DVD may represent the first semi-permanent pairing of the two films. It's taken a long time, but I think it's been worth the wait.

Girlfriend's value as a critique of its predecessor isn't just because it inverts some of *David Holzman*'s theoretical premises — by being a real personal documentary with some of the characteristics of a fiction, chronicling McBride's excited and enraptured discovery of his attractive new girlfriend Clarissa. ("At the time I made it," he told me when I interviewed him for the French magazine *Positif* in the early '70s, "I was fond of referring to it as a fiction film, because it was very much my personal idea of what Clarissa was like, and not at all an objective or truthful view.")

In fact, the dialectic it forms with *David Holzman* operates on several clearly conscious levels, starting with its possessive title, which is now in the first person, as well as an overt early reference to Herman Melville's "Bartleby the Scrivener" (which figured at the very end of the previous film) and a re-introduction of the same Éclair 16 mm camera. The English girlfriend in question, in flight from her upper-class background, is indeed the ostensible focus, as is her irreverent decision to marry a yippie activist she met only a week ago in order to remain in the states. (Perhaps for legal reasons — which also presumably accounts for some of the blipped-out names — the fact that McBride was married to though separated from someone else at the time goes unmentioned.) But in the very first shot we can also hear and then see McBride as he asks Clarissa to hold up a mirror facing him and Wadley, prompting her until she gets it right — an apt metaphor for much of what follows. And there's a similar sense of displacement in the way he asks her to identify the contents of her purse; for much as Holzman loves to inventory his own possessions, including his attractive girlfriend Penny (Eileen Dietz), in front of his own camera, McBride is asking Clarissa to describe her own possessions while implicitly showing her off as a possession of his.

Some of the other rhyme effects between the films are less immediately obvious, but no less telling for that. The counterpart to David's fragmented record of an entire evening spent watching television — one frame per shot change adding up to 3,115 separate shots in less than a minute — is Jim's far more exuberant home-movie montage chronicling his drive with Clarissa from New York to San Francisco. And this points in turn to a radically redefined relation to both life and politics expressed in the two films. David virtually begins by telling us he just lost his (nameless) job and has been reclassified A-1 by his draft board, but the issue of being unemployed and potentially drafted into the Vietnam war never comes up directly again after that. By contrast, the issue of Clarissa having a job (as a coffeehouse waitress) and the impact of her father's war experience are discussed at some length, and there's hardly anything else in the film that isn't politically inflected. If *David Holzman* explores how to think about various matters, *My Girlfriend's Wedding* fearlessly explores and even proposes how to live.

This is even more true of this film's forty-six-minute sequel (or footnote), *Pictures from Life's Other Side* (1971), which focuses almost entirely on a later cross-country trip, this one also including Clarissa's illegitimate, preadolescent son Joe and a couple of dogs, with Clarissa and Joe taking over the commentary and the whole family trading off various sound and camera duties. Funded by an American Film Institute grant, the film was eventually suppressed by the same organization, undoubtedly because of its unabashed countercultural stances — in particular, one suspects, the occasional nudity of all the family members, including Clarissa in the final stages of her pregnancy with her and Jim's son Jesse — so that it remains to this day even more unseeable than its predecessors.

Significantly, the intertitle in *My Girlfriend's Wedding*, "Four days later we leave for San Francisco," refers to Jim and Clarissa but not to Wadley. And because Wadley was left behind on that trip, this segment clearly paves the way for the more family-made *Pictures*, where McBride's curiosity in *My Girlfriend's Wedding* about what his creative role as director actually consists of becomes even more relevant. Incidentally, Clarissa and the two dogs — not to mention other members of the McBride tribe, such as Lorenzo Mans and Jack Baran — are seen once more, this time playing fictional parts, in McBride's wonderful 1974 sex comedy *Hot Times*.

Concluding on a personal note: the fact that I've known several members of this tribe slightly longer than I've known these films probably enhances their value for me, but perhaps not as much as one might expect. I think anyone who watches these works winds up on a first-name basis with most of these people. That's what continues to make *David Holzman's Diary* and *My Girlfriend's Wedding* contemporary and vital as well as precious time capsules.

Essay in booklet accompanying DVD of *David Holzman's Diary* and *My Girlfriend's Wedding*, issued in the U.K. by Second Run Features in 2006; see also www.jonathan rosenbaum.com/?p=16032 and www.jonathanrosenbaum.com/?p=14850

Two Early Long-Take Climaxes: *The Magnificent Ambersons* and *A Star Is Born*

Only about nine minutes into *The Magnificent Ambersons*, we enter the front door of the Amberson mansion along with a few guests to attend their grand ball, and the film not only moves into high gear; it leaps to a summit so high that in a way all that the remaining seventy-odd minutes of the film can do after this sequence is refer back to it, recall it, cross-reference it in numerous ways.

It's almost twenty-two minutes into the 1954 *A Star Is Born* when, along with Norman Maine, we enter the front door of a sleepy after-hours cabaret where swing musicians and a vocalist, Esther Blodgett, are performing exclusively for themselves. Esther casually slides into a chorus of "The Man Who Got Away," and slowly she builds from there. Once again, a film suddenly leaps to such a high level of intensity, in this case for about four minutes, that all the remainder of the film — in this case, 150 minutes — can do is fitfully and wistfully remember that pinnacle, refer back to it musically and emotionally in a variety of ways.

Both films, of course, survive today in the form of ruins, so we can't speak about them as integral works with any confidence; even the "restored" *A Star Is Born* is an incomplete simulacrum. Yet it seems that even in their original forms, they suffered as well as thrived on the peculiar fact that they peak so early. All of the ensuing and interminable anticlimax has to proceed as a kind of slow recovery from that initial stretch of ecstasy.

Posted on www.jonathanrosenbaum.com, November 1, 2008

Wrinkles in Time:
Alone. Life Wastes Andy Hardy

Wearing suspenders, Mickey Rooney as Andy Hardy steps behind his mother (Fay Holden), clutching her left shoulder and right forearm with his two hands, and firmly kisses the back of her neck while she slowly nods her head with a stoic, worldly-wise expression. In a series of stuttering, staccato jerks, he does the same thing again, to the throbbing strains of eerie, ghostly music. Then he does it a third time, pausing first to rock back and forth from one foot to another a good many times, as if he had ants in his pants. When he kisses the back of his mom's neck this time, his lips seem to remain glued there. This embrace, his barely perceptible jaw movements, and her steadily bobbing head all conspire to suggest something vaguely obscene and depraved. Could Andy have become some kind of Dracula, sucking blood from his mother's neck? Or do the slow pumping rhythm and repeated nervous thrusts represent some kind of sexual motion?

When Andy breaks away, this gesture too is repeated compulsively, his mouth twisting back and forth between amorous solemnity and a delighted grin, as if he couldn't make up his mind about how he feels. Finally, when he moves away from his mother entirely, his body turning in a semicircle, the camera cuts to a new and more distant angle that shows he's wearing an apron; apparently he's been washing dishes at an unseen sink. Her eyes steadily follow him as he moves, and she smiles. Picking up a plate and a towel, he turns further around in the same direction, showing his back to us and his mother, stepping toward a table with a checkered tablecloth. Meanwhile his mother, looking at him adoringly, says something both wordless and inhuman.

I'm trying to describe the first two and a half minutes of Martin Arnold's creepy fifteen-minute experimental film *Alone. Life Wastes Andy Hardy* (1998), but I can't be confident that my account is either complete or entirely accurate. For one thing, the somewhat stocky, stolid older woman Andy Hardy kisses may not be his mother; theoretically it could be his Aunt Milly, another character in the series. I know that MGM released fifteen Andy Hardy pictures between 1937 and 1946 — seven in 1938 and 1939 alone — and a final one in 1958. But with the possible exception of the last, I don't believe I've seen any of them apart from occasional snatches while channel surfing. I'm not even sure which of the Andy Hardy features furnished the extracts for this film — assuming it was only one — though the presence of Judy Garland in later segments of *Alone* narrows the possibilities to three: *Love Finds Andy Hardy* (1938), *Andy Hardy Meets Debutante* (1940), and *Life Begins for Andy Hardy* (1941) (Garland plays a character named Betsy Booth in all of them).

And finally, because I never saw the sequence before Arnold got his hands on it, I don't know with certainty if the perverse meanings he's gleaned from it grow out of only one gesture. Does Andy Hardy simply and briefly peck at his mother's neck in the course of washing dishes? That's what it looks like, but I can't be sure.

Arnold — an Austrian who manipulates fragments of black-and-white Hollywood features through optical printing and editing — is presenting a program of his films, including *Alone. Life Wastes Andy Hardy*, on Friday, February 18, at Columbia College's Ferguson Hall through the auspices of Kino-Eye Cinema. Two earlier items on the program are described as parts of a trilogy with *Alone*, though they seem to me merely setting-up exercises by comparison: neither packs the same punch, establishing most of Arnold's procedures but doing much less with them. These films lack *Alone*'s narrative and internal complexity — its ability to connect a good many scenes and characters while actually telling a story part of the time.

Pièce touchée (1989, sixteen minutes) shows a woman reading in a chair as a door behind her repeatedly opens and closes; a man finally enters and engages in some kind of interaction with her. It's difficult to tell what it is because Arnold essentially turns the two figures into epileptic dolls with his relentless repetitions and reversals: he prints the same shots backward and/or upside down in rapid alternation with the originals, producing various aggressive flicker effects. (According to the French rock magazine *Les Inrockuptibles* — which reviewed Arnold's short films earlier this month, just after their video release in France — this fragment is drawn from Joseph M. Newman's 1954 police procedural *The Human Jungle*.)

Passage à l'acte (1993, twelve minutes) is much more interesting to me because its source is recognizable, which makes Arnold's perversions more diabolical. It takes a few short fragments of a scene from *To Kill a Mockingbird* (1962), with a father (Gregory Peck) and mother figure, little girl, and little boy sitting at the breakfast table. Arnold submits this material to the same sort of looping, inverting, and scrambling as in *Pièce touchée*, but this time the effect is much more bizarre.

To Kill a Mockingbird is certainly ripe for deconstruction: this rather self-satisfied 1962 adaptation of a pretty good southern novel occupied thirty-fourth place in the American Film Institute's stupid poll of the best American movies — and was ludicrously praised by Jack Valenti as the first Hollywood film to deal honestly with racial issues. But what Arnold chooses to deconstruct is to all appearances a fairly ordinary family scene. The boy runs out through a rattling screen door at the beginning and later returns; at the end, both the boy and girl leave by the same door, though the girl first does something with the lower part of the door and then either kisses her father or whispers something in his ear. (In the background of many of the shots with the boy is a black cook, seen from behind.)

It's all quite obscure in terms of narrative, but most unsettling of all is the way various manipulations transform the dialogue into a series of unearthly and meaningless noises. What may start out as "yes" from Peck is quickly transmuted into "byah," "weh," "bam," and "jam," immediately followed by volleys of what sound like gunshots or an onslaught of attacking woodpeckers, then further remarks from Peck that sound like "haffa-now," "flupper," and "patoot." Then there's a frenetic dialogue between the boy and girl in which he seems to be saying "hoy-ya" and she quacks back, followed by repeated rapid cuts between the woman raising a cup of coffee to her lips and the girl doing the same with a glass of milk.

All this unnervingly dehumanizes the actors as well as the characters they're playing. Arnold's distortions remind us of the mechanical nature of film projection, which we take for granted as representing reality: altering this mechanism can turn people into inhuman geeks at the drop of a hat. *Alone* carries this principle even further — most notably with Judy Garland's singing, which moves in and out of recognizable as well as freakish registers — and makes its point even more effectively by allowing us to comprehend a few of the words being uttered by Garland, Rooney, and an unidentified actor. (Indeed the title, *Alone*, comes from one repeated recognizable portion of her song.)

Does this progression make each film in the trilogy "better" than the last? For me it does: the recognizable movie and actor in the second and the comprehensible dialogue in the third allow for more dialectical play, enabling Arnold to exploit various registers of discomfort. But someone who can identify the movie used in *Pièce touchée* and can't recognize Gregory Peck or *To Kill a Mockingbird* in *Passage à l'acte* may well assess these films differently.

The few critical commentaries I've read about Arnold's trilogy imply that he's doing something psychoanalytical. For instance, a blurb from the San Francisco Cinematheque states that the trilogy's targets are "the conventions of Hollywood filmmaking and its inherent repressions." This suggests that Arnold's manipulations bring the repressed to light—exposing, as it were, the "unconscious" of the Andy Hardy movies.

The problem is that Freud's theory of the unconscious refers to the minds of individuals—not to movies, which don't have minds. And if we bring in Jung's notion of the collective unconscious, we have to establish what collectives we're thinking of. Do we mean all the people who made creative contributions to the Andy Hardy movies, all the people in the audience who saw the originals, or some combination of the two? I think we have to opt for the third possibility—and in the case of *Alone* also consider the audience of Arnold's film, which includes many people like me who don't know the Hardy movies. And despite the differences among these groups, I think we can safely assume there's a lot of shared cultural baggage. Robert B. Ray in his 1995 book *The Avant-Garde Finds Andy Hardy* notes that while practically nothing analytical has been written about these extremely popular movies, "they continue to be mentioned . . . as the principal source of television's sitcoms (from *Ozzie and Harriet* and *Father Knows Best*, the series most obviously derived from the Hardy series, to *Family Ties* and *The Cosby Show*)." Which is another way of saying that we all know these movies indirectly, probably at several removes.

Neal Gabler in his persuasive 1988 book *An Empire of Their Own: How the Jews Invented Hollywood* (which offers a much better argument than the oversimplified 1997 TV documentary based on it, *Hollywoodism: Jews, Movies and the American Dream*) suggests that the Hardy films can be seen as the propagandistic version of the American dream that evolved out of MGM studio chief Louis B. Mayer's denial of his European Jewish roots. Gabler cites Billy Wilder's recollection of a scene at MGM while he was scripting *Ninotchka*: "We looked out the window because there was screaming going on, and Louis B. Mayer held Mickey Rooney by the lapel. He says, 'You're Andy Hardy! You're the United States! You're the Stars and Stripes. Behave yourself! You're a symbol!'"

Does *Alone* unpack the dark underside of that symbol? To some extent I think it does, even though I don't immediately see European Judaism on the surface of Arnold's nightmarish film. Or maybe I do and don't recognize it, sharing a certain denial with Louis B. Mayer. Shortly after we see Andy and his mom committing incest in the kitchen, we see Andy suddenly slapped by his father, Judge Hardy, who simultaneously yells at him in fury, "Shut up!" It's a genuinely shocking moment, in part because Arnold has isolated the sound of that explosion so that it erupts from total silence. Arnold then lingers over

Andy briefly touching his cheek and slowly registering pain, disbelief, and shame — before replaying Judge Hardy's slap and command twice again, this time allowing Andy a short verbal response after his pain, disbelief, and shame register: "All right." In the final replay he follows this with "Dad."

Is Jewish patriarchal rage rearing its ugly head in an Andy Hardy movie, courtesy of Arnold's analytical editing? Perhaps, but on the other hand I can't even be sure that the white-haired man slapping Andy in the chops is Judge Hardy, because he doesn't seem to resemble the images of that character reproduced in Ray's book. So Arnold's extract could be turning another character into a father figure, according him a mythic function he might not have had in the original movie.

Whatever the details of Arnold's project, he's certainly transforming a key image of American paradise from our past into a very bad dream. In Arnold's archetypal Hollywood small town, lovers kiss repeatedly in a park, then start hissing and emitting ducklike wheezes. This is a blighted cosmos where Judy Garland sings "alone" first like a melancholy foghorn and then as if someone has just stepped on her foot — and where a door repeatedly opens and closes as if attacked by some poltergeist until Mickey Rooney finally enters in a top hat and tails and gets stuck in a perpetual dance shuffle, caught in an endless loop that makes us realize he's actually in hell.

Chicago Reader, February 18, 2000

Martha:
Fassbinder's Uneasy Testament

Margit Carstensen: You really are a wretched person.
Rainer Werner Fassbinder: That's what I've been saying all along.
Margit Carstensen: How am I supposed to pull myself together after this?

The following exchange, appearing at the end of a dialogue that took place between the writer-director and his lead actress after the completion of their film *Martha* in 1973,[1] helps to pinpoint what continues to make that film politically lethal. Fassbinder's sarcasm, which becomes oddly comforting in most of its onscreen as well as offscreen manifestations, offers a particular kind of challenge to the viewer in *Martha* that becomes inextricably tied to how one regards its title heroine. Accepting the self-rationalizations and denials of a woman trapped in a monstrous marriage to a sadist is made to seem intolerable, a cause for squirming, and the fact that Fassbinder plays this game as poker-faced high comedy only makes the challenge more formidable.

Vacationing in Rome, a virgin librarian in her early '30s (Carstensen) abruptly loses her domineering father, who collapses from heart failure on the Spanish Steps. Shortly afterwards—and following the snatching of her purse by Fassbinder regular El Hedi ben Salem, who has already entered her hotel room in the opening scene, as if to confirm her status as victim—she meets a macho and abusive bridge and dam builder (*Peeping Tom*'s Karlheinz Böhm) whom she shows an immediate interest in, and winds up marrying him. It's a match made in heaven between a masochist and a sadist, with the husband's contempt, cruelty, and absurdly escalating demands mainly received by this fragile heroine as her proper due and the prescribed duty of any good wife in any bourgeois marriage. It's an excruciatingly open question whether she finally achieves absolute fulfillment, complete enslavement, or some grotesque combination of the two.

For Fassbinder in his dialogue with Carstensen, it's a happy ending: "When Martha can no longer take care of herself, she has finally gotten what she wanted all along," he maintains. Carstensen counters, "I wouldn't go that far. I really think that this is a resignation on her part."

The radical cleavage between these positions produces the candy-colored, acid-coated valentine delivered by *Martha* to viewers, inflected by what may well be Carstensen's greatest performance in a Fassbinder film. And if we choke on the bittersweet confection, it might be said that the film is functioning politically.

I hasten to add that this proposition is debatable. It was debated, at any rate, by Richard Roud and myself over three issues of *Film Comment* in the mid-seventies[2]—with Roud maintaining that the film wasn't "believable" without "some notion that Martha is sensually chained" to her husband, and the "super-cool" treatment of the characters making this impossible. For him, therefore, "*Martha* [has] neither the intensity nor the compassion of *The Bitter Tears of Petra von Kant, Ali,* or *The Merchant of Four Seasons,*" three earlier and better-known Fassbinder features. My own intemperate counterthrust was to argue that the latter three films seemed "to operate as flattery machines . . . designed to make one conclude *I'm compassionate/ironic, therefore I am,* while *Martha,* which makes its social victim as hard to 'understand' as its oppressor, brings one back to the more radical theory of Descartes." A less fancy version of this argument would be to say that *Martha* prompts more analysis than attitude, thereby making its difficulties purposeful and ultimately educational in a Brechtian manner, by testing the viewer's implicit notions of what a bourgeois marriage should be.

But *Martha* had more practical difficulties to cope with at the time, at least in reaching an American audience. Unlike those three earlier Fassbinder films and many later ones, it failed to surface at the New York Film Festival (which Roud was the director of at the time) or land a stateside distributor, and subsequent legal problems with the Cornell Woolrich estate about its adaptation of a Woolrich story[3] kept it out of reach for a good many years afterwards. Consequently it never had a chance to be become canonized when Fassbinder was still in vogue in the states—making its release on DVD its first real opportunity, apart from a few appearances at Fassbinder retrospectives, to reach an American public.

■ ■ ■ ■ ■ ■ ■ ■ ■

Part of my reluctance to join the Fassbinder bandwagon in the '70s was that I couldn't accept without qualms the critical industry's interpretation of his work as left-wing and subversive—an interpretation that was intricately bound up with the rediscovery of Douglas Sirk's '50s Hollywood movies by Fassbinder and others. For academics who argued — and in many cases still argue — that Sirk soap operas like *Imitation of Life* were subversive critiques of American life rather than conformist endorsements, a certain historical sleight of hand was necessary, particularly when it came to dealing with the reception those movies were given back in the '50s. Sirk — a leftist stage director in pre-Nazi and Nazi Germany and something of a closet intellectual and campy commercial director in both Germany and the U.S. — made movies with conservative, defeatist, and conformist as well as skeptical and subversive elements. The conservative elements played most indelibly to his producers and his contemporary audiences; the skeptical and subversive ingredients were more often cynically and carefully buried, waiting to be discovered by future generations.

Reconciling Sirk's or Fassbinder's cynicism with a leftist political agenda has always struck me as somewhat problematic. Both directors tend to deal with characters incapable of understanding their own social victimization and, more often than not, incapable of change; regarding these doomed characters with ironic compassion, Sirk and Fassbinder are to my mind more defeatist than progressive because their sophistication often consists of recognizing corruption and stupidity, not of imagining situations where they might be overcome. The worlds both directors conjure up resemble more stylish versions of the repressed world found in W. C. Fields comedies — bounded on all sides by irritations and petty frustrations. ("There are no lighthearted moments in any Fassbinder film that I can recall," Gary Indiana wrote in the February 1996 *Artforum*. "If a character's happy, it's because he hasn't yet heard the bad news.") Fassbinder differs most strikingly from Sirk in focusing much more often on working-class and petit bourgeois characters, at least through the mid-seventies — *Martha* is a notable exception — but the sense of entrapment is no less pronounced.

Sirk's stylistic hallmarks include theatrical uses of lighting, color, and mirrors, and his thematic hallmarks include blindness; in the most general terms, one could say his movies are about ways of seeing and not seeing. Fassbinder's self-conscious and relatively low-budget appropriation of these hallmarks make them at once more overt and more overtly campy, so that contemporary readings of Fassbinder films are fully in tune with these attitudes in a way that contemporary readings of Sirk films were not. (For the record, the heroine of *Martha* is named Martha Hyer — after an actress who played in one Sirk feature, the 1956 *Battle Hymn*, though Hyer's association with a genteel and somewhat bookish upscale repression is probably tied more directly to her role in the 1959 Vincente Minnelli melodrama *Some Came Running*.)

Openly bisexual, tyrannical on his sets, and habitually dressed in a leather jacket, Fassbinder cut a starlike figure in the firmament of New German Cinema, though in this respect he was hardly alone. If the French New Wave of the '60s was mainly about films, the New German Cinema of the '70s was mainly about filmmakers, and each of its best-known directors had a claim to fame that was largely a matter of public image: eccentric exhibitionism crossed with German romanticism (Werner Herzog), existentialist hip crossed with black attire and rock 'n' roll (Wim Wenders), Wagnerian pronouncements (Hans-Jürgen Syberberg), a dandy's stupefied worship of shrines and divas (Werner Schroeter), and so on. When it came to Fassbinder, who improbably evoked both John Belushi and Andy Warhol, one was made to feel that the real drama in film after film wasn't so much in the makeshift characters or the fruit-salad images but in the offscreen intrigues of a baby Caligula manipulating his players and technicians.

Although it was made for German TV, *Martha* benefited from having a bigger budget than was usual for Fassbinder at the time — which allowed for some Italian location shooting as well as a more baroque and elaborate camera style than one finds in most of his other features (such as a spectacular 720-degree tracking shot encircling Martha and her husband-to-be, Helmuth Salomon, when they first encounter one another in Rome, immediately after her father's death). It's tempting to ascribe this kind of high style — also apparent at the banquet back in Germany where Martha first gets introduced to Helmuth — to personal factors. Fassbinder appears to have had a particular investment in this material that his collaborators have noted, including cinematographer Michael Balhaus and Karlheinz Böhm in Juliane Lorenz's *Chaos as Usual: Conversations About Rainer Werner Fassbinder* (New York/London: Applause Books, 1997). The latter reports that Fassbinder consciously based the portrayal of Helmuth Salomon on his own father, and even dressed like his father in conservative neckties, shirts, and suits throughout the film's production — an association that seems echoed by Helmuth surfacing magically as a kind of doppelganger-replacement for Martha's own father immediately after his death.

Certainly the tension that we briefly observe at the outset between father and daughter paves the way for her equally conflicted determination much later in the story to accede hilariously to Helmuth's desire for her to read a book on dam construction during his absence. (Typically, she initially rebels against this directive, then winds up memorizing entire passages that she can recite to him.) And even without reading the Woolrich story that inspired the plot, one can infer that the paranoia and masochism that underlie Woolrich's special brand of suspense and horror are perfectly suited to Fassbinder's ideological project. This obliges us to identify with Martha's anguish even at those selected moments when we can't be entirely sure how much her masochism is inflected by her paranoia, thereby obliging us to question how much her imprisonment is a function of her own will. Part of the luminosity and passion of Carstensen's performance is to make us feel that ambiguity and ambivalence, all the way up to the impending sense of doom carried in the final shot.

Essay in booklets accompanying DVD issued by Fantoma (www.fantoma.com) in the U.S. (2004) and by Madman (www.madman.com.au) in Australia (2008); see also www .jonathanrosenbaum.com/?p=15547 and www.jonathanrosenbaum.com/?p=15788

Notes

1. "Rainer Werner Fassbinder Talking about Oppression with Margit Carstensen," translated by Eric Rentschler, in Rentschler's collection *West German Filmmakers on Film: Visions and Voices* (New York/London: Holmes & Meier, 1988), 168–71

2. "London Journal," Jonathan Rosenbaum, January–February 1975, 83; "Rotterdam Journal," Richard Roud, May–June 1975, 2, 62; "London Journal," Jonathan Rosenbaum, January–February 1976, 4.

3. "For the Rest of Her Life," *Ellery Queen's Mystery Magazine*, May 1968. To the best of my knowledge, this has been reprinted only twice — in *Ellery Queen's Murder Menu* (1969) and, much later, in *Tonight, Somewhere in New York: The Last Stories and an Unfinished Novel by Cornell Woolrich* (New York: Carroll & Graf Publishers, 2005), where the editor, Francis M. Nevins, erroneously claims that the story also appeared in his classic posthumous 1971 collection of Woolrich stories, *Nightwebs* (New York: Harper & Row).

One should add that although Woolrich's story — reportedly "the last of his stories that [he] lived to see published," five years before *Martha* was made — begins, like the film, with the couple meeting by chance on a street in Rome (although her father doesn't figure in the plot) and ends quite similarly with the heroine in a wheelchair, most of the details in between are substantially different. (For one thing, the story is much more explicit about the husband's sadism than it is about the wife's masochism.)

India Matri Buhmi

From the beginning, film has owed part of its fascination to ambiguous overlaps between documentary and fiction. Just after the war, Roberto Rossellini came to prominence as a filmmaker through combinations of this kind — popularly known as Italian neorealism in *Open City* (1945) and *Paisan* (1946), and quickly expanding into other adventurous mixtures of reality and invention, culminating in his 1959 *India Matri Buhmi*, whose title means "India, Mother Earth." It's a sublime symbiosis of fable and nonfiction that poetically interrelates humans and animals, city and village, society and nature.

At war's end, Rossellini was primarily concerned with the human devastation in Italy and Germany. But once he began working with Ingrid Bergman, with whom he was living after their affair busted up both their marriages, domestic issues started coming to the fore, particularly in such features as *Europa 51*, *Voyage to Italy*, and *Fear*. The Bergman films flopped both critically and commercially, though for the young critics of *Cahiers du cinéma* they were models of personal independent filmmaking that would help spark the French New Wave. Rossellini's other bold forays during this period include a feature about Saint Francis of Assisi, a comic fantasy called *The Machine That Killed Bad People* (about a still camera that turns its subjects into statues), and a direct-sound recording of a play starring Bergman, made at a time when all films in Italy were dubbed.

From this standpoint, *India* can be regarded as the pinnacle of Rossellini's richest period, his crowning masterpiece. Jean-Luc Godard once referred to it as "the creation of the world," and unlike many other films about India made by Westerners — Jean Renoir's *The River* (1951) is prototypical — it can't be accused of either presumption or pretension. It's remained one of the hardest to see of Rossellini's major works, in part because of the complex and chaotic conditions under which it was made and initially received. Then fifty-one, Rossellini became romantically involved with his main script collaborator, twenty-seven-year-old Sonali Senroy Das Gupta, a traditional Brahmin who was married with two small children and, ironically, went to work for Rossellini only at her husband's insistence. The ensuing scandal forced her and Rossellini to leave the country before the film was finished. (It was completed in French and Italian studios.) Its French producers were so dissatisfied with it after its Cannes premiere that they refused to give it a commercial release, and the Italian reception was lukewarm at best.

Lamentably, the only print to have circulated with English subtitles is the badly faded and dubious 1987 restoration of the Italian version, which is missing almost ten minutes, including most of the final sequence. By common consensus, the Paris Cinematheque's only slightly faded 1994 restoration of the French version — which survives in only one print, without subtitles — is the closest thing we have to a definitive edition. It's never been available commercially, on film or on video, and it's doubtful it ever will be. But now that it's been privately subtitled in English and on video by Rossellini biographer Tag Gallagher, it can finally be seen by a wider audience. (The Chicago Cinema Forum is screening it twice this weekend.)

India, like *Paisan*, is divided into separate stories with different characters and settings, but with a strictly documentary prologue and epilogue. Originally it was supposed to have nine episodes, but five were eventually discarded. (It was also originally meant to be called *India 57* — dating it by year, like *Europa 51* and *Germany Year Zero* [1947] — but the number was dropped after its release was delayed.) Like most of Rossellini's greatest work, it conforms to what Godard once called "the definitive by chance." It has the spontaneous, unpredictable feel of a jazz improvisation while remaining so simply and lucidly focused it's difficult to imagine it any other way.

The four stories not only move between nonfiction and fiction, but develop more broadly from youth to middle age to old age to death while charting interactions between humans and nature. In all but the second episode nature is represented by animals: elephants in the first, a tiger in the third, a monkey in the fourth. In the second, it's represented by a manmade lake: a laborer is preparing to leave Hirakud with his wife and young son after five years of helping to build an enormous dam with a crew of 35,000 workers.

Deceptively, the documentary prologue is conventional to a fault: scenic pans across cityscapes, a standard voice-of-God male narrator intoning, "For anyone coming from the West, Bombay has been the traditional gateway to India." We're told about endless quantities of people, ethnic and linguistic mixes, as the pans continue across pedestrians. The tone briefly turns more personal when the ugliness of some of the architecture is briefly noted; then the narration and editing converge in a virtual parody of a conventional travelogue. We hear countless synonyms for "carrying" over a montage of people transporting assorted objects, followed by a long string of different verbs as the action in the montage changes.

Eventually we see an elephant and the exposition becomes specific: "The elephant has been brought to the city for a religious ceremony. It comes from the immense jungle Karapur, where it works, lived wild, was captured and trained. The elephant is the bulldozer of India." The next thing we know, we're in the jungle, and gradually introduced to a procession of elephants guided by men who clear away trees. We learn that the elephants can only work three hours a day, from seven to ten in the morning, after which it becomes too hot. The rest of the day is spent tending to them. This leads to a sequence of elephants being bathed and scrubbed in a river that's one of the most hypnotic, magical, and beautiful sequences in all of cinema, illustrating a kind of utopian interaction and harmony between men and animals. By this time it's become apparent that the narrator is one of the bathers, and for the remainder of this story he recounts courting a peddler's daughter, told in counterpoint with an account of the mating habits of the elephants.

There's an assertion I've only ever heard secondhand, attributed to French critic Alain Bergala in his critique of the French version, that *India* is the first film to incorporate morphing, specifically the transitional portions of the narration between the separate episodes. Real morphing — the seamless digital transformation of one image into another — was first used extensively in *Willow*, released in 1988. But I assume Bergala meant morphing as a concept and structure — when one narrator or character imperceptibly merges into another and documentary morphs into fiction. It's a narrative method with metaphysical and spiritual connotations, relating to reincarnation, transubstantiation (in Rossellini's own Catholic context), and metamorphosis, summed up by the laborer/narrator of the second episode when he passes a corpse burning on a funeral pyre and reflects, "Maybe it's beautiful to dissolve into nature." This episode is as melancholic as the first is jubilant, mainly due to the sorrow and anger of the laborer's wife about leaving their home again five years after being ousted from East Bengal because of the partition with Pakistan.

The third episode is narrated by an eighty-year-old man, happily married, who spends his days communing with his cows and the animals in the jungle near his home. His contemplative life is disturbed one day by the sounds of trucks prospecting for iron, causing most of the birds and animals to flee. With no other prey, a tiger attacks a porcupine and is wounded in the process. Vulnerable and threatened, the tiger becomes dangerous to men for the first time, and a hunt ensues. But the old man, believing "the world is big enough for everyone," ultimately carries out a plan of his own.

Like the prologue and epilogue, the fourth episode features third-person narration. An old beggar with a monkey, en route to a fair at Bagdel, collapses and dies from the heat. The monkey finds himself caught between the human and animal worlds, and after warding off the vultures circling the beggar's corpse, he travels alone to the city, where he continues to perform and collect money out of habit. The monkey's adventures eventually lead him to a circus, and as a shot of the circus audience morphs into a street crowd, the narration morphs into the recitation of another catalog, this one all-embracing, encompassing sheep, goats, cows, people, and even trees. It ends with a shot of birds that closely resemble the vultures, but like the tiger in the third episode, they're simply part of the world — no more and no less.

Chicago Reader (published as "When Fable and Fact Interact"), August 31, 2007

Radical Humanism and the
Coexistence of Film and Poetry
in *The House Is Black*

The Iranian New Wave is not one but many potential movements, each one with a somewhat different time frame and honor roll. Although I started hearing this term in the early 1990s, around the same time I first became acquainted with the films of Abbas Kiarostami, it only started kicking in for me as a genuine movement—that is, a discernible tendency in terms of social and political concern, poetics, and overall quality—towards the end of that decade.

Some commentators—including Mehrnaz Saeed-Vafa—have plausibly cited Sohrab Shahid Saless's *A Simple Event* (1973)[1] as a seminal work, and another key founding gesture, pointing to a quite different definition and history, would be Kiarostami's *Close-up* (1990).[2] Other touchstones would include Ebrahim Golestan's remarkable *Brick and Mirror* (1965), Dariush Mehrjui's *The Cow* (1969), Massoud Kimiaï's *Gheyssar* (1969), and Parviz Kimiavi's *The Mongols* (1973). But I'd like to propose a lesser-known short film preceding all of these, Forugh Farrokhzad's *The House Is Black* (1962)—a twenty-two-minute documentary about a leper colony outside Tabriz, the capital of Azerbaijan. For Mohsen Makhmalbaf, it is "the best Iranian film [to have] affected the contemporary Iranian cinema," despite (or maybe because) of the fact that Farrokhzad "never went to a college to study cinema."[3] It is also, to the best of my knowledge, the first Iranian documentary made by a woman. It won a prize at the Oberhausen Film Festival in 1963 and was also shown at the Pesaro Film Fesrival three years later. For me it is the greatest of all Iranian films, at least among the sixty or seventy that I've seen to date. More than any other Iranian film that comes to mind, it highlights the paradoxical and crucial fact that while Iranians continue to be among the most demonized people on the planet, Iranian cinema is becoming almost universally recognized as the most ethical, as well as the most humanist.

Farrokhzad (1935–67) — widely regarded as the greatest of all Iranian women poets *and* the greatest Iranian poet of the twentieth century, who died in a car accident at thirty-two — made *The House Is Black*, her only film, at twenty-seven, working over twelve days with a crew of three. The following year, in an interview, she "expressed deep personal satisfaction with the project insofar as she had been able to gain the lepers' trust and become their friend while among them."[4] I mainly want to consider it here for its anticipation of "the Iranian New Wave" as I know it. On a more personal level, Mehrnaz Saeed-Vafa and I worked with three others in subtitling *The House Is Black* in English prior to its screening at the New York Film Festival in 1997, on the same program as Kiarostami's *Taste of Cherry*.

Though it was dismissed in a single sentence by the *New York Times*'s reviewer, it clearly made a strong impression on many others who saw it there and in subsequent screenings at the annual Robert Flaherty Seminar and at Chicago's Film Center, before the print was returned to the Swiss Cinémathèque. The same version is what is now being released by Facets Video, and though it doesn't appear to be quite complete — one abrupt edit looks like a censor's cut, and a few stray details visible in some other versions are missing — this is the best version of the film available in North America.[5]

A few relevant facts about the film: its producer, Ebrahim Golestan (born in 1922) — also a pioneering filmmaker in his own right, as I've already noted, as well as a novelist and translator (who translated, among other things, stories by Faulkner, Hemingway, and Chekhov into Persian) — was Farrokhzad's friend and lover for the last eight years of her life, and she worked with him as a film editor before making her own film.[6] Her most notable editing job was on *A Fire* — an account of a 1958 oil well fire near Ahvaz that lasted over two months until an American firefighting crew managed to extinguish it. As Michael C. Hillmann accurately describes it, the film juxtaposes the fire with "the sun and moon, flocks of sheep, villagers eating, harvest time, and the like."

Prior to working on *A Fire* in 1959, Farrokhzad studied film production as well as English during a visit to England. Shortly afterwards, she traveled to Khuzestan and worked on films there in several capacities — as actress, producer, assistant, and editor.[7]

According to Karim Emami, a writer and translator who worked for Golestan Films during this period, her first experience in handling a movie camera was shooting streets, oil wells, and petroleum pumps on a handheld super-8 camera in Agha-Jari, shooting from the interior of a touring car — an image that immediately calls to mind Kiarostami, *Taste of Cherry* in particular. She also appeared in the Iranian segments, filmed by Golestan, of an hour-long 1961 National Film Board of Canada TV production, *Courtship*—a discussion of the rites of betrothal in four separate countries—playing the sister of a working-class bridegroom in Tehran. She acted in another Golestan film that was never finished called *The Sea*, and another, in 1961, called *Water and Heat* or *The View of Water and Fire*. She also made one other film after *The House Is Black*—"a short commercial for the classified ads page of *Kayhan* newspaper" which Emami regards as relatively inconsequential.[8] She is also said to have worked on still another Golestan film entitled *Black and White*, and plays an almost invisible cameo in his *Brick and Mirror*—the pivotal part of a young mother who abandons her infant.

In an interview last year, Kiarostami credited Golestan as the first Iranian filmmaker to use direct sound—a common attribution, I believe. But it's worth noting that *The House Is Black*, which clearly uses direct sound in spots, was made prior to *Brick and Mirror*, raising at least the possibility that Farrokhzad might have been a pioneer in this technique in Iranian cinema.

Defying the standard taboos and protocols concerning lepers—especially the injunction to avoid physical contact with them for her own safety—Forugh Farrokhzad wound up permanently adopting a boy in the colony named Hossein Mansouri, the son of two lepers, who appears in the film's final classroom scene, taking him with her to Tehran to live at her mother's house. Yet some of the film's first viewers criticized it for exploiting the lepers—employing them as metaphors for Iranians under the shah, or more generally using them for her own purposes and interests rather than theirs.

When I first heard about the latter charge I was shocked, for much of the film's primal force resides in what I would call its radical humanism, which goes beyond anything I can think of in Western cinema. It would be fascinating as well as instructive to pair *The House Is Black* with Tod Browning's 1932 fiction feature *Freaks*—which oscillates between empathy and pity for its real-life cast of midgets, pinheads, Siamese twins, and a limbless "human worm," among others, and feelings of disgust and horror that are no less pronounced. By contrast, Farrokhzad's uncanny capacity to regard lepers without morbidity as both beautiful and ordinary, objects of love as well as intense identification, offers very different challenges, pointing to profoundly different spiritual and philosophical assumptions.

At the same time, any attentive reading of the film is obliged to conclude that certain parts of its "documentary realism" (perhaps most obviously, its closing scene in a classroom, as well as the powerful shot of the gates closing, which occurs just before the end)—working, like the subsequent films of the Iranian New Wave, with nonprofessionals in relatively impoverished locations—must have been staged as well as scripted, created rather than simply found, conjuring up a potent blend of actuality and fiction that makes the two register as coterminous rather than as dialectical. (Much more dialectical, on the other hand, is the relation between the film's two alternating narrators—an unidentified male voice, most likely Golestan's, describing leprosy factually and relatively dispassionately, albeit with clear humanist assumptions, and Farrokhzad reciting her own poetry and passages from the Old Testament in a beautiful, dirgelike tone, halfway between multi-denominational prayer and blues lament.)

This kind of mixture is found equally throughout Kiarostami's work, and raises comparable issues about the director's manipulation of and control over his cast members. Yet without broaching the difficult question of authors' intentions, it might also be maintained that the films of both Farrokhzad and Kiarostami propose *inquiries* into the ethics of middle-class artists filming poor people and are not simply or exclusively demonstrations of this practice. In Kiarostami's case, it is often more obviously a critique of the filmmaker's own distance and detachment from his subjects, but in Farrokhzad's case, where the sense of personal commitment clearly runs deeper, the implication of an artist being unworthy of her subject is never entirely absent.

The most obvious parallel to *The House Is Black* in Kiarostami's career is his recent documentary feature *ABC Africa* (2001) about orphans of AIDS victims in Uganda—a film which goes even further than Farrokhzad in emphasizing the everyday joy of children at play in the midst of their apparent devastation, preferring to show us the victims' pleasure over their suffering without in any way minimizing the gravity of their situation.[9] But it's no less important to note that one of Farrokhzad's poems is recited *in toto* during the most important sequence of Kiarostami's most ambitious feature to date, whose title is the same as the poem's, *The Wind Will Carry Us* (2000).

The importance of Farrokhzad in Iranian life and culture—where even today, and in spite of the continuing scandal that she embodies and represents, she's commonly and affectionately referred to by her first name—points to the special status of poetry in Iran, which might even be said to compete with Islam. *The House Is Black* is to my mind one of the very few successful fusions of literary poetry with film poetry—a blend that commonly invites the worst forms of self-consciousness and pretentiousness—and arguably this linkage of cinema with literature is a fundamental trait underlying much of the Iranian new wave.

I hasten to add that "film poetry" is one of the most imprecise terms in film aesthetics, whether it's used to describe Alexander Dovzhenko or Jacques Tati, so a few precisions are in order about why I'm using this term here. Much of what I have in mind is the suspension — or extension — of what we usually mean by "narrative" or "story" so that a certain kind of descriptive presence supersedes any conventional notion of an event. After a leper is seen walking outside beside a wall, pacing back and forth, intermittently hitting the wall lightly with his fingers, we hear Forugh very faintly offscreen reciting the days of the week over this image, the rhythm of her voice sounding a kind of duet with the man's repeated gesture. Two notions of time are being superimposed here so that they become impossible to separate: an event lasting a few seconds and a duration stretching over days (and, by implication, weeks, months, and years).

Similarly, in the film's penultimate sequence, while a one-legged man limps on crutches between two rows of trees towards the camera, we hear Forugh's voice evoke a cluster of other images, some of them with very different time frames, over this single movement: "Alas, for the day is fading, / the evening shadows are stretching. / Our being, like a cage full of birds, / is filled with moans of captivity. / And none among us knows how long / he will last. / The harvest season passed, / the summer season came to an end, / and we did not find deliverance. / Like doves we cry for justice . . . / and there is none. / We wait for light / and darkness reigns." Again there is a kind of duet, ending this time in a kind of rhyme effect as her last two lines give way to the loud, clumping sound of the man's footsteps in the foreground as his dark body directly approaches the camera, dramatically blotting out everything else.

Although the film is mainly framed by two scenes in a classroom, the second of these is briefly interrupted by what can only be called a poetic intrusion — a shot I've already mentioned that is unrelated in narrative terms but enormously powerful in descriptive terms: a crowd of lepers is suddenly seen outdoors, approaching the camera, only to be blocked from us when a gate abruptly closes on them, bearing the words "leper colony" (or more precisely "leper house," tied more directly to the film's title). In narrative terms, this shot has no relation to what precedes and follows it apart from the most obvious thematic connection: lepers. Yet it functions almost exactly like a line in a poem — parenthetically yet dramatically introducing the brutality of our social definition of lepers and how it shuts them away from us — before returning us to the classroom.

That Farrokhzad was the first woman in Persian literature to write about her sexual desire, and that her own volatile and crisis-ridden life (including her sex life) was as central to her legend as her poetry, helps to explain her potency as a political figure who was reviled in the press as a whore and placed outside most official literary canons while still being worshipped as both a goddess and a martyr. Despite her enormous differences (above all, in gender and sexual orientation) from Pier Paolo Pasolini, it probably wouldn't be too outlandish to see her as a somewhat comparable figure in staging heroic and dangerous shotgun marriages between eros and religion, poetry and politics, poverty and privilege — and a figure whose violent death has been the focus of comparable mythic speculations. She and her film remain crucial reference points because of their enormous value as limit cases, as well as artistic models. And as far as I'm concerned, if the Iranian New Wave begins with *The House Is Black*, there's no imagining where it can still lead us.

Cinéma/06 (automne 2003); developed from a lecture delivered on April 1, 2001, at the conference "Women and Iranian Cinema," held at the University of Virginia and organized by Richard Herskowitz and Farzaneh Milani; also published as an essay in the booklet accompanying the DVD issued by Facets Video (U.S.) in 2005; see also www.jonathanrosenbaum.com/?p=8338

Notes

1. See Mehrnaz Saeed-Vafa, "Sohrab Shahid Saless: A Cinema of Exile," in *Life and Art: The New Iranian Cinema*, edited by Rose Issa and Sheila Whitaker (London: National Film Theatre, 1999), 135–44.

2. See Godfrey Cheshire, "Confessions of a Sin-ephile: *Close-Up*," in *Cinema Scope* 2 (Winter 2000): 3–8.

3. Mohsen Makhmalbaf, "Makhmalbaf Film House," translated by Babak Mozaffari, in *The Day I Became a Woman* (bilingual edition of screenplay) (Tehran: Rowzaneh Kar, 2000), 5.

4. Michael C. Hillmann, *A Lonely Woman: Forugh Farrokhzad and Her Poetry* (Washington, DC: Three Continents Press/Mage Publishers, 1987), 43.

5. A still better version — with French subtitles, taken mainly from the print shown in Oberhausen, and authorized by producer Ebrahim Golestan — was issued on DVD along with *A Fire* as part of the [then] biannual French magazine *Cinéma* (07 [printemps 2004]), edited by Bernard Eisenschitz and published by Editions Léo Scheer.

6. See also Mehrnaz Saeed-Vafa, "Ebrahim Golestan: Treasure of Pre-Revolutionary Iranian Cinema," *Rouge* #11, 2007 (www.rouge.com.au/11/golestan.html). [2009]

7. Michael C. Hillmann, op. cit., 42–43.

8. Karim Emami, "Recollections and Afterthoughts" (undated lecture delivered in Austin, Texas), quoted on Forugh Farrokhzad web site, www.forughfarrokhzad.org (unfortunately no longer available at this address).

9. See also Mehrnaz Saeed-Vafa and Jonathan Rosenbaum, *Abbas Kiarostami* (Urbana and Chicago: University of Illinois Press, 2003), 37–40, 83–84, 119–23.

WR, Sex, and the Art of Radical Juxtaposition

Between the mid-1960s and the mid-1970s, it was generally felt among Western intellectuals and cinephiles that cutting-edge revolutionary cinema came from Western Europe, Latin America, and the United States. Among the touchstones were Jean-Luc Godard's films in France, Newsreel's agitprop documentaries and their spin-offs (such as Robert Kramer's *Ice* and *Milestones*) in the United States, diverse provocations like Lindsay Anderson's *If . . .* and Godard's *1+1* in the United Kingdom, and, in Latin America, such films as *Lucía* (Cuba), *The Hour of the Furnace* (Argentina), and *Antonio das Mortes* (Brazil).

By contrast, the wilder politicized art movies coming out of Eastern Europe at the time—such as those of Verá Chytilova, Miklós Jancsó, and Dusan Makavejev—were treated as curiosities, aberrations that wound up getting marginalized by default. The fact that they came from Communist countries made them much harder for Westerners to place, process, and understand; in most cases, an adequate sense of context was lacking.

Part of the problem was a certain intellectual as well as sensual impoverishment arising from the one-dimensional view of Communism fostered by the Cold War, even among some of the better-educated leftists and cinephiles, which tended to lump together all the Eastern European countries as if they were all part of the same stereotypical gray wasteland. Communists across the board were supposed to be prudish, and sexual liberation and Communism were seen as competing forms of radicalism rather than as separate parts of the same struggle. (Minor exceptions to the rule were "free love" experiments in Russia, exemplified by the *ménage à trois* in Abram Room's 1927 *Bed and Sofa*, and in some bohemian leftist circles in the West, as suggested rather timidly in Warren Beatty's 1981 *Reds*.)

Yet for all their substantial disparities, Chytilova's Czech *Daisies* (1966), Jancsó's Hungarian *Red Psalm* (1971), and Makavejev's Yugoslavian WR — *Mysteries of the Organism* (1971) share two striking traits: they're significantly *less* prudish than any of the examples of so-called revolutionary cinema cited above, and they're quite adventurous formally. Indeed, their erotic candor and their formal boldness are interconnected. In the case of Makavejev's masterpiece, both are integral aspects deriving from the film's dialectical structure, which explores sexual freedoms and their perils in both New York and Belgrade, using each city and set of practices and problems to help define the other. Maybe because Makavejev qualified as a post–Cold War intellectual even while the Cold War bureaucracies were still fully in force, he was bound to court certain misunderstandings on both sides of the Atlantic — much like his hero Wilhem Reich, the maverick Austrian psychologist whose work the film explores and celebrates (and whose initials comprise the first part of its title).

Born in Belgrade in 1932, Makavejev studied psychology at the local university before entering film school in the same city, and these two preoccupations are yoked together more insistently in WR than in any of his other features (though his 1967 *Love Affair: or, The Case of the Missing Switchboard Operator* offers a clear precedent). He first encountered Reich's work in the early fifties, during roughly the same period he was studying Freud and Gestalt psychology, discovering French surrealist and Soviet silent cinema via the French Cinémathèque's Henri Langlois, and making his first amateur films (some of which had some early brushes with Yugoslav censorship). Eventually, a Ford Foundation grant financed a pilgrimage to the United States to trace the final, desperate stages of Reich's career.

Reich, born in the German Ukraine in 1897, into a family of well-to-do Jewish farmers, became a medical student in Vienna after serving in the Austrian army in World War I. A respected analyst by his early twenties who was selected by Freud as a first assistant physician at his clinic, Reich subsequently joined the teaching staff there and became vice director, shortly after he published his first major book, *The Function of the Orgasm* (1927), which already began to chart his deviation from Freud. In 1930 he moved to Berlin and joined the Communist Party, which expelled him three years later because of his unorthodox ideas. The same year, he published *Character Analysis* and, partly in response to Hitler's rise to power, *The Mass Psychology of Fascism*, shortly before he left Germany for Denmark, where his controversial notions eventually occasioned further decampments to Sweden, Norway, and, by the end of the '30s, the U.S.

Settling in New York, Reich conducted experiments over the 1940s deriving from his concepts about sexuality that by the mid-fifties led to government persecution, lengthy legal battles, and finally a prison sentence, during which he died in 1957. By this time, his increasingly radical theories about sexual health — his view of the libido as a flow of energy that orgasms regulate, and his concept of muscular armor, a neurotic symptom preventing the regulation of this energy — had made him as embattled as he had previously been in European Freudian and Marxist circles.

It wasn't only the politics of sexuality but also the sexuality of politics represented by Reich that sparked Makavejev's interest. In WR, he's less concerned with the pseudoscientific aspects of Reich's late theories about "orgone energy" than he is with Reich's overall privileging of sexuality in relation to politics and psychology. And training this emphasis on sexual lifestyles and issues in both America and Yugoslavia, Makavejev offers diverse applications of Reichian therapy (both happy and desperate), as well as documentary segments in New York involving various sexual preferences and practices, and, in Belgrade, a fictional story about a Reichian feminist named Milena (Milena Dravic) trying to seduce Vladimir Ilyich (Ivica Vidovic), a repressed Bolshoi ice skater named after Lenin. All this leads irresistibly to the significance of Joseph Stalin as an erotic and phallic symbol — explored at length via fictional representations of Stalin in films as well as actual appearances in newsreels.

■ ■ ■ ■ ■ ■ ■ ■ ■ ■

WR represents the apotheosis of radical juxtapositions through editing that can be traced back to the silent features of Sergei Eisenstein — a procedure of cutting between seemingly autonomous and disparate blocks of fictional and nonfictional materials, revived decades later in such edgy yet marginalized fare as the aforementioned 1+1 (the "director's cut" of the Godard film better known as Sympathy for the Devil, 1969), Edgardo Cozarinsky's Argentinean Dot Dot Dot or . . . (1971), and Mark Rappaport's American Casual Relations (1973) — films whose similar formal preoccupations are reflected in their titles. These filmic collages stage shotgun marriages between seemingly incompatible elements to see what kind of sparks spring from the encounters, and Makavejev is clearly the supreme master of this subgenre — not only in WR, but in his earlier features, Man Is Not a Bird (1965), Love Affair (1967), and Innocence Unprotected (1968).

This is how WR operates on a macro scale, but the same principal of juxtaposition can be found within individual scenes. Milena, for instance, who tends to talk about sex more than practice it — even though she preaches free love to crowds of neighbors and fellow workers in her apartment house — has a randy flatmate, Jagoda (Jagoda Kaloper), who cheerfully reverses those priorities. And the fact that both Milena and Jagoda are played by actresses with the same first names suggests at least traces of a documentary impulse behind the film's only sustained story.

Too nuanced and complex in his thinking to be a simple utopian, however, Makavejev perceives sex as an unleashing of potentially dangerous energies that threaten not only puritanical and authoritarian systems but also, in some limited cases, sanity — especially if we acknowledge that the latter term is commonly defined socially and legally more than it is psychologically or medically. So in WR, Milena's eventual success in seducing Vladimir Ilyich ultimately leads to her getting beheaded by him, with one of his ice skates — exposing certain dark mysteries of orgasms as well as organisms. To cite a suggestive formula proposed by the late Raymond Durgnat, Makavejev's vision is that of a tragic Rabelaisian Marxist — an artist so dialectical in spirit that he can juxtapose his politically incorrect celebration of Nancy Godfrey in New York sculpting a plaster-cast replica of *Screw* editor Jim Buckley's erect penis with a satirical song by Tuli Kupferberg about the destructive links between sex and capitalist ownership: "I'm gonna kill myself over your dead body if you fuck anybody but me." (Kupferburg and fellow poet Ed Saunders headed a New York rock band called The Fugs — one of whose tart songs, "Kill for Peace," we hear while Kupferberg appears in army fatigues and helmet, with a machine gun, on a street near Lincoln Center. I have a cherished memory of this quintessential sixties group performing "Coca-Cola Douche" at a free concert in the Lower East Side's Tompkins Square Park, with elderly Poles and Ukrainians comprising the bulk of their appreciative audience.)

The American episodes of WR also offer segments involving both transvestite and Andy Warhol Superstar Jackie Curtis and lesbian and feminist artist Betty Dodson, who paints friends while they masturbate. But the film's dialectical enterprise goes much further than explorations of the various highs, lows, and diversities of sexually related activities. Makavejev alternates his rough-and-ready 16mm documentary footage of Kupeferberg, Godfrey, Buckley, Curtis, and Dodson in New York with the slick 35mm fictional footage shot in Belgrade. And following this latter allegorical story into outright fantasy, he can show us Milena's severed head continuing to speak, as if to underline the fact that none of the questions he's raising is considered closed.

Makavejev also uses clips from Nazi as well as Stalinist propaganda films (including footage of patients receiving electroshock and waterboarding), many kinds of folk tunes (along with both circus and classical music), and accounts of Reich's persecution in America. In short, one might say that this Serbian filmmaker was clearly asking for trouble, and he got it in spades: WR — *Mysteries of the Organism* was banned in Yugoslavia for sixteen years, leading to his own exile, and his subsequent and in some ways even more transgressive *Sweet Movie* (1975) fared no better.

One could argue that he was risking not only censorship but also the possibility of being misunderstood as some sort of ideologue. That is, undertaking the same sort of interrogative/exploratory juxtaposition of clashing ideological discourses proposed by Godard in *La chinoise* (1967) and by Spike Lee in *Do the Right Thing* (1989), he risks being misread as a simplistic anticommunist libertarian — much as Godard could be (and often was) misread as a Maoist, or Lee could be misread as a Malcolm X supporter dismissing the pacifism of Martin Luther King.

In fact, Makavejev is attempting something far more difficult and valuable: a critical account of the possibilities and limits of two contradictory societies in relation to sex. In his cogent book about the film, Durgnat plausibly summarizes part of the results as "The USA has more freedom than Socialism, Yugoslavia has more Socialism than freedom." But one should stress that the comparison never takes the form of a simple contest in which there can only be one winner.

Essay in booklet accompanying Criterion DVD (U.S., 2007)

Revisiting *The Godfather*

Although I vastly prefer *Citizen Kane* (1941) to *The Godfather* (1972), one facet of both films that gives me some pause — especially because I believe that this facet has something to do with the current and unquestioned status of both movies as towering masterworks — is their special capacity to view corruption from a corrupt vantage point. Both movies are melancholy and wistful about their conviction that corruption is an inescapable part of American life in general and The American Dream in particular, and maybe I wouldn't mind this attitude quite so much if its metaphysics weren't so glib and absolute in its defeatism.

After all, accepting gangsterism along with its built-in denial as essential and inescapable parts of our condition has a lot to do with what made the gangsterism/denial of the Bush era so rampant, everyday, and taken for granted, at least until the possibility of overcoming it was implicitly posed by the Obama campaign. In his book *GWTW: The Making of Gone with the Wind* — published the year after *The Godfather*'s release, when some commentators were already touting it as that late '30s blockbuster's natural successor — Gavin Lambert perhaps said it best: "When the most ruthless level of private enterprise becomes widely taken for granted, a film like *The Godfather* finds there are no questions left to be asked. Its characters exist in a nightmare which they (and the audience) accept as everyday reality."

What *Citizen Kane* has that Orson Welles' other films lack is the contribution of Herman G. Mankiewicz, whose caustic wit is valued by some for its complacency about the inevitability of corruption. The more innocent view of corruption shared by all of Welles' other films — that is to say, their lack of cynicism — surely has something to do with their failure to be fully assimilated into the mainstream of American taste. And for the Pauline Kael who viewed

Kane as "*kitsch* redeemed," the notion that *The Godfather* might be viewed as a different kind of *kitsch* rather than as a noble Shakespearean tragedy is never entertained, because there are some ideological givens about American violence, even at its most infantile and unreasoning, that are too serious to be scoffed at, especially when they're bathed in "Rembrandt" lighting.

By contrast, consider all the depictions of violence in such otherwise very different films as Renoir's *The Rules of the Game* and Jarmusch's *Dead Man*, which refuse the very possibility of violence having any kind of dignity whenever or however it occurs. Mythologies about macho power and the pride of wanton blood-spilling are arguably at the roots of what put George W. Bush twice into office, but this is something we've generally allowed ourselves to laugh at only after it's too late to undo most of the damage. This also helps to explain why American reviewers generally showed themselves to be incapable of stepping beyond the critical framework dictated by the press book of Oliver Stone's *Nixon* and insisted on employing the word "Shakespearean" in their reviews — thereby glamorizing the film and, more implicitly, Nixon's own skuzzy exploits. (At least Herman Mankiewicz never tried to position himself as a Shakespeare — apparently being content to accept the more modest mantle of, say, a bush-league Thackeray.)

This development can perhaps be traced in part back to Pauline Kael's use of the adjective "Shakespearean" near the end of the first paragraph of her review of *The Godfather, Part II*. Her second paragraph — which casually identified its predecessor as "the greatest gangster picture ever made," immediately after announcing that *Part II* "enlarges the scope and deepens the meaning" of its predecessor — marked the lamentable suspension of her Orwellian scoffing at pretension that was perhaps the strongest virtue of her early criticism. In terms of her own unapologetic trash aesthetic, a far better candidate for "greatest gangster picture" would surely be the Hawks-Hecht-Hughes *Scarface*, no less arty than Coppola's blockbuster but far more exuberant and irresponsible (and far more honest about its own amorality), and in most respects closer to the starkness of Greek tragedy, incest and all, than to any Shakespearean tragedy or historical melodrama.

It's a moot point whether Coppola intended this, but the ethical contrast between Vito Corleone (Brando) as an earthy, charismatic gentleman Mafiosi and his cold-blooded son and successor Michael (Pacino), a Machiavellian who winds up engineering the deaths of family members — a brother-in-law in the first film, a brother in the second — tends to mystify or at least detract from the degree to which both men are killers. If we're being asked to brood about the moral and stylistic decline of the Corleones, we're less likely to be attentive to the continuity of violence between the nostalgically depicted past and the more coarsely perceived near-present.

Both *Citizen Kane* and *The Godfather* (all three parts) qualify as what Manny Farber called White Elephant Art—the sort of studio sucker-punch that Kael was usually able to see through, until she capitulated without qualm to this particular brand of it, inviting her more uncritical fans to follow. (I may be alone in finding campy rather than profound the incongruous and multiple recurrences of Nino Rota's omnipresent *Godfather* theme in *Part II*—performed on a church organ at the communion of Michael Corleone's son at the beginning, and later sung as a folk ballad with guitar accompaniment in Little Italy almost half a century earlier, just before the intermission.) If what Kael called "the Promethean spark in [Mario Puzo's] trash" was really and truly ignited by the movie version, the Stalinist grandiosity and monumentality that made it all possible seemed to fly by her shit-detector without registering so much as a blip. And one possible reason for this, I would submit, is that she bought into its ideological underpinnings, perhaps unconsciously.

Even though Lee Strasberg's performance as Hyman Roth in *Part II* represents a triumph of what Farber called Termite Art—especially in relation to the White Elephant Oscar-mongering of Brando's cheek-stuffing masquerade, to which Strasberg offers a kind of lesson in Method simplicity and understatement—I'd still single out the original *Godfather* as the one worthier of its classic status. Yet it's still always been tainted for me by the response of the New York audience to the final scene, the first time I saw this movie, at a huge theater just north of Times Square: when Michael Corleone lies to his wife Kay (Diane Keaton) about ordering the killing of his brother-in-law, they applauded and cheered. At the time I thought they were being crass; today I'm more apt to think that they may have understood the movie better than Kael or perhaps even Coppola did.

Broadly speaking, the first *Godfather* is a generic gangster film with arthouse trimmings and the second is an arthouse film with generic gangster trimmings, but both blockbusters encompass masterful American adaptations and appropriations of recent Italian cinema. The first and best sequence in the first film, built around a wedding, is indebted to the remarkable, protracted ball in Visconti's *The Leopard* (1963) while the stylish, nostalgic handling of period décor in the second appears to owe something to Bertolucci's *The Conformist* (1971); and both would of course be diminished considerably without the catchy music drawn from Fellini's habitual composer. The outsized success of both *Godfathers* helped to mark the eclipse of foreign film distribution in the U.S. for the sake of glossy American art movies, a little bit before Woody

Allen's (and Martin Scorsese's and Paul Schrader's) mining of similar fields started to take hold.

I'm certainly not claiming that *Godfathers I* and *II* lack moral ambiguity and nuance and that cherished hits necessarily lack such qualities. Lambert made a very good case for those qualities in *Gone with the Wind*, though I think he went overboard when he claimed—after conceding that "thirty years will have to pass before we can know if *The Godfather*'s appeal is momentary or lasting"—that, unlike its predecessor [*Gone with the Wind*], "the involvement [that *The Godfather*] demands never rises above the level of sensation, since its impact lies in showing the organization of violence, painstakingly detailed." Surely the complex irony milked out of the interfacing of family values, capitalism, and remorseless murder—a kind of irony shared with the much greater *Monsieur Verdoux* and *Psycho*—also has a great deal to do with the dynamic impact of the first two *Godfathers*. But I don't think Chaplin's film or Hitchcock's encourages any of the same complacency, which in the case of Coppola's films amounts to a kind of political defeatism: in both *Godfathers*, Michael can't break away from his awful family heritage of obligation, vengeance, and crime, including murder. Presumably neither can we when we accept his resignation. But there's nothing remotely noble about this resignation, Shakespearean or otherwise; it's a cowardly form of pathos, and one which Americans have been living with on an intimate basis for the past eight years.

"Slow Criticism" dossier, *de Filmkrant* (January 2009)

Part 4

Criticism

Film Writing on the Web:
Some Personal Reflections

There's a part of me that understands perfectly why a minimalist like Jim Jarmusch and a nineteenth-century figure like Raúl Ruiz won't have anything to do with email. "You can't *smell* email," Ruiz once said to me, to explain part of the reason for his distaste. But I find it tougher to feel nostalgic about film criticism before the Internet, because even though you *could* smell it, the choices of what you could lay your hands on outside a few well-stocked university libraries were fairly limited. Similarly, the choices of what films you could see outside a few cities like New York and Paris before DVDs were pretty narrow, and possibly even more haphazard than what you could read about them.

These two developments shouldn't be considered in isolation from one another. The growth of film writing on the web — by which I mean stand-alone sites, print-magazine sites, chatgroups, and blogs — has proceeded in tandem with other communal links involving film culture that to my mind are far more important than the decline in the theatrical distribution of art films and independent films, so I'll be periodically discussing those links here.

When I started out as a cinephile in New York in the early '60s, the English-language magazines that counted the most were the ones that went furthest in gathering together diverse constituencies: *Sight and Sound*, *Film Culture*, and *Film Quarterly*. Even the more local and partisan *New York Film Bulletin* was translating texts from *Cahiers du cinéma*. Of course the film world was much smaller then, and some of the nostalgia for that era undoubtedly focuses on the coziness. By the time film writing on the web started, film culture had spread and splintered into academia and journalism, which often lamentably functioned as mutually indifferent or sometimes even mutually hostile institutions.

So the theoretical golden age, I assume, took place before all the institution-alizing.

Significantly, the most enterprising early efforts to disseminate film writing on the web were neither American nor English but Australian — most notably the academic and peer-reviewed *Screening the Past,* founded by classical and fine arts scholar Ina Bernard in Melbourne in 1997, and the more journalistic *Senses of Cinema,* founded by filmmaker Bill Mousoulis in the same city in 1999. Both publications are still going strong — having published nineteen and forty issues respectively by late 2006, and continuing to keep all their previous issues online, although *Senses* underwent several changes after the departure circa 2002 of Mousoulis and another editor, critic Adrian Martin, the latter of whom went on to cofound the no less ambitious *Rouge* in 2003. It's easy to hypothesize that this Australian concentration came from both a highly devel-oped and interactive local film community and a desire both to be recognized by and to communicate with the wider world of cinephilia.

Other extremely useful film sites that have by now become regarded as staples [a brief list revised and updated in August 2009] include the English and academic film-philosophy.com and filmstudiesforfree.blogspot.com and, in the U.S., the basically journalistic (and industry-oriented) moviecitynews .com, theauteurs.com, and girishshambu.com — all especially valuable as con-duits to other sites. Then there are the sites maintained by film magazines (e.g., *Sight and Sound, Film Comment, Cineaste, Cinema Scope*), which offer samples rather than exhaustive duplications of their latest issues, and those sites that have replaced former magazines on paper, such as *Bright Lights.*

My acquaintance with blogs and chatgroups has been more limited, but a few of each might be mentioned here. Among the more notable critics' blogs are ones devoted to Serge Daney in English (sergedaney.blogspot.com) and to Raymond Durgnat [since removed, alas], and ones maintained by Fred Camper, Steve Erickson, Chris Fujiwara, and Dave Kehr. [My own web site, jonathanrosenbaum.com, was subsequently launched in May 2008.] And the main chatgroups I'm familiar with are the auteurist "a film by," "film and politics" (which started out as a splinter group deriving from the former, and is also on Yahoo), and a few separate chatgroups located on the elaborate site wellesnet.com ("the Orson Welles web resource"). The latter calls to mind a slew of other director-based sites, including especially impressive ones devoted to Robert Bresson, Carl Dreyer, Jonas Mekas, and Jacques Tati.

■ ■ ■ ■ ■ ■ ■ ■ ■

How wide are the readerships of such resources? Klaus Eder, who for many years has been the general secretary of FIPRESCI, the international film critics organization, recently told me that *Undercurrent*—an online, English-language magazine established on their web site in 2006, edited by Chris Fujiwara, that has so far published only three issues—had about 100,000 readers per month. Considering how specialized the magazine's turf is—encompassing such topics as the late film critic Barthélemy Amengual, Alexander Dovzhenko, the acting in Don Siegel's *Madigan*, Austrian cinema, sound designer Leslie Schatz, assorted short films, and recent features about Cameron Crowe, Philippe Garrel, Danièle Huillet, Terrence Malick, Park Chan-wook, and Tsai Ming-liang—and considering that 100,000 readers seems to comprise more than those of all film magazines on paper combined, this was a startling piece of information, and one that initially beggared belief. It was also hard to square this figure with one given to me by Gary Tooze regarding a recent piece of mine called "Ten Overlooked Fantasy Films on DVD (and Two That Should Be!)" on his much more commercial and consumer-oriented web site, DVD Beaver. (In that case, he estimated about 10,000 hits during the first week the article was posted.)

But once Klaus added that the average length of time spent by each reader of *Undercurrent* was roughly two minutes, I started to realize that my shock was premature, and that my superimposition of two incompatible grids—one devoted to subscribers and readers of paper magazines such as *Cahiers du cinéma, Film Quarterly*, and *Sight and Sound*, the other devoted to web surfers—could only lead to muddled conclusions. And I'm not sure that the comparison with DVD Beaver is very meaningful without the average length of time of each hit in that case, which I don't know.

I also recently learned from David Bordwell that his web site at davidbordwell.net "receives between 250–450 unique visitors each day, with an average of 2–3 pageloads per visitor. Most visitors on any day are first-time visitors, with about 60–100 coming back from a previous day. Heaviest usage is from the US and Europe, which you'd expect." I don't think we can meaningfully compare these figures with the sales of Bordwell's books (which I didn't ask him about), and I'm not even sure how meaningfully we can compare Bordwell's site with *Undercurrent*, given the range of things that web surfers are looking for. Bordwell largely uses his site to update and expand many of his writings on paper, and this already points to functions that are qualitatively different from those of published works.[1]

Extrapolating from all this, I started to realize that current claims that film criticism is becoming extinct, and counterclaims that it's entering a new golden age, are equally misguided if they assume that film criticism as an institution functions the same way on paper and in cyberspace, as two versions of the same thing rather than as separate enterprises. Related debates about the distribution of foreign films in the English-speaking world (drastically shrinking in theaters, drastically expanding in the production and distribution of DVDs), or the sophistication of young filmgoers regarding film history (growing if you follow some chatgroups, declining if you follow certain others), or the number of films that get made (even more difficult to determine if videos and films are treated interchangeably) seem equally incoherent due to the disparity of reference points, creating a Tower of Babel in a good many discussions. It's a central aspect of our alienated relation to language that when someone says, "I just saw a film," we don't know whether this person saw something on a large screen with hundreds of other people or alone on a laptop — or whether what he or she saw was on film, video, or DVD, regardless of where and how it was seen.

In short, we're living in a transitional period where enormous paradigmatic shifts should be engendering new concepts, new terms, and new kinds of analysis, evaluation, and measurement, not to mention new kinds of political and social formations, as well as new forms of etiquette. But in most cases they aren't doing any of those things. We're stuck with vocabularies and patterns of thinking that are still tied to the ways we were watching movies half a century ago.

If we consider briefly just the question of email and chatgroup etiquette, we already encounter a daunting array of new kinds of behavior. If sending an email to someone can sometimes partake of the kind of intimacy associated with whispering, there are also arguably new forms of interpersonal brutality that crop up periodically in chatgroups, obliging some leaders of such groups to impose certain standards of civility between members. Even definitions of what constitutes a stranger or evaluations of the importance of typos has undergone a certain amount of transformation within the new context of chatgroups, and there are few of us who aren't still finding our bearings within such contexts.

■ ■ ■ ■ ■ ■ ■ ■ ■

In order to grasp some of the new tricks that some of the old dogs are failing to learn, it helps if we start redefining what we mean by community in relation to geography, which is central to all these paradigmatic shifts. It becomes relevant, for example, that Fujiwara edits *Undercurrent* from Tokyo as well as from Boston, and that the editor of *Film Quarterly*, published by the University of California Press, works out of London — and perhaps even that this sentence is initially being written on a plane between Chicago and Vancouver — especially if we persist in regarding the discourse of both magazines as a discourse being aimed at a specific geographically based constituency seen in relation to a particular nation-state, town or city, university, or other institution. Speaking as someone who currently feels that he lives on the Internet more than he lives in Chicago, I consider this distinction vital to the ways that I function as a writer. Maybe it's also relevant that *Rouge*, the most ambitious of the international online film magazines (translating some of its texts into English from Chinese, French, German, Italian, Japanese, Portuguese, and Spanish sources), originates from Australia — or at least from three Australian editors, who may at any given time be in France, Greece, or elsewhere while doing part of their editorial work. But if it *is* relevant, this is largely because Australia is itself multicultural, also yielding a multicultural, state-run TV channel, SBS, that similarly has few counterparts.

It's my own conviction that the nation-state itself is fast becoming an outdated and dysfunctional concept, apart from the special interests of politicians and corporations and their own highly functional designation of countries as markets. It seems bewildering that while most of the world appears to detest George W. Bush as much as I do, this fact has been deemed totally irrelevant to political strategy and activity within the Democratic Party, so that the U.S. currently appears to be more isolated from the rest of the world than it was during the cold war — in spite of the unprecedented possibilities of communication and interactivity made possible by the Internet. And if we scale down this striking paradox to the more modest dimensions of film culture, the same anomalies are apparent. The choices of ordinary filmgoers are said to be steadily shrinking at the same time that most of the riches of world cinema are becoming internationally available for the first time on DVD.

Part of our problem in assessing our new conditions is a bad habit of often assuming by reflex that they're either bad or good — which is about as futile as arriving at such a simplistic conclusion about globalization. Let me try to illustrate this with a couple of extended personal anecdotes. Shortly after September 11, 2001, attacks, I was invited by the *Chicago Reader*'s editor to write something reflecting on its aftermath. After she decided not to run my article, I received a similar invitation from *Senses of Cinema*, and emailed them the same piece, somewhat rewritten.

I wrote about my fear of what I described as American as well as Middle Eastern terrorists — by which I meant Americans who suddenly started thinking about the vanished World Trade Center as if it were their own private property and the attacks of September 11 as if they were simply and unambiguously an "attack on America," thereby allowing the Middle Eastern terrorists and their assumed positions to set all the terms of the discussion and automatically dismissing the non-Americans from over eighty countries who were destroyed in the attacks as irrelevant. I was especially upset by a poster with an American flag over the words "September 11, 2001 / We Will Not Forget" placed on the front door of the building where I live in Chicago by an upstairs neighbor, who didn't bother to consult anyone else in the nine-unit building about it. Feeling that flags were already being used to intimidate, to stop conversations rather than start them, I objected at our next condo meeting that "we will not forget" in this context meant that we *will* forget all the non-Americans killed — at which point my neighbor left the room and refused to discuss the matter further, with the result that his poster remained up for many weeks afterwards. I concluded that I was tempted to attribute part of this terrible climate to a certain "narcissism about mourning" that a visiting German filmmaker had recently mentioned to me about some of her New York friends and acquaintances.

Less than an hour after the issue of *Senses of Cinema* containing my article appeared online, I received an abusive email from a New York film critic whom I knew only slightly and who wrote me, in a fit of rage, that I had no moral right to accuse people like him of being narcissistic about mourning when he could still smell the ashes of burnt flesh from his apartment. So three extremely disparate and irreconcilable definitions of community were affecting me all at once: a feeling of repression, censorship, and bullying in the building where I live; an ability to express this feeling freely and openly to like-minded individuals on a web site located on the other side of the planet; and an almost traumatic sensation of being assaulted by an acquaintance 800 miles away for expressing the same feeling. The first and last of these experiences were nightmarish and dystopian, the second was utopian, and the second two were possible only because of the Internet — because I can't imagine that the New York acquaintance would ever have phoned me with the same message. And only the first was geographically matched with where I happened to be.

My second anecdote relates to the recent death of Danièle Huillet, the filmmaking partner of Jean-Marie Straub, and how this was both discovered and dealt with by many people via "a film by." Shortly after I learned about this shocking and upsetting occurrence, when a friend in New York, critic Kent Jones, phoned me, I posted what little information I had in this chatgroup, and for roughly the first twenty-four hours there was little if any response. But when responses then started to come, they were detailed and far-ranging, and came from such diverse quarters as Los Angeles, Paris, the American Midwest, and Melbourne. They included photographs of Huillet as a little girl growing up on a farm (posted at kinoslang.blogspot.com) which I had never even known existed, information about the first digital video of Straub-Huillet (which later proved to be obtainable online), links to an article in *Libération* and many older English-language texts — and a detailed (and somewhat contentious) discussion about an obituary written by Dave Kehr for the *New York Times*, an obituary that conceivably might not have been written if the news about Huillet's death hadn't been posted in "a film by."

More generally, the kind of discourse and behavior one encounters in "a film by" seems to run the gamut from news and critical analysis to childish and protracted exchanges of insults — a mix that is by no means restricted to chatgroups dealing with film, and which also can be characterized as split between occasional and habitual (or even compulsive) contributors — those who periodically visit and those who appear to do very little apart from exchange comments. Significantly, this particular group was initially formed by critics Fred Camper and Peter Tonguette to counter the impolite behavior in other film chatgroups, and it continues to be monitored for that reason, but this hasn't prevented the discussions from periodically descending into invective that overwhelms other forms of communication. It would be interesting to hear from psychologists and/or psychoanalysts about the psychic reservoirs and "family plots" that appear to be tapped into by these exchanges, leading to forms of behavior that seem to be specific to the Internet and periodically undermine some of the more progressive and utopian possibilities.

Thanks to the site of cinema-scope.com, where I write a regular column called "Global Discoveries on DVD" that usually appears online, I received one of the most exciting glimpses of the utopian possibilities inherent in film writing on the web. For some time, I have been fantasizing that ciné-clubs, a major spur to French cinephilia over most of the past century, could be making a comeback, this time in global terms, thanks to DVDs. These ciné-clubs could be situated almost anywhere, in houses and apartments as well as in storefronts, and a model configuration might be touring "retrospectives" on DVD in which the DVDs could be sold at the screenings (perhaps along with relevant books and/or pamphlets), in much the same way that CDs are now often sold by music groups in clubs between their sets. And if enough circuits for these retrospectives could become established in this fashion, this could ultimately finance the production of these packages. In some ways this dream has already been realized in the U.S. by moveon.org and the way it has arranged private showings of such Robert Greenwald documentaries as *Uncovered*, *Out-Foxed*, *Wal-Mart*, and *Iraq for Sale*, but it doesn't appear to have caught on with other kinds of films.

While attending the Mar del Plata film festival last spring, I met a schoolteacher based in Córdoba named Roger Alan Koza who had established a few ciné-clubs in separate small towns that he visited on a regular basis, and the films he showed included some of the more specialized and esoteric films I had written about, including Forough Farrokhzad's *The House Is Black* (1962) and Kira Muratova's *Chekhov's Motifs* (2002). He told me the combined audiences of such screenings for each film was somewhere between 700 and 800 people. Considering how unlikely it would be to fill single auditoriums of that size in most major cities of the world for such films, I realized that the shifting paradigms of today might also transform what we normally regard as a minority taste. Once the paradigm of a single geographical base changes, all sorts of things can be transformed. Maybe Muratova's craziest feature is too difficult for most New Yorkers and Parisians, but once it can be acquired globally on DVD with the right subtitles, anything becomes possible — including a sizable group of viewers in Córdoba.

Film Quarterly 60, no. 3 (March 2007); slightly revised and updated, August 2009

Note

1. I was chagrined to discover that an essay of mine on *Eyes Wide Shut* reprinted in *American Movie Critics* by the Library of America, a publisher celebrated for its "definitive" editions, introduced a typo in the opening paragraph that reversed the meaning of the sentence, changing "argue" to "agree"—a typo that hadn't occurred in any of the article's three other appearances on paper. Ironically, if such a typo had occurred in the *Chicago Reader*, where the article first appeared, it could have been corrected a day later in the *Reader*'s online edition, whereas the Library of America's typo, barring a second edition, is permanent. [2009 postscript: although a correction sent to the Library of America went unacknowledged, thereby provoking the previous sentence, the subsequent paperback did correct the error.]

But this doesn't necessarily make the *Reader*'s online system superior. For the past several years, due to space restrictions regarding the *Reader*'s paper edition, all its capsule film reviews that run past a particular length now have to be permanently shortened for both the paper and its online editions. Thus the older issues on paper preserve longer capsules that are no longer available anywhere else, while the capsules available online can theoretically be altered on a week to week basis and thus have none of the same archival status and value.

Goodbye, Susan, Goodbye:
Sontag and Movies

I don't think that Susan Sontag was a great film critic; to hear her tell it, she wasn't really a critic at all. But it's still hard to overestimate her importance as an American writer in relation to movies. The last of the great New York intellectuals associated with *Partisan Review*, she was the only one in that crowd who understood and appreciated film in a wholly cosmopolitan manner, as a part of art and culture and thought — something that couldn't be said of Hannah Arendt, Saul Bellow, Irving Howe, Alfred Kazin, Mary McCarthy, Philip Rahv, Harold Rosenberg, Edmund Wilson, or any of the editors at the *New York Review of Books*. Even if one considers the most sophisticated members or fellow travelers of that group who functioned as film critics — James Agee, Manny Farber, Pauline Kael, Dwight Macdonald, Delmore Schwartz, Parker Tyler, Robert Warshow — none of them could claim quite the same global, cultural, and historical reach that Sontag had. Farber possibly came closest; and also undoubtedly, like most of the others, he came much closer than her to grasping particular surfaces as well as moments in film. Her turf was closer to being philosophical, though the paradox for acolytes like myself is that we learned things from her that made her into a sort of intellectual journalist — precisely what she didn't want to be once she established her name, aside from a few exceptional forays such as "Trip to Hanoi." To a certain extent, the same was true of Godard, who was only a couple of years older, and who in the '60s also became a kind of cultural journalist in spite of himself, in his films and his interviews. "What I don't like [in *Against Interpretation*]," Sontag wrote in 1996, "are those passages in which my pedagogic impulse got in the way of my prose. Those lists, those recommendations! I suppose they are useful, but they annoy me now."

No less annoyed, it seems, were some of her editors: in the first chapter of my book *Movie Wars* (2000), I went into detail about the censorship of her essay "A Century of Cinema" the same year, when it first appeared in English, in the *New York Times Magazine*, under a different title ("The Decay of Cinema") — a systematic deletion of names of filmmakers and film titles that weren't already thought to be familiar to *Times* readers. Yet even though this may be my least favorite of Sontag's essays about film (second only to "Novel into Film: Fassbinder's *Berlin Alexanderplatz*," the only other one collected in *Where the Stress Falls* — which for me founders in part on the common misperception that *Greed* is simply a paragraph-by-paragraph adaptation of *McTeague*), its saving grace for me is precisely its useful lists and recommendations, all intended as exceptions to her apocalyptic argument about cinema when I'd rather regard them as refutations. After all, it was earlier references of this kind in her essays that had first introduced me to writers like Francis Ponge and Carlo Emilio Gadda. And I suppose that her gloom and doom about the death of cinephilia, so deeply inflected and in many ways determined by her refusal of TV and video, was ultimately defensible in those terms given that her love of movies was chiefly visceral. It only became "film" as opposed to movies when she wound up writing about the subject, which she liked to do less and less.

■ ■ ■ ■ ■ ■ ■ ■ ■

When I suggested to a friend and fellow English major at Bard College that our literary speakers club invite Sontag to give a talk (it was late fall or early winter, 1964), I'd read her two theater chronicles and "Notes on 'Camp'" in *Partisan Review* and her essay on *Vivre sa vie* in *Moviegoer*. I'd also seen her once on a literary panel at Columbia with Ralph Ellison and Stanley Edgar Hyman. What impressed me most in her writing was the polemics of the theater chronicles, which included discussions of *Dr. Strangelove*, *The Great Dictator*, and *Point of Order* (that is, her performance as a critic — which I suspect is the very reason why these were the only pieces in *Against Interpretation* that she said she disliked when she wrote "Thirty Years Afterward . . ." in 1996, which also recorded her misgivings about her lists and recommendations), the forms of the other two pieces (with their numbered sections), and the fact that all four articles treated film as part of art and thought without any sort of self-consciousness or special pleading — an approach that seemed virtually unprecedented at the time. It wasn't because I agreed with much of what she was writing about particular films; it was because it seemed like she was reinventing some of the rules by which such films could be written about.

When the invitation to Susan went out, "Notes on 'Camp'" had either just provoked an article in the *New York Times Magazine* or was about to, but neither *Time*'s December 11 story about the Camp piece (which is reportedly what catapulted her into the mainstream) nor the essay "Against Interpretation" in the December *Evergreen Review* had appeared. When I finally met Susan on campus, where she had driven up with a friend, she was livid about just having encountered a smart-ass student who'd asked her, after recognizing her name, whether she was "real or intentional Camp." As she said later, "I didn't know whether to burst into tears or kick him in the balls."

It was a memorable evening. She read and discussed portions of her just-completed essay "On Style," and I was especially gratified by some of her film references — Josef von Sternberg, *The Lady from Shanghai*, Leni Riefenstahl — which in effect ratified recent inclusions of mine in the Friday night campus film series that I'd been criticized for showing. But what really won me over to her was, after speaking about my desire to write an article for *Moviegoer* about *Sunrise*, my favorite film at the time, her account of how the film had made her weep at the same Columbia University screening I'd attended a couple of years earlier.

Later, with a group of other instant acolytes, we went off to a local bar, where some of the passions she expressed were for Godard's *Contempt* (which she'd already seen four or five times on 42nd Street), the literary critic Jean Starobinski, and whatever rock song was playing on the jukebox as she sashayed over to the cigarette machine. Above all, it was the singular mix of such enthusiasms that made her so sexy and vibrant, combined with an almost Latin fusion of mind and body that felt liberating in the same way that living in Paris did, when I eventually moved there towards the end of the '60s.

It's hard to convey now how threatening she used to be to English department types (among others) during that period, when her influence was first beginning to take hold. I recall Stanley Edgar Hyman, on a visit to Bard, once admitting to me how friendly he found her when he met her — which surprised him given how much he associated her with "the homosexual mafia." When I attended graduate school at Stony Brook, Long Island, after graduating from Bard, simply mentioning her name was often all it took to provoke a violent response from some of my colleagues, who often lunged at her sexuality, as if that immediately explained everything. ("I wouldn't trust her around my daughter," the novelist Jim Harrison declared to me, with a touch of bravado, when I once suggested inviting her to campus to give a talk.) But it's also important to recall that Godard was hated by many of the same people in that period and for similar reasons, so the homophobia in Susan's case was something of a smokescreen, a diversionary tactic. Despite her bohemian taste for dressing in black, she wasn't really a beatnik, yet the sense of fun as well as freedom that she projected in relation to the arts often made her seem like a kindred spirit. Even her slang was that of a hipster.

■ ■ ■ ■ ■ ■ ■ ■ ■ ■

Another thing that enhanced this quality over the years to come was her un-categorical resistance to academic film study as it slowly began to rear its head in the '70s. The only time I recall her ever expressing this resistance overtly was the last occasion when I spent an evening with her, in Chicago in the early '90s. She'd been invited by Miriam Hansen to speak at the University of Chicago's inauguration of its Film Studies Center, a fairly posh event, and her talk, entirely improvised, was essentially an extremely tactful and graceful repudiation of academic film study, delivered in a way calculated to offend no one. This basically took the form of recalling her early encounter with Ken-neth Anger films when she attended the University of Chicago as an under-graduate, and her subsequent regular attendance in New York at the Theodore Huff Film Society, a mainly all-male congregation of hardcore film buffs (in its latter years presided over by William K. Everson), and some of its cultish habits and fetishistic rituals. Implicit in all this was a declaration of allegiance for the very sort of maniacal, unreasoning cinephilia that most Anglo-American aca-demic film study is dedicated to undermining or eliminating, though she never said this directly. (The fact that French academic film study is generally more friendly to cinephilia is worth noting, though the reverse isn't always true, and Susan's regular visits to the Paris Cinémathèque didn't necessarily make her any closer to French film academics. But she didn't ignore film academics the way mainstream critics usually do, either; I once learned from David Bordwell that his book on Dreyer prompted her to send him a fan letter.)

Afterwards, at a small gathering held in Miriam's apartment, we spoke for a bit about Orson Welles. *This Is Orson Welles*, the book by Welles and Pe-ter Bogdanovich that I'd recently edited, had just appeared, and Susan asked me to go through the index of Miriam's copy and read aloud to her all the references to *Danton's Death*—Welles had mounted a stage production of the George Büchner play in the '30s—which she was interested in directing herself. Later, when I drove her back to the Quadrangle Club, where she was staying, I recall her mentioning that her best friend when she'd attended the University of Chicago as a teenager was Mike Nichols. This put an interest-ing spin on a comment she'd once made to me about two decades earlier, at the Cannes Film Festival, when I was enthusing about *Gravity's Rainbow* and saying what a great movie I thought it could make. "Let's just hope that Mike Nichols doesn't get his hands on it," she said, obviously thinking of *Catch-22*.

■■■■■■■■■

Most of my other encounters with Susan over the years were film-related. A characteristic one: watching Louis Feuillade's seven-hour silent serial *Tih Minh* at the Museum of Modern Art in the late '60s, then joining her and Annette Michelson at a nearby coffee shop, where I invited her to update her Bresson essay to include discussions of *Au hasard Balthazar* and *Mouchette* for an anthology I was editing (never published). She explained that she was more interested in what Bresson's earlier films did, which is what she'd already written about, adding that she wasn't too keen to write more about film anyway. And if she were, I asked, who would she want to write about? Vertov, she said, without a moment's hesitation.

I also recall a private screening in Paris of her third film, a documentary about Israel called *Promised Lands* (1974); Bresson himself attended, and she greeted him, effusively, as *"Cher maître."* I still haven't caught up with her fourth and last film, *Unguided Tour* (1983), but then again it's hard to think of any well-known filmmaker whose films are harder to see than hers — which makes me more cautious about dismissing them than some of my fellow reviewers. How can we be sure? The one time I saw *Duet for Cannibals* (1969), it meant almost as little to me as her first novel, *The Benefactor* (1963) — or her last, for that matter, which I couldn't finish. But when I saw *Brother Carl* (1971) at the Directors' Fortnight at Cannes, I liked it enough to defend it in the *Village Voice*, and still found it interesting, albeit problematic, when I got to see it again at a New York screening with Susan in attendance in the early '80s.

It was also at the Cannes festival in the early '70s that I told Susan about the screenplay I'd been commissioned to write adapting J. G. Ballard's *The Crystal World* for a fledgling producer, Edith Cottrell, who owned the rights and was hoping to find someone interested in directing it. *"I'm* interested," Susan declared, and back in Paris I wound up spending an afternoon with her in her garage flat behind Nicole Stéphane's house, engaged in what I suppose could be called a script conference. She wasn't too enthused about what I'd written so far, but insofar as I'd been interested in the script mainly as a way of paying my rent — and had so little confidence in it being filmed that I wasn't even making a carbon copy — I could hardly blame her. Still, the prospect of working for Susan made it much more interesting, so I eagerly went off to follow her suggestions about making the whole thing "sexier," not realizing at the time that her own interest in the project most likely evaporated on the spot. She was rather awkward in explaining this when I finally managed to reach her again on the phone, and by the time she'd arranged to return a copy of Olaf Stapledon's *Last and First Men* that I'd lent her, it finally dawned on me that we wouldn't be having a second script conference.

I never held it against her. But I did start to harbor a grudge for another reason in 1980, when we were both back in New York. At a New York Film Festival party, she asked me what I'd been working on, after speaking favorably about my 1978 collection *Rivette: Texts and Interviews,* and when I told her I'd just written an experimental autobiography called *Moving Places: A Life at the Movies* that Harper & Row was about to publish, she brought me up short by saying, "You're too young to write an autobiography!" Her snap judgment was nonnegotiable; the implication was that at thirty-seven, I'd been wasting the past couple of years of my life doing such a stupid thing, and my having previously regarded her as the book's ideal reader could only have been a profound misconception.

I can still find some traces of that grudge in the mixed (though respectful) review of *Under the Sign of Saturn* that I published in *Soho News* a month later — although I must say that I still agree with most of its conclusions. (It was in that book, after all, where she momentarily seemed to come dangerously close to replacing Godard with Woody Allen and Hans-Jürgen Syberberg.) After praising her first two collections, I added, "Speaking as someone who used the parenthetical examples of those essays rather like the way an earlier generation used Eliot's footnotes to *The Waste Land*—as a central tool in my liberal arts education—I am disappointed at not being able to appropriate Sontag's recent, more inner-directed essays in quite the same fashion. As an old college friend observed recently, 'She doesn't belong to us anymore.'"

Some time later, when we met again at the *Brother Carl* screening, she graciously deferred to me during the discussion, asking me to explain to the audience who her actor Laurent Terzieff was, and afterwards she said to me something like, "I have the impression that you're sore at me because I didn't want to read your book." Since she professed never to read the reviews of her own books, I wasn't quite sure how she'd arrived at this correct assumption, but I stammered out a shameful disclaimer on the spot. And the next day made the even bigger mistake of sending her an inscribed copy of *Moving Places,* which I'm fairly sure she never read. Yet once my book was eventually praised by Godard, her supreme idol, in one of his interviews, I could safely assure myself that her validation no longer mattered, and that I could revere her just as much without it.

Over the years, at various times, we had many friends in common — Stephen Koch, Annette Michelson, Paul Thek, Elliott Stein, Marilyn Goldin, Gary Indiana, Noël Burch, Edgardo Cozarinsky, Béla Tarr — so it was often possible to feel in touch or at least *au courant* with Susan even when I didn't see her for long stretches. I was delighted to hear from Edgardo about what a breakthrough *The Volcano Lover* had represented for her — not simply because it put her in touch with a wider public, but more crucially because it allowed her to write fiction and essays at the same time. And what remained an inspiration about her up to the very end (and beyond) was the sheer will to live that delayed the death sentence handed to her by her cancer for longer than most people expected, including her doctors, and the courage to fight whatever obstacles stood in her way. In short, what I think Susan taught me and countless others by her example was her way of being in the world. What she had to say about film was ultimately an extension of that.

"Susan Sontag's Readers Respond, Remember, Re-Read," edited by Colin Burnett, *Synoptique* 7 (February 14, 2005), www.synoptique.ca/core/en/articles/sontag_index/

Daney in English:
A Letter to *Trafic*

CHICAGO, NOVEMBER 13, 2000

Dear Jean-Claude, Patrice, Raymond, and Sylvie,

Trying to find a useful way to discuss Serge Daney in an Anglo-American context, it's hard not to feel a little demoralized. I recently looked up the letter I wrote to a university press editor in early 1995, not very much shorter than this one, enumerating — to no avail — all the reasons why bringing out a collection of Serge's film criticism in English was an urgent matter and a first priority, almost comparable in some ways to what making Bazin available in English had been in the '60s.

I believe this might have been the longest "reader's report" I've ever written for a publisher. I was trying to persuade the editor to publish a translation of Daney texts that in fact had already been commissioned and completed in England, but, for diverse reasons, had never appeared in print. All the texts chosen came from *Ciné journal* and *Devant la recrudescence des vols de sacs à main*. I thought this translation needed some revision to make it more graceful and user-friendly, and I would have preferred a broader selection. (The essays in *La rampe*, for instance, were completely ignored, as were all the P.O.L. writings.) But I was also careful to insist that even if the manuscript were published exactly as it was, it would automatically constitute an intervention of major importance in American film studies. I even made a special point of citing the "Diderot to Daney" lineage at the end of Godard and Miéville's *2 × 50 ans du cinéma français* (*Two Times Fifty Years of French Cinema*, 1995)[1] — naïvely hoping that this pride of place would somehow make Serge seem more necessary to American film teachers and students rather than more esoteric.

What's discouraging isn't simply that I failed to convince this editor, but that we're even further now than we were from the prospect of having Daney in English—at least in any proper sense, with a book of his own. Not, I think, for the reason recently suggested to me by an American colleague—that the time for this project has already passed. After all, the Castellian translation of *Persévérance*, published by the Argentinian film magazine *El Amante*, appeared only two years ago. And in the academic world we're no longer speaking of journalistic time, which is where critics like me and those of *El Amante* mainly live, but of geological time. (Considering that your first collection in English, Raymond, has only just appeared, I'm sure you know exactly what I mean.)[2] The problem, rather, is that the vested interests of academic film study in America have become still more narrow and entrenched. It's also worth stressing that from an American perspective, Serge never truly belonged to this world, and to make him a lecturing professor even now might take a bit of doing. The capacity to traverse the discourses of academia and journalism with ease, however common in France and Italy, is much harder to pull off in the English-speaking world, and even though Bazin was a journalist who managed to enter the gates of English-speaking universities, others can't necessarily expect to follow in his footsteps. Maybe this is because the questions Serge was broaching finally had too much currency and too many political consequences to enter the academy without raising a few hackles.

What questions? The two most obvious ones that come to mind are: films viewed on television screens and world cinema seen from a truly global perspective—two areas in which Serge was an obvious pioneer and in which the U.S. seems woefully behind other large segments of the industrialized world. But I believe the first of these issues remains much more of an obstacle than the second. The sad fact is that in the many hundreds of film courses now being taught in the U.S., films have increasingly been phased out of the curriculum for budgetary as well as practical reasons (failing projectors, tattered prints, the cost of film rentals) to be replaced by videos, laser discs, and DVDs. And in the overwhelming majority of these cases, the videos, laser discs and DVDs are being discussed not as what they actually are but as if they were films. In short, a massive denial is taking place, with all the alienation and confusion that one might expect, so that many of the essential properties of what we've been calling cinema for the past hundred years—qualities and directions of light (projected and otherwise), definition, shape, composition, size, and texture, diverse relations between sound and image, conditions of social and communal reception—are now deemed inessential, specialized, even "elitist."

Knowing that we were living through a transition, Serge took it upon himself to chart some of the material consequences of what it meant to watch a

Minnelli musical or melodrama, a Fellini fantasy, a Ford western, a Preminger noir, a Disney cartoon, or even something like *Diva* (1982) on television, knowing that neither the object nor the spectator was quite the same as before, and that therefore the transactions between the two were undergoing evolutionary changes. Two decades later we're still living through that transition, still trying to figure out what it means. When I cotaught a course in Chicago three years ago with a video artist, Vanalyne Green, a course called "Film and Video: What's the Difference?," essays by Serge on the subject that had been translated into English — including four from *Le Salaire du zappeur*, in a collection edited by Jacques Kermabon and Kumar Shahani and printed in New Delhi[3] — became an important part of our syllabus. But I also discovered something distressing — something that made our subject relatively inaccessible to younger students, and something that I'm sure applies in other countries today as well: that the degree to which many of the differences between film and video matter a great deal is in part generational.

Does this mean that Daney's positions are already becoming out of date, or at least relatively specialized? I hope not, because I regard his formulation of the dilemma as a critical prerequisite — the eye of the needle that has to be passed through before one can pretend to discuss cinema as it exists today, in all its ambiguity. And because American film criticism hasn't yet learned how to thread that needle, and hasn't even figured out why it's important to learn, it's doomed to remain transcendental in the worst sense, by which I mean immaterial.

On the other hand, maybe it's the very nature of the American vision to regard materiality as irrelevant, or at least as secondary. In her 1947 essay "America the Beautiful: The Humanist in the Bathtub," Mary McCarthy wrote, "The strongest argument for the un-materialistic character of American life is the fact that we tolerate conditions that are, from a materialistic point of view, intolerable. . . . Where for a European, a fact is a fact, for us Americans, the real, if it is relevant at all, is simply symbolic appearance."[4] From this point of view, a small screen on a portable TV can be as much of a silver chalice as a giant screen in a movie house: if it's only a portal to something else — a means to an end, like that passageway in *Being John Malkovich* (1999) — then the only thing that counts is whether or not you can pass through it. It doesn't even matter whether you have to walk or crawl.

But I fear I'm being far too negative here. After all but concluding that young American cinephiles couldn't possibly appreciate what Daney has to offer, I have to come clean and admit that when I looked up "Serge Daney" in a search engine on my computer today, I suddenly found myself staring directly at something called "Chronicle of a Passion: The Homepage of Steve

Erickson"—where, in addition to many reviews, articles, and interviews by this young New York critic, I also discovered a fairly extensive section of texts by and about Serge in English, practically all of them reproduced from fugitive appearances in American, English, and Australian publications. This includes three early reviews from *Cahiers du cinéma* in the '60s, of *Chimes at Midnight* (1966), *The Great Race* (1965), and *The Family Jewels* (1965) (all three criticized as "rather turgid" by Erickson, adding that "the dismal translations don't make matters better, [but] I've included these mostly for completist purposes"); "Sur *Salador*" and "Le Thérrorisé (pédagogie godardienne)" in the '70s; an excellent interview with Serge and accompanying article by Bill Krohn commissioned (along with the translation of "Le Thérrorisé") by Jackie Raynal when she was programming the Bleecker Street Cinema in 1977; texts from the early '80s on *Stalker* (1979) and the death of Jean Eustache (both translated wholly or collaboratively by Erickson himself), *Trop tôt, trop tard* (translated by me in 1982 for a catalogue accompanying a Straub-Huillet retrospective in New York—the last one to date held in the U.S.), *One from the Heart* (1982), and "Zoom interdit"; four *Libé* texts about television from 1987; lamentably, only one text from the '90s, albeit a crucial one, on Annaud's *L'amant* (*The Lover*, 1992); and finally texts about Daney by Malcolm Imrie (in England) and Adrian Martin (an obituary published in Australia).

I've never met Erickson, though he phoned me a few times in Chicago several years ago. What I find so touching about his act of passionate and semiclandestine appropriation is its underlying generosity; in his introduction to the Daney section he reveals that he managed to get ahold of the same unpublished manuscript of Daney in English that I myself read and went to the trouble of copying in 1995 (knowing even then, alas, that the odds of its being published weren't great), and adds, "If anyone out there would like a copy, please contact me." In the final analysis, this *sotto voce* invitation—almost as if he were offering pornographic postcards to strangers passing on the street— may turn out to be a more authentic way of introducing Daney to American cinephiles than attempting to smuggle him into a classroom. It reminds me of a remark made to me a few years back by Edgardo Cozarinsky, when he compared friends duplicating films on video for one another to medieval monks dutifully copying illuminated manuscripts—a way of secretly keeping culture alive during the dark ages, passed from hand to hand. Indeed, keeping Daney alive like this no doubt comprises a more lasting and more valuable legacy than trying to force, say, *L'Exercice a été profitable, Monsieur* into the same universe of discourse—not to mention the same genre of classroom assignments—as *The Classical Hollywood Cinema* or *Film Art*.

I realize, of course, that this either/or dilemma is a peculiarly American one because of the absolute rift that exists here between journalism and academia, and in most cases between cinema and other academic subjects within universities. This wasn't always the case: when I was a college student in the '60s, running the local cine-club at Bard College before film was taught there as an academic subject, one could invite a film critic like Dwight Macdonald to speak on campus and assume that all sorts of people there would be interested. But when I returned to Bard to give a reading from *Moving Places*[5] in the early '80s, after a film department was fully established there, I was depressed to discover that no one apart from film students were even informed about my visit.

■■■■■■■■■

For Serge, the fact that he considered the passage between cinema and television as a kind of physical voyage, and one that could even induce jetlag — precisely in the sense that Gilles Deleuze speaks in French of "voyage" (usually translated as "journey") in his preface to *Ciné journal*, as a means of generating optimism as well as pessimism — made it another part of his itinerary as a world traveler. An essential part, because as Deleuze points out in a by-now familiar formulation, to travel is to verify, to compare, to see: "Your travels, in other words, have left you with mixed feelings. Everywhere, on the one hand, you find the world turning to film, and find that this is the social function of television, its primary function of control — whence your critical pessimism, despair even. You find, on the other hand, that film itself still has endless possibilities, and that this is the ultimate journey, now that all other journeys come down to seeing what's on TV — whence your critical optimism."[6]

To travel to different parts of the world is also to change one's image of that world, and Daney's early forays to Asia, the Middle East, India, and North Africa were path-clearing ventures that ultimately provided some of the West's initial routes towards the cinemas of those regions. "World cinema" as it was known during the postwar period and then during the nouvelle vague was a very different entity from what we know it to be today, not only because certain nationalities and ethnicities have subsequently been coaxed out of hiding but because nationality itself is beginning to mean something different. In this case, I would stress that the lagging behind of America, while still a problem, is not nearly as serious as it was a few years ago. For all the isolationism that continues to rule our media, the dawning recognition of figures like Hou and Kiarostami is finally taking place, and, yes, the world has gotten even smaller since the '80s, the period I regard as the Daney decade.

One reason why it's gotten smaller is the huge multinational corporations that have begun to displace or at the very least dominate the national governments — the "brands," as they're often called. This has unified the globe in two diametrically opposed ways: by making McDonald's hamburgers, Nike sneakers, Coca-Cola, and Disney animated features seemingly omnipresent, and by creating a significant counterforce — destructive dreams and plots of resistance to these and comparable brands that are no less universal, even if they're generally, at least so far, much less evident.

Perhaps this counterforce is still mainly a matter of potentiality rather than one of active power (a way of dreaming about the Internet); but I'm also beginning to realize that the brands have a vested interest in minimizing whatever threatens them, and that significant political gains have in fact already been made. Last August, while reviewing an independent American video documentary that was premiering in Chicago, Rustin Thompson's 30 *Frames a Second: The WTO in Seattle,* I was also reading an interesting book about the same global movement, Naomi Klein's *No Logo: Taking Aim at the Brand Bullies.*[7] The video was made by an American TV news cameraman and film critic who is nostalgic enough about the '60s to include video clips from both Haskell Wexler's *Medium Cool* (1969) and Godard's *Le petit soldat* (1960). (The latter even inspired the first part of Thompson's title; if film, for Godard, was the truth twenty-four frames a second, video is the truth thirty frames a second — although, as Thompson fully realizes, given his own acknowledged subjectivity, six additional frames per second don't amount to any additional truth.) He was apparently politicized in December 1999 by demonstrations against the World Trade Organization in Seattle, yet he saw these events as essentially American — populist proof that his fellow citizens weren't as politically apathetic as he had previously assumed, thereby inspiring him to include a third clip, from the final scene of Ford's *The Grapes of Wrath* (1940), about the survival and resilience of The People. In short, one might say that because Thompson comes from a big country — big in the sense that China and Russia are also big — he becomes lost inside its boundaries, and practically everything he sees becomes translated into national events and groupings. And the same thing has been happening since the presidential election a week ago, when both the innocence of Americans and the appalling lack of meaningful choices have suddenly become a comic spectacle for the rest of the world. (While many of my friends have been calling the ambiguous and tortured election results a "worst case scenario," I've been entertaining the notion that it may at least temporarily function as a "best case scenario" — at least if one views these results as a kind of protracted deconstruction of American electoral politics, and surmises that from a global standpoint, a petrified America might possibly yield a safer and healthier planet.)

In contrast to Thompson's video, the book is by a Canadian who sees the movement against the brands as global first and last, as global as the brands themselves. Consequently, even though Klein's book appeared in 1999 and therefore omits the December demonstrations in Seattle, she has much more to say about them than the video, starting with the fact that two days prior to the fiftieth anniversary of the WTO in Geneva, in May 1998, an international movement called Reclaim the Streets successfully staged thirty events in twenty countries—a "Global Street Party" involving "Indian farmers, landless Brazilian peasants, unemployed French, Italian, and German workers and international human-rights groups" and ranging from 800 people dancing on a six-lane highway in Utrecht to even larger bashes in Prague, Sydney, Berkeley, and Birmingham—although these were "rarely reported as more than isolated traffic snares" in the press. (Klein also devotes one chapter to substantial victories in the campaigns against Nike, Shell, and McDonald's— convincing Nike to eliminate its sweatshops in Burma, for instance—which I hadn't heard about on the evening news, either.) For the average American— myself included, at least before I read No Logo—the global movement of May 1998 took place exclusively in backwaters whereas the one in December 1999 was supposedly a "world-class" event by virtue of converging in Seattle. But if the world consists mainly of backwaters—which is certainly one of the main impressions one carries away from the films of Dreyer, Godard after he left Paris, Hawks, Hou, Kiarostami, Kramer, Kurosawa, McCarey, Mizoguchi, Paradjanov, Pialat, Rocha, Sembène, Straub-Huillet, Tarkovsky, and van der Keuken, among other Daney favorites—then it has to be Seattle (or Paris, or New York, or Chicago) that's relatively slow in catching up. I believe Serge was one of the first film critics who had a dawning awareness of this fact—an awareness made especially evident through his choices of what films were the most important, and one even dramatized by the photograph of him on the cover of Persévérance.[8]

I'm not sure if this global flexibility was always the case with Serge, even if he traveled to the U.S. as early as 1964 (with Louis Skorecki, to interview Hawks, McCarey, Tourneur, Lewis, Sternberg, and Keaton), the same year he started writing for Cahiers du cinéma. In fact, I have to confess that the period in his career that I still find most difficult to use today is during the following decade, when his focus became more parochial: the Maoist era of the Cahiers and its immediate aftermath, part of which has recently (and paradoxically) been commemorated in English by the belated publication of the fourth and (avowedly) last volume of essays translated from that magazine.[9] Here indeed is still more Daney in English—perhaps most notably "The Aquarium," his reflections on Robert Kramer and John Douglas' Milestones (1975). And notwithstanding the extremely prohibitive price of this volume (about a hundred dollars!) that makes it highly unlikely for classroom adoption, there's an undeniable logic in commencing the project of publishing Daney in English between hardcovers with portions of the first decade of his collected work in French. (It was towards the end of that decade that Jackie Raynal first introduced Serge and me to one another in New York, shortly before he invited me to become the New York correspondent for the *Cahiers*. My first true act in that endeavor undoubtedly remained the most important, for him as well as for me: introducing him to the euphoria and what Barthes might have called the "circulation" of the *Rocky Horror Picture Show* cult one Saturday night at the 8th Street Playhouse.)[10]

Still, I remain somewhat stumped about what Americans and English students can do with many of these mid-seventies texts a quarter of a century later — such as a roundtable discussion and then an essay critiquing that same discussion about an American film (*Milestones* again) that remains almost completely unknown today outside of France: unavailable and undistributed on film and on video alike in both the U.S. and the U.K. Perhaps the neglect is unjust and maybe the publication of this book can help change this situation, but without wanting to sound at all cynical or cavalier about this, I'm not holding my breath. I have only the vaguest recollection of having seen the film at the London Film Festival in 1975, and, rightly or wrongly, remember it now only as an early harbinger of a certain new age sensibility that would eventually overtake the American counterculture. In contrast to *Ice*, Kramer's 1969 film — which I saw years earlier in Paris and which for me captured the neurosis and paranoia of the American radical left with disturbing accuracy and indelible brilliance (for which it was mainly scorned in New York) — *Milestones* continues to fascinate me almost exclusively as a site of French contemplation.

Admittedly, I used to feel the same way about Lang's two Indian films, which are now particular favorites of mine, so I hope I'm not being short-sighted in assuming today that *Milestones* probably has fewer secrets to divulge, at least to me. Here is where I begin to understand what makes Serge more difficult to "translate" than Bazin, beyond a specific French and European context. Even though I've always loved *Moonfleet* (1955), ever since it came out — unlike *Der Tiger von Eschnapur* (1959) and *Das indische Grabmal* (1959), which I could only see in Paris and in a dubbed *version française* prior to the late '70s — I can't begin to imagine how one could translate the title of *L'Exercice a été profitable, Monsieur* into a context that would make much sense to American cinephiles except as an exotic emblem of French cinephilia. Even starting with the English line spoken in the Lang film by Stewart Granger — "The exercise was beneficial" — would get one nowhere.

Yet at the same time, I must confess that my own fascination with Jacques Rivette's *Out 1* (1971) as a statement about the French counterculture, and my consternation that French criticism has almost completely ignored it, corresponds closely to my dismay about the privileged treatment accorded by Serge and his friends towards *Milestones*, and perhaps their own dismay that Americans including me tended to recoil from it. (In a more postpolitical context, I can recall Serge openly acknowledging to me and to Bill Krohn on separate occasions the injustice of the *Cahiers* siding with the status quo and refusing to cope with the challenges offered by Rivette's subsequent *Duelle* [1976] and *Noroît* [1976]—a refusal accompanied by some feeling of embarrassment, as if those two films had both undertaken certain unsuccessful acts of psychoanalysis.)

In fact, the reasons why France (including Serge) was in denial about *Out 1* and why the U.S. (including me) was in denial about *Milestones* may have been almost the same—along with the reasons why a certain kind of otherness inflected with sameness can convert a certain kind of foreign film into a good object worthy of extended study. I suspect that what we both truly needed in relation to our leftism in the '70s was a site of mourning, and a close look at our own countries in relation to this grief might have simply been too debilitating. (Perhaps the Paris he knew became a fit subject for analysis again only after it had become sufficiently depoliticized—past the point of negation, as in Eustache's *La Maman et la putain* [1973].) Looking too directly at political failure was too apt to turn us both into pillars of salt, so we took detours through each other's countries and vernaculars in order to approach "the awful truth," to cite it in terms of the McCarey title. And, based on my few encounters with Kramer, when he expressed his frustration about being virtually invisible in the States, it was a dilemma that no doubt tormented him more than anyone. (For me, the most beautiful thing about "L'aquarium" is the spirit of an endless quest, bordering on the Proustian: "What holds the tribe together? What does it consist of? A glob of spittle, one might say.")[11]

■ ■ ■ ■ ■ ■ ■ ■ ■

Another reason why the planet has been shrinking is a vision of exchange and circulation that Serge already recognized around him and helped to foster in others, a vision embodied in the very name of *Trafic*. It's fascinating to me how that vision, when it was still only a spark at the end of Serge's cigar—a concept for a film magazine first described to me at some point during the '80s, in the cafe of the Hilton lobby in Rotterdam—was perceived from the outset as international, yet also French: a very special combination. In contrast to the internationalism that is also American, which resembles the brands whether it wants to or not, the internationalism of Serge — like that of Tati, one of his great loves and reference points — was already apparent in the franglais of the title of his magazine. But the full significance of the Frenchness wasn't clear to me until a few years later, in late 1991, when I held the first issue in my hands and discovered something that it hadn't occurred to Serge to tell me: that *Trafic* was also a literary magazine. That's why I found, among other things, an opening quote from Ezra Pound, a journal kept by Serge, a poem by Godard, personal reflections from Monteiro and Kramer, one letter from Rossellini and another from Bill Krohn. So that by the time I became a contributor myself in the second issue, it seemed perfectly natural, even logical, for me to be comparing *Playtime* (1967) to *Ulysses*.

Perfectly natural in *Trafic*, but hardly anywhere else. This perhaps explains why, years later, when I came to revise and update an essay from *Trafic* about *Histoire(s) du cinéma* for *Film Comment*,[12] I felt it necessary to suppress nearly all of the references to *Finnegans Wake*. And for similar reasons, when I recently included some of my *Trafic* texts about film festivals in a polemical book of mine that is coming out in the U.S. this week,[13] my editor insisted on cutting these texts substantially, simply in order to reduce the number of filmmakers and films that he's never heard of. For I take it that part of any literary project worth its salt is an acknowledgement of a certain ignorance, a sense of potential knowledge that always and necessarily exceeds one's grasp (which for me is central to the mystery and beauty of Faulkner, for instance, or Proust, or *Wuthering Heights*), whereas the *sine qua non* of film criticism in the U.S. is its utter reliance on the consumption model: if you can't already see a film, you're much better off not knowing that it exists. I would argue, in fact, that this is what prevents my country from being truly global in outlook as well as truly literary, the problem with the Thompson video: an excessive absorption in the local that has currently lodged itself in the Florida polls. Didn't Serge rightly point out, in one of his last TV interviews, that Marshall McLuhan's '60s description of television as a "global village" was still valid — but only if one placed the emphasis on "village"? (In the case of film criticism, this also usually means attending only to either academic or journalistic writing while ignoring the other — the major reason, I think, why we still don't have a volume of Daney in English: because he's too academic for mainstream publishing and too literary for academic publishing. The fact that he's interested in cinema and television, art and the Gulf War, already makes him too interdisciplinary for easy classification and marketing.)

For this notion of cinema as an extension of literary discourse — already fundamental to Alexandre Astruc's *caméra-stylo*, and elaborated still further in the nouvelle vague, initially by Alain Resnais' choice of screenwriters and the fact that most of his younger colleagues were writers themselves — has actually been an implicit theme of French cinephilia from the beginning, already present in Louis Delluc and Jean Epstein: a notion, finally, that the cinema is literature by different means, but literature none the less. Hence the importance of film criticism, which Godard realized from early on was just another way of "making cinema"; and the means by which words become coextensive with sounds and images becomes one of the first essential steps towards realizing with the Lettrists that words are both sounds and images. Writing about *Finnegans Wake* in 1939, shortly after it was published, William Troy had the perspicacity to point out that "a word, in the terminology of modern physics, is a time-space event. It is not too much to say that for the poet no word in a language is ever used twice exactly in the same way."[14] No word, no sound, and no image; and the coming together of all three in a united yet disparate poetic front might be said to equal Godard's most basic film aesthetic.

For Serge, I suspect, this wasn't so much a part of any conscious program as it was part of the air he breathed. That's why *Trafic*, which he knew from fairly early on would be his final resting place — *Le Tombeau de Serge*, one might call it, thinking of Marker[15] — immediately became a literary magazine not so much methodically as instinctively, indirectly, and altogether naturally, a product of accumulated wisdom more than deliberation. Sylvie, I'm reminded of your lecture about Serge in Rotterdam in 1993 — the first annual "Serge Daney Lecture" at that festival, when you and Robert Kramer both spoke. You addressed the "coherence" of Serge's "liberation" — "the liberation to be oneself, to be receptive to the voice of others" — linking together "the three different periods of Serge's critical work — the *Cahiers du cinéma* period (20 years), *Libération* (10 years), and *Trafic* (only one year, although he'd been preparing *Trafic* for five)." (I should add that these latter quotations are drawn from yet another small publication of texts by and about Serge in English, issued by the Rotterdam Festival. So each time I think I've offered a nearly exhaustive inventory of how much — or how little — Serge has been allowed to function in my language, another exception immediately rises to the surface.)

This, finally, must be what Godard is referring to in the "Diderot to Daney" lineage — literature as liberation, cinema as discourse — and why, alas, my own citation of this tradition in my reader's report five years ago couldn't establish a clear place for Serge in American film studies, much less American literature. Maybe this is partly because *Trafic* functions for me as *Out 1* has — and as portions of the American cinema function for you, much as they functioned for Serge: as a form of global circulation, a way of being in the world by remaining in motion. In these terms, what matters most about Kiarostami may not have much to do with being Iranian — and what matters most about Serge and

Trafic may have little to do with being French. That all three are literary may count for much more — at least in the online global village we inhabit, with the emphasis firmly on "global."

Faithfully and affectionately,
Jonathan

2009 postscript: The two most significant events to have occurred regarding Daney in English in the nine years since this article was written have been Paul Douglas Grant's translation of Daney's posthumous *Persévérance* (1994) as *Postcards from the Cinema* (Oxford/New York: Berg, 2007) and the launching of the web site sergedaney.blogspot.com.

Trafic, no. 37 (printemps 2001): "Serge Daney: après, avec"; see also "The Missing Image," *New Left Review* 34 (July–August 2005), and www.newleftreview.org/?view=2575

Notes (by Adrian Martin, added for subsequent online publication in English in *Senses of Cinema*)

1. The title on the video itself is *Deux fois cinquante ans de cinema français*, subtitled as *Twice Fifty Years of French Cinema*. However the "phrase book" of this work prepared by Godard and published by P.O.L. in 1998 is called 2 × 50 *ans de cinéma français*.

2. Rosenbaum is here alluding to the publication of Raymond Bellour's *The Analysis of Film* (Bloomington and Indiana: Indiana University Press, 2000), an edited and translated version of his *L'Analyse du film* (Paris: Editions Albatros, 1979).

3. Jacques Kermabon and Kumar Shahani, eds., *Cinema and Television: Fifty Years of Reflection in France* (London: Sangam Books, 1991).

4. Mary McCarthy, *On the Contrary: Articles of Belief, 1946–1961* (New York: Noonday Press), 12–13. This essay originally appeared in *Commentary*, September 1947.

5. Rosenbaum, *Moving Places: A Life at the Movies* (Berkeley: University of California Press, 1995).

6. Gilles Deleuze, "Letter to Serge Daney: Optimism, Pessimism, and Travel," *Negotiations: 1972–1990*, translated by Martin Joughin (New York: Columbia University Press, 1995), 78.

7. Naomi Klein, *No Logo: Taking Aim at the Brand Bullies* (New York: Picador, 1999).

8. The cover image by Françoise Huguier, stretching over the front and back jackets, is of "Serge Daney in Japan," showing him at rest while a local child plays nearby.

9. *Cahiers du cinéma*, vol. 4, 1973–1978: *History, Ideology, Cultural Struggle*, edited by David Wilson (London and New York: Routledge, 2000).

10. Rosenbaum, "Lettre des U.S.A.," *Cahiers du cinéma* 307 (January 1980); English language version in *Sight and Sound*, Spring 1980.

11. Daney, "The Aquarium (*Milestones*)," *Cahiers du cinéma*, vol. 4, translated by David Wilson, 155.

12. Rosenbaum, "Godard in the Nineties: An Interview, Argument, and Scrapbook," *Film Comment* 34, no. 5 (September/October 1998): 52–63.

13. *Movie Wars: How Hollywood and the Media Conspire to Limit What Films We Can See* (Chicago: a cappella books, 2000).

14. William Troy, "Notes on *Finnegans Wake*" [1939], in *Selected Essays* (New Brunswick, NJ: Rutgers University Press, 1967), 97.

15. The allusion is to the French title of Chris Marker's video essay about Alexander Medvedkin, *The Last Bolshevik* (1993): *Le Tombeau d'Alexandre* ("Alexander's Tomb").

Trailer for Godard's
Histoire(s) du cinéma

The following text derives from two particular film festival encounters: (1) a roundtable on the subject of Jean-Luc Godard's *Histoire(s) du cinéma*, held in Locarno in August 1995; (2) some time spent with Godard in Toronto in September 1996. I participated in the first event after having seen the first four chapters of Godard's eight-part video series; unlike the other members of the roundtable — Florence Delay, Shigehiko Hasumi, and André S. Labarthe — I'd been unable to accept Godard's invitation to view chapters 3a and 3b, devoted to Italian neorealism and the French New Wave, in Switzerland a few days prior to the event. A little over a year later, Godard brought these chapters and a still more recent one — 4a, on Alfred Hitchcock — with him to Toronto, where he was presenting *For Ever Mozart*, and showed me these three chapters in his hotel room over two consecutive evenings. We also had some opportunities to discuss the series (in English); some of our conversation was recorded, but much of it wasn't. Then, in mid-December, just as I was beginning to write this article in Chicago and Godard was working on the final episode, he generously assisted me by sending me copies of all the completed chapters to date.(The first two of these chapters are each fifty minutes long; the remaining five are each twenty-five minutes long.)

At the moment, *Histoire(s) du cinéma* remains a "work in progress"[1] and the same thing has to be said for this tentative examination, a trailer which can at best be described as fragmentary first impressions by someone who, among other limitations, knows cinema better than he knows French. (And, like most trailers, this is being made while the finished work is still in production.) In the text that follows, all quotations from my conversations with Godard in Toronto are indicated by the abbreviations "JR" and "JLG." For invaluable assistance throughout this adventure, my particular thanks to Nicole Brenez, Bernard

Eisenschitz (the organizer of the roundtable in Locarno), Jean-Michel Frodon, Piers Handling, Bill Krohn, Marco Müller, and Rob and J. K. Tregenza.

Video as a Graveyard

> JR: Whenever you recount a history, there's an implication that something is over, and it seems to me that one implication of *Histoire(s) du cinéma* is that cinema is over.
>
> JLG: The cinema we knew. We also say that of painting.

If one wants to be "up to the minute" about cinema, there's no cause to be concerned that *Histoire(s) du cinéma* has been in production for at least nine years—after having been sketched out rather differently, in the form of an illustrated lecture series given in Montreal, a decade prior to that.[2] After all, James Joyce's *Finnegans Wake*, the artwork to which *Histoire(s) du cinéma* seems most comparable, written between 1922 and 1939, was first published in 1939, but if one read it for the first time this year, one would still be ahead of most people in literary matters. For just as *Finnegans Wake* figuratively situates itself at some theoretical stage after the end of the English language as we know it—from a vantage point where, inside Joyce's richly multilingual, pun-filled babble, one can look back at the twentieth century and ask oneself, "What was the English language?"—Godard's babbling magnum opus similarly projects itself into the future in order to ask, "What was cinema?"

Joyce's province was the history of mankind as perceived through language and vice versa, both experienced and recapitulated through a single, ordinary night of sleep—that is to say, through dreams. Only superficially more modest, Godard's province is the twentieth century as perceived through cinema and vice versa, both experienced and recapitulated through technology—that is to say, through video. Clips and soundtracks are examined and juxtaposed—partly through the ordinary operations of a video watcher (fast forward, slow motion, freeze frame, muting, and programming) and partly through more sophisticated techniques like editing, sound mixing, captioning, and superimposition. *Finnegans Wake* considers both the English language and the twentieth century as something that's over, and in the same way *Histoire(s) du cinéma* treats both the twentieth century and the history of cinema as something that's liquidated, finished. (This isn't entirely a new position for Godard. In January 1965, responding to a questionnaire in *Cahiers du cinéma* which inquired, "What do you think of the immediate and the long-range future of the French cinema? Are you optimistic, pessimistic, or do you have a 'Let's wait and see' attitude?," he replied, "I await the end of Cinema with optimism.") This is one of the reasons why, to my mind, the fact that *Histoire(s) du cinéma* is a video is of enormous importance, because video in certain respects is the graveyard of cinema, and it's also the graveyard of the history of the twentieth century — or at least of the popular perception of that history. ("*Cogito ergo vidéo*" reads a title at the beginning of chapter 1b.)

As "unwatchable" and "unlistenable" in many respects as *Finnegans Wake* is "unreadable," *Histoire(s) du cinéma* remains difficult if one insists on reading it as a linear argument rather than as densely textured poetry; in my experience, it is most rewarding when approached in a spirit of play and innocence. It reminds me of a time when I once played a record of Cyril Cusack reading aloud from *Finnegans Wake* at a friend's apartment, and it provoked sustained giggles of delight from her two grammar-school children, neither of whom had the same sort of problem with Joyce's prose encountered by most university professors. As Godard says in chapter 1b, "The cinema, like Christianity, isn't founded on historical truth. It gives us one account of the story and asks us to believe it." *Histoire(s) du cinéma* is neither cinema nor Christianity, but it asks for a similar act of faith.

It is also, like *Finnegans Wake,* a work constructed in layers, aurally as well as visually — a dimension made especially evident by the dense weave created by the separate channels of the soundtrack. If you look at the separate drafts and manuscripts of *Finnegans Wake,* you can see that the work became more and more complex as it developed, and in the same way, if you look at the working notes and treatments of *Histoire(s) du cinéma,* you can tell that it went all the way from Godard's view of film criticism during the '70s to something which is perhaps closer to philosophy, or maybe even psychoanalysis. Just as most animated films are constructed in layers over extended periods — with the result that probably the best newsreels and documentaries about certain countries are animated films because they bear the imprints of their own periods through their steady accumulations of thoughts and impulses — Godard's video needs to be read in relation to its own period of composition (1988–97), not merely in relation to the preceding periods during this century that it covers.

> JLG: For me, the reason why I was not so commercial was that it wasn't very clear to me whether I was writing a novel or writing an essay. I like both of them, but now, in *Histoire(s) du cinéma,* I'm sure it's an essay. It's easier for me and it's better that way.
>
> JR: So it isn't simply a matter of video versus film?
>
> JLG: No. But video permits certain things. The sound is the same. The good thing in video, too, is that you don't have to pay when you use music, as you

do in a movie or on TV because of the copyright. For example, in *Détective*. I used some Bartók music, and the Bartók estate refused permission; we had to change it at the last minute. But I could use the same Bartók music in *Histoire(s) du cinéma* without asking anyone. [See "*Histoire(s) du cinéma* as Legal and Political Precedent," below.]

JR: It seems to me that a different kind of energy goes into your films and your videos. It's clear, for instance, that *Histoire(s) du cinéma* couldn't be a film. Why is this the case?

JLG: Well, I'd say for technical reasons, because video is closer to painting or to music. You work with your hands like a musician with an instrument, and you play it. In moviemaking, you can't say that the camera is an instrument you play through; it's something different. And then there's the possibility of superimposition, which isn't the same in movies, where it has to go through different technical processes. The image isn't good enough in video, but it's easier. You only have two images to work with in video; it's like having only two motives in music, and the possibilities of creating a relationship between two images are infinite. The big difference is that if you shoot the three stone lions of Eisenstein in video, it can be an entire Warhol movie.

Criticism versus *Hommage*

A central aspect of *Finnegans Wake* is the multilingual pun (and it's important to bear in mind that *Histoire(s)* is a work in at least seven languages: French, English, Russian, German, Spanish, Italian . . . and Latin). And a no less important aspect of *Histoire(s) du cinéma* is the multiple quotation — that is, quoting from different films at the same time, which plays an almost equivalent role.

The notion of multiple film quotation has of course been important for Godard since the '60s. Consider, for example, the degree to which *Alphaville* (1965) offers a complex critique of the silent German expressionist cinema on many registers at once — not only through the thematic and plastic importance of light and darkness, day and night, but also such quotations (or paraphrases) as the camera's moving through a hotel's revolving door (from *The Last Laugh*), figures clinging to walls like Cesare in *The Cabinet of Dr. Caligari*, and a brief passage in negative (as in *Nosferatu*), combined with allusions to later films influenced by expressionism (Akim Tamiroff evoking *Mr. Arkadin*, *Touch of Evil*, and *The Trial*; the flight from the city at the end conceived in relation to *Orpheus*): in short, an updated version of Lotte Eisner's *The Haunted Screen*, but expressed in terms of film rather than prose. Chapter 3b of *Histoire(s) du cinéma* acknowledges this relationship by superimposing extracts from Fritz

Lang's *Destiny* over the opening of *Alphaville* and even tracing certain visual rhymes (such as ones between Lemmy Caution's cigarette and candles in the Lang film). Yet during my conversation with Godard, I was surprised to hear him say that when he made *Alphaville,* most of his references to German cinema were made unconsciously; it was only when he looked back at the film years later that he realized what he had done, and chapter 3b — dealing, as it does, with the nouvelle vague — records that discovery.)

Dominating the first four chapters (1a, 1b, 2a, 2b) are the alternating sounds of typing and of film turning on an editing table: staccato and legato, the sounds of Godard's two activities as a critic. (The style becomes exclusively — and beautifully — legato in 3a, on Italian neorealism, the most moving episode to date.) The continuity between writing and filming is apparent in many respects here, above all in the important role played by *The Wrong Man* (1956) — the subject of the longest, most serious, and most detailed critique written by Godard for *Cahiers du cinéma*[3] — in episode 4a, devoted to Hitchcock, which shows Godard coming full circle back to the preoccupations of his writing forty years ago. Insofar as Godard, like Rivette, has remained a film critic throughout most of his career as a filmmaker, it is important to clarify how methods of quotation, paraphrase, and allusion, unlike those of practically every other filmmaker, generally remain critical. When Allen, De Palma, Scorsese, and Tarantino echo shots or sequences from other filmmakers, the gesture is always one of postmodernist appropriation, not one of critical transformation, and the same thing can be said about the *hommages* of (among others) Truffaut and Bertolucci. (For me, the only time when Truffaut as a filmmaker continues to function as a critic is in the powerful act of self-criticism implied in *The Green Room* [1978] regarding the morbidity and rigidity of *la politique des auteurs* as a personal system.) When Rivette literally quotes the Tower of Babel sequence from *Metropolis* in *Paris Belongs to Us,* thereby criticizing the metaphysical presuppositions of his characters, or when Resnais virtually duplicates a sequence of shots from *Gilda* inside Delphine Seyrig's room in *Last Year at Marienbad,* thereby locating the romantic mystifications of Robbe-Grillet within the even larger romantic mystifications of Hollywood, a certain kind of critical commentary is taking place, even if it's only implied in the second instance. The same process is at work on a much more elaborate scale in *Celine and Julie Go Boating,* when Rivette takes the critical discoveries of doubling in Hitchcock, made by Truffaut in relation to *Shadow of a Doubt* ("Skeleton Keys"—a major piece from 1954 inexplicably omitted in both volumes of Truffaut's criticism in English, but available in *Film Culture* no. 32, Spring 1964, and *Cahiers du Cinema in English* no. 2, 1966) and by Godard in relation to *The Wrong Man* (translated without its original title,

"The Cinema and Its Double," in *Godard on Godard* [New York: Da Capo, 1986], 48–55), and then applies these principles to the same evolving "double" structure of his own film, doubling shots as well as scenes. But the same thing obviously can't be said for Allen and DePalma appropriating the baby carriage from *Potemkin* in *Bananas* and *The Untouchables*, for Schrader and Scorsese using part of the plot of *The Searchers* in *Taxi Driver*, for DePalma borrowing a 360-degree dolly around a kissing couple (along with Bernard Herrmann) from *Vertigo* to use in *Obsession*, for Tarantino getting Uma Thurman in *Pulp Fiction* to imitate Anna Karina's dance around a pool table in *Vivre sa vie*, or, for that matter, Rivette dressing Juliet Berto and Dominique Labourier in black tights *à la* Musidora when they steal a book from a library in *Celine and Julie Go Boating*.

Part of Godard's critical activity is classification, which comes into play whenever multiple quotation is employed. *Made in USA* is full of combined references to violent noir thrillers and animated cartoons, some contained in the dialogue ("a film by Walt Disney, but played by Humphrey Bogart," "Walt Disney plus blood"), some contained in the colors and iconography, some contained in the performances (Laszlo Szabo imitating Tweety Pie), and some even contained in the names of characters, so that the surname of Jean-Pierre Léaud's character, Donald, might well be either "Duck" or "Siegel." The murder of a provincial aunt in *Weekend* evokes the knife thrusts in *Psycho* and the incinerator used for burning a corpse in *Monsieur Verdoux*, two films that associate murder with business; and *Les Carabiniers* teems with references to war films ranging from Walsh's *What Price Glory?* to Sirk's *A Time to Love and a Time to Die*.

The same tendency is carried over directly into *Histoire(s) du cinéma*. Early in chapter 1a, Godard creates a very beautiful montage by intercutting clips from Murnau's *Faust* (Mephistopheles greeting Faust at a crossroads) and Minnelli's *The Band Wagon* (Cyd Charisse dancing around Fred Astaire in a bar during a production number) while we hear portions of both Beethoven's Tenth Quartet and the incantatory narration in *Last Year at Marienbad* in which the hero speaks to the heroine about how she hasn't changed. Leaving aside Beethoven, it appears that what we have here are three very different versions of the Faust theme involving hypnotic persuasions, invitations into a world of narcissistic fantasy and self-fulfillment. (The dance number in *The Band Wagon*, one should recall, is part of a stage musical based on *Faust*, and Charisse dancing around Astaire in a gangster setting is explicitly linked in the editing to Mephistopheles tipping his hat to greet Faust.)

Other multiple quotations of this kind in the early chapters of *Histoire(s) du cinéma* include such pairings and clusters as the burning of a witch from

Dreyer's *Day of Wrath* with Rita Hayworth singing "Put the Blame on Mame" in *Gilda* (followed by allusions to *Witchcraft Through the Ages* and *Ordet*, accompanied by dialogue from a film by John Garfield which I can't identify); the wicked witch from Disney's *Snow White and the Seven Dwarfs* with Bernard Herrmann's *Psycho* score; D. W. Griffith, Charles Chaplin, Mary Pickford, and Douglas Fairbanks posed together, identified collectively as *"Les Enfants Terribles"*; the title *I Confess* with a still from *Pickpocket*; *Elena et ses hommes* with "The Night They Invented Champagne" from *Gigi*, along with erotic sequences from *Silk Stockings* and *Prénom: Carmen*, a photograph of Renoir, and a recording of Renoir speaking.

For Godard, the functions of critique and *hommage* sometimes overlap: in *JLG/JLG* and in *2 × 50 ans de cinéma français*, it is the latter that predominates, even if the deliberate obscurity of certain references in *2 × 50 ans* arguably corresponds in certain cases to a particular critical position. (Characteristically, the touching *hommage* to Roger Leenhardt in the latter — included not in the Diderot to Daney "pantheon" of writers at the end but much earlier, in what is probably the longest clip in the video — is an unattributed extract from Godard's own *The Married Woman*.) There is nothing critical about the groupings of stills and portraits in chapter 1a organized around Eisenstein, Welles, Renoir, and Vigo. But an *hommage* becomes a critique when it defamiliarizes the material, as the Russian formalists might say — which is why the clips in *Histoire(s)* that tend to be the most mysterious are usually the ones that one recognizes: James Gleason drunkenly rocking back and forth in a rocking chair in *The Night of the Hunter* (in chapter 3a — an image recalling Lillian Gish in *Intolerance*, reminding one of how closely Laughton studied Griffith), the screen test on board a ship in *King Kong* (recycled repeatedly throughout the series). And when Godard wants to cite a particular director within a given context, his choices are sometimes anything but obvious. In 3a, which details some of the sources of the New Wave ("It's all over the place," I recall Godard saying to me in Toronto, "because the New Wave was all over the place"), the major reference to Robert Aldrich is a pair of female wrestlers at work in . . . *All the Marbles*, and the major reference to Preston Sturges is by way of *The Beautiful Blonde from Bashful Bend*. . . .

Hitchcock, Master of the Universe

> JR: Have there been many cases where you can't acquire the clips you want?
>
> JLG: If I don't have it, I take another one, and then I tell another story, more or less, with no problem. In the last episode [4b], any shots can be good. I need documentary shots that are both strong and of no importance.

JR: What are for you the main differences between the early episodes and the late ones?

JLG: The early episodes are more linked to cinematography; the last ones are more about the philosophy of what cinema is in this century, more about what is specific to cinema.

JR: You certainly concentrate more on specific film subjects in 3a, 3b, and 4a: neorealism, la nouvelle vague, and Hitchcock.

JLG: I put in Hitchcock because during a certain epoch, for five years, in my opinion, he really *was* the master of the universe. More than Hitler, more than Napoleon. He had a control of the public that one else had.

JR: What about Ronald Reagan? Didn't he have the same control?

JLG: No, because Hitchcock was a poet. And Hitchcock was a poet on a universal level, not like Rilke. He was the only poet maudit to have a huge success. Rilke wasn't one, Rimbaud wasn't. He was a poet maudit for everyone; *Notorious* wasn't like James Joyce. I remember André Bazin was very angry with us. And something which is very astonishing with Hitchcock is that you don't remember what the story of *Notorious* is, or why Janet Leigh is going to the Bates Motel. You remember one pair of spectacles or a windmill — that's what millions and millions of people remember. If you remember *Notorious*, what do you remember? Wine bottles. You don't remember Ingrid Bergman. When you remember Griffith or Welles or Eisenstein or me, you don't remember ordinary objects. He is the only one.

JR: Just as with neorealism, as you show, you remember only people.

JLG: Yes, it's the exact contrary. You remember feelings, or the death of Anna Magnani. It's very clear.

JR: It was a very important moment for me in 4a when you included almost an entire sequence from *The Wrong Man*, of Henry Fonda alone in his jail cell, because that linked your video with one of your major critical pieces for the *Cahiers*. By contrast, I don't recall you including any clips from *Bitter Victory* or *A Time to Love and a Time to Die*.

JLG: No.

JR: And it's interesting that you call Hitchcock the only filmmaker apart from Dreyer who could film miracles, because some people have argued that the miracle in *The Wrong Man* isn't believable.

JLG: But it was based on a true story! And *Ordet* and *The Wrong Man* were both commercial flops; that's another connection.

Cinema and the Twentieth Century

> JLG: Everything came from the New Wave. First it was spreading and then it
> disappeared. That's why I said to Anne-Marie [Miéville], "At the time of Jean
> Vigo, it was the same as it is for us now: 'difficult,' a flop, no one's seeing it."
> But because of what happened at the time of neorealism and then at the time
> of the New Wave — because of the theory of all that — attendance went up.
> And now it's going down again. It's always been like that. I say what I mean in
> the third episode of *Histoire(s) du cinéma*: it's evident that movies are capable
> of thinking in a better way than writing and philosophy,[4] but this was very
> quickly forgotten. So this is what happened. The New Wave was a miracle. It
> was a crystallization of what James Agee wrote about.[5]

In terms of the overall myth of *Histoire(s) du cinéma*, the cinema and the
twentieth century — almost interchangeable in Godard's terms — are contextu-
alized by two key countries (France and the United States), two emblematic
studio chiefs (Irving Thalberg, Howard Hughes), and two emblematic world
leaders (Lenin, Hitler); two decisive falls from cinematic innocence (the end
of silent film that came with the talkies and the end of talkies that came with
video); two decisive falls from worldly innocence (World War I and World
War II); and two collective cinematic resurgences that took place in Europe,
affecting the moral and aesthetic consciousness of the rest of the world (Italian
neorealism and the New Wave).[6]

In chapter 2a, Serge Daney explains to Godard why he is uniquely qualified
to recount the history of cinema by coming from the New Wave, which started
midway through the twentieth century and midway through cinema itself.
(Coming midway through *Histoire(s) du cinéma*, in an episode that concludes
the second of four hours, it is an ideally timed moment of stock-taking.) He
also stresses the degree to which Godard's desire to place himself in history is
a characteristic French trait. And because "The cinema authorizes Orpheus to
turn around without making Eurydice die" (the final title in this chapter, apart
from a Latin motto), the implication of many things being almost over — above
all, the century and the cinema — establishes the basis for Godard's extraordinary monologue at the end of 2b, "Beauté fatale," about cinema itself as an
act of mourning.

What Is History?

> JR: There's a sequence from *Que Viva Mexico* in chapter 2a that seems edited in a
> very Eisensteinian way. Is this editing yours?

JLG: No, it's Marie Seton's. In a sense, I think I'm virtually unassailable in *Histoire(s) du Cinéma*. I used Marie Seton's because it was the very first one that we knew about, *Time in the Sun*. Jay Leyda had not yet done his critical work on it, and I never saw that version; it was the kind of movie we never saw. And so, since I was speaking of the New Wave, it has to be Marie Seton. Because Marie Seton belongs to the same epoch as Jean-Georges Auriol, who was so fond of Marie. If it was another episode, maybe I would have edited the footage myself. I'm not ashamed to re-edit another filmmaker.

How much of a historian is Godard? A complex question, almost as complex in a way as asking the same question about Joyce. "That which has never taken place is the work of the historian," reads an early title in chapter 2a. Much of Godard's work since the '80s is concerned with amnesia—a subject that becomes especially important in his *King Lear* (1987) and *2 × 50 ans de cinéma français*—but there are times when Godard's own amnesia seems as much of an issue as everyone else's.

Case in point: The epigraph of *Contempt* (1963), attributed to André Bazin and appearing also in the beginning of episode 1a and in *For Ever Mozart*, is "Cinema substitutes for our gaze a world that corresponds to our desires." But it appears that neither the quotation nor the attribution is correct. A more probable source is a sentence that appears in "Sur un art ignoré" by Michel Mourlet (*Cahiers du cinéma* no. 98, août 1959, 34, nine months after Bazin's death): "Since cinema is a gaze which is substituted for our own in order to give us a world that corresponds to our desires, it settles on faces, on radiant or bruised but always beautiful bodies, on this glory or this devastation which testifies to the same primordial nobility, on this chosen race that we recognize as our own, the ultimate projection of life towards God."

Another example: in excerpts from a document (published in English in *Jean-Luc Godard: Son + Image*, edited by Raymond Bellour with Mary Lea Bandy [New York: Museum of Modern Art, 1992], 132) written and assembled by Godard alongside *Histoire(s) du cinéma*—an early version of a book scheduled to be published by Gallimard at the same time that the complete video series premiered in Cannes—Godard incorrectly describes Howard Hughes as the "producer of *Citizen Kane*."

False quotations and false attributions are, of course, quite common in film criticism. Although Godard himself is correctly credited for having made the famous remark "Tracking shots are a moral question," what is almost invariably omitted from this attribution is that Godard was merely inverting a sentence by Luc Moullet published four months earlier: "Morality is a question of tracking shots." (Moullet's sentence appears in "Sam Fuller: In Marlowe's

Footsteps" [March 1959], translated in *Cahiers du Cinéma: The 1950s* [Cambridge: Harvard University Press, 1985], 148; Godard's sentence appears in a July 1959 roundtable on *Hiroshima, mon amour*, translated on page 62 of the same volume.) Godard's version of the epigram is perhaps the more memorable of the two, and it's theoretically possible that Moullet was only paraphrasing something he heard Godard say at an earlier date. For that matter, Moullet may (or may not) have been paraphrasing something he might have read or heard from Bazin. The point, in any case, is I don't know, and the history of film and film criticism abounds with such cases of not knowing. A surfeit of not knowing, however, produces only confusion, and the advantage of false or at least dubious quotation and attribution in this case is that they produce some form of history — or, more precisely, *histoire(s)*. . . . Is it true, as Godard asserts in 2b, that F. W. Murnau and Karl Freund invented Nuremberg lighting while Hitler still couldn't afford a beer in a Munich café? Whether true or not, it is certainly a form of history, poetry, and criticism, transforming the object of our gaze.

Puns, for Joyce, are the stuff of dreams, and the same could be said for the multiple quotations of Godard: neither is a proper vehicle for history in any rigorous way, but they both reflect history and cast reflections upon it. (There is no precise equivalent to Vico or a theory of circular history in *Histoire(s) du cinéma* as there is in *Finnegans Wake*, but the sense of eternal recurrence is very much present in the repetition of various images and phrases.) After all, "History," said Stephen Dedalus in *Ulysses*, "is a nightmare from which I am trying to awake." And the history from which *Histoire(s) du cinéma* is trying to awake is also a history of science, painting, literature, and music — in short, the same history of modernism that Joyce is also trapped inside, offering a surfeit of significations that film scholarship will be decoding in the century to come. (If we have film and if we have scholars, that is; the implication of Daney's discourse is that we won't.)

In Dreams Begin Responsibilities

In Godard's first phase as a filmmaker (roughly 1959–68), he functions very much as a historian of the present, literally as well as figuratively — a major dimension of his work that becomes diminished once he forsakes Paris for Grenoble and then rural Switzerland. Arguably, it is only when Switzerland functions as Switzerland in his films of the '90s, as in *Nouvelle vague* (1990) — or when Germany functions as Germany in *Germany Year 90 Nine Zero* (1991) — that the Godardian sense of both place and period survives intact; in *Hélas pour moi* (1993) and, even more, *For Ever Mozart* (1996), by contrast, there is a sense of relative "placelessness" that also seems to locate both films outside of time, in spite of their many topical references. Interestingly enough, this ceases to be a problem in his videos (in *Histoire(s)*, for instance, the only ongoing "place" that counts is cinema, not Switzerland), and perhaps for this reason, it has recently been in video, not film, that he functions most comfortably as a historian.

This historical impulse can already be seen in a mocking juxtaposition of shots reportedly eliminated by the French censors from *Breathless* (1960) — a cut from Charles de Gaulle in a car following Dwight D. Eisenhower in a car in a procession down the Champs-Elysées to Jean-Paul Belmondo following Jean Seberg down the sidewalk. This conflation of the sexual with the military/political rhymes with the rude simile proposed by Godard in chapter 1a of *Histoire(s) du cinéma* over a frenzied montage synthesizing a musical number ("Ladies in Waiting") from *Les Girls*, Max Ophüls, Molière, Madeleine Ozeray, Louis Jouvet, and even Bogart: "1940, Geneva, *L'École des femmes*, Max Ophüls. He falls upon Madeleine Ozeray's ass just as the German army takes the French army from behind." The reference is to Ophüls's unfinished filming of a stage performance of the Molière play, and the significance here is again the simultaneity of what's happening in cinema and what's happening in the world outside — a point made equally in the same chapter when Godard rhymes a figure in a skeleton costume at a masked ball in *The Rules of the Game* (1939) with concentration camp victims, or when, in 3a, he links Elina Labourdette's penultimate line in *Les Dames du Bois de Boulogne* (1945), "*Je lutte*" ("I struggle"), to de Gaulle saying to the free French, "We must struggle," around the same time. The latter linkage has prompted Godard to call *Les Dames du Bois de Boulogne* the "only" film of the French Resistance, and even if one chooses to reject such a notion, it becomes possible to appropriate it as a *critical* insight into the early films of Robert Bresson. For it might be argued that some of Bresson's most important identifying traits as a filmmaker — such as his uses of offscreen sounds to replace images, or the sense found in all his films of souls in hiding, of buried identities and emotions — might be traceable in part to his nine months (1940–41) in a German prison camp and his subsequent experience of the German occupation of France. This applies not only to his masterpiece *about* the French Resistance, *A Man Escaped* (1956) — where the sounds of the world outside Fontaine's prison cell create as well as embody his very notion of freedom — but also to his other early features. Such an interpretation can of course be debated, but it seems to me a far more fruitful approach to Bresson's style to see it growing out of concrete and material historical experience than to treat it as a timeless, transcendent, and ultimately mysterious expression of abstract spirituality. (Judging from Michel Ciment's recently published interview with Bresson in *Positif* no. 430, decembre 1996, Bresson may share this bias himself: "To treat me like a Jansenist is insane: I'm the opposite of a Jansenist, I search for an overall impression. When I'm on the grand boulevards, I ask myself straightaway, 'What sort of impression do they make on me?' And in fact this impression is of a jumble of legs which makes a sharp sound on the pavement. I've tried to render this impression with sound and image.") And Godard's historical linkage, without actually propounding this critical argument, at least points us in the proper direction. It's a way of saying that cinema is concerned with the world, not with an alternative to it, and that cinema belongs to the world, including us.

Histoire(s) du cinéma as Legal and Political Precedent

JR: There's an important legal precedent in the way *Histoire(s) du cinéma* uses clips. There are some other very interesting recent videos that use clips critically — Mark Rappaport's *Rock Hudson's Home Movies* and *From the Journals of Jean Seberg* and Thom Andersen and Noël Burch's *Red Hollywood* — without acquiring rights. It's usually impossible to get rights for the clips in works of this kind, so they've all been made outside the system.

JLG: Gaumont, which owns *Histoire(s) du cinéma*, probably has a big worry now, because if it's me it's one thing, but if it's Gaumont . . . The first two episodes were shown on five separate European TV channels, so it *is* a precedent, because if it wasn't me with the friendship of Gaumont, no other producer would have done it due to the rights problem. But for me there's a difference between an extract and a quotation. If it's an extract, you have to pay, because you're taking advantage of something you have not done and you are more or less making business out of it. If it's a quotation — and it's more evident in my work that it's a quotation — then you don't have to pay. But it's not legally admitted in pictures.

JR: Yes, but it also isn't legally acknowledged that films and videos can be criticism.

JLG: It's the only thing video can be — and should be.

One could argue that the decline of film criticism in recent years — observable in the habits of most newspaper and magazine editors in both Europe and North America as well as most films academics in North America — is not so much a reflection of the changing tastes of audiences (as these editors and academics often insist) as it is the power of multicorporations to eliminate everything that interferes with their promotion. Just as the so-called "American independent" filmmakers promoted by the Hollywood studios via Sundance usually means the filmmakers who have lost their independence, "film criticism" in the mainstream now refers mainly to promotional journalism; true independents and critics have to function in the margins. In more ways than one, the traffic is moving underground.

Philosophically speaking, *Histoire(s) du cinéma* is a dangerous work because it dares to raise the issue of whom cinema, film criticism, and film history belong to. Truthfully, they belong to everyone today with a VCR, but contractually, they belong to the state, and the state today — especially from the standpoint of an American like myself — is Disney. It is Disney and its client states such as Miramax that set our cultural agendas and rewrite our official film histories and critiques via the mass media. By writing his own film history and criticism on video, using means that are readily available and relatively inexpensive, Godard is proposing a direction that filmmakers and video artists everywhere could explore with benefit — the direction of appropriation, a movement already inaugurated by the critical and historical reappraisals of the New Wave, and continued in *Histoire(s) du cinéma* by other and more subterranean means, such as poetry and autobiography. Recalling *Paris Belongs to Us*, Jacques Rivette's first feature, I propose a slogan: Paramount belongs to us.

Trafic, no. 21 (printemps 1997); revised and updated, January 2009; see also www.jona thanrosenbaum.com/?p=15581

Notes

1. When Godard completed this work in 1998, he revised all the episodes apart from the last, based on the film clips to which Gaumont couldn't acquire the rights. In 1999, the soundtrack to the series was issued on CDs by ECM along with an abbreviated version of Godard's text in English, French, and German and some frame enlargements in four books. My text minus the final section was included in English in the fourth volume. I still don't know whether Godard himself performed this censorship, presumably on the pretext that this section was now "out of date." [2009]

2. See Jean-Luc Godard, *Introduction à une véritable histoire du cinéma* (Paris: Editions Albatros, 1980). One should also note that some of Godard's other recent videos — *Les enfants jouent à la Russie* (1993) and *2 × 50 ans de cinéma français* (1995) — might be regarded with profit as "annexes" to *Histoire(s) du cinéma*.

3. See my article *"Le vrai coupable*: Two Kinds of Criticism in Godard's Work," *Screen* 40, no. 3 (Autumn 1999): 316–22.

4. Compare the following sentence from "Le cinéma et son double," *Cahiers du cinéma* 72 (June 1957): "Once again, Alfred Hitchcock proves that the cinema today is better fitted than either philosophy or the novel to convey the basic data of consciousness" (*Godard on Godard*, translated by Tom Milne [New York: Da Capo, 1986], 50).

5. For example: "The films I most eagerly look forward to will not be documentaries but works of pure fiction, played against and into, and in collaboration with unrehearsed and uninvented reality" (Agee in the *Nation*, January 25, 1947).

6. A skeptical afterthought: "Missing from this highly skewed view of the world is practically all of Asia and the Pacific, the Middle East, and Africa — not to mention most experimental cinema made everywhere. At least two major Japanese filmmakers, Kenji Mizoguchi and Yasujiro Ozu, are given some recognition, and a still from Souleymane Cissé's *Yeelen* is seen, but the latter is the only fleeting allusion to African cinema, and the cinemas of Iran, India, and Australia (for instance) can't be said to exist at all in this scheme. Even worse, adding a certain amount of complacent and (at times) neocolonialist insult are the references to Fritz Lang's *The Indian Tomb*, George Cukor's *Bhowani Junction*, and Marguerite Duras's *India Song* that seemingly 'replace' Indian cinema (three great films, to be sure — but hardly adequate substitutes) and an even more dubious evocation of other 'darker' cultures in which Philippe Garrel's *Marie pour mémoire*, Jean Grémillon's *Lumière d'été*, John Coltrane's jazz piece 'Africa,' *White Shadows [in the South Seas]*, *Captain Blood*, Glauber Rocha's *Antonio das Mortes*, and Jean Rouch's *Moi, un noir* are invited to rub shoulders with *Yeelen*.

"To be fair, Godard was among the first Europeans who recognized the importance of Abbas Kiarostami, and this recognition took place while he was still working on *Histoire(s) du Cinéma*. Nevertheless, it's clear and perhaps also understandable according to his 'closed book' policy that he decided Kiarostami played no role in the (hi)story he had to recount. Here is only one clear instance of a collision between history as it's written and the history that remains to be told, and it points to a much wider weakness and absence in much contemporary film criticism that attempts to generalize about the state of the art, past and present." (Taken from a 2003 essay, "Godard's Myth of Total Cinema," commissioned by the Rotterdam International Film Festival.)

Moullet retrouvé

Almost thirty years passed between my extended defense of Luc Moullet in *Film Comment*[1] and the long-overdue launch of his first American retrospective and a DVD box set with English subtitles. But it was worth the wait. In the spring of 2006, "Luc Moullet: Agent Provocateur of the New Wave," including eight of his thirty-two films, showed at Chicago's Gene Siskel Film Center. And three years later, a complete Moullet retrospective was shown in Paris, accompanied by much fanfare, including the publication of a DVD (unsubtitled) featuring ten of his best short films, *Luc Moullet en shorts*, and three separate books: a lengthy interview with Emmanuel Burdeau and Jean Narboni (*Notre Alpin Quotidien*, 130 pages) and a long-overdue collection of his film criticism (*Pige Choisies [De Griffith à Ellroy]*, 372 pages), both published by Capricci, and a study of King Vidor's *The Fountainhead* (Le Rebelle de King Vidor: les arêtes vives*, 112 pages), published by Yellow Now.

Moullet started out in the mid-1960s as a neoprimitive, brandishing his lack of technique while reflecting some of the tenderness of François Truffaut's films of that period as well as some of the boorish satirical humor of Jean-Luc Godard's. (His cinema is basically and fairly consistently one of sweet and lovable assholes.) Then he gradually became a *petit maître* by the mid-1980s — both as a director and as an athletic comic performer with a sense of small moments worthy of Jacques Tati. Not quite a minimalist, he still has a way of deflating pretension with earthy, deadpan simplicity. His *Essai d'Ouverture* (*Opening Tries*, 1987), the funniest fifteen minutes he's ever filmed, consists of virtually nothing but him trying to open a large bottle of Coke. (One might regard this as an apotheosis of the comedy of domestic frustration virtually minted in the 1950s by MGM's *Pete Smith Specialties*. When I was on the selection committee of the New York Film Festival in the mid-1990s, I persuaded the other members that we should include it in that year's program, roughly a decade after it was made, thereby making it the festival's first Moullet film.)

I especially regretted the absence from the Film Center series of his very great and politically potent non-comic documentary, *Genèse d'un repas* (*Origins of a Meal*, 1978) and *Les sièges de l'Alcazar* (1989), Moullet's hilarious fifty-two-minute account of an edgy 1955 flirtation between Parisian film critics from rival magazines, *Cahiers du cinéma* and *Positif*, during a Vittorio Cottafavi retrospective, as well as two '90s shorts—his passionate defense of slag heaps (*Cabale des oursins*, 1991) and a very odd documentary about Des Moines, the home town of both Jean Seberg and John Wayne, *Le ventre de l'Amérique* (1996). I also missed his 1984 short *Barres*, which celebrates and inventories all the ingenious ways one can get onto the Paris *métro* without paying, and *Parpaillon* (1992), a delightful comedy feature about a bicycle rally held in the Alps, the full title of which is *Parpaillon ou à la recherche de l'homme à la pompe Ursus d'après Alfred Jarry*—a film celebrated at length (and in English) by Fabien Boully in the online *Rouge* (www.rouge.com.au/ 6/parpaillon.html). Fortunately, the first five of these films are now available on DVD, the first two with English subtitles. And the polemical force of these strange low-budget comedies is especially relevant now, when the low cost of digital cinema is a posing a challenge to blockbuster mentality in all its oppressive ramifications.

A filmmaker of economy in every sense of that term who has produced most of his own films, Luc Moullet has argued that "Each person can realize a good film at least once in his life," so access to filmmaking for 50 million French people should be facilitated—"especially since there is room for 30 French films a year costing $1 million, but also for at least 500 features costing $6,000." He's also claimed of *The Smugglers* (1967)—a personal testament and would-be mountain adventure offering a multifaceted metaphor for filmmaking—that if it had cost 20 percent less it would have been better "because there would have been something in the film that emphasized this austerity. . . . One of the great advantages of poverty is to develop a sense of responsibility on the part of the director."

Moullet is still a tough sell for some people, including many in France—though his first feature, *Brigitte et Brigitte* (1966), was an unexpected hit—because his defiant way of challenging glitz remains an affront to the film industry. The son of a mail sorter and a typist, he grew up in the sticks—like the title heroines of *Brigitte and Brigitte*, who hail from separate mountain villages, and become Paris roommates. (One of them, who reappears in *The Smugglers*, drops out of a degree in English at the Sorbonne, just as he did.) And mountains are even more important in his movies than country smarts. In

A *Girl Is a Gun*, the English-dubbed version of his crazed, erotic *Une Aventure de Billy le Kid*—which cross-references Sergio Leone, Anthony Mann, *Duel in the Sun*, and Luis Buñuel's *L'Age d'or*—the vistas are so breathtaking and the colors so gorgeous that they make the absence of any "production values" irrelevant.

The most neglected of the *Cahiers du cinéma* critics in the 1950s who became filmmakers in the '60s, and the only one who still writes and publishes criticism today, Moullet was the first to write at length about Samuel Fuller and Edgar G. Ulmer and the first at *Cahiers* to champion Buñuel. Neither a formalist nor an ideologue, he has the sort of attentiveness to film style that once led him to compare William Faulkner's run-on sentences in *Pylon* to the gratuitous camera movements in Douglas Sirk's film adaptation, *The Tarnished Angels*. He also wrote in the same period, anticipating his own virtues as a filmmaker, "The young American filmmakers have nothing to say, Sam Fuller even less than the others. He has something to do, and he does it, naturally, without forcing it. This isn't a small compliment."

The range of his taste is impressive: a recent list of favorites includes two silent films by Cecil B. DeMille, a short by Godard, Rose Troche's *Go Fish*, Raúl Ruiz's *The Blind Owl*, Catherine Breillat's second feature, and King Vidor's *Ruby Gentry*. Brigitte Bardot is seen reading his book on Fritz Lang in Godard's *Contempt* (1963) and his *Politique des Acteurs* came out in 1993, but as with Jacques Rivette, much of his major writing remains uncollected.

Interestingly enough, *Pige Choisies* uses the titles of both *Essai d'Ouverture* and *Le ventre de l'Amérique* in his table of contents. The first of these introduces a fascinating, self-disparaging preface about Moullet's career as a film critic (including his early entry into *Cahiers du cinéma* as a cantankerous groupie of Godard, Rivette, Rohmer, and Truffaut), which is still very much in progress. In the same introduction, Moullet takes up the issue of anti-Semitism that has been debated recently in relation to Godard (by Richard Brody's biography and by Bill Krohn's very critical review of it in *Cinema Scope*), maintaining that, in opposition to his "very antisemitic" father, Moullet specialized in panegyrics to Jewish filmmakers—and he then offers a rather eclectic parenthetical list of examples consisting of Lang, Preminger, Lubitsch, Ulmer, Gance, Truffaut, Fuller, and DeMille. (Personally I hadn't known about Gance or DeMille being Jewish, and Moullet himself couldn't have known about Truffaut before Truffaut himself did. Furthermore, in some of these cases—including Lang and DeMille and possibly others—Moullet is apparently defining half-Jewish as Jewish, much as many people insist on defining Barack Obama as black. But I'm grateful that at least he leaves out Chaplin, who was misidentified as either a Jew or a half-Jew—most often by anti-Semites—for decades.)

The second title in the table of contents packages the fifth section (there are a dozen sections in all), with reviews or articles about W. C. Fields, Richard Brooks' *The Last Hunt*, Anthony Mann's *Men in War*, Chaplin's *A King in New York*, Joseph L. Mankiewicz's *The Quiet American*, Raoul Walsh's *The Naked and the Dead* (a review subtitled, "Better than *The Bridge over the River Kwai*"), Nicholas Ray's *Wind Across the Everglades*, John Ford, and Edgar G. Ulmer. My main disappointments are the absence of Moullet's reviews of *Jet Pilot* and *The Tarnished Angels*. The main pleasant surprise is Moullet's notorious but formerly unavailable polemic at Pesaro that, according to him, scandalized Barthes, Metz, and Pasolini but delighted Godard, during which Moullet memorably declared, "Language is theft." (His celebrated celebration of Samuel Fuller is also included — but missing its last two paragraphs, which attempt to connect Fuller with Christopher Marlowe, and which Moullet confesses he now finds incomprehensible.) There's also an attack on Spanish cinema in general (dubious) and Pedro Almodovar in particular (welcome) that he couldn't publish anywhere else, his wonderful and extravagant 1996 defense of Raúl Ruiz's *The Blind Owl* (available in English at http://www .rouge.com.au/2/blind.html), and much, much more. (By contrast, the interview book, judging from what I've sampled so far, is fun and interesting, but relatively slight compared to the shorter interview included in *Luc Moullet le contrebandier*, a 1993 monograph.)

Regarding Moullet's multifaceted and sometimes ambivalent politics, *Brigitte and Brigitte* features both a right-wing Brigitte and a Communist one. (Meanwhile, the small-scale gags and the episodic narrative easily accommodate guest-star appearances by Chabrol, Michel Delahaye, Fuller, Rohmer, Andre Téchiné, and Moullet himself, as well as his own parents.) *The Comedy of Work* (1987) seems to admire as well as satirize malingering freeloaders in a welfare state, some of whom are also mountain climbers. (As the late Jill Forbes once wrote, Moullet seems characteristically amused that an organization dedicated to keeping people in work should in fact turn out to keep them out of work in order to keep itself in work.) Both of these features are preoccupied with the absurdities of bureaucracy. Most of the squabbles in *Shipwrecked on Route D 17* (2002) — Moullet's slickest effort to date, perhaps because it was produced not by him but by Paulo Branco — are between various city and country folk during the beginning of the first Gulf War, though some oafish French soldiers in search of Saddam Hussein are also in evidence. But the epitome of his deadly irony can be seen in the narration for *The Smugglers*. Over a shot of a rushing stream, we hear, "Look closely: this used to be a totalitarian state." The camera pans over to the embankment on the right. "Now it was to know freedom and democracy. All at once, everything would change." Then it pans back to the stream. "Look at it now!" The narrator is saying something and the camera is doing something. But you might say that the deed speaks louder than the words.

Adapted in 2009 from "The Modest Master," *Chicago Reader*, March 31, 2006, and "Two (Out of Three) Luc Moullet Books and One DVD," www.jonathanrosenbaum .com, posted May 3, 2009

Note

1. See "À la recherche de Luc Moullet," this volume.

The Farber Mystery*

ollowing *James Agee: Film Writing and Selected Journalism* (2005) and *American Movie Critics* (2006), *Farber on Film* is the Library of America's third and so far most ambitious effort to canonize American film criticism — a daunting task that's been lined at every stage with booby traps, at least if one considers the degree to which film criticism might be regarded as one of the most ephemeral of literary genres. And this is certainly the volume that adds the most to what has previously been available; by rough estimate, it easily triples the amount of film criticism by Manny Farber that we previously had between book covers.

As Karl Marx once pointed out, quantity changes quality, but this doesn't entail any lessening of Farber's importance. I would even argue that both the nature and evolution of his taste and writing over thirty-odd years, before he gave up criticism to concentrate on his painting, still make him the most remarkable figure American film criticism has ever had.

Bringing a painter's eye to film criticism and couching even his most serious observations in a snappy, slangy prose, Farber was perhaps the first American in his profession to write perceptively about the personal styles of directors and actors without any consumerist agendas or academic demonstrations. You couldn't quote him in ads because it wasn't always clear or even necessarily relevant whether he liked the movie or not.

Sometimes he showed the discernment of an aficionado: one remembers "a Cagney performance under the hands of a [William] Keighley . . . as a sinewy, life-marred exactness that is as quietly laid down as the smaller jobs played by

Farber on Film: The Complete Film Writings of Manny Farber, edited by Robert Polito. New York: Library of America, 2009. 825 pp.

the Barton MacLanes and Frankie Darros." Other times he went after poetic approximations: "Howard Hawks is a bravado specialist who always makes pictures about a Group. Fast dialogue, quirky costumes, the way a telephone is answered, everything is held together by his weird Mother Hen instinct."

The editorial processes at work in all three Library of America volumes of film criticism have raised as many questions as they've answered. The same applies to *Britton on Film*, published this year and subtitled *The Complete Film Criticism of Andrew Britton*—even though, as Brad Stevens pointed out in *Sight and Sound* last April, it's far from complete. (From this standpoint, the enlarged 2001 edition of Robert Warshow's *The Immediate Experience* looks irreproachable—though Warshow's entire published oeuvre apparently still runs to only 300 pages, making things a lot simpler.) The title of the Agee volume seems to imply that all of his film writing but only a selection of his other journalism is included, which is far from the case. Agee published well over 200 unsigned film-review columns and film-related profiles in *Time* between 1942 and 1948, and editor Michael Sragow added only twenty of these to the thirty-eight included in the previously collected *Agee on Film* (1958). On the other hand, Farber, who died in 2008, requested that all fifteen of his own *Time* movie columns in 1949–50 be excluded from his collected criticism because they were so often rewritten by editors that he didn't want to claim authorship—an exclusion that Agee apparently had neither the opportunity nor the expressed desire to make regarding his own prose in *Time*.

My objection to Sragow's work has less to do with any inclusion than with its omission of Agee's greatest single essay, unrelated to film and unpublished during his lifetime—"America, Look at Your Shame!" (1943), which can be found in the January–February 2003 issue of *The Oxford-American* and the collection *James Agee Rediscovered* (edited by Michael A. Lofaro and Hugh Davis [Knoxville: University of Tennessee Press], 2005). And Philip Lopate's selections and exclusions in *American Film Critics* often regrettably seem to have more to do with social pecking orders than with literary or aesthetic criteria, at least regarding living figures. (When it comes to the pioneers, I may simply have a blind spot about his major discovery, Otis Ferguson, whose collected works have never affected my perceptions of either film or jazz, his two specialties, much less literature.)

The main issues raised by the canonized Farber are exclusions: his art criticism (forty-odd pieces)—which does get discussed, along with Farber's painting, in Robert Polito's introduction—and a major interview conducted with Farber and Patricia Patterson (his partner and writing collaborator since the mid-1960s) by Richard Thompson in 1977. The latter comprises the last forty-three pages of the superb 1998 expanded edition of *Negative Space*, Farber's only previous book. In both cases the losses are conceptual as well as textual, and despite the generosity of what remains, they are huge.

Segregating the art criticism from the film criticism and the TV criticism (all of which apparently *is* included) distorts the meaning of Farber's work in much the same way that isolating Jorge Luis Borges's fiction and nonfiction in separate canonizing volumes has done. You can't and shouldn't distinguish between the separate cultural branches of Farber's criticism because they all have things to say to one another. One can fully understand the niche-market rationale at the same time that one deplores the consequences. Similarly, I both understand and deplore the absence of the 1977 interview—a major and climactic critical statement that Farber and Patterson revised and worried over at length—as well as the inclusion of a Guggenheim grant proposal (clearly not intended for publication, unlike the interview) as the book's final Farber text, implausibly dated the same year. In fact, I moved permanently from London to San Diego in early 1977, to replace Farber as a teacher while he was on leave for his Guggenheim—which is why I can attest to his and Patricia's attitude toward that interview, conducted around the same time. Moreover, Manny had already hired me in 1976, whereas his proposal mentions me as one of the critics he expected to be "working with" in London.

On the other hand, I'll concede that sometimes "precise" memories are mistaken. The first time we met in San Diego, Farber admitted he'd misremembered having met me eight years before, in New York. For that matter, in my 1993 essay about him, I recorded my apparent discovery that when he came to my house in Del Mar to watch Preston Sturges's *Christmas in July*—which I was preparing to show in a class, and which he subsequently screened and lectured on many times himself—he'd never actually seen it before, though having cowritten what clearly remains the definitive Sturges essay, he was too embarrassed to tell me this. Or so a mutual friend informed me. But "Preston Sturges: Satirist" in the December 21, 1942, issue of the *New Republic* makes it clear that Manny had seen *Christmas in July* back then. Ergo, it would probably be more accurate to say that thirty-odd years later, in my living room, he rediscovered it.

In fairness to Polito, he does reprint a four-page fragment from the missing 1977 Farber interview in his notes (which is where the Guggenheim proposal should have gone), and he can't be accused of de-radicalizing Farber's work in his ambitious introduction, thoughtfully titled "Other Roads, Other Tracks." (The only error of his I spotted is misattributing an image described by Farber of boys sniffing a bicycle seat to *Jules and Jim* rather than Truffaut's earlier *Les mistons*.) Indeed, one of the best bits in the interview fragment is Farber's reply to the question, "Are there things in common in painting and criticism as you practice them?": "The brutal fact is that they're exactly the same thing." One could easily argue that the performative side of his film criticism, highlighted in both the interview and in his volatile teaching, is every bit as important as its relation to art criticism. As a contemporary of the action painters, born only five years after Pollock, Farber knew as much about brutal painterly facts as he knew about enactments, onscreen and off, and for anyone who attended his brilliant 1979 lecture at the Museum of Modern Art comparing '30s and '70s iconography (with *Toni* and *The Honeymoon Killers* among the key exhibits), it was difficult even to coherently separate the two. Yet this collection skimps them both, apparently for niche-market reasons.

Nevertheless, the wealth of what's offered is astonishing, both as historical chronicle and as a multilayered clarification. Like many of the clarifications about art/criticism coming from Farber, these gifts are frequently *deepenings* of mysteries — clarifications, in short, about what we don't know (or in some cases didn't know). There are even swamps and detours that one can get lost in, such as two separate pieces entitled "Nearer My Agee to Thee," written seven years apart. (The first, included in *Negative Space*, is a measured assessment of his late friend's film criticism; the second is more a grumble about the rising stock of both Susan Sontag and Andrew Sarris in 1965.) Given Farber's demurrals when I knew him about Chaplin, it's startling to read his raves for the 1942 rerelease of *The Gold Rush* (his third movie column) and for *Limelight* a decade later. He's also more positive about *The Best Years of Our Lives*, Hitchcock, and *Native Land*, and more critical of Renoir, *To Have and Have Not*, and *Sullivan's Travels* than I would have imagined.

Reviewing Brahm's *Hangover Square*, Lang's *Ministry of Fear* and *The Woman in the Window*, and Siodmak's *The Suspect* in one 1945 column, he settles on the last and least known of these today as his favorite. In 1944, he can write that the "two things" Gene Kelly "does least well — singing and dancing — are what he is given most consistently to do," yet reviewing *Anchors Aweigh* the next year, he calls him "the most exciting dancer to appear in Hollywood movies." For a critic who devoted his final piece in 1977 to Chantal Akerman's *Jeanne Dielman*, it's a nonlinear career of nonlinear writing and painting that encompasses a continuously unfolding education, and following its various curves, leaps, and dips is exhilarating.

Most striking of all, as Polito rightly stresses, is how few of Farber's boosts or pans are unmitigated. After paragraphs of relentless abuse meted out to *The Magnificent Ambersons* ("It stutters and stumbles as Welles submerges Tarkington's story in a mess of radio and stage technique") — peppered with the hyperbolic sarcasm that would remain in his prose, making him often sound as up-to-date as a cranky blogger — he adds that Orson Welles "wants realism and there's no one in Hollywood to touch him in its use." Even after dismissively scoffing at *My Darling Clementine*—his misgivings about John Ford appear to have settled in early—he pays sincere respects to five of its cast members.

These mixed or splintered evaluations are congruent with an overall resistance to methodical, empirical argument, so that pathways, as in his paintings, seem to overlap or encircle one another, backtrack or veer off the initial course, rather than pursue any logical succession. (As Polito puts it, "His writing can appear to be composed exclusively of digressions from an absent center.") Sometimes the best way to read Farber is to adopt some of the same contradictory, nonacademic principles—seeing him as both right and wrong (in the same review, paragraph, or even sentence), as pre-auteurist (in his early recognition of the directorial styles of Fuller, Hawks, Karlson, and Mann, well ahead of French critics or Sarris) and non-auteurist (as when he avoids mentioning Nicholas Ray, Jean Renoir, and Otto Preminger while reviewing *On Dangerous Ground*, *This Land Is Mine*, *The Lusty Men*, and *Angel Face*—attributing the first of these to no one, the second to Dudley Nichols, and the latter two to Howard Hughes).

Some of the cultural limitations of Farber's positions might be said to belong to their periods as much as to Farber himself: the machocentric harping on male performers and poses that seems to make him not only blanch at Maya Deren's films in 1946, but also call them "lesbianish" and their compositions and lighting "pansyish"; or, in that Guggenheim proposal about "Munich Films," the innocent confusion of labeling Jean-Marie Straub a "Frenchman" and making no distinction at all between Germans and Austrians (so that Murnau, Sternberg, Wilder, and Lang all get hastily shoveled into the same clause). Yet it's no less striking how his considered and principled invectives against segregated racial stereotypes in *Tales of Manhattan* (1942), *Cabin in the Sky* (1943), *Song of the South* (1946), and even *The Purple Heart* (1944) all seem ahead of their times, at least within the white press. If, compared to Warshow, he seems unperturbed by the political insanity of *My Son John* (1952), he's far more attentive to the brilliance of Robert Walker's acting in it. Similarly, in contradistinction to the jejune swagger of some of his '60s wisecracks (whereby Jean-Pierre Léaud becomes Jean Pee Loud) are the deep appreciations of Akerman, Duras, Godard, Rivette, Snow, and Straub-Huillet when virtually all his colleagues were studiously ignoring them.

We should also remember that Farber wrote mostly during periods when production information of the kind that would inform our later readings of *Ambersons* and *My Son John* was unavailable and beyond the critical radar. And part of the bountiful history lesson afforded by this mammoth collection can be gleaned even from the uncorrected errors—such as Farber alluding to

Fuller's *Fixed Bayonets*, almost a year after he boasted "I wouldn't mind seeing it seven times," as *Broken Bayonets*, at a time when neither his editors nor much of his readership were likely to notice the difference.

Moving Image Source, September 22, 2009; see also "They Drive by Night: The Criticism of Manny Farber," in *Placing Movies: The Practice of Film Criticism* (Berkeley/ Los Angeles: University of California Press, 1995), and at www.jonathanrosenbaum .com/?p=14534; www.rouge.com.au/12/farber_rosenbaum.html; and www.jonathan rosenbaum.com/?p=6399

The American Cinema Revisited*

Ironically, my enemies were the first to alert me to the fact that I had followers.
—Andrew Sarris, *Confessions of a Cultist* (1970)

One of the main emotions aroused in me by the forty or so contributions to the millennial Festschrift *Citizen Sarris* is nostalgia — specifically, a yearning for the era three or four decades ago when something that might be described as a North American film community was slowly emerging and recognizing its own existence.

This was just before academic film studies, radical politics, drugs, and diverse other developments splintered that community into separate and mainly non-communicating cliques and ghettos, accompanied by an intensification of studio promotion that eventually took infotainment beyond its status as a minor industry and into an arena where advertising was coming close to defining as well as monitoring the whole of film culture, thus phasing out individual voices — or at the very least bunching them together in sound bites, pull quotes, bibliographies, and adjectival ad copy.

It's not as though a single film community can't or won't ever exist again. More precisely, it's changed its stripes and certain portions of it have gone back underground — "underground" in the present situation often meaning online. And occasionally representations of that lost community crop up in books such as this one, where academics (ranging from John Belton to James Naremore to Elizabeth Weis), journalists (from Roger Ebert to Leonard Maltin to Gerald Peary), programmers, distributors, and producers (including

Citizen Sarris, American Film Critic: Essays in Honor of Andrew Sarris, edited by Emanuel Levy. Scarecrow Press, 2001.

Geoffrey Gilmore, Daniel Talbot and James Schamus), and filmmakers (including Robert Benton, Budd Boetticher, Peter Bogdanovich, Curtis Hanson, and John Sayles) are once again juxtaposed cheek by jowl, as they used to be in the pages of *Film Culture*—as if they all still listened to one another. (To be fair, sometimes they still do, and this book demonstrates how it can still happen—and how Sarris could and can make it possible.) Through Emanuel Levy hasn't quite succeeded in making this group international—despite a one-page essay by Serge Losique entitled "The International Film Critic" and a Todd McCarthy memoir entitled "Sarris and Paris"—he's at least made it North and South American in orientation rather than simply "American," with Piers Handling contributing a useful piece about "Auteurism in Canada" and Richard Peña doing something similar with Latin America in "Andrew Sarris and the Romantic Rebellion."

My nostalgia for that era and lost community is personal as well as tribal. I'm speaking of the decade during which I left Alabama for Vermont and New York and discovered art cinema as well as film criticism, the French New Wave as well as the auteurist styles of Hollywood—the latter as propounded in a sixty-eight-page essay called "The American Cinema" by Andrew Sarris that lead off the Spring 1963 issue of *Film Culture*, which I still own, minus its lurid cover of chained chorines in a surreal '30s musical. (By contrast, hardly anyone seems to recall Sarris' pantheon of actors' performances, "Acting Aweigh!," which appeared in the Fall 1965 issue and was clearly designed as a companion piece, though it inspired much less comment or controversy.) I was already a buff at the time who ran the Friday night film series at Bard College, but I didn't start getting involved professionally with film criticism until 1968, just as I was quitting grad school in English and American Lit, when a classmate hired me to edit an anthology of film criticism (never published) structured around directors—which lead me to meet, among others, Andrew Sarris.

I moved to Paris the following year, and on trips back wrote a few movie pieces for the *Village Voice* that Andy either assigned or approved: first a pedestrian account of a thrilling experience—being an extra on Bresson's *Four Nights of a Dreamer*; then reviews of such independent fare as Jim McBride's *Glen and Randa*, a documentary about the first moon landing called *Moonwalk One*, and Jonas Mekas' *Reminiscences of a Journey to Lithuania*; and my first two years of Cannes festival coverage—thereby paving the way for book reviews of everything from *Gravity's Rainbow* and *Myron* to *Theory of Film Practice*; Martin Gardner's *Science: Good, Bad and Bogus*; *Jerry Lewis: In Person*; and Dwight Macdonald's *Discriminations*. I also contributed ten best lists to Sarris' year-end wrap-ups, along with a slew of others—not really the same thing as the *Voice*'s recent annual polls, because it was still a genuine community newspaper in the early '70s, closer to a bulletin board than anything else, with a letters column that was typically more fun to read than anything else in the paper.

How did Sarris figure in all this? As one of the main connecting threads and references for me and my friends, and in many ways as a passionate rallying point. Also as a facilitator and friend in his own right. During the same period, I can recall Andy once gleefully referring to Vidor's *Street Scene* as "pre-Bazinian" after a Paris Cinémathèque screening, and offering a wonderful rap to me about what was so special about Eustache's *The Mother and the Whore* as a kind of "first-person" testament, and as an uncommon stretching of a filmmaker's limits, after its first Cannes screening.

The names I miss most in this volume of tributes are those of various Sarris disciples and comrades-in-arms with whom I feel or once felt a particular kinship, such as Stuart Byron, David Ehrenstein, Tag Gallagher, Stephen Gottlieb, Roger Greenspun, Joseph McBride, Richard McGuinness, Michael McKegney, Roger McNiven, George Morris, William Paul, and James Stoller. The reasons for these absences are quite diverse (some of these people are no longer alive, and others no longer write) and I'm not bringing them up as reproaches to Levy's ample list of contributors — simply as indicators of the sort of history that sometimes escapes textbooks and Festschrifts alike. Along with many of the writers who *are* included, they and I qualified in some ways as Sarrisites — a motlier crew than the Paulettes (also known as the Kaelites) by and large, though surely no less passionate, and surely different in vocation insofar as we were all entirely and exclusively self-appointed. (I can still recall Todd McCarthy's voluminous, single-spaced letters to me in the mid-seventies, running through weeks and months of auteur-oriented filmgoing with heartfelt thumbnail evaluations attached to every feature, often complete with Sarris-like alliteration). Only later would come the revisions, retractions, and even defections. It was a shock, for instance, once I came to know Samuel Fuller, that, contrary to what Andy wrote, he wasn't either a primitive or a right-winger — not the man who organized a fund-raising party for Adlai Stevenson in the '50s. But Manny Farber wasn't entirely accurate about those aspects of Sam either. Yet if it weren't for both of these pioneering critics, I might never have discovered Fuller's movies in the first place.

Furthermore, as Molly Haskell puts it in one of *Citizen Sarris'* best pieces, "Life with Andrew . . . and Film" — even more valuable for its many corrective insights than for its biographical information — "Although he attracted a great many followers (and detractors: he received more mail, hate and otherwise, than anyone at the *Voice*), Andrew never set out to acquire acolytes, or form a flock of disciples to whom he would issue the party line on every film, or whose straying members he would whip back into the fold . . . or excommunicate!" It doesn't take too much imagination to figure out who Haskell is distinguishing her husband from, and it's important to stress that her point isn't a wife's wishful thinking or idealistic gloss but the gospel truth: not only did Sarris fail to encourage disciples, unlike his most visible opponent; one way or another, he — unlike the enduring example of his work — wound up doing his best to discourage them, Another of Haskell's corrective insights distinguishes him from practically everyone else in his critical generation: a refusal to use such Frankfurt-school epithets as "trash" or "kitsch," perhaps underlining the degree to which he developed in reaction to analysts such as Siegfried Kracauer, and in concert with what he once called "the Parisian heresy (in New York eyes) concerning the sacred importance of the cinema."

■ ■ ■ ■ ■ ■ ■ ■ ■

The interesting thing about Andy in the '60s was that he became polemical almost in spite of his normal and mainly gentle inclinations — a taker of hard and fast positions that disconcertingly created dissension wherever he went, when it wasn't really his nature to sustain such battles for long. In the back pages of the Spring 1963 *Film Culture*, he assigned five stars to Renoir's *The Elusive Corporal* and Hitchcock's *The Birds*, no stars to *Lawrence of Arabia* and *To Kill a Mockingbird*, and only one star to Antonioni's *Eclipse* — judgments bound to give offense to all sorts of people as well as a certain kind of passionate sustenance to a hardcore group of followers, myself included (even though I preferred *Eclipse* to *The Birds*, and still do today, and despite the fact that Andy later offered a thoughtful semi-defense of *Zabriskie Point* in contrast to practically everyone else in New York at the time, reprinted in *The Primal Screen*.) Because what Andy stood for was a revolution in taste — a new kind of syllabus founded on the excitements stirred up by the personal styles of directors. It led to a lot more than his defense of certain American directors; he was also one of the few American critics at the time to defend both *Muriel* and *Gertrud*.

Above all, it was a declaration that movies were important — a position that still gave one a lot of leeway for change and development. Here are two key sentences by Sarris drafted four years apart for *Film Culture*, each one retaining its own kind of legitimacy. 1962: "After years of tortured revaluation, I am now prepared to stake my critical reputation, such as it is, on the proposition that Alfred Hitchcock is artistically superior to Robert Bresson by every criterion of excellence and further that, film for film, director for director, the American cinema has been consistently superior to that of the rest of the world from 1915 to 1962." 1966: "All in all, no film I have ever seen has come so close to convulsing my entire being as has *Au hasard Balthazar.*"

It was the passion that finally counted the most, and one might add that similarly, the best pieces in this collection aren't always or necessarily the ones that have the most to say about Sarris. In contrast to the more gingerly or dutiful tributes that seem to be walking on eggshells — no need to name names here, because most of them can be spotted at once — is a lengthy and deeply felt piece of invective by Ed Sikov, an avowed ex-Kaelian, about the homophobia he finds in Pauline Kael's review of George Cukor's last feature, *Rich and Famous*, which he briefly juxtaposes with Sarris' review of a Cukor biography, as well as Sarris' public apology for gay-baiting when he wrote about Parker Tyler. In his preface, Levy records his regrets that neither Kael nor any of the "Paulettes" he approached agreed to contribute anything to this volume, though he neglects to add that the fury of this former Paulette — almost recalling in certain respects one of the essays in *The God That Failed* about defection from the Communist party — is in some ways as revealing as the silence of the others. The degree to which some auteurists and anti-auteurists split over issues of politics, religion, and even sexual orientation testifies to the urgency these kinds of debates had when certain basics of critical programs were still being established and defended. Which is another way of saying that these people weren't just fighting about movies; they were fighting about world views, lifestyles, and personal philosophies — a far cry from the thumbs up and thumbs down of simple consumerism. (If you want to get a sense of the decanted essence of this position, see if you can hunt down *The Films of Josef von Sternberg*, a Museum of Modern Art monograph of 1966 that qualifies as Sarris's first book — and for me as well as a certain number of contributors to *Citizen Sarris* remains his best.) In the same period that I became a Sarrisite and some others became Paulettes, I also became, after I moved to Paris, a Burchite — hunting down the unseen films mentioned in Noël Burch's *Praxis du cinéma* (the original French edition of *Theory of Film Practice*) with some of the same fanaticism that led me to stay up all night in Manhattan (before the era of VCRs) to catch unseen features by Nicholas Ray or Samuel Fuller. Maybe the agendas of *The American Cinema* and *Praxis du cinéma* were too incompatible to make much sense together, but not for a crazed cinephile in Paris with time on his hands. Things were still growing then, which meant that everything was still possible.

I don't doubt that things are still growing and still possible for various crazed cinephiles today, so I'm not trying to pull any rank here. The point is that, cinema-is-dead theorists to the contrary, film history never even comes close to repeating itself, for better and for worse. And the prime lesson to be learned from *Citizen Sarris, American Film Critic* isn't how much things were changed forever by one book called *The American Cinema*, because ultimately there is no forever in film criticism. The point is how much they're still changing because of it, because with or without forever, ripples can last for centuries.

Cinema Scope, no. 6 (Winter 2001)

Raymond Durgnat

Note: In their original publication, Durgnat's "interpolations" were run as a separate article; here they are laid out all through my text, as Ray once told me he would have preferred it. Most of the notes have been added to the original by Adrian Martin—who has also made a few slight and judicious editorial changes, such as correcting Ray's Latin.

1

Raymond Durgnat was born in London of Swiss parents in 1932. He studied English literature at Cambridge, was a staff writer for the British Elstree Studios, and did research in film at the Slade School of Fine Art. He is currently head of General Studies at St. Martin's School of Art. In 1963, he cited Jerry Lewis and Clara Bow as his favorite movie stars and published *Nouvelle Vague: The First Decade*, an analysis of the films of thirty-four French directors that has long been out of print and remains the most thorough single work ever done on the subject, in English or French.

Seven more books on film by Durgnat have been published over the last decade. He has also written an uncountable number of uncollected articles and reviews, including a first-rate appraisal of six Josef von Sternberg films for *Movie* (under the name of O. O. Green, which permits Durgnat to quote appreciatively from his own work twice), an indispensable genre survey ("Paint It Black: The Family Tree of Film Noir"), and a book-length study of Alfred Hitchcock that appeared serially in *Films and Filming* (February–November 1970).[1] In 1969, he listed as his ten favorite films *Quai des brumes* (Marcel Carné, 1938), *La Ronde* (Max Ophüls, 1950), *Vampyr* (Carl Dreyer, 1932), *Miracle in Milan* (Vittorio De Sica, 1951), *Duel in the Sun* (King Vidor, 1946), *The*

Saga of Anatahan (Sternberg, 1953), *Allegretto* (Oskar Fischinger, 1936/43), *Duck Soup* (Leo McCarey, 1933), *The Thief of Bagdad* (Ludwig Berger, Tim Whelan, and Michael Powell, 1940), and *French Cancan* (Jean Renoir, 1955); and as his ten favorite directors Len Lye, Norman McLaren, Tex Avery, F. W. Murnau, G. W. Pabst, Dreyer, Sternberg, Renoir, Vidor, and Tony Conrad.

> *Raymond Durgnat*: I was a staff writer for Associate British Pictures at Elstree Studios, did postgraduate research in film at the Slade School of Fine Art, and lectured in film at the Royal College of Art. Faber and Faber is publishing a thorough revision of the *Films and Filming* Hitchcock series as *The Strange Case of Alfred Hitchcock*. As for the *Movie* Sternberg piece, I'd been asked by another interested party to write for *Movie* anonymously, so what looks like nutty self-indulgence was my only way of getting a credit out of it.

2

Many (if not all) critics tend to fall into two categories, which might be called the Big Game Hunters and the Explorers. The Big Game (read: masterpiece) Hunters are basically out for trophies to possess, stuff, and hang on their walls; the Explorers usually poke around simply to see what they find. The Hunters are a relatively Apollonian group — disciplined, academic, and generally traditional in their aesthetic values: immediate examples that come to mind are Robin Wood,[2] James Agee, William Pechter, Stanley Kauffmann, Dwight Macdonald, John Simon, and historians like Georges Sadoul, Jean Mitry, and Lewis Jacobs. The Explorers, a more Dionysian group, are relatively cranky, kinky, and eclectic: Jean-Luc Godard, Manny Farber, Robert Warshow, and Raymond Durgnat are four eminent examples.

If the Hunters are mainly concerned with what Farber has called White Elephant Art — monoliths, like Kubrick's in 2001: *A Space Odyssey*, that leave lasting traces — the Explorers are more drawn to Farber's contrasting category of Termite Art, which "goes always forward eating its own boundaries, and, likely as not, leaves nothing in its path other than the signs of eager, industrious, unkempt activity."[3]

For the last ten years or so, Durgnat has remained the most active and far-reaching Explorer in British criticism. He is something of a wandering troubadour in his profession — in the variety of publications that he writes for, the range of subjects that he takes on, and even in the wayward drifts and occasionally strangled clauses of his prose style, a dense thicket of uncertainly placed commas and quotation marks that only rarely seems to do justice to the speed and rhythm of his thought.

RD: "Uncertainly placed commas"—I can't proofread—"and quotation marks"—this was the result of an unhappy, early compromise between my academic bent and journalistic constraints. Quotation marks were meant to imply "I know this is a loose use of the word, but it has sense." Now I either define it or don't, and trust the reader to get the idea.

His penchant for surrealism and sociology has made his critical approach closer to that of the French magazine *Positif* than to the general orientation of *Films and Filming*, a slick English fan magazine where he has presided as house intellectual for over a decade. But in fact, his idiosyncratic methods and manners place him well beyond the pale of *any* established school of critical thought. In a letter replying to an unfairly abusive review of his book *Films and Feelings* in *Sight and Sound*, Durgnat asserted at one point, "I'm out to follow an argument, not seduce people."[4] Walking alone, he tends to cast a long shadow.

RD: I was close to *Positif*, especially in its 1960–7 period. Surely *Positif* is an established school, and surely I'm within their pale, albeit writing from an Anglo-Saxon tradition (nearer I. A. Richards than F. R. Leavis).

An essential aspect of his wanderlust is that he rarely stays with any one subject for long, at least not in the rigorous, methodical way that characterizes André Bazin, Warshow, or Wood. Even when he devotes a book to a single figure, like Luis Buñuel or Georges Franju, his characteristic approach is multilayered and varied, a continual shift of strategies, rather than the systematic pursuit of any single argument.

The business of criticism seems to me "matters arising," and naturally varies from film to film. I'd rather be wrong but open up a perspective than be prematurely right, i.e., dismiss opportunities for the full intellectual, sensual, emotional experience of reflective hesitation—which seems to me to be of the essence of art, as opposed to brusquer communication (e.g., moral saws, the human sciences).

On the few occasions when he *does* stick to one procedure—as in his study of character traits in *Johnny Guitar* in *Films and Feelings* and his sociological commentary on Panama and Frank's *Li'l Abner* in *The Crazy Mirror*—the results are usually somewhat flat and academic. (A more successful example, also in *Films and Feelings*, is his extended psychological-political analysis of

This Island Earth, which anticipates Susan Sontag's essay on science fiction films, "The Imagination of Disaster," in many important respects.)[5]

As Robert Mundy points out, Durgnat "is often at his best writing about *moments*, rather than about films or directors."[6] He can also be quite strong on individual aspects of films, as the following sampling of quotes demonstrates.

> One craves, perhaps, a venture into those dark interiors where the fantasies of *The Thief of Bagdad* interpenetrate with those of *Peeping Tom*. Whence their centrifugality? The comparison with the director of *The Citadel* is pertinent. Vidor, intellectually, perhaps, less cagey and sophisticated than Powell, has retained an authenticity of emotional excess which endows his films with their genuine mysticism, founded on human energy. But Powell lived in a class, and a country, and a generation which suspects, fears and undermines emotion. Thus his diversity of qualities rarely finds their holding center.[7]

> [Emil] Jannings allowed himself to stray as far from "realism" as comedians do — one can speak of "slow" expressionism, like Jannings', and "fast" expressionism, like Chaplin's (or Jerry Lewis'). The middle term between them is exemplified by Catherine Hessling in Jean Renoir's *Nana* (1926), where she gives what is both the best and worst performance in the history of the French cinema. With her petal-light limbs flung out into Napoleonic postures, her bee-sting mouth pouting in her heart-shaped face, her eyes narrowed till the pupils disappear under a palisade of lashes, her fluttering precocity and jagged stances, this awkward blend of Chaplinesque, quicksilver and marionette fixity comes, if only the spectator will adapt his response, to make at least as much sense as modern "Method"-ism.[8]

> Hell [in *Hellzapoppin'*], by an atmospheric pun, is a combination of the traditional Hell (devils with horns roast blonde angels trussed to spits), and of a modern factory, where devils pedal away at grindstones and produce "Canned Guy" and "Canned Gal" (just at this time, of course, America was arming for war, and soon to draft people into munitions factories).[9]

Of course, not all of Durgnat's strengths can be observed in short quotations. It is his special knowledge of and sensitivity to the surrealist tradition in France, for instance, that makes his study of Franju particularly valuable, and richly evocative in a way that most Anglo-American criticism of Franju is not. And on a few occasions, when Durgnat grasps a film as the meeting ground of several interconnecting influences, traditions and social forces, he is able to treat it as a complex but homogenous unity: his essays on *Kiss Me Deadly*,[10] and *Judex* (1963) in the Franju book, are probably the best things that have been written on either film.

Finally, one can value Durgnat for the wealth of movies that he's seen, and the unknown delights that he often brings to our attention. While I find it difficult to share his enthusiasm for *Li'l Abner*—particularly since nothing he says about it even remotely convinces me to go back to it—I can only applaud his frequent allusions to such unjustly neglected works as *Her Man* (Tay Garnett, 1930), *The 5,000 Fingers of Dr. T.* (Roy V. Rowland, 1953), *It's In the Bag!* (Richard Wallace, 1945), and the cartoons of Tex Avery, even if none of these has received the extended treatment from Durgnat that one would hope for.

> *RD*: Is "going back to it" the only response a critic can hope for? I had a different end in view: to spell out some of the ways in which comedy calls on reality. Lawrence Alloway, of all people, couldn't understand what I was trying to do in the not dissimilar piece on *This Island Earth*, a film which I've no particular enthusiasm for, either. I was out to show that there are more meanings in ordinary meanings—of the shallow type required for entertainment—than usually spotted by critics, who imagine that only important art can involve people and make poetic and ideological points. I'm looking at movies which are run-of-the-mill yet saturated with something too shallow really to be myth (in the full sense), but too ambivalent to be merely cliché. I'm trying a kind of micro-criticism, more concerned with the molecules of a film's meaning than the implications of its meaning.

3

When Durgnat attacks Pauline Kael's "Fantasies of the Art-House Audience"[11] at some length in *Films and Feelings* for its puritan assumptions, one feels the confrontation of two critics on a common turf. Quite simply, Kael and Durgnat are two of the most accomplished sociological film critics since the death of Robert Warshow, and the differences between their approaches are instructive. It is frequently said of Kael that she reviews audiences as much as films; one might add to this that her moral evaluations of each tend to precede her analyses. In Durgnat's case, analysis of what theoretically takes place *between* the film and the audience comes first, and any moral evaluation of this occurrence is usually either postponed or suspended. Within the terms of Durgnat's sociology, concepts of good and bad, right and wrong are relatively nonexistent—or at least nonessential.

> *RD*: No, they're essential, but . . . no more so than some other non-moral spiritual axes. Does my work really give an impression of amorality? Surely I often talk morally, even in the case of *This Island Earth*.

This is not to suggest, of course, that Durgnat doesn't evaluate films, or that he avoids moral judgments: he periodically makes his tastes and preferences known, and some of his judgments — like his notorious dismissal of Godard — are couched almost exclusively in moral terms:

> Godard wears dark glasses to hide from the world the fact that he's in a constant state of ocular masturbation, rubbing himself off against anything and everything on which his eye alights. The flickering glance of his camera is the constant dribble of premature ejaculation. It is an unseeing stare. Godard keeps babbling on about the world being absurd because he can't keep an intellectual hard-on long enough to probe for any responsive warmth.[12]

RD: This passage of mine was rude so that the reader *wouldn't* take it too solemnly as a moral point. At that time, the consensus was taking Godard as a sort of sage of solipsism. I wanted to say that his films weren't just about triumphs over the medium, but about a predicament too absurdist to be tragic in the traditionally dignified way. And, after all, he did a right-, or rather left-about turn intellectually soon afterwards. This sort of Portnoy's Complaint of the bourgeois intelligentsia is the shadow side of the "reflective hesitation" I was advocating earlier — hence the suddenly violent metaphor! Besides, those same "Asides" do describe Godard's first two features as "masterpieces," which is high praise, surely.

But while Kael discusses contemporary films as interactions and encounters between screen and audience, Durgnat isolates mythic and archetypal structures that bind the two into an indissoluble whole.

RD: The danger is of binding them into an over-schematized, stylized whole — merely a set of conventions. But the alternative sense, of "baseline possibilities" within which each audience reacts differently, is neatly suggested by your "court" metaphor.

If film watching suggests the back and forth movement of a tennis game, Kael's eye is on the players, while Durgnat's is on the court.

RD: I wonder if three subjects for moral judgment are being telescoped here: (1) The moral impact on an audience of a film (what real spectators, in groups, make of it, in fact); (2) The moral assumptions and conclusions of a film when fully and correctly apprehended by a kind of ideal spectator, an *ami inconnu*; and (3) Durgnat's own moral attitudes. Obviously, they interconnect in his writing. But so far as (1) is concerned, Durgnat's moral polarity revolves around the question of honesty and insight (good) as against mystification and easy cliché (bad). Thus, Billy Wilder's *Stalag 17* is a better description of capitalist processes than George Stevens' *Giant*. But nihilist or Fascist films may be good insofar as they undermine everyone else's complacencies, and state uncomfortable truths.

4

Durgnat's unwavering hatred for the elitist and middlebrow stances of *Sight and Sound*, which crops up periodically in his work, has probably provided his career with as much sustained focus as Robin Wood's admiration for F. R. Leavis has unified the thrust of Wood's work.

> *RD*: I'd say "consistent disagreement"; I hope I don't read as if I'm negative or rooted in hatred. It's true that *Sight and Sound* has often given me a useful chopping block, and that it did deserve attack, if only because it was both so generally accepted, and itself so extremely destructive and dismissive, during its very bad period (1956–68, roughly). Probably there isn't any sustained focus for my work, in the sense of an overriding preoccupation, because, like your traditional liberal humanist, I'm interested in everything to do with art — and with art because it has to do with human experience. *Homo sum, humani nihil a me alienum puto* ["I am a man, and consider nothing human to be foreign to me"], as Terence said circa 150 BC.

The striking contrast between Durgnat and Wood, who are quite likely the two most ambitious English film critics in their generation, is a remarkably complementary one in many respects. The somewhat explicit relationship of Wood to Freud is balanced by the more implicit (but equally crucial) link of Durgnat to Jung. In a certain sense, Freud/Wood seek to civilize the unconscious by exposing its mysteries and terrors to the light of day, while Jung/Durgnat are more bent on achieving a truce and partnership between night and day, mystery and logic.

> *RD*: I know the contrast is only an analogy, but I'm nearer Freud than Wood in my pessimism about moralistic rationalization, and about any hope of civilizing the unconscious. Wood, like F. R. Leavis, is puritanical, and I'm not; but it's worth remembering that puritanism is only one moral position, and a minority one. I suspect that Buñuel's mixture of Jesuitical casuistry, inverted Marxist "pessimism of the intelligence," and the surrealist inversion of Freud is beyond the capabilities of the puritan position, however evolved. To understand Buñuel, you have either to be innocent of puritanism, or to have taken it beyond the point where its internal incoherencies appear. Otherwise, you either dismiss it or just goggle at the shock and riddle of it all.

This sharp division was particularly evident when conflicting reviews of Buñuel's *Belle de jour* (1967) by Durgnat and Wood were printed side by side in *Movie*.[13] Durgnat's response is characteristically sympathetic:

By liberal standards, the film *is* a fairy tale, its psychology is strange indeed. But its serene indifference to liberal notions is the condition of its insidious freshness. It can treat a psychopathic case in the Lubitsch style because bourgeois manners are psychopathic anyway.

Wood concludes, on the contrary, that:

For an adherent of an "ism" explicitly dedicated to revolution, Buñuel, on the evidence of his films, seems remarkably defeatist, steering his characters towards their preordained hopelessness by eliminating any possibilities of health.

Earlier in the review, he states:

I don't think that Buñuel feels anything much for Séverine as a human being; if the film evokes no disgust for her, it evokes no compassion or affection either. What one does take away is an impression of a pervasive nastiness.

Wood's rejection of *Belle de jour* seems partially a function of the callousness with which he feels other people, including Durgnat, respond to it; George Kaplan attacks the potato-sack sequence in *Frenzy* (1972) with a similar attitude.[14] Speaking for myself, I was revolted by the audience's reactions to the murders in *The Godfather* when I saw it, and disliked the film at the time for its capacity to elicit these responses. But are such judgments really legitimate to the films themselves, as opposed to how the audience chooses to take them? Wood asserts that in *Belle de jour*, "there is no attempt . . . to explore the potentialities of life; there is no sense of what normality is or more important, could be." But surely the film *does* attempt to explore at least some of life's possibilities; and a sense of what normality both is and could be is precisely what Buñuel conveys, in his treatment of Séverine's acceptance of her masochism. It is hardly necessary to *agree* with Buñuel's definitions of normality in order to accept the film.

RD: I agree with you, but your tone implies that normal people can hardly be expected to agree with Buñuel's definitions of normality. I think many normal people would. We know that his "normality" involves a fullness of passion, an *amour fou*, a "real"ization of the essence of dream-life, as against hypochondriacal notions of emotional decorum. If you can accept Marlene Dietrich's saloon girl in *Destry Rides Again* (1939), or Norman Mailer on the wisdom of prostitutes, you can accept Buñuel's Séverine. Buñuel's film is full of saddening ironies, and I'm sure he knows it. It's sad and intricate because we can sense that Séverine and her husband should accept her re-pressed life and they don't, forcing her to live it out in that imperfect, indeed tragic, way. Buñuel is asking us to consider the myopia, errors and cowardice which everyone in the film shows, at one time or another — just like us — all tangled up with misdirected hopes and acts of courage — just like us — and ending in frustration — which is common enough.

Real people are not the size they assume on large movie screens, and music doesn't accompany our lives in quite the same way as soundtrack scores; birds are not intent on destroying mankind, and many of the temporal and spatial conditions of life in *Only Angels Have Wings* are patently unreal; if Wood can accept these and countless other conventions — including, say, the brutal sex-ist assumptions of *Klute* — why can't he accept the compassion that Buñuel so visibly displays towards his heroine, by having her deepest desires gratified?[15]

RD: I don't quite see her afternoons as quite so fine as "deepest" might suggest, although I agree with your general drift. A major reason for art is to enable us to share — and sensitize ourselves to both the surfaces and the structures of experiences existing on temperamental and moral coordinates different from our own. It's what you're slowest to approve of that teaches you the most. (I don't say that whatever you disapprove of is therefore good.)

For Wood, the discovery of what he considers to be positive moral values in a film is a prerequisite to his appreciation of it — a requirement that Durgnat seems in no way bound to. When Wood finds what he's looking for, he can take hold of a film with a precision that few other critics can master, convey-ing its total impact with a passionate clarity that seems well beyond Durgnat's range. But when he confronts those films whose "positive values" are problem-atical, at least from a traditional standpoint, it often appears that he either dis-misses these films unjustly — as he does with *Belle de jour* — or supplies them with moral resonances that they don't have; which I think he does, even more damagingly, with Nicholas Ray's *Bigger Than Life* (1956).[16]

RD: Do you really think that there is just one tradition of positive values in our culture? Then how do you square, say, George Eliot, Nietzsche, Kafka, Bessie Smith? I'd have thought that one of our problems was precisely the cynicism induced by our multitude of conflicting moral and spiritual cul-tures, and the very great difficulty of creating a synthesis which is neither weak nor narrow.

Bigger Than Life is a profoundly upsetting exposure of middle-class aspirations because it defines madness — the drug-induced psychosis of Avery (James Mason) — as taking these values seriously. Each emblem of the American dream implicitly honored and worshipped by Avery in the opening reel is systematically turned on its head, converted from dream to nightmare, by becoming only more explicit in his behavior. The dramatic function of his incurable disease and his taking of cortisone, carrying the respective promises of death and superlife, is to act on the slick magazine ads that Avery and his wife try to inhabit in much the same way that expressionist lighting works on actors' faces (or, to cite an analogy from the film, the X-ray of Avery's torso); it highlights details that are already actively present.

Wood seems somewhat aware of this aspect of the film, and shows much sensitivity towards certain manifestations of it; but his Leavis-inspired concern for moral centers ultimately leads to a taming of the film's subversive implications. After noting persuasively that the basic creative tension in Ray's work is between "conscious, rational control" and "the promptings of spontaneous, anarchic impulse," he minimizes this tension by avoiding the film's anarchic thrust, virtually turning Ray into a safe social democrat. "It would be quite wrong to see *Bigger Than Life* as a simple endorsement of the American bourgeois family," he soberly states, in a tragicomic understatement that brutalizes the film's meanings (does he consider it a complex endorsement?). To say *this* about one of the most scathing portrayals of the American bourgeois family that the cinema has given us! Turning away from the film's powerful negativity and despair in his search for "an impulse towards the formation of human norms," he reaches for the unconvincing closing scene of family reconciliation — an ending that, as we learn from an interview with Ray, was composed hastily just before it was shot, and is completely unsatisfactory to the director himself.[17] Wood then concludes that the film's "message (in so far as a complex work of art can be said to have one) is not 'Be satisfied with what you've got' but 'Work with what you've got, empirically and realistically. And know yourself.'"

RD: Oh, I obviously must see *Bigger Than Life*!

But does *Bigger Than Life* really offer us the luxury of such Sunday school lessons? One could probably summarize two of Mr. Wood's other favorite films with equal justice by saying that *Marnie* teaches us that "Honesty is the best policy," while the message of *Rio Bravo* is "A friend in need is a friend indeed."

RD: Perhaps Wood does take some moral as a precondition of a film's being artistically satisfying, but he does distinguish the full experience from the moral summary thereof.

The weaknesses and strengths of any critic are likely to be bound up with one another: without Wood's moral piousness and liberal squeamishness, or Durgnat's occasional solipsisms and unwieldy structures, one suspects that the talents of each would be less than they are. Yet the feeling persists that these two gentlemen could learn a lot from each other.

> RD: I've disagreed with Robin Wood throughout my Hitchcock book. I hope I've done so in a way that shows how much I respect him, and how much I've learned from him — which is a lot. Critics hope to be learned from (or else why write?) and to learn (or else why read?). It would be interesting to know whether Robin Wood has ever learned anything from Raymond Durgnat, or whether he thinks Durgnat is as morally sick as Rosenbaum's account implies he ought. Certainly, another neo-Leavisite, David Holbrook, thinks Durgnat is revolting ("d for dirt, or Durgnat, section"). I wrote about *Belle de jour* without knowing Robin Wood was writing about it too, and remain unconvinced, along Rosenbaum's lines.
>
> Yet the feeling persists that Rosenbaum's real interest is his "friendly enemy" relationship with Wood, and that the Durgnat bit is a framework around it! Perhaps Durgnat disappears behind his own eclecticism, and even the critical persona can't be seen — or seems relatively sloppy or boring. I'd hate to think it really was!

Afterword (2002)

Having written this almost thirty years ago, when I was living in Paris, I'm surprised to discover that I still agree with a lot of it, even though it seems to be written by someone else. It led, quite unexpectedly, to the first exchange I ever had in print with another film critic — an event masterminded by Richard Corliss, the editor of *Film Comment* at the time, who sent Ray the galleys of my article, and then kindly sent me the galleys of his responses. Under the circumstances, I'm still grateful to Ray for letting me off so easily. In fairness to him, I should stress that his comments were intended by him to be run as footnotes to some of my points, so he wasn't prepared for the prominence they were given in the magazine as a separate article titled "Apologia and Auto-Critique." As he put it to me when we met for the first time, in London, a few months later, he felt more comfortable "sniping" at me from the sidelines — a preference that points to what I regard as his dependable underground instincts, which I suspect have accompanied him throughout his career.

Ray has argued that the dated aspects of films directed by William Wellman are more valuable than the relative "timelessness" of those directed by Howard

Hawks because they have more to tell us about the worlds they came from—which is another way of saying that film criticism can and should be a way of writing about the world.[18] By the same token, I'd like to think that this ancient essay of mine about Durgnat might be worth reading today precisely for its outdatedness—not only in relation to Ray and myself, but in relation to the world we were both inhabiting in the early '70s. When I wrote it, "Durgnat" was simply a prominent name in my well-thumbed library of film books and magazines, shipped from New York to Paris—a library that hadn't yet included his hefty books on Renoir, Hitchcock, and King Vidor, *Sexual Alienation in the Cinema* and *WR—Mysteries of the Organism* (the latter my second favorite Durgnat book to date, after *Films and Feelings*), not to mention an uncountable number of articles in English and American magazines, including many that I still haven't managed to track down.

In other words, Ray wasn't yet a friend or one-time housemate (as he became in a San Diego suburb in 1977, when both of us were teaching in the same department nearby), but he was already a major reference point.[19] Consequently, it was easy to misread him as a person even more than as a critic. Knowing that he had Swiss parents, I regarded him in part as a conduit into French culture—the New Wave and surrealism, Franju and Renoir—and therefore as a guide of sorts into the international underground, without imagining that he was also capable of wearing Union Jack socks, as I would discover a few years later, and English to the core. Similarly, viewing Durgnat as a refreshing opponent of the puritanical streak in '60s Anglo-American film criticism, as represented by Penelope Houston (in his memorable polemic "Standing Up for Jesus"—a critical touchstone for, among many others at the time, the late Jill Forbes, whom I knew in Paris)[20] as well as Pauline Kael (in his extended response to her "Fantasies of the Art-House Audience" in *Films and Feelings*), I misread his opposition as "unwavering hatred" rather than good-natured snipe-shooting—and was pleased to discover later that his critique of Kael actually led to a friendly correspondence with her.

By the same token, I was much too eager to square Ray off against Robin Wood—an indication of my temperament rather than his, which understandably led him to the incorrect suspicion that Robin was the real focus of my piece. In fact, this was merely an effort to shoehorn an argument about *Bigger Than Life* that was preoccupying me at the time into an article where it didn't belong—justified (or, at least, rationalized) in my mind by Ray's own almost Sterne-like digressions. But I should have realized that no two writers ever digress in the same way or for the same reasons, and three decades later, I hope Ray will accept my apology for confusing my bugaboos with his own. Such are the perils of mimetic criticism, to which fledgling critics are especially susceptible.

Note: Ray Durgnat died on May 19, 2002, around the same time that this article and afterword, as part of an online tribute to him, were being posted.

Film Comment, May–June 1973; notes and afterword originally published in (but subsequently removed from) the online *Senses of Cinema*, no. 20 (May–June 2002); see also www.jonathanrosenbaum.com/?p=15842

Notes (mostly by Adrian Martin)

1. O. O. Green, "Six Films of Josef von Sternberg," *Movie*, no. 13 (Summer 1965): 26–31, reprinted under Durgnat's name in Ian Cameron, ed., *Movie Reader* (New York: Praeger, 1972), 94–99; Durgnat, "Paint It Black: The Family Tree of the Film Noir," *Cinema* (UK), no. 6/7 (August 1970): 48–56, reprinted in Alain Silver and James Ursini, eds., *Film Noir Reader* (New York: Limelight Editions, 1996), 37–51, and also condensed into a chart (under the title "The Family Tree of Film Noir") in *Film Comment* (November–December 1974): 6–7; the Hitchcock essay series appeared in *Films and Filming* (February–November 1970).

2. For Robin Wood's response to this characterization see the chapter "Big Game" in his *Personal Views*, revised ed. (Detroit: Wayne State University Press, 2006), 17–42.

3. Manny Farber, *Negative Space* (New York: Da Capo, 1998), 135.

4. Philip French, "*A World on Film* and *Films and Feelings*," *Sight and Sound* (Autumn 1967): 210–11; Raymond Durgnat, "Correspondence," *Sight and Sound* (Winter 1967/68): 52.

5. Susan Sontag, *Against Interpretation and Other Essays* (New York: Dell, 1969), 212–28.

6. Robert Mundy, "Raymond Durgnat," *Cinema* 7 (U.S.), no. 2 (Spring 1972): 59.

7. Durgnat, *A Mirror for England: British Movies from Austerity to Affluence* (London: Faber and Faber, 1970), 215.

8. Durgnat, *Films and Feelings* (London: Faber and Faber, 1967), 89–90.

9. Durgnat, *The Crazy Mirror: Hollywood Comedy and the American Image* (Latimer Trend and Company, 1969), 174.

10. Durgnat, "The Apotheosis of Va-Va-Voom," in *Eros in the Cinema* (London: Calder and Boyars, 1966).

11. Pauline Kael, *I Lost It at the Movies* (New York/London: Marion Boyars, 1966), 31–44.

12. Durgnat, "Asides on Godard," in Ian Cameron, ed., *The Films of Jean-Luc Godard* (London: Studio Vista, 1969), 153. It is worth mentioning that later, in the same collection, Durgnat comes to the defense of Godard in his essay on 1+1 (1968).

13. Wood and Durgnat, "*Belle de jour*," *Movie*, no. 15 (1968).

14. George Kaplan, "Alfred Hitchcock: Lost in the Wood," *Film Comment* (November–December 1972): 46–53. [Editor's note: Kaplan was in fact Robin Wood.]

15. The words of a traditionalist critic might be helpful here. Samuel Johnson has

argued that anyone entering a theatre can imagine that a couple of chairs and fake pillars are, say, Ancient Egypt: "Surely he who imagines this," Johnson wrote, "can imagine more." Why, then, couldn't he imagine that Séverine attains fulfillment at the end of *Belle de jour*?

16. Robin Wood, "Film Favorites: *Bigger Than Life*," *Film Comment* (September–October 1972): 56–61.

17. *Movie*, no. 9 (1963): 19–20.

18. Durgnat, "Hawks Isn't Good Enough," *Film Comment* (July–August 1977): 13.

19. *Editor's note*: Subsequent to their meeting, Rosenbaum and Durgnat (and David Ehrenstein) collaborated on the roundtable discussion "Obscure Objects of Desire" in *Film Comment* (July–August 1978): 60–64, available online at www.jonathan rosenbaum.com/?p=15471; and Durgnat discussed the first edition of Rosenbaum's *Moving Places: A Life at the Movies* (New York: Harper and Row, 1980), available online at www.escholarship.org/editions/view?docId=ft3s2005n8;brand=ucpress, in the review essay "Nostalgia: Code and Anti-Code," *Wide Angle* 4, no. 4 (1981): 76–78.

20. Durgnat, "Standing Up for Jesus," *Motion*, no. 6 (Autumn 1963): 25–42.

Surviving the Sixties*

You know, I'm not someone who ever survived the Depression," the great American film critic and painter Manny Farber once said to me, back in the late 1970s. "It's not the sort of experience you ever really get over." This was in part a gentle rebuke to someone born after the 1930s who tended to romanticize that era — seeing glimmers of communal warmth and common cause leaking through all that picturesque poverty, especially in Hollywood pictures. For me, the 1930s were a legendary period — the time in the U.S. when socialism came closest to being a mainstream position. Indeed, the next two decades in American history might be viewed as a series of desperate holding actions against the dreams nurtured in that epoch.

By contrast, the 1960s was a period of prosperity that nurtured outsized utopian dreams of its own — dreams so grandiose that the succeeding decades up to the present could be viewed as another set of fearful responses. Having spent part of my teens and all of my twenties during the countercultural uprisings, I'm not sure I can say with confidence that I ever fully survived that period myself. But for J. Hoberman, six years younger than me, one feels it was more a pivotal than a terminal stage in his education — making him unusually well suited to chart its developing mythologies and unpack its excesses, because he's no longer living there.

In *The Dream Life: Movies, Media, and the Mythology of the Sixties,* Hoberman is working as neither a film scholar nor a film critic in the usual sense — roles he has taken on with distinction in such previous books as his definitive

The Dream Life: Movies, Media, and the Mythology of the Sixties, by J. Hoberman. New York/London: New Press, 2003. 461 pp.

history of Yiddish cinema (*Bridge of Light*) and his no less authoritative *On Jack Smith's* Flaming Creatures (*and Other Secret-Flix of Cinemaroc*), as well as his two critical collections (*Vulgar Modernism* and *The Magic Hour*, designed successively as chronicles of the 1980s and 1990s). Hoberman veers closer to the kind of social and ideological history he broached in *The Red Atlantis: Communist Culture in the Absence of Communism*, although this time with a more specific narrative line. Usefully defining the American sixties as a fifteen-year "decade" stretching from the launch of *Sputnik* in 1957 to "the media-driven debacle known as Watergate" in 1972, he offers a provocative demystification that is also, curiously enough, a wry celebration of that era's dream life as reflected as well as informed by commercial movies.

Over the course of three successive U.S. presidents and four elections, with Vietnam hovering in the background as a constant, anxious undertow, Hoberman tracks the emergence of a bewildering and generally obfuscating trend in public life—the interfacing of media and politics: "Given the post-1960 tele-saturation of the American marketplace, the corresponding development of political image-building and the advent of a self-conscious Pop Art, as well as the relaxation of long-standing codes that governed the protocols of mass-media content, the distinction between passive consumer and active participant blurred. Movies might be political events, and political events were experienced as movies."

After establishing in his introduction that "there was a sense" during this period "that electoral politics, the mass media, and publicity had combined in a new totality—an additional atmosphere, a second nature, the dream life of the nation," Hoberman proceeds to chart the manifestations of this "new totality" chronologically over half a dozen chapters, forging a rich tapestry in which high-profile film releases and diverse social, cultural, and political events become increasingly interchangeable as expressions of the same collective mythology. Thus the 1964 military-coup scare thriller *Seven Days in May* is examined from its origins in a best seller the previous year (juxtaposed with both the Cuban Missile Crisis and Andy Warhol's first one-man show in New York) to its release after the Kennedy assassination in Dallas, with disquieting production information along the way. ("The opening scene of right-wing pickets scuffling with Ban-the-Bombers outside the White House was shot a few days after the 1963 Nuclear Test Ban Treaty was initialed in Moscow, and according to *Variety*, actual anti–Test Ban demonstrators had to be dispersed to facilitate the staged disturbance.")

■ ■ ■ ■ ■ ■ ■ ■ ■

As an intellectual journalist, Hoberman has many traditions to draw upon, but two in particular stand out: the more detached (albeit pessimistic and unforgiving) cultural analysis practiced by the Frankfort School and the more genial, humorous, and appreciative style associated with American muckraking. The first of these functions as a kind of adult conscience, the second as a kind of lively sport. But it would be inexact to say that Hoberman generally chooses between these separate traditions or seeks to employ them dialectically, as alternative strategies. More often, he seems to work with them in tandem, and a good deal of the ambiguous flavor of this book derives from the various ways he combines the rigors of an analyst with some of the instincts of a spoiler.

To address the issue somewhat differently, and more concretely, is it possible to reconcile the separate agendas of Siegfried Kracauer (1889–1966, cited in the book's second sentence) and H. L. Mencken (1880–1956, not cited at all)? I'm not sure it is, despite their common Germanic roots and the fact that they were only a decade apart from being precise contemporaries. But it has to be conceded that Hoberman comes closer than anyone else I can think of to performing this impossible shotgun marriage — with a giddy kind of verve driving his most scathing prose. Here are a few treasures among many:

[Kracauer]
Freedomland is consecrated to the Hegelian notion that history is rational and that the history of the world has achieved full consciousness — in the existence of the United States. The past is petrified, and so is the future. The present is somewhat less certain.

[Mencken]
Three weeks after [Barry] Goldwater was nominated, [Lyndon] Johnson demonstrated total control over the Democratic convention held in Atlantic City — a tawdry town of ancient fan-dancers and geriatric flagpole-sitters where, in addition to kewpie dolls and saltwater taffy, the boardwalk's souvenir stands hawked plastic wall hangings inscribed with JFK's imagined beyond-the-grave message to his wife.

[Kracauer/Mencken]
Had there ever been an American Western in which humanity was so consistently venal, cowardly, and cruel as in The Wild Bunch? The law is represented by the railroad company; its agents are moronic bounty hunters riding behind the unwilling ex-convict Deke Thornton (Robert Ryan). The Bunch are less like [John] Wayne's Green Berets than the Commanches that Wayne battled in The Searchers; they kill their own wounded and leave

them unburied. Western morality is obliterated. In this scenario, there are no good guys. A postscript shows Thornton recruited to the Mexican revolution, but this faint echo of *Magnificent Seven* idealism glosses *The Wild Bunch's* real pleasures — the thrill of invasion and massacre of foreigners.

America was involved in the most elaborate military operation since World War II, except that only a small percentage of society seemed directly affected. There was no food rationing, no gas coupons, no Liberty Bonds, no real home front. *Dirty Harry's* belligerent invocation of martyred police — a prophecy, in its list of names, of the eventual Washington, DC, Vietnam Memorial — proposed cops as our foot soldiers. (*Dirty Harry's* concern for the war at home is reinforced by those images, then unique, of choppers hovering over San Francisco, as if the city itself were a free fire zone — which is what it turns out to be.)

One of the teasing ambiguities arising from this sort of blend is the question of agency: is Sam Peckinpah, the auteur of *The Wild Bunch*, exhibiting American xenophobia, criticizing it, or some of both? And what about Don Siegel, the supposedly (or at least usually) liberal auteur of *Dirty Harry*? Not that Hoberman necessarily needs to resolve these questions. But the degree to which the fantasies are driving the films rather than vice versa is a matter he most often prefers to broach and then leave unsettled — understandably, because intentionality is generally a hornet's nest. After all, we can probably safely say that *The Searchers* is both objectively racist and one of the most insightful depictions of racism found in American cinema. Choosing between those descriptions might ultimately mean short-changing the film's impact and importance, and ascribing either or both attributes to John Ford only complicates matters further. (Even so, Hoberman is not above offering critical annotations when they serve his argument — as in his hilariously apt thumbnail description of *The Man Who Shot Liberty Valance* as "Ford's going-out-of-business sale.")

On the other hand, when Hoberman suggestively juxtaposes *Spartacus* with *The Alamo* as an articulation of the 1960 presidential campaign in which Kennedy opposed Goldwater — ticking off the veiled references to the Hollywood blacklist in the first film's dialogue, written by formerly blacklisted Dalton Trumbo — he's letting a few intentions creep into the picture. And this raises the question of how legible such subtexts might have been at the time: surely more evident than similarly veiled references to the blacklist were in *The Robe*, scripted without credit by the blacklisted Albert Maltz in 1953, but still probably more meaningful today than they were in 1960.

The critical part of my nature flinches a little when Hoberman, after noting that JFK essentially green-lighted the production of *The Manchurian Candidate*, goes on to call it "a bit Bondlike in its futuristic technology, robotic hit men, sinister Asians, and joking violence"—as if Ian Fleming and satirist George Axelrod were really brothers under the skin. But then he goes on to concede that "Once the spectator realizes that the Cold War is the nightmare from which the hero Frank Sinatra is trying to awake," the film "is genuinely self-reflexive." And it's certainly legitimate to conclude that the film is also one of the "Kennedy scenarios" (along with *Advise and Consent*, *Seven Days in May*, *Dr. Strangelove*, and *Fail-Safe*) that "conceived American democracy as the province of demagogues, extortionists, traitors, megalomaniacs, and assassins." Even if JFK didn't write those scripts, his carefully manufactured image presided over their executions.

■■■■■■■■■

On his cooler Kracauer side, Hoberman does a brilliant job of analyzing the social fantasies of both the right and left during this period as if they were all a string of overblown movies, or finding diverse other ways of interrelating films and public events—as politicians and filmmakers were themselves often doing then. (A particular favorite: "LBJ's entire Vietnam visit lasts two hours and twenty-four minutes—only three minutes longer than the eventual running time of *The Green Berets*.") In this respect, his enterprise recalls at times the methods of Hans-Jürgen Syberberg in *Hitler, A Film from Germany*. Some of the early portions of his own juicy narrative could in fact be called *JFK, A Film from the U.S.* if it weren't for the fact that the U.S. becomes the designated recipient as well as the deliverer of this national message. This is more or less where Mencken steps in. As a muckraking satirist who took a great deal of pleasure in celebrating the American excesses that he skewered for the benefit of his compatriots—characteristically attaching flyers for hog-calling contests and the like to the letters he sent to friends—Mencken was something of a grandstander as well as an analyst, and this becomes part of Hoberman's style as well; those plastic wall hangings are partially there to be perversely enjoyed, not simply noted.

In fact, a good deal of *The Dream Life* unfolds like a Menckenesque scrapbook of American folly and hyperbole fed by the more hysterical social myths of the period coming from the left as well as the right, the freaks as well as the straights. Thus *Alice's Restaurant* is viewed with the same sort of skepticism as *Easy Rider*; while "both movies articulate a general sense of failure" in American culture, they're also "equally devoid of political analysis and deep in political denial." More comically, on the left we find Twentieth Century-Fox chairman Darryl F. Zanuck, after gleaning from a survey in *Fortune* magazine that Che Guevara was more popular on college campuses than LBJ, Nixon, Hubert Humphrey, or George Wallace, rushing to the Côte d'Azur with director Richard Fleischer in order to wrest Omar Sharif away from a bridge tournament so he can be cast as the revolutionary superstar in a blockbuster biopic—which Sharif reluctantly submits to only if a special "conscience clause" is written into his contract. After a production budget "bigger than Castro's" ("It costs more to make a movie about a revolution than it does to make a revolution," reports John Leonard in the *New York Times*, calculating the cost at "about $10,000 an hour"), the movie finally opens disastrously in the spring of 1969 to empty theaters.

And on the right? Apart from the various statements and personal projects of John Wayne, a key player and reliable buffoon in these pages, we learn that the "Reverend [David A.] Noebel, a preacher with the Christian Anti-Communist Crusade, had revealed 'a systematic plan geared to making a generation of American youth mentally ill and emotionally unstable' in his 1965 pamphlet, *Communism, Hypnotism and the Beatles*."

Beyond the parameters of left and right, one finds the overweening self-importance of the period's commentators. During the summer when *Apollo XI*, the manned rocket to the moon, was launched, and a third of a million freaks turned up at the music festival in Woodstock, Hoberman reports that "The *New York Times* editorialists were sufficiently delirious to imagine the last half of July 1969 'the most revolutionary and significant fortnight of the entire twentieth century.' Covering the Apollo launch for *Life*, [Norman] Mailer scarcely hesitated in calling the moon mission 'the climax of the greatest week since Christ was born.'"

It makes for lively reading, yet there are times when celebratory skeet-shooting of this kind can interfere with analysis or a precise sense of history, especially when parts of it sound almost too good to be true. Though there are some unadorned facts in this study that leap out of the page, and deserve to be better known—we learn that "The Pentagon eventually revealed that a third of all enlistees [during the war in Vietnam] had tried heroin, with nearly two-thirds of those developing a habit"—the bulk of the survey is devoted to media representations, and it suits Hoberman's purpose that a disproportionate number of them are over-the-top extravaganzas of one kind or another. It's hard to resist alluding to *The Woman on Pier 13* only by its prerelease label, *I Married a Communist* (used by producer Howard Hughes to "test" the political credentials of the Hollywood directors he offered it to), even if few ever actually saw a movie with that title. Or to resist converting a peevish and jokey aside of Nikita Khrushchev on a New York TV talk show, "We will bury you," into an ominous "[threat] to bury capitalism," much as American media mavens were doing at the time. You might say it makes good copy, but insofar as it does, this is a loophole that Hoberman shares with some of his targets.

And there are other times when restricting the mad American spectacle to American spectators on their native soil needlessly limits the focus. This is a drawback I'm especially keen to because during the latter parts of the book's chronology I was living in France, where certain aspects of *The Dream Life* were thrown into even bolder relief. When I attended the world premiere of *Woodstock* in Cannes in 1970, director Michael Wadleigh, a hippie himself, dramatically dedicated this Hollywood release to the students just killed at Kent State and solemnly passed out black armbands after the screening. Within days, black armbands were selling briskly in the local boutiques, implicitly serving as plugs for Warner Brothers — a prime instance of how quickly a gesture of political solidarity could instantly become part of someone else's promotional campaign when one wasn't looking.

On the other hand, I luckily missed much of the feeding frenzy in the alternative press occasioned by the grotesque countercultural celebration of the bloody exploits of Charles Manson and his extended "family," which Hoberman chronicles in depressing detail, and which might well have tarnished some of my radical idealism if I'd still been around for it. This was only one of the sour turns taken by the radical left in the early 1970s — though Hoberman suggests it may have been largely the establishment that encouraged the immediate identification of the counterculture with mass murder: "While Los Angeles district attorney Vincent Bugliosi complained that Manson had become a 'cause,' the *Berkeley Barb* noted that prison authorities fostered Manson's countercultural image, permitting the monster to keep his long hair, bellbottoms, and fringe leather shirts, repeatedly presenting him to be photographed in full hippie regalia."

As with so much of the evidence in the book, the media mechanisms set in motion by the fearful fever-dreams of the right — mechanisms by which the most graphic fantasies of the left were blatantly encouraged and even advertised so that they might then overtake and ultimately supplant the political discourse underlying them — turned practically every rebellious blade-thrust into a two-edged sword, a frontal attack that became a form of self-immolation. (According to the recent research of American independent filmmaker Jay Craven for his feature *The Year That Trembled*, there is some reason to suspect that the burning of an ROTC building at Kent State that sparked the shooting of students may have actually been done by an FBI agent provocateur posing as a radical.)

For all his all-American appreciation of yahoo excess, Hoberman, unlike Mencken, doesn't hail from Baltimore. Although *The Dream Life* isn't obvious about this, a New Yorker's view of American culture subtly inflects its view of the zeitgeist, especially when it comes to the vantage point of its own research. Bosley Crowther, for instance — the stuffy *New York Times* reviewer who figured as a favorite *bête noir* of local film buffs — is possibly accorded more significance as a mainstream commentator on commercial movies than he would have likely had outside Manhattan and Hollywood.

Pauline Kael, who deservedly receives still more attention, is inexactly described as a "Berkeley-based freelancer" when she published her famous 9,000-word defense of *Bonnie and Clyde* in the *New Yorker* in 1967, the same year that Crowther retired — and two years after she moved to New York. More importantly, Hoberman is attentive to the impact this essay had both in establishing Kael at the *New Yorker* and in ratifying the cultural credentials of *Bonnie and Clyde*. But one could expand on this notion and posit Kael's manifesto as a turning point in American film criticism as well as American filmmaking that veered it away from the relative internationalism then being spearheaded by Andrew Sarris, her arch rival at the time, and towards a more home-grown patriotism that also implied a certain isolationism. *Bonnie and Clyde* was itself pivotal in this respect, because its script by Robert Benton and David Newman was inspired by the unstable genre mixes of the French New Wave and in fact had been offered to François Truffaut and Jean-Luc Godard to direct at separate junctures before the assignment went to native son Arthur Penn. What made Kael's defense of the film partisan in a nationalistic way was her differentiation between Americans and "the French." Consider the following paragraph:

> If this way of holding more than one attitude toward life is already familiar to us — if we recognize the make-believe robbers whose toy guns produce real blood, and the Keystone cops who shoot them dead, from Truffaut's *Shoot the Piano Player* and Godard's gangster pictures, *Breathless* and *Band of Outsiders* — it's because the young French directors discovered the poetry of crime in American life (from our movies) and showed the Americans how to put it on the screen in a new, "existential" way. Melodramas and gangster movies and comedies were always more our speed than "prestigious," "distinguished" pictures; the French directors who grew up on American pictures found poetry in our fast action, laconic speech, plain gestures. And because they understood that you don't express your love of life by denying the comedy or the horror of it, they brought out the poetry in our tawdry subjects.

Now Arthur Penn, working with a script heavily influenced — one might almost say inspired — by Truffaut's *Shoot the Piano Player*, unfortunately imitates Truffaut's artistry instead of going back to its tough American sources. The French may tenderize their American material, but we shouldn't. That turns into another way of making "prestigious," "distinguished" pictures.

One could argue that the most ideologically pertinent words in this polemic are all first-person plural pronouns: "us" and "our" in the first sentence, "our" (used twice) in the second, and "we" in the fifth. All imply a fundamental cleavage between French and American sensibilities, and what could be called French and American property in terms of both life and history, including film history. (One might even conclude from the syntax that French crime isn't a tawdry subject until — or unless — it becomes Americanized.) Thus both French cinephiles who might have regarded certain American crime pictures as "our movies" — not necessarily to the exclusion of Americans, but in concert with them — and Americans who might have felt the same way about certain New Wave pictures become excluded from Kael's line of reasoning; the very notion of a shared tradition is deemed inadmissible by definition. In more ways than one, the xenophobic underpinnings of Cold War rhetoric are faintly echoed in this discourse, and such strains were to become more rather than less pronounced — and not only in Kael's prose — in the years to come. Furthermore, once it became established that Americans could make their own art films — Kael favorites like the first two *Godfather* pictures come to mind — the very notion that they might learn something from foreigners got swept under the rug, with an audible sigh of relief.

Hoberman, who knows better than to use personal pronouns the way Kael does, can't be accused of replicating any part of this discourse. Yet there are times when one wonders if he's still become the unwitting beneficiary of some of its assumptions, if only through the way he intermittently treats *The Dream Life* as a kind of master text bound on either side by the Atlantic and the Pacific. This assumption is by no means monolithic — which is why he can implicitly link the mythologies of Ian Fleming and George Axelrod without blinking, and, in spite of my own flinches, with some justice. (Indeed, the "urbanity" of both writers might be said to be routed through the fantasies of *Playboy* as well as the scenarios of JFK.) But he does tend to sidestep the degree to which many facets of American and European myths overlapped and interfaced in the 1960s.

I'm thinking, for instance, about how the week-long run of Godard's film about Maoist students, *La chinoise*, at New York's Kips Bay Theater in early April 1968, preceded the student takeover of Columbia University campus buildings by only a couple of weeks, and how the student uprisings in France in May 1968 were less than two weeks after that. What I'm stipulating aren't simple chain reactions — even if I had radical friends at Columbia who saw the Godard film more than once, and radical friends in Paris who were inspired in part by the events at Columbia. What I'm thinking about, rather, are the crosscurrents that made those two cities a lot closer to one another in shared aspirations and, yes, mythologies than many younger people, including possibly Hoberman, are apt to assume today.

Even though it's hard to imagine a serious student radical at the Sorbonne expressing "hallucinated solidarity with the Manson Family," as Hoberman shockingly reports Weather and former SDS activist Bernadine Dohrn doing ("Dig it: first they killed those pigs, then they ate dinner in the same room with them, then they even shoved a fork into the victim's stomach. Wild!") — in part because widespread use of hallucinogens never took hold in Paris they way it did in New York or London — the more utopian fantasies of the period might be said to have galvanized Paris Maoists and Berkeley anarchists (as well as London squatters) with common and interlinking passions. I can even recall attending a comically confused mass meeting at the Sorbonne in 1969 or 1970 presided over by Jerry Rubin with a French translator — though if any comparable rallies occurred on U.S. campuses at the time, these would have likely been grouped around Jean-Luc Godard and Jean-Pierre Gorin, not Daniel Cohn-Bendit.

For most of this review I've been expressing demurrals, yet it's central to the strengths of *The Dream Life* that it provokes dialogue and counterarguments rather than simple acquiescence. The sardonic cast of the prose guarantees that nostalgia for the 1960s is kept perpetually at bay — to the consternation of aging hippies and the enlightenment of everyone else, including younger reformists who've grown understandably weary of their elders' stale reveries. It's a nostalgia that nowadays is just as apt to rhapsodize about how great the movies were than how great the sex, drugs, rock-and-roll, and demonstrations could be, and to mix metaphors, the bracing wet blanket that Hoberman tosses on these manifold delights functions as a useful and even timely wakeup call. He's not out to spoil our fun but to help us understand it better, delusions and all.

Cinema Scope, no. 17 (Winter 2003)

L.A. Existential

I think there's this weird thing at work now with the way people relate to, specifically, mainstream cinema. When they watch those movies, they like to be on the receiving end . . . and the sound is so loud, and the images are so powerful, they want to be totally passive. But then, a few months later, the same film is on DVD, and they can watch it and they own it. And the relationship is inverted. They own that moment, that scene, they also control that diverse, complex relationship they have with film actors. They can watch this or that in slow motion, or image by image.
—Olivier Assayas in a 2003 interview

The paradigmatic shift in moviegoing described above is fundamental, profoundly altering what we mean by film history as well as film criticism. But if you keep your focus trained on theatrical releases, and regard the subsequent surfacing of the same items on video and DVD only as faint echoes, you're less likely to be aware of what's been happening lately, which is in fact affecting the entire corpus of cinema and our access to it. From this more global point of view, the full year that it's taken for my favorite movie at last year's Toronto film festival to reach Chicago — it's playing now for a week's run at the Gene Siskel Film Center — is still only the second stage in a three-step process. The culmination will be when you can take *Los Angeles Plays Itself* home with you and watch it again at your own speed, as I just did while preparing to write this review.

Thom Andersen's compulsively watchable, endlessly quotable 169-minute essay film is already a pertinent consequence of this change, because it derives from him reclaiming and mastering his own previous experience of watching movies. Designed specifically to ape an old-fashioned double feature, with an intermission planted about two-thirds of the way through, it lies outside the mainstream because it lacks studio backing and distribution, yet it's far too plainspoken and witty to qualify as esoteric or marginal. It's an essay that qualifies as social history, as film theory, as personal reverie, as architectural history and criticism, as a bittersweet meditation on automotive transport, as a critical history of mass transit in southern California, as a wisecracking compilation of local folklore, as "a city symphony in reverse," and as a song of nostalgia for lost neighborhoods such as Bunker Hill and unchronicled lifestyles such as locals who walk or take buses.

Most of all, it qualifies as film criticism on the highest level — analytical, transformative, and profoundly political. But it's also sufficiently engrossing and funny to persuade some viewers that it isn't being political or seriously critical at all, at least until its closing stretches — a clever ruse it shares with Ron Mann's documentary *Go Further*, an engaging piece of environmental propaganda that also turned up at the Toronto film festival (as well as Chicago's) last year, and which will open at the Landmark in early December.

Like Los Angeles itself, politics and criticism sometimes need to be disguised or de-emphasized in order to register with effectiveness as entertainment. Such is our tortured ambivalence about fun as well as edification that we virtually demand to be hustled. Curiously, the same subterfuge in reverse is used with certain kinds of mindless entertainment. The sour and unvarying sitcom made out of the presidential campaign by most current TV news coverage can coast along as chewing gum for the eyes and ears with minimal amounts of information only because it carries the pretense that it's informing us about something vital.

So it might be argued that parts of *Los Angeles Plays Itself*, even its exemplary simplicity, lightness, and clarity, carry some elements of a con job — because if Andersen owned up to doing something serious and complex we'd be less likely to pay close attention. The American taboo against discussing class — brilliantly explored in Thomas Frank's recent book *What's the Matter with Kansas?* — is part of what necessitates this deception, and the unreasoning conviction that anything that educates us can't be pleasurable probably accounts for much of the rest.

This mask, which often takes the form of crankiness and sarcasm, also runs the risk of creating a false impression about Andersen's relation to his material. Though most responses to his film have been enthusiastic and supportive, a few of the smarter critics, such as Gary Indiana and A. O. Scott, have registered piqued demurrals. "Do I really feel superior to Hollywood movies, as A. O. Scott claimed in the *New York Times*?" Andersen asks in an article in the current Fall issue of *Cinema Scope* (where he also offers appraisals of two major films not covered by *Los Angeles Plays Itself*, *Mulholland Drive* and *Collateral*). "I would say that I take them more seriously than someone who has to write about them twice a week can afford to" (www.cinemascope. com/cs20/ar andersen_collat.htm). Indeed, Andersen has also accurately noted in interviews that virtually all his clips and the ways that they're edited by Yoo Seung-Hyun convey appreciations of the movies in question, even when the same movies are being tweaked on the sound track. Brandishing his indifference to what passes for both high and low fashion in his academic neck of the woods, he quotes approvingly from both Richard Schickel and Pauline Kael, stomps twice on David Thomson, and has the following to say about Los Angeles's most chic spokesperson: "Forget the mystical blatherings of Joan Didion and company about the automobile and freeways. They say, 'Nobody walks.' They mean, 'No rich white person like us walks.'"

You might say that paradoxically he's a traditionalist who refuses to play by the rules. Significantly, even the boiler-plate "directed and written by" credit that's traditionally given to auteurs is dispensed with — as it is in the films of Chris Marker, another essayist who prefers to have his highly distinctive, personal, and literary commentaries spoken by other people on his soundtracks. Choosing, with a deceptive kind of false modesty, to credit himself merely with "research/text/production," Andersen serves up clips from almost 200 American movies whose only point in common is their being set in Los Angeles, and uses the voice of Encke King to deliver his text about how these movies — and movies in general — have treated his home town. (Though actually born in Chicago, in 1943, he moved to Los Angeles four years later.)

As the film observes early on, Los Angeles is the most photographed city in the world, yet it's also one of the most invisible, because we usually aren't supposed to notice it except as "background": "If we notice the locations, we're not really watching the story. It's what's up front that counts . . . but what if we watch with our own voluntary attention instead of letting the movies direct us?" For all the offhanded way he and Assayas evoke the revenge of the passive spectator, it isn't the least of Andersen's achievements to alter the ways we look at all 191 films he has excerpted, some of which he excerpts more than once — an assembly ranging chronologically from early silents to the present, and generically from an experimental film like *Meshes of the Afternoon* (1943) to *The Terminator* (1984).

■ ■ ■ ■ ■ ■ ■ ■ ■

A good example of Andersen's criticism at its finest is a single simple sentence about the films of John Cassavetes: "His comedies face up to tragedy and reject it." What's startling about this terse observation is that none of Cassavetes' films, with the possible exceptions of *Husbands*, *Minnie and Moskowitz*, and

Gloria, has been regarded by critics as a comedy—certainly neither of the films Andersen has chosen to show us brief segments of, *A Woman Under the Influence* (1974) and *Love Streams* (1984), though both segments exhibit extreme forms of behavior.

Andersen is onto something both elusive and special about Cassavetes, and if one also starts thinking about *Faces* (1968) and *The Killing of a Chinese Bookie* (1976), both of which also have Los Angeles settings, his meaning becomes more apparent. Apart from scattered evidence of comedy in all these films, what's most comic about them is their dialectical relation to tragedy—the way that they "face up to tragedy" dramaturgically and then "reject" tragedy as a dramaturgical solution. It might be argued that even the compulsive laughter heard throughout *Faces* functions dialectically, initially as a rejection of comedy that makes it tragic, and finally as a rejection of tragedy that makes it comic.

What, one might ask, has any of this to do with Los Angeles? In a film that has by now moved through three epic chapter headings—"The City as Background," "The City as Character," and "The City as Subject"—before arriving at this brief interlude towards the end, sandwiched between considerations of Steve Martin's *L.A. Story* (1991) and Diane Keaton's *Hanging Up* (2000), the relevance of Cassavetes to the ongoing discussion is mainly implied. *L.A. Story*, though deemed "an honorably failed romantic comedy," has at least two strikes against it: one is its title, because Andersen has much earlier discoursed at length about why he despises "L.A." as "a slightly derisive diminutive" ("Only a city with an inferiority complex would allow it"); the other is its racial profiling. (We're told that there are only "two blacks with speaking parts" in the movie, "both restaurant employees.") Then the narration adds, "The comedies of John Cassavetes cut deeper," leading us directly into the aforementioned Cassavetes clips and other comments. And once *Hanging Up* is gently but firmly skewered for professing to be about Los Angeles while restricting its exposure of public space to a tunnel that the upper-class characters drive through, it becomes clearer that Cassavetes is trusted because he shows us a more comprehensive view of life in Los Angeles in terms of both class and behavior.

■ ■ ■ ■ ■ ■ ■ ■ ■

All cities are palimpsests, just as any historical period is a combination of previous historical periods, and part of Andersen's modus operandi is to show us why the example of Philip Marlowe continues to have a solid grip on our perception of a layered text such as Los Angeles. A detective's job is to look at the same surfaces everyone else sees and tease out a formerly unseen layer, and that's what Andersen does — not only when he's showing us clips, but also when he's generating footage of his own, shot by experimental filmmaker Deborah Stratman, to make some of his points. Early on, we're shown a series of signs in otherwise unremarkable landscapes directing crews to film locations, and the signs themselves wouldn't register as such if Andersen didn't alert us to their covert meanings.

From there it's only a logical step to introduce us to some of the more famous locations and sites in various films — including the outdoor steps in Silver Lake navigated by Stan Laurel and Oliver Hardy when they attempt to move a piano in *The Music Box* (1932); the Spanish colonial revival house occupied by Barbara Stanwyck in *Double Indemnity* (1944); the Bradbury building at 3rd and Broadway, inspired by Edward Bellamy's evocation of a socialist utopia — built in 1893 and discovered by movies half a century later, where it plays a Burmese hotel in *China Girl* (1943), a London military hospital in *The White Cliffs of Dover* (1944), and eventually, many noirs and SF programmers later, an apartment house of the future in *Blade Runner* (1982); Frank Lloyd Wright's Ennis house (1924), in numerous appearances stretching over sixty-six years, from *Female* (1933) to a 1999 music video, often with different interiors; and Union Station, a favorite site for movie kidnappings.

The fact that *Blade Runner* also uses the last two locations, with Union Station doubling as a police station, contributes to Andersen's investigation of the ways in which reality and fantasy mingle in all the films he cites. Sometimes the sources of reality are as unexpected as the sources of fantasy. A low-budget 1952 programmer called *The Atomic City* in which we see a real crowd of spectators leaving a baseball game — a sequence that might have defied the production code's prohibitions at the time about the "social intermingling of white and colored people" had it employed extras — "suggests that Los Angeles may have been more comfortably integrated in 1952 than it is today." On the other hand, counter-illustrating Andersen's biases against films that take geographical license with the city is the "literalist" thriller *Kiss Me Deadly* (1955), scrupulously respecting every location it uses, even though its plot veers towards science fiction and Greek mythology.

Eventually this develops into a fascinating simultaneous appreciation of modernist architecture in Los Angeles and a caustic denigration of the way it's invariably used (as in hillside homes designed by John Lautner and Richard Neutra) to house villains in crime pictures. More generally, Andersen often takes the transgressive but defensible position that films are to be valued for what they reveal to us regardless of their own intentions. After noting that cop Joe Friday "thinks like a computer" and "walks and talks like a robot," the narration confesses, "Actually, I love *Dragnet*" — referring to the 1968 TV show more than the 1951 feature, although both are sampled. "Its creator and star Jack Webb directed each episode with a rigor equaled only by Ozu and Bresson, the cinema's acknowledged masters of transcendental simplicity. *Dragnet* admirably expressed the contempt the LAPD had for the law-abiding citizens it was pledged to protect and to serve." And after maintaining that the parade of grotesque crazies in these episodes contributed to the national image of Los Angeles as Cuckooland, Andersen can't resist asking rhetorically, "Is there any other city that puts its [police force's] motto ('To protect and to serve') in quotation marks?"

■■■■■■■■■

Andersen teaches film and video at the California Institute of the Arts, and *Los Angeles Plays Itself* grew out of one of his lectures there. But it's also clear that he's been storing up material for this feature for most of his life. And it's important to recognize that one doesn't have to agree with any of his judgments in order to learn something from them. "People who hate Los Angeles love *Point Blank*," he remarks with irritation while ruminating on the subject of "high tourists" and "low tourists" who shoot in Los Angeles. High tourists include Jacques Demy (*Model Shop*, 1969), Michelangelo Antonioni (*Zabriskie Point*, 1970), and Jacques Deray (*The Outside Man*, 1973); low tourists include Alfred Hitchcock (only one of whose thirty American films is set even partially in Los Angeles — the first ten minutes of the 1942 *Saboteur*), Woody Allen (*Annie Hall*, 1977), and John Boorman (*Point Blank*, 1967).

As someone who loves both Los Angeles and *Point Blank*, I'm not sure what to make of Andersen's declaration, but at least he helps me to see the grotesquerie of this modernist thriller's interior decoration in a different light. And when it comes to Robert Altman, the narration is brilliant both in decrying his "condescension towards the outer suburbs" and how his characters "lead lives of noisy desperation" in *Short Cuts* (1993) and in appreciating how Elliott Gould's Marlowe in *The Long Goodbye* ("Altman's best film," 1973) serves to deconstruct and expose aspects of the city's environment.

His two most substantive critiques pertain to two overpraised and underexamined crime pictures that put Los Angeles on the map as a respectable movie subject, *Chinatown* (1974) and *L.A. Confidential* (1997). Andersen's concern is less with how these films misrepresent local history — though he's highly informative on this topic in both cases — than with why these misrepresentations have been so widely embraced, and how they've functioned ideologically as pretexts for political defeatism: "Cynicism has become the dominant myth of our time and *L.A. Confidential* preaches it. . . . Cynicism tells us we are ignorant and powerless and *L.A. Confidential* proves it."

But in many ways the film's most touching passage is its last — a celebration of the neorealist depictions of minorities in Bunker Hill and Watts in four neglected features: the late Kent Mackenzie's *The Exiles* (1961), Haile Gerima's *Bush Mama* (1975), Charles Burnett's *Killer of Sheep* (1977), and Billy Woodbury's *Bless Their Little Hearts* (1983). The first of these, about Native Americans from Arizona who've emigrated to Bunker Hill, had some currency in the early '60s but has been almost completely forgotten ever since until Andersen revived it. (It has played at a few festivals and other venues alongside *Los Angeles Plays Itself*; as a piece of filmmaking and as a fragrant time capsule, it's worthy of being placed alongside Cassavetes' *Shadows*, which was released the previous year.) The other three are often made to seem as remote from contemporary film culture as Bunker Hill is from contemporary Los Angeles, but Andersen vividly resurrects them with sharp and deeply felt appreciations.

Finally, by changing our relationship to both his title city and the movies filmed there, Andersen alters our options both as moviegoers and as Americans. The very fact that he dares to see a relation between these two identities may be his boldest step of all. If you're looking for some redemption in either capacity, this film, a monumental act of recovery, is the place to go.

Chicago Reader, October 1, 2004; see also www.jonathanrosenbaum.com/?p=7866 and www.jonathanrosenbaum.com/?p=6725

Index